LAW AND THE "SHARING ECONOMY"

LAW AND THE "SHARING ECONOMY"
Regulating Online Market Platforms

EDITED BY

Derek McKee, Finn Makela, and Teresa Scassa

in collaboration with Sabrina Tremblay-Huet

University of Ottawa Press
2018

University of Ottawa **Press**
Les **Presses** de l'Université d'Ottawa

The University of Ottawa Press (UOP) is proud to be the oldest of the francophone university presses in Canada and the only bilingual university publisher in North America. Since 1936, UOP has been "enriching intellectual and cultural discourse" by producing peer-reviewed and award-winning books in the humanities and social sciences, in French or in English.

Library and Archives Canada Cataloguing in Publication

Law and the sharing economy : regulating online market platforms / edited by Derek McKee, Finn Makela, Teresa Scassa.

(Law, technology and media)
Includes bibliographical references and index.
Issued in print and electronic formats.
ISBN 978-0-7766-2751-9 (softcover).--ISBN 978-0-7766-2752-6 (PDF).--
ISBN 978-0-7766-2753-3 (EPUB).--ISBN 978-0-7766-2754-0 (Kindle)

1. Technology and law. 2. Cooperation--Law and legislation. 3. Labor laws and legislation. I. McKee, Derek, 1975-, editor II. Makela, Finn, editor III. Scassa, Teresa, editor IV. Series: Law, technology and media

K487.T4L39 2018   344'.095   C2018-903496-3
                                                                   C2018-903497-1

Legal Deposit: Third Quarter 2018
Library and Archives Canada

Printed and bound in Canada

Copy editing   Michael Waldin
Proofreading   Robbie McCaw
Typesetting   Édiscript enr.
Cover design   Édiscript enr.
Cover illustration   Jean-Guillaume Blais

The University of Ottawa Press gratefully acknowledges the support extended to its publishing list by Canadian Heritage through the Canada Book Fund, by the Canada Council for the Arts, by the Ontario Arts Council, by the Federation for the Humanities and Social Sciences through the Awards to Scholarly Publications Program, and by the University of Ottawa.

ONTARIO ARTS COUNCIL
CONSEIL DES ARTS DE L'ONTARIO
an Ontario government agency
un organisme du gouvernement de l'Ontario

Canada Council   Conseil des arts
for the Arts   du Canada

Canada

u Ottawa

Table of Contents

Part IV: Regulating Markets

Part V: Regulating Labour

Acknowledgements

The workshop and public panel discussion that led to the publication of this volume were made possible by a grant from the Social Sciences and Humanities Research Council of Canada (SSHRC). We would like to thank SSHRC for its generous support for this project. Additional financial support for the workshop and panel discussion came from the Faculty of Law at the Université de Sherbrooke, the Critical Legal Research Laboratory, the City of Longueuil, Borden Ladner Gervais, and Melançon Marceau Grenier et Sciortino. We are grateful to all of our sponsors. Thanks as well to the Université de Sherbrooke for its support from its fund Appui aux activités de création et d'édition savants; to the Canada Research Chairs program; and to the University of Ottawa's fund for open-access publication.

We would also like to thank our colleagues and collaborators who supported this project through their intellectual and organizational work. Particular thanks are due to Sabrina Tremblay-Huet, whose role in planning the workshop and editing the publication was so significant that we thought it appropriate to include her name on the title page. Julien Fitzgerald, Siobhan Mullan, and Andrée-Anne Perras-Fortin also made important contributions as research assistants. At the Université de Sherbrooke, additional thanks are due to Annie Bezeau, Marie-Luce Cheney, Geneviève Dufour, David Jobin, Sébastien Lebel-Grenier, Hélène Mayrand, Nicolas Ouimet, and Véronique Fortin. We are particularly grateful to the members of the Critical Legal Research Laboratory for their individual and collective support for this project. Outside the faculty, thanks are due to Orly Lobel, who took part in the public panel discussion and the workshop, providing important feedback on other participants' contributions; to Ariane Krol, who generously donated her time and her critical insight as moderator of the public panel discussion; and to the anonymous peer reviewers who assessed the articles and helped us to improve them. Many thanks as well to the editorial team at the University of Ottawa Press, with particular appreciation to Elizabeth Schwaiger and Michael Waldin for their work on the manuscript.

The "Sharing Economy" through the Lens of Law

Finn Makela, Derek McKee, and Teresa Scassa

Introduction

In the last few years, websites and mobile applications permitting the rental of goods and the provision of services have attracted hundreds of millions of users and have had an enormous economic impact. The best-known examples of this phenomenon include Airbnb (short-term accommodations) and Uber (short car rides). These websites and mobile applications (often referred to as "platforms") rely on their users to offer their own physical and human resources to clients. Many of those who offer rentals and services through these sites (often referred to as "providers") do so on a part-time or casual basis. Many providers seek to generate revenue on the basis of existing household assets, such as spare rooms or personal vehicles. Because these platforms allow for the more widespread use of such assets, they are often collectively identified as parts of the "sharing economy."[1] However, as we shall explain below, there is considerable debate as to the appropriateness of this label.

In general, sharing economy platforms provide users with a forum for interaction, a standard set of contractual terms, and a secure method of payment. They do not themselves own the physical capital, nor do they directly employ the labour required to provide the services in question. They typically provide a platform to facilitate exchanges and charge a commission on each transaction in return. This online marketplace model is not unique: eBay pioneered it in the 1990s for sales of goods. However, the provision of services is more complex than the sale of goods; there are more things that can go wrong, and higher levels of security and trust are required. Sharing economy platforms therefore ask providers and clients to rate one another's performance and rely on these rating systems as trust systems and as a form of quality control. Nevertheless, the rapid expansion of platforms like Airbnb and Uber has generated enormous controversy. Well-publicized cases of vandalism, assault, and even murder among platform users suggest that the platforms' screening and trust mechanisms will never be perfect. Controversies have also arisen from the platforms' economic impact. This impact is felt most acutely in certain sectors: Uber drivers compete with taxi drivers; Airbnb hosts compete with hotels. But the platforms are also understood to have broader impacts: Uber is associated with a trend toward low-paying, precarious work, whereas Airbnb is accused of exacerbating real estate speculation and adversely affecting the availability and cost of long-term rental housing. While governments in some jurisdictions have attempted to rein in the platforms, these companies' technological infrastructure has in some cases allowed them to bypass conventional regulatory frameworks, generating accusations of unfair competition as well as debates about the merits of existing regulatory regimes). Indeed, the platforms blur a number of familiar distinctions, including personal versus commercial activity; infrastructure versus content; contractual autonomy versus hierarchical control. These ambiguities can stymie legal regimes that rely on these distinctions as organiz-ing principles, including those relating to labour, competition, tax, insurance, information, the prohibition of discrimination, as well as specialized sectoral regulation.

It was with a view to exploring these challenges—and potential responses to them—that we brought together scholars from across Canada and elsewhere for a workshop held at the Université de Sherbrooke (accompanied by a public panel discussion at the Grande Bibliothèque in Montreal) in January of 2017. The scholars offered a rich variety of insights, both in terms of the traditional areas of law they brought to bear on the sharing economy and the theoretical perspectives that informed their analysis. The workshop papers com-prise the present volume, and contribute to the ongoing discussions on legal regulation of the sharing economy.

At the time we launched this project, early in 2016, legal scholars were only just beginning to publish research on the sharing economy.[2] As this book goes to press, in 2018, the volume of research has substantially increased. Hundreds of articles on the topic have now appeared in academic law journals, especially in the United States. After an initial period of exuberance, it appears that the debate has now matured. The practical and conceptual challenges presented by sharing economy platforms are now well recognized.[3] At the same time, it is recognized that different platforms present different challenges, and that different jurisdictions might legitimately respond to these challenges in different ways. From a singular phenomenon, understanding of the sharing economy has expanded to a multifaceted inquiry that defies easy categorization.[4]

The Object of Regulation: Is There Such Thing as the "Sharing Economy"?

Platforms like Airbnb and Uber have come to be associated with the idea of a sharing economy. We have chosen to use this term in the volume's title because of its widespread recognition. However, we enclose it in quotation marks in the title to acknowledge that this is an imperfect label. Indeed, there seems to be a general consensus that platforms like Airbnb and Uber have little to do with sharing. Nevertheless, due to divergent interpretations of the underlying economic phenomenon, no consensus has emerged around an alternative label.

The term "sharing economy" evokes values of altruism or solidarity. Indeed, some authors use this terminology to describe a very different phenomenon, that is, attempts to develop more egalitarian, communitarian, and ecologically sustainable forms of economic organization.[5] A related use of this phrase can be found in Yochai Benkler's descriptions of carpooling and distributed computing as economic activities organized through sharing.[6] Benkler emphasized the fact that these forms of economic organization helped to make use of underused resources. However, Benkler identified sharing as an *alternative* to the market; an essential feature of his case studies was that no money was exchanged.

The association of platforms like Airbnb and Uber with sharing stems from the fact that individuals use the platforms to give others access to personal assets that might otherwise sit idle.[7] In this light, the platforms may seem to echo Benkler's case studies. However, Airbnb and Uber clearly fall outside Benkler's definition of sharing. The platforms are explicitly commercial, market-driven undertakings. Providers are commercially oriented as well; while their activities may generate social connections, they also have financial goals. Moreover, it has become clear that such platforms are not only used to share idle capacity, but that they are used to bring new resources to market, as when providers buy secondary apartments in order to rent them on Airbnb, or buy new cars in order to drive for Uber. Indeed, Uber encourages such investment by financing car purchases, and Airbnb does little to discourage it. And while physical assets like apartments and cars are an important part of the story, human resources—labour—may be just as, if not more, important.

Given the explicitly commercial nature of many platform enterprises, the altruism or solidarity associated with the label "sharing economy" may be misleading. Some authors attempt to reconcile the different uses of this label and to think about how to encourage genuine sharing in a digitally mediated environment.[8] Others have abandoned the label when writing about platforms like Airbnb and Uber. Some authors have proposed expressions that are arguably more accurate, such as the "platform economy,"[9] "peer platform markets,"[10] or "crowd-based capitalism."[11] However, the latter labels may make it difficult to circumscribe the phenomenon at issue. Platforms have arguably become a defining feature of twenty-first-century economic organization, including not only rental- and service-oriented platforms such as Airbnb and Uber, but also others such as Google, Facebook, and Amazon.[12] Other authors prefer terms that frame the platforms' activities from the perspective of workers ("crowdwork"[13] and "the gig economy"[14]). Such terms emphasize the role of labour rather than that of physical assets. They imply that Uber belongs in a category with platforms like Instacart and TaskRabbit that focus on pure service delivery. However, the issue of low-paid, precarious work is not unique to the digital environment, so a focus on workers may shift the focus away from platforms. Finally, others have rejected attempts at generalization, insisting instead on the particularities of different platforms and the economic sectors in which they operate.[15] It goes without saying that one's views on the legal issues generated by the platforms are likely to be influenced by one's answers to these conceptual questions, and vice versa.

The contributors to this volume are similarly troubled by the "sharing economy" label. Several contributors also explicitly problematize the notion of sharing (Arthurs), pointing out that platforms rely upon the "fundamental falsehood" (Gautrais) that they are involved in sharing to do rhetorical "heavy lifting" in policy debates (Valverde). While most of the contributors agree that the sharing economy has little or nothing to do with genuine sharing, we have not sought agreement on a definite concept to which the label attaches. Several workshop participants insisted on the specificity of individual platforms and warned against using them synecdochically to stand in for a more general phenomenon. This approach is reflected in contributions that concentrate on one or the other of the two most well-known platforms: Uber (Kaplinsky, Tucker, Valverde) and Airbnb (Sheffi, Tremblay-Huet). Other contributors chose to focus on regulators and their techniques (Gautrais, Geist, McKee) or on objects of regulation (Ducci, Scassa), using different platforms to provide examples of how policy goals are formulated, frustrated, achieved, or betrayed.

These approaches support the view that while specific aspects of the sharing economy may pose particular challenges for legal regulation and may even incite us to rethink traditional categories, it is unlikely that the platforms' activities are shaping the emergence of a new and unified area of law. Indeed, there is no more reason to believe that the twenty-first century will be characterized by a "law of the sharing economy" than to believe that the eighteenth and nineteenth centuries were characterized by a "law of the horse."[16] What we have instead, in this volume, is a set of diverse lenses through which we can examine both the sharing economy and its broader social impacts, and from which certain key themes emerge.

Technologies of Regulation

Thinking about regulating the sharing economy requires us to consider the various ways in which policy objectives can be achieved through regulation. Traditional approaches to this appeal to the notion of a toolbox of policy instruments, that is, to different *technologies of regulation*.

One such technology is the state licence. Derek McKee's contribution uses the cases of Uber and Airbnb to explore the contours of licensing regimes more generally. Both the taxi and hotel industries have typically been regulated, at least in part, through licensing, and platforms that operate in these areas provide an opportunity to re-evaluate these regimes and their pathologies. One conclusion that flows from this re-evaluation is that licensing is not a single technique that responds to a predetermined set of problems. Rather, the state uses licences for myriad ends with varying degrees of success. Furthermore, a licensing regime is not a static solution; over time, it generates new problems, some of which may have been unforeseen by regulators. Finally, attention to the internal logic of licensing allows us to see how platforms themselves act as private licensors; a perspective that challenges the view that regulation is the exclusive purview of the state.

A licence, according to the definition adopted by McKee, constitutes the conditional permission to engage in activity that would otherwise be prohibited. A licensee thus benefits from immunity in exchange for complying with the terms of the licence. However, licences do not grant third parties rights opposable either to the licensor or the licensee; the distribution and enforcement of rights (and correlative duties) obey a different logic.[17] In this case, adjudication can operate as a mode of regulation. Here again, sharing economy platforms provide an occasion to confront our preconceptions. As Nofar Sheffi's contribution documents, platforms may use the adjudicative form to avoid state regulation. Airbnb sets up a private mechanism of adjudication and enforcement whereby it situates itself as the umpire of the competing claims of "hosts" and "guests." This shifts attention from any claims that users may have against the platform itself, which—combined with an arbitration clause that makes pursuing a claim against Airbnb unrealistic if not impossible for most users—insulates it from potential liability. Sheffi questions whether such private adjudication (disguised as a form of customer service) is necessarily problematic, despite the fact that it provides neither the procedural safeguards nor the transparency that characterize state law. On the one hand, her chapter poses the implicit question: If the private "court of Airbnb" is cheaper, faster, and more accessible than a traditional rental board and if the "litigants" are generally more satisfied with the outcomes it generates, then why should it be considered any less legitimate? On the other hand, given the obvious shortcomings of "Airbnb law," her chapter incites us to interrogate the basis on which we would attribute legitimacy to any given legal order.

Whereas adjudication determines the winners and losers of individual disputes, sudden and significant changes in technology, political economy, and law can generate entire categories of winners and losers. This is the subject of Harry Arthurs' contribution. Using examples from labour market regulation and consumer protection, Arthurs shows how sharing economy platforms pose "category problems" for aspiring regulators. Despite claims to innovation, platforms did not create these problems, but exacerbate them, revealing both continuity with historical regulatory challenges and the limits of traditional approaches. Although "pop-up" or "flash" regulation that treats specific pathologies of the sharing economy may provide a promising avenue for addressing these problems, their success would depend on the capacity of citizens to organize and formulate coherent demands and on the state to be responsive to them. Ultimately then, for Arthurs, regulating the sharing economy is not a *technical* problem, but a *political* one.

Regulating Technology

The ubiquity of digital communications systems, smartphones in particular, was a precondition for the emergence of sharing economy platforms. Indeed, Uber has consistently sought to avoid regulation by claiming that it is neither a taxi company nor an employer, but a technology company. Asking how the sharing economy might be regulated thus necessarily raises questions about how to regulate the technologies upon which they are based.

Vincent Gautrais' contribution argues that though the technology used by sharing economy platforms may be disruptive of traditional legal concepts, it does not operate in a vacuum. Rather, state law contains many resources that may be applied to the platforms' activities. Thus statutes—supplemented by traditional rules of interpretation and by the development of case law—do not cease to have effects simply because the technologies we seek to regulate were not specifically envisioned by the drafters. On the other hand, statutes and case law are not the only sources of law; they interact with other sources of normativity, including not only contracts, but also industry standards and—since technology is never neutral—even algorithms, in a "normative ecology" that bears little resemblance to the Kelsenian pyramid of validity. Regulating digital technology thus may require new tools of oversight to be mobilized by multiple actors. For instance, documentation and reporting allow for supervision by contracting parties and consumers, and data retention allows for supervision by auditors. These mechanisms and institutions need not replace courts and administrative agencies; just as technology multiplies sources of normativity, regulatory responses should multiply opportunities for their oversight.

In order to exercise oversight, one must have access; this is especially true of data. By virtue of the very information technology that has enabled their meteoric rise, platforms generate vast amounts of data in which others may have an interest. When it comes to their data, platforms may find themselves in a different position vis-à-vis regulation: rather than seeking to avoid it, they may want to mobilize it to protect what they consider to be a strategic business asset. Ironically, sharing economy platforms decidedly *do not* want to share their data. As Teresa Scassa explains in her contribution, platforms may seek to prevent "opportunistic businesses" from scraping their data and using it either to provide tailored services to users of the platform or information to competitors. They may also want to deprive potential regulators of the information needed to effectively regulate. A patchwork of laws is leveraged by platforms to protect their data. Although the most obviously applicable legal regime is that of intellectual property, notably copyright, Scassa argues that exclusively framing the platforms' data as property risks occluding the public interest.

The Site of Regulation: Local to Global

Recognizing the dual nature of sharing economy platforms foregrounds the question of the *site* of regulation. Considering platforms as new vectors for providing traditional services invites the application of local law and, in particular, municipal bylaws and regulations. Conversely, understanding platforms as primarily technology companies entails the possibility that their activities may be subject to global regulatory regimes. The contributions that focus on the opposite ends of this spectrum do more than simply argue for the applicability of global or local regimes. Rather, they see sharing economy platforms as opportunities to reflect on the possibilities and limits of the regimes themselves.

Taking the local perspective, Mariana Valverde's contribution shows how Uber's "cowboy capitalism" approach to regulation takes advantage of historical attributes of municipal governance that make it particularly vulnerable to industry capture. Valverde situates taxi licensing within the context of municipal business licensing, which has its roots in pre-modern governance structures that generally target marginal economic activities and have not evolved to adequately regulate large transnational business enterprises. Thus, despite the inherently local nature of the services offered through Uber, we ought to be skeptical of the possibility of effective municipal regulation of platforms.

Perhaps, then, global regulation offers a more promising alternative. Since many sharing economy platforms operate across national borders, one might think that multinational trade regimes may contribute to the regulation of their activities. But, here too, we may have reason to doubt, as Michael Geist's contribution demonstrates. On one hand, the development of bilateral and multilateral trade treaties has shown that the global trade regime is also vulnerable to industry capture. Due to their market and political power, incumbent players may be able to influence rules governing new technology in ways that disadvantage sharing economy upstarts. On the other hand, the increasing focus in global agreements on reducing non-tariff barriers to trade may hamstring national governments in their efforts to regulate technology companies. In both cases, Geist argues, global regulation may hinder, rather than enable, national regulation of sharing economy platforms in the public interest.

Regulating Markets

Despite their appeal to the concept of sharing, sharing economy platforms are clearly engaged in market behaviour. In some sense then, any attempt to regulate such platforms is an attempt to regulate markets. Yet, it is not always evident what market is the object of regulation. Are platforms new entrants in already existing markets for services with established players, such as taxis and hotels, or have they created entirely new markets? What other conceptions of a market could contribute to the regulation of sharing economy platforms?

Eran Kaplinsky's contribution shows how regulation may not only *apply* to markets, but *create* them. Though taxi licensing regimes were initially conceived of as mechanisms for countering market failures such as destructive competition and negative externalities, the licences (often called "medallions" or "plates") themselves acquired many of the characteristics of property, creating a secondary market with its own problems. New regulations would thus not only affect the primary market but could potentially destroy the secondary market, with disastrous consequences for licensees who are significantly invested therein. Any attempt to reform the licensing regime must therefore address the question of compensation for what may amount to a regulatory expropriation. As Kaplinsky points out, there are good arguments both for compensation and for "letting the chips fall where they may." Furthermore, if compensation *is* pursued, a coherent approach would require a nuanced understanding of both the legal forms of different categories of licences, and of their economic effects.

Regulating sharing economy platforms using competition law also requires a definition of the relevant market. In his contribution, Francesco Ducci explains how sharing economy platforms may be understood not only as actors *within* a market to be regulated but as the private regulators *of* a market. However, whereas states regulate markets in pursuit (presumably) of the public interest, sharing economy platforms regulate prices—often via algorithms—in order to internalize indirect network externalities; that is, to capture the value generated by their matchmaking. Platforms thus raise different questions for competition law than the traditional service providers with whom they are often seen to be in competition (for example, taxis and hotels). Yet, despite this difference, Ducci argues that existing doctrine and case law on so-called two-sided markets address the relevant attributes of "sharing economy" platforms and thus provide the tools necessary for their regulation.

Regulating Labour

One market in which sharing economy platforms intervene massively is the labour market, though their business model depends on obfuscating this fact. Rather, platforms hold themselves out to be in the business of matching excess capacity with unmet demand. According to this story, the Uber "partner" monetizes her vehicle when it is not being used for personal transport and the Airbnb "host" does likewise with an unused spare room. Capital, not labour, is what is ostensibly being "shared" via platforms.

Despite platforms' claims to innovation, firms have a long history of externalizing labour costs by situating workers outside of their boundaries. In legal terms, this is done by classifying workers as independent contractors rather than employees, a (mis)classification that is at the heart of the category problem identified by Harry Arthurs. In her contribution to this volume, Marie-Cécile Escande-Varniol documents the French experience in trying to address the difficulties caused by the category problem without calling into question the fundamental distinctions upon which it is based. The French solution was to adopt an intermediate category, specifically designed to apply to "self-employed workers using electronic remote connection platforms." Escande-Varniol argues that the result is ambivalent: on one hand, the new category imposes some obligations on platforms vis-à-vis workers, while on the other hand, it confirms their exclusion from the employee category and from the robust protections that it entails.

Legal categories are clearly important, but restricting one's attention to them risks concealing important facets of the political economy of production. Eric Tucker's detailed history of the taxi industry in Toronto allows us to see that not all workers are simply "employees in disguise." On the contrary, capturing the value generated by petty commodity production (or, in the case at hand, petty *service* production) is a distinct mode of labour exploitation. Though this mode has often been described as pre-capitalist, it has continued to exist alongside the wage relationship in capitalist economies and may even become a defining characteristic of the twenty-first-century gig economy. Insofar as the traditional categories of employment law are the *consequence* rather than the *cause* of the wage relationship, we ought to be careful about using them as lenses through which to apprehend the relations of production. Tucker's contribution is an example of how historical analysis rooted in political economy can help us understand how sharing economy platforms function in a given industry, which is an important precondition for their effective regulation.

Notwithstanding their attempts to obscure it, platforms that connect users with service providers, like Uber, Deliveroo, and TaskRabbit, are clearly in the business of providing labour. This is less obvious in the case of Airbnb. Nonetheless, Sabrina Tremblay-Huet's contribution shows that behind the *appearance* of the rental of property lies the *reality* of labour. Like the commodity, the Airbnb rental unit is thus "in reality, a very queer thing, abounding in metaphysical subtleties and theological niceties."[18] The Airbnb rental economy is dependent on labour in two different ways. First, many "hosts" in fact operate as businesses and use workers to clean rooms and communicate with "guests." This shifts employment away from the heavily unionized hotel industry to precarious grey-market employment. Second—and this is the dominant theme in Tremblay-Huet's contribution—even when hosts do the work themselves, it is not perceived of as work, since the neoliberal discourse of empowerment casts it as entrepreneurship or investment. Thus the "host's" freedom from accountability to a boss who schedules work translates into the platform's freedom from accountability for sick days, overtime pay, pension contributions and so forth.

Conclusion

Just as there is no distinct phenomenon that is entirely and exclusively captured by the notion of a sharing economy, the contributions to this volume demonstrate, by their variety, that there is no single regulatory response to the social and economic disruption caused by online market platforms. As with any large-scale change, the advent of the sharing economy not only raises questions about the objects of regulation but invites us to rethink our hypotheses about what regulation can accomplish, how, and for whom.

Notes

1. See e.g. "All Eyes on the Sharing Economy," *The Economist* (9 March 2013), online: <www.economist.com/news/technology-quarterly/21572914-collaborative-consumption-technology-makes-it-easier-people-rent-items>; Juliet Schor, "Debating the Sharing Economy" (2014) A Great Transition Initiative, online: <http://www.greattransition.org/publication/debating-the-sharing-economy>.
2. See e.g. Orly Lobel, "The Law of the Platform" (2016) 101:1 Minn L Rev 87; Christopher Koopman, Matthew Mitchell & Adam Thierer, "The Sharing Economy and Consumer Protection Regulation: The Case for Policy Change" (2015) 8:2 J Bus, Entrepreneurship & L 529; Sofia Ranchordás, "Does Sharing Mean Caring? Regulating Innovation in the Sharing Economy" (2015) 16:1 Minn J L Sci & Tech 413; Brishen Rogers, "The Social Costs of Uber" (2015) 82 U Chicago L Rev Dialogue 85; Molly Cohen & Arun Sundararajan, "Self-Regulation and Innovation in the Peer-to-Peer Sharing Economy" (2015) 82 U Chicago L Rev Dialogue 116.
3. See e.g. Shu-Yi Oei & Diane M Ring, "Can Sharing Be Taxed?" (2016) 93:4 Wash UL Rev 989; Brishen Rogers, "Employment Rights in the Platform

Economy: Getting Back to Basics" (2016) 10:2 Harv L & Pol'y Rev 479; Katrina M Wyman, "Taxi Regulation in the Age of Uber" (2017) 20:1 NYUJ Legis & Pub Pol'y 1.

4. The statistics that we have used to define the size and scope of Airbnb and Uber are proof of the rapid growth and acceptance of these platform technologies by consumers around the world. The figures used by the authors were accurate at the time of writing.

5. See e.g. Jenny Kassan & Janelle Orsi, "The LEGAL Landscape of the Sharing Economy" (2012) 27:1 Journal of Environmental Law & Litigation 1; Bronwen Morgan & Declan Kuch, "Radical Transactionalism: Legal Consciousness, Diverse Economies, and the Sharing Economy" (2015) 42:4 JL & Soc'y 556.

6. Yochai Benkler, "Sharing Nicely: On Shareable Goods and the Emergence of Sharing as a Modality of Economic Production" (2004) 114:2 Yale LJ 273.

7. An alternative phrase, "collaborative consumption," performs a similar elision. See Rachel Botsman & Roo Rogers, *What's Mine Is Yours: The Rise of Collaborative Consumption* (New York: Harper Collins, 2010).

8. See e.g. Koen Frenken & Juliet Schor, "Putting the Sharing Economy into Perspective" (2017) 23 Envtl Innovation & Societal Transitions 3.

9. Lobel, *supra* note 2.

10. OECD, Committee on Consumer Policy, *Protecting Consumers in Peer Platform Markets: Exploring the Issues*, Background Report for Ministerial Panel 3.1, Doc No DSTI/CP(2015)4/FINAL (2016), online: <http://www.oecd.org/officialdocuments/publicdisplaydocumentpdf/?cote=DSTI/CP(2015)4/FINAL&docLanguage=En>.

11. Arun Sundararajan, *The Sharing Economy: The End of Employment and the Rise of Crowd-Based Capitalism* (Cambridge, MA: The MIT Press, 2016).

12. See Nick Srnicek, *Platform Capitalism* (Cambridge, UK: Polity Press, 2017); Julie E Cohen, "Law for the Platform Economy," 51 UC Davis L Rev 133.

13. Jeremias Prassl & Martin Risak, "Uber, Taskrabbit, & Co: Platforms as Employers? Rethinking the Legal Analysis of Crowdwork" (2016) 37:3 Comp Lab L & Pol'y J 619.

14. Valerio De Stefano, "The Rise of the 'Just-in-Time Workforce': On-Demand Work, Crowdwork, and Labor Protection in the 'Gig Economy'" (2016) 37:3 Comp Lab L & Pol'y J 471.

15. See e.g. Wyman, *supra* note 3.

16. But see Lobel, *supra* note 2 at 142–44 (arguing that "there is something new and unique about the law of the platform" at 144).

17. See Wesley Newcomb Hohfeld, "Some Fundamental Legal Conceptions as Applied in Judicial Reasoning" (1913) 23:1 Yale LJ 16.

18. Karl Marx, *Capital: A Critique of Political Economy, Volume I–Part I* (New York: Cosimo Classics, 2007) at 81.

PART I

TECHNOLOGIES OF REGULATION

CHAPTER I

Peer Platform Markets and Licensing Regimes

Derek McKee[1]

I. Introduction

Recent debates about Airbnb, Uber, and similar "sharing"[2] platforms have generated an apparent consensus. According to policy reports published by governmental and intergovernmental organizations, the platforms have benefits, but they also pose risks. The platforms give consumers access to a wider variety of services at lower costs; they also provide a flexible source of income for providers. However, peer-to-peer rentals and services threaten consumers' safety and privacy; they may also give rise to contractual unfairness. Most commentators agree that these problems would be appropriately addressed through some form of regulation.

What form of regulation? This is where the consensus breaks down. Some government authorities have tried to subject platform-mediated services to rules designed for their analog counterparts, such as hotels and taxis. However, proponents of the platforms are generally critical of these rules. They claim that "self-regulation" by the platforms would be more appropriate.

This debate over the appropriate form of regulation is complicated by the presence of public licensing regimes. In many places around the world, it is illegal to drive a taxi without some form of prior authorization. Some jurisdictions also require licences for operators of hotels. The platforms achieved their initial success by ignoring such licensing regimes, claiming (more or less plausibly) to be exempt from them.

Debates over the "sharing economy" have therefore brought to the fore a set of debates about the merits and demerits of licensing as a form of governance. While licensing provides regulators with a powerful instrument, licences have also been seen as an overly blunt tool—and one that can fall into the wrong hands. Many scholars have argued that licensing regimes are likely to generate economic inefficiencies, political conflicts of interest, and arbitrary exercises of power. In view of these pathologies, some scholars have argued that licences would be better replaced with other policy instruments.

While acknowledging these critiques, this chapter emphasizes that much depends on the details of licensing regimes. Such regimes are highly variable. They can concentrate control in government hands, or delegate it to private actors. They can impose major or only minor barriers to entry, and they can do so formally or informally. In short, the presence or absence of licensing is never an all-or-nothing question.

The recent experience of regulatory responses to sharing econom" platforms bears witness to this need for nuance. In response to the market disruptions generated by "sharing economy" platforms, few governments have dispensed with licensing entirely. Instead, they have made adjustments to existing licensing regimes; they have also created new licences for platforms and providers. Moreover, even if governments eliminate public licensing regimes, the platforms' regulation of service providers who operate through their platforms is akin to privately managed licensing. There is no guarantee that such a regime will operate in the public interest; indeed, there are reasons to suspect it will mainly serve the platforms' private interests. The alternative of platform "self-regulation" therefore provides no escape from the dilemmas associated with licensing.

The argument proceeds as follows. In section II of the chapter, I summarize recent policy discussions undertaken by governments and international organizations. These discussions have produced an apparent consensus around certain issues, especially the need to protect consumers from possible harms. However, they have also revealed disagreement around other issues, including the application of labour or employment law as well as the potential application of competition law. Moreover, policy makers disagree over the proper mechanisms for implementing consumer protection goals, especially where licensing regimes are present.

In section III of the chapter, I take a closer look at licences as a legal technology. Licences have a long history; they are also a ubiquitous feature of contemporary legal systems. Governments use licences to pursue various forms of social and economic regulation. Licences are useful to regulators because they provide an effective means of enforcing standards. Nevertheless, licensing regimes have often been the object of critiques, stemming from economic concerns, political concerns, or various combinations of the two.

In section IV, I examine how these issues have been manifested in the context of debates over "sharing economy" platforms, using the licensing of hotels and taxis in Quebec as a case study. These platforms have encroached on economic sectors historically subject to licensing. In response, many jurisdictions have undertaken legislative reforms; to clarify the applicability of the older licensing regimes, to adapt them to the realities of new, digitally mediated services; or to create new, bespoke licensing regimes for the platforms and their users. Many governments have effectively implemented some kind of compromise, treating incumbents and newcomers differently, recognizing each as occupying a certain niche in the market. In doing so, not only have governments not abolished older licensing regimes, they have often created new, separate licensing regimes for the platforms or for providers. These regimes impose barriers to entry and they often contain some form of supply management.

In section V, I consider the fact that, in functional terms, the platforms operate more or less like private licensing regimes. Even without state-imposed licensing, then, the platforms may be perfectly capable of replicating the pathologies historically associated with licensing regimes: there are tensions between the public interest goals that platforms are expected to fulfill and the platforms' private interests; platforms are likely to engage in rent-seeking behaviour, and they often behave arbitrarily. The superimposition of a public licensing regime for platforms or providers may counter some of these tendencies, but it may also reinforce them.

II. Policy Consensus and Conflict

In the last few years, national and local governments around the world have tried to respond to the policy challenges posed by peer platform markets, such as Airbnb and Uber. Although responses vary from one jurisdiction to another, it is also possible to identify an emerging consensus. This consensus focuses on consumer protection, understood to include issues of safety, privacy, and contractual fairness. It also includes taxation. However, the consensus does not extend to the labour issues arising from platform-mediated services, nor does it extend to the application of competition law. Finally, despite agreement on consumer protection objectives, there is no consensus as to how these goals should be achieved. This last disagreement is partly due to the presence of licensing regimes.

This consensus is on display in a number of policy documents published by national governments and international organizations in 2016. I will review three of these documents in particular: a report published by the Organisation for Economic Co-operation and Development (OECD) in June 2016;[3] a communication by the European Commission (EC), also published in June 2016;[4] and finally a report by the staff of the United States Federal Trade Commission (FTC), published in November 2016.[5] Of these three reports, the EC's is the only one that purports to represent the official views of the organization that published it. Nevertheless, all three reports attempt to stake out common ground among a diverse range of participants, and all have received some kind of official endorsement.

The OECD report in question was prepared by a consultant, Professor Natali Helberger of the University of Amsterdam, and provided as a "background report" for the OECD's "Ministerial Meeting on the Digital Economy: Innovation, Growth and Social Prosperity" in Cancun in June 2016. The declassified document is entitled "Protecting Consumers in Peer Platform Markets: Exploring the Issues." As the title suggests, the report deals exclusively with consumer protection issues; it excludes issues of taxation, labour, sectoral regulation, and competition. The report proposes that, in general, consumer protection laws (such as prohibitions on fraud and other deceptive practices) should apply to peer platform markets. It identifies a number of issues for discussion, including the reliability of the platforms' own trust mechanisms (such as pre-screening and user ratings) and how these interact with more formal kinds of regulation and self-regulation, as well as to what extent platforms should be responsible (and legally liable) for the behaviour of their users.

In June 2016, the EC issued a communication entitled "A European Agenda for the Collaborative Economy," outlining its views on the issues.[6] In this document, the Commission highlights the economic opportunities associated with the new platforms and argues that Europe should not miss out. It also acknowledges a number of problems with the platform model, however, including uncertainty surrounding application of existing laws (and possible exploitation of these ambiguities, to the detriment of the public interest), as well as divergent and fragmented regulatory approaches. It notes that under European Union (EU) law, market access requirements for providers (in effect, licensing requirements) must be non-discriminatory, minimally restrictive, justified, and proportionate. It also notes that under the EU's e-Commerce Directive, platforms that are merely offering an intermediation service (and not themselves providing the underlying service) cannot be subject to prior authorization requirements.[7] It also notes issues related to protection of consumers and workers, although it mainly focuses on legal ambiguities surrounding these issues, without taking a particular stance.

The last report I will discuss is the FTC staff report, published in November 2016, on the basis of a workshop that brought together a series of experts in June 2015.[8] In this report, the FTC staff deals with a wide range of policy issues, although it explicitly excludes questions of labour as well as questions of discrimination, finding that these issues fall under the jurisdiction of other government agencies. It calls for a "balanced" approach to regulation, taking into account a number of policy priorities such as innovation, competition, and consumer protection.

These policy reports bear witness to a consensus surrounding the protection of consumers (and users more generally) in peer-to-peer marketplaces. There is general agreement that consumer protection is an important regulatory goal. In a world of peer-to-peer rentals and services, consumers need protection from accidents and assaults. They also need protection against fraud and other deceptive practices. Finally, they need protection against misuse of their personal information. In the context of the "sharing economy," consumer protection thus refers to the protection of platform users' safety and privacy as well as protection against fraud and other contractual abuses. In many cases these concerns apply to users on both sides of the transaction—to providers as well as consumers. In some cases, as with regard to safety, it is a question of protecting users from other users. In other cases, as with privacy, it is a question of protecting users from the platforms.

The emerging policy consensus also addresses the question of taxes. When the platforms first appeared, taxes were a controversial

issue. The platforms initially took the position that, as mere technological intermediaries, they were not responsible for any tax obligations
that might arise from the transactions. But under pressure from tax
authorities, the platforms have largely conceded this point; in many
jurisdictions, they have begun to collect and remit taxes directly on
behalf of providers, and to cooperate with tax authorities in other
ways.[9] In the United States context, Shu-Yi Oei and Diane Ring have
noted that "sharing economy" services raise enforcement challenges,
but that they do not really challenge the basic concepts of tax law.[10]
This consensus is reflected in the reports I have summarized. The
OECD report does not address the issue of taxes. However, the EU
Commission's communication concludes that platform economy services should be subject to the *same* taxes as other services. The FTC
staff report notes a consensus that Airbnb hosts should be subject to
local hotel taxes, but also notes disagreement over the adequacy of
Airbnb's tax collection efforts.[11] The policy consensus surrounding
taxation can be seen as reflecting the maturity of "sharing economy"
economic activities. Governments recognize that platform-based
services are playing a big role in the economy, and have concluded
that these services should contribute to public revenue.

However, there are three notable places where the policy
consensus surrounding peer platform markets breaks down. The
first area of disagreement has to do with labour. The platforms
mobilize millions of individual service providers. The platforms
consider these providers to be independent contractors, and they
have fought hard against legal challenges aimed at characterizing
them as employees. Indeed, the independent-contractor designation
is central to the platforms' business model. Some commentators argue
that peer platform markets thus herald "the end of employment"
and the transition to a new age of entrepreneurship.[12] However, as a
number of commentators have noted, including Harry Arthurs and
Marie-Cécile Escande-Varniol in this volume, there are significant
policy concerns surrounding the platforms' treatment of service
providers. Providers often work long hours for limited revenue.
Moreover, their characterization as independent contractors rather
than as employees brings various disadvantages. It generally means
that they lack job security; they are precariously employed in the
"gig economy." In many jurisdictions, the independent-contractor
designation also serves to exclude providers from protections, such

as minimum wages, workplace accident insurance, and the right to bargain collectively.[13]

The second disputed issue concerns competition. The platforms are essentially networks, and they generate network effects. As with a telephone network, or Facebook, the platforms' interest for any given user depends on who else joins the network. At the early stages of development, platforms face the chicken-or-egg problem of attracting a critical mass of users.[14] Once the platforms have attained critical mass, however, network effects may suffice to pull in everyone else. Indeed, the major platforms' business strategies (and their investors' behaviour) are consistent with a winner-take-all competition for market share. There are signs that network effects have enabled certain platforms to dominate their respective markets.[15] This dominance may enable these platforms to hold off competitors and to collect rents.

However, it is not clear how competition law might respond to this situation. In competition law, before one can reach a conclusion about market power, it is necessary to define the relevant market. Even in conventional industries, market definition is a notoriously difficult exercise. Competition authorities typically use economic tests to determine to what extent similar products are substitutable, and within what geographic area, either on the demand side or on the supply side. But there is no neutral criterion for determining at what point a partially substitutable product constitutes a separate market. This is inevitably a value-laden line-drawing exercise.[16]

In the context of "sharing economy" platforms, market definition raises particularly difficult questions. To what extent do the services offered through the platforms compete with those of incumbent industries? Do taxi drivers and Uber drivers offer basically the same service? Or is the different process for obtaining a ride sufficient to place them in a separate market? Do Airbnb hosts compete with hotels, or are they offering something new? Market definition in the "sharing economy" is further complicated by the distinction between the platforms' intermediation services and the services provided *through* the platforms, such as rides and accommodations.[17] Are these part of a single integrated service, or are they two different kinds of services, existing in two different markets? To the extent that they can be separated, platforms may be intermediating "two-sided markets." The application of competition law to such markets is unclear.[18]

As Francesco Ducci notes in his contribution to this volume, competition law has previously faced similar problems—but that doesn't mean that such problems are easily resolved. Of the reports I have discussed, the FTC staff report is the only one to devote significant attention to competition issues. The report acknowledges the possibility that certain platforms have achieved market dominance. However, it avoids taking any particular stance on this issue.

The third area of conflict concerns the *means* for achieving consumer protection objectives. While there is a consensus as to these objectives, opinions diverge as to the appropriate mechanism for achieving them: whether the platforms can effectively protect consumers through their own business practices, or whether state regulation is required. The platform companies have often argued for the effectiveness of their own bespoke systems of background checks, inspections, peer ratings and reviews, insurance, and arbitration. Some commentators have championed platform self-regulation, arguing that the state should only regulate where self-regulation is inadequate.[19]

The reports I have summarized show no signs of a consensus on this issue. The FTC staff report notes disagreement as to what standards should apply, or who should set them. It endorses calls for a "level playing field," arguing that the same rules should apply to new platforms as to traditional suppliers, although it notes a debate over whether rules should be strengthened or relaxed. It devotes considerable attention to user ratings and the debate over whether these function as an effective mechanism for consumer protection. The OECD report identifies a number of issues for discussion, including the reliability of the platforms' own trust mechanisms (such as pre-screening and user ratings) and how these interact with more formal kinds of regulation and self-regulation, as well as to what extent platforms should be responsible (and legally liable) for the behaviour of their users.

The debate over the means for achieving consumer protection objectives is related to the debate over competition. This linkage is due to the fact that the major platforms have encroached on industries that have historically been subject to licensing regimes: taxis and, to a lesser extent, hotels. In these and other industries, consensus policy objectives such as safety and contractual fairness have often been pursued through the mechanism of licensing. But licences, even if merely intended to protect consumers, also have an impact on competition. Indeed, without exploring the issue in depth, the OECD noted this relationship in its report:

> [...] some consumer protection issues in peer platforms are inextricably linked with competition concerns. For example, providers of goods and services in regulated sectors of the economy often argue that failure to apply existing laws and regulations to peer platform markets creates an unfair competitive advantage, favouring market entrants at the expense of incumbents who may be subject to regulatory structures that often are decades old. Conversely, outdated regulations can entrench the status quo and protect incumbents from competition by, for example, maintaining overly restrictive measures that discourage entry by innovative new providers. In addition, peer platform markets tend to feature "network effects" that may lead to market concentration and potential competition issues.[20]

The presence of licensing regimes therefore drives another set of cracks through the consumer protection consensus. If they are going to protect consumers, governments and legislators must decide whether to do this within the framework of existing licensing regimes or through some other mechanism. In order to understand what is at stake in these choices, it is worth taking a closer look at licences as a policy instrument.

III. Public Licensing Regimes

Licences are a ubiquitous yet poorly understood feature of contemporary law and governance. Governments use licences to pursue an enormous variety of policy objectives. The details of licensing regimes are just as varied. Nevertheless, licensing regimes have also been the object of strident critiques. Critics have alleged that such regimes give rise to arbitrary exercises of power, that they are economically inefficient, and that they serve the private interests of particular groups rather than the public interest.

A number of authors have noted the ubiquity of licensing regimes and their application to a wide range of subject matters, ranging from drilling for oil to keeping a dog.[21] Typical objects of licensing regimes include professions, other occupations and commercial activities, the marketing of certain products, and certain uses of land.[22] Official terminology varies, with some licences labelled as permits, approvals, authorizations, and so on (or, in the case of taxis, plates or medallions); in this paper, I use "licence" as a generic category.

A licence is best defined in functional terms. Issalys and Lemieux describe a licence as "a permission, often subject to conditions, given by a government authority to a natural or legal person, to carry out an act or to exercise an activity that would otherwise be illegal"[23] [author's translation]. In this chapter, I have chosen to adopt Issalys and Lemieux's definition because it succinctly expresses common-sense understandings of licences in Canada and in related legal systems.

This definition specifies that the underlying activity would be illegal without authorization. This requirement serves to distinguish licences from other legal forms, such as contracts or corporate organization, in which the state recognizes (and agrees to enforce) certain private arrangements that would nevertheless be legal even in the absence of state approval. Marriage belongs to the same category: although many jurisdictions retain the formality of a "marriage licence," one can enter into a conjugal relationship without one. The fact that licences are mandatory also serves to distinguish licences from certification schemes, which may confer advantages on those who comply with their terms, but are legally optional.[24]

The definition I have adopted is largely functional. However, it also contains a formal element in its reference to government authority. This term links licences to the exercise of *public* power. Although the concept of a "licence" plays a prominent role in private law (and by extension, in intellectual property law), the "licence" granted by a possessor of property is excluded from the definition. Moreover, this definition excludes private certification schemes that operate without a formal grant of state authority, even when they effectively serve to control access to a particular activity, as is the case with many sports associations.[25] However, as I shall argue in section V, below, such private arrangements may closely resemble public licensing regimes in functional terms.

The power to issue public licences may nevertheless be conferred upon various kinds of authorities. Licences may be issued by government departments or by arm's-length agencies. As Mariana Valverde has noted, licensing may be a preferred technique of local authorities in Canada and in other countries where municipal powers have evolved from pre-modern modes of governance.[26] Licensing powers may also be delegated to private organizations, as occurs most typically when professional associations act as self-governing bodies.

When licensing is delegated to private entities, it may operate as a form of co-regulation or self-regulation, with a governmental authority setting general objectives, and a private body authorized to develop these goals into detailed requirements. Such self-regulatory arrangements may be seen as more efficient than top-down, governmental command-and-control arrangements. In principle, they allow regulated entities to make use of their knowledge and expertise in order to determine the most cost-effective way of complying with public standards.[27] In addition, under such self-regulatory arrangements, the costs of running the regime may be borne by the regulated industry or profession, through the payment of fees, rather than imposed on taxpayers.

Not only the identity of the issuer but also the design features of licensing regimes may vary considerably. Licences may be issued for an indeterminate period, or they may be subject to periodic renewal. Licences may be free, or they may be subject to fees. The fees may be calculated to cover the costs of running the licensing regime. Licences may attach to particular individuals (as with driver's licences or with professional qualifications), or they may be transferable. Licences may be issued to anyone who asks, or they may require the applicant to prove compliance with certain standards.[28] Licensees may or may not be subject to ongoing testing or inspection to ensure that they continue to meet these standards. The licensing regime may also be coupled with a system for price regulation, in which licensees agree to market their services only at prescribed rates. The licensing regime may or may not set a limit on the total number of licences issued, or delimit geographic areas in which licensees can exercise their activities; to the extent that it does so, it may come to resemble a public franchise or a quota system.[29] In practice, high standards for licensing may also implicitly function as quantitative restrictions, as with London's "knowledge" requirement for cab drivers.[30]

In addition to these variable design features, licences can also have various formal legal characterizations. In some cases, especially where licences are transferable, they may be treated as a form of property.[31] In other cases, especially with regard to public franchises, the relation between the issuing authority and the licensee may take the form of a contract.[32]

Licensing regimes nevertheless have certain features in common. By definition, licences involve authorization for some activity, often subject to conditions. A standard feature of licences, then, is the possibility of suspension or revocation should the licensee fail to respect the conditions. Performance of the activity without the licence may be punishable with more directly coercive sanctions, including fines or imprisonment. Licences therefore provide regulators with a "big stick": even if licences are rarely revoked, the mere threat of such a severe sanction may induce licensees to cooperate. Authors such as Ayres and Braithwaite have therefore endorsed the use of licensing as part of a "pyramid of enforcement strategies."[33]

Licensing may serve multiple purposes. Licences are typically associated with the enforcement of standards for quality or safety. The prior verifications required to obtain or renew a licence may be seen as a way of preventing accidents or frauds. All kinds of licences, from professional qualifications to aircraft safety certificates, are typically justified on such public interest grounds. As I have noted, the standards associated with licensing may be coupled with implicit or explicit quantitative restrictions. Such restrictions are usually justified as ways of limiting negative externalities (such as pollution) or forestalling wasteful competition (in situations that approximate natural monopolies). In addition, licensing regimes may have other primary or secondary purposes. In some cases, the licence mechanism mainly serves to raise revenue: it is an indirect tax. In other cases, the information gathering and surveillance associated with licences may become ends in themselves, contributing to techniques of social control.[34]

It is important to note that licences are only one possible way of enforcing standards, and that other policy instruments might be more or less able to achieve the same goals. Alternatives include prohibitions backed by penalties (perhaps backed by powers of investigation); tort liability; taxes; subsidies; government contracting; information and propaganda; or public ownership and management. Indeed, in many circumstances, licences are used in combination with some of these other instruments. For example, the goal of road safety is achieved not only through the licensing of drivers but also through speed limits, criminal prohibitions on drunk driving, manufacturing standards for cars, public ownership and maintenance of highways, awareness campaigns that warn of risks, and so on.[35]

Given the power of licences and their application to so many areas of governance, licences have attracted certain critiques. Four major strands of critique can be identified. The first strand, associated with liberal values of individual freedom and the rule of law, stresses the enormous power associated with licensing and its potential for abuse. In his 1964 article "The New Property," Charles Reich identified licensing (alongside grants, benefits, services, employment, procurement contracts, and so on) as a form of "government largess" that was playing an ever greater role in modern society.[36] Reich highlighted the fact that licences could often be refused or revoked arbitrarily, on the basis of prejudices or political biases, and that those subject to such decisions often had little access to procedural protections. In Canada, similar concerns emerged from the case of *Roncarelli v Duplessis*, after the premier of Quebec had a restaurateur's liquor licence revoked in retaliation for the latter's support for the distribution of "seditious" literature by Jehovah's Witnesses.[37]

In order to overcome official arbitrariness in licensing decisions, critics such as Reich have looked to administrative law, arguing for substantive limits on refusals and revocations, procedural protections, such as the right to a hearing, and an obligation for licensing authorities to offer reasons for their decisions. Indeed, since the 1970s, administrative law in some jurisdictions has evolved in such a way as to respond to these critiques. In Canada, relevant developments include the sidelining of the distinction between administrative and quasi-judicial decisions and the recognition of a generalized duty of fairness in administrative decision-making.[38] Relevant developments also include judicial review of the reasonableness of discretionary decisions and the recognition that administrative authorities may (under some circumstances) have a duty to provide reasons for their decisions.[39] In Quebec, the legislature has codified licence holders' and applicants' rights to be heard as well as licensing authorities' duty to give reasons.[40] Nevertheless, the procedural protections associated with licensing regimes are nowhere near as strong as those associated, for example, with criminal law. Although the common law provides a default set of procedural principles, it is generally open to legislatures to derogate from these requirements.[41]

A second strand of critique is closely related to this first strand, but focuses on licences that restrict the use of private property, such as building permits and pollution controls. For libertarian critics of the administrative state like Richard Epstein, such licences constitute another form of government overreach, and should be severely curtailed.[42]

The third strand of criticism comes from economists, who are wary of the inefficiencies associated with licensing. Where licensing regimes restrict the use of private property, they may be seen as hindrances to development, diminishing the general welfare.[43] Alternatively, where licences restrict particular economic activities, they may be seen as imposing barriers to market entry, limiting supply.[44] Depending on the dynamics of the market, such regimes may generate higher prices for consumers and corresponding rents for licence-holding producers. These effects are most likely exacerbated when authorities place explicit quantitative restrictions on the number of licences. Some economic analysts argue that (voluntary) certification schemes could substitute for licensing regimes in many circumstances. Such regimes could arguably be used to uphold standards, providing consumers with reliable information about quality and safety, while lowering barriers to market entry.[45]

A fourth strand of critique, associated with public choice theory, focuses on the politics as well as the distributive effects of licensing. This fourth strand of critique is often coupled with the third strand— the critique of economic inefficiency. Noting the cartel-like effects of licensing regimes, public choice critics have argued that such regimes serve the private interests of licence holders more than they serve the public interest.[46] Such critics argue that licensing regimes have a regressive impact on distribution, by limiting the supply available to consumers and enabling licence holders to extract rents. These critics also argue that the existence of many licensing regimes can best be explained in terms of regulatory capture: the regulated industry manages to exert a disproportionate influence over the authority meant to regulate it. The exercise of licensing powers by private entities, such as professional bodies, may be seen as the ultimate form of regulatory capture.

These four strands of critique are not mutually exclusive. Indeed, the fourth strand combines elements of the third strand, and may borrow from the first and second strands as well. In the worst-case scenario, licensing regimes may be seen as the exercise of coercive state powers, serving private or bureaucratic interests at the expense of the general welfare, and often exercised in an arbitrary or capricious manner. To the extent that these charges are accurate, licensing regimes have a lot to answer for.

Nevertheless, even those who are critical of licensing regimes acknowledge that they may serve legitimate public purposes. Epstein admits that "we cannot (and should not) strive for a permit-free society."[47] From an economic standpoint, Anthony Ogus identifies cases where licensing helps to provide private actors with relevant information, to reduce externalities, to paternalistically protect individuals from the poor choices they might otherwise make, or to implement a distributive policy.[48] The persistence of licensing regimes therefore cannot be wholly explained in terms of interest group politics. In economic terms, whether the benefits of licensing regimes outweigh their costs is likely to depend on the circumstances. Moreover, when undertaking such a cost-benefit analysis, one must consider the fact that alternative policy instruments would also have costs as well as benefits.[49] In addition, where tradable licences are already in place and have acquired a significant value, the dilution or elimination of these licences raises important distributive concerns—as Eran Kaplinsky highlights in his contribution to this volume.

Finally, it is important to recall that licensing regimes often serve multiple purposes, which may not be easily separated. If a licensing regime is dismantled, it may not be easy to find an appropriate substitute. Moreover, even if one can conceive of an alternative, this does not mean that it will be easy to implement: one must keep in mind that there are limits to human beings' capacity for collective organization.[50] In particular, policy makers never start with a blank slate; they often face the challenge of creating new systems of governance out of old ones that have outlived their usefulness. However, these older systems of governance may also help define the ends that are deemed to be worth pursuing.[51] Licences are therefore destined to remain part of the regulatory apparatus of the administrative state, at least for the foreseeable future.

IV. Public Licensing Regimes and the Arrival of "Sharing Economy" Platforms

The arrival of "sharing economy" platforms has created dilemmas for policy makers, especially with regard to licensing regimes. Many such platforms encourage individuals to undertake economic activities that have historically been subject to licensing. How should legislators and governments respond? In this section, I illustrate the complexity of these dilemmas through a study of hotel and taxi licensing in the province of Quebec. These examples demonstrate that when licensing regimes are challenged, legislators may respond in a number of ways. These responses include modifying existing regimes or creating new ones. These solutions may help mitigate the problems associated with older licensing regimes, but they may also create new problems, including new barriers to entry and new concentrations of market power.

In Quebec, "establishments providing accommodation to tourists in return for payment" are subject to a mandatory classification system.[52] Anyone operating such an establishment must first obtain a classification certificate, which means that the system is, in effect, a licensing regime. Although legislation empowers the minister of tourism to issue certificates, the minister has delegated the management of the system to an industry association, the Corporation de l'industrie touristique du Québec (CITQ).[53] To obtain a classification certificate, one must apply to the CITQ. If the CITQ approves, it issues the certificate, with a rating from zero to five stars, along with a physical sign, which must be prominently displayed at the main entrance to the establishment. The CITQ also conducts inspections to verify that certificate holders maintain quality standards appropriate to their classification. Certificate holders must pay an annual fee to the CITQ (starting at $247.78 in 2017).[54] The Act establishes significant fines (starting at $2,500) for anyone operating a tourist accommodation establishment without a certificate.[55]

Taxis, in Quebec, are subject to three different kinds of licences: owners' permits,[56] drivers' permits,[57] and intermediaries' permits.[58] Owners' permits are issued by a provincial arm's-length agency, the Commission des transports (which also sets taxi fares).[59] The Commission also issues intermediaries' permits for places outside Montreal. Drivers' permits, outside Montreal, are issued by the Société de l'assurance automobile du Québec (SAAQ), the provincial motor vehicle regulator and insurer. In Montreal, a municipal arm's-length agency, the Bureau du taxi, is responsible for issuing drivers' permits as well as intermediaries' permits. Four out of eleven seats on this agency's board are reserved for industry representatives. It is an offence to offer taxi transportation services without an owner's and a driver's permit,[60] and it is an offence to provide taxi advertising, dispatching, or similar services in certain areas without an intermediary's permit.[61]

The licensing regime for taxis clearly establishes barriers to market entry for would-be providers. Owner's permits (equivalent to other jurisdictions' plates or medallions), are subject to quantitative restrictions. Although the Commission stopped issuing transferable owner's permits in 2000, permits issued before November 15, 2000, are fully transferable; they can be bought, sold, and leased. According to media reports, some owner's permits for Montreal were traded for over $200,000, prior to the arrival of Uber.[62] The high cost of owner's permits means that many drivers must either lease these from permit owners or borrow heavily in order to purchase one for themselves.[63] Driver's permits, for their part, are subject to examinations[64] and police background checks.[65] Drivers must also be sufficiently fluent in French.[66] In some locations, a prospective driver must also complete a training course.[67]

With regard to hotels, the CITQ's classification certificates are not subject to such quantitative restrictions. Nevertheless, fees and bureaucratic processes are likely to discourage those who might have entered the short-term rental market on a casual basis.

It is important to recognize that barriers to entry are not just a product of these licensing regimes themselves, but also of the way these regimes interact with other systems of public and private regulation. For example, under the CITQ's classification scheme, municipalities may veto applications for tourist accommodation establishments located in their territory if they consider that the proposal would be inconsistent with their zoning bylaws.[68] Such bylaws may restrict tourist accommodation establishments to commercial areas or impose separation distances between such establishments.[69]

In addition, the CITQ's classification scheme intersects with the legal regime for rental property. Quebec tenants must obtain their landlord's approval before subleasing.[70] In 2016, Quebec's rental housing tribunal, the Régie du logement, made it clear that this provision applies to short-term Airbnb rentals.[71] Shortly thereafter, the same tribunal authorized a number of landlords to evict tenants who had been subleasing their apartments on Airbnb without permission.[72]

In the case of taxis, the sectoral licensing regime intersects with the general licensing regime for drivers and vehicles. In Quebec, the SAAQ is responsible for testing all drivers, registering all vehicles, and managing a public system of insurance for driving-related injuries. Taxi drivers in Quebec must not only have regular drivers' licences, they must have higher, commercial-grade licences, known as "Class 4C."[73] In order to obtain such a licence, the driver must undergo a medical examination, have his or her vision checked, and pass a written test.[74]

When "sharing economy" platforms like Airbnb and Uber arrive on the scene, lawmakers in jurisdictions with licensing regimes like Quebec's have faced a set of interconnected normative questions. First, should platform-based service providers be subject to the existing licensing regimes, or should they be exempt? Second, should existing licensing regimes be preserved, or does the arrival of the platforms mean that they should be modified or even dismantled?

In Quebec, the government's initial response (beginning in 2014) was that the existing regimes should apply to these new services. In 2015, the Quebec legislature reformed the *Act Respecting Tourist Accommodation Establishments* and its accompanying regulations in order to provide for more inspectors and to toughen the penalties for unlicensed establishments.[75] The minister of tourism explained the reform as part of a crackdown on "illegal hotels."[76] The Quebec government took a similar line in response to Uber. The minister of transport emphasized that Uber drivers' activities were illegal.[77] In 2015 and 2016, the Bureau du taxi of Montreal seized hundreds of vehicles from Uber drivers.[78] Defenders of the existing licensing regimes, especially those in the conventional taxi industry, accused Uber and its drivers of unfair competition and launched a class action against Uber.[79] Tax authorities also targeted Uber's Quebec offices for investigation, leading to protracted litigation.[80]

The new platforms and their defenders generally responded to these attacks in two ways. On one hand, they dodged the legal questions, claiming that the informal, digitally mediated nature of the activities undertaken by their providers somehow fell outside the existing licensing regimes.[81] On the other hand, they mounted a full-throated critique of existing licensing regimes. In the case of Uber, they argued that taxi licensing was a thing of the past, and that Uber represented the future.[82] They described the taxi industry as a legalized cartel, extracting rents and providing mediocre services to the public.[83] In effect, these arguments turned the "unfair competition" argument on its head: the platforms and their allies presented themselves as the true champions of a competitive marketplace.

In fact, the government's defence of the existing licensing regimes was not absolute. The government showed a willingness to compromise. With regard to tourist accommodations, the government issued a regulation specifying that the classification scheme only applies to spaces that are offered for rent, for periods of thirty-one days or less, "on a regular basis."[84] The Ministry of Tourism subsequently issued an interpretation bulletin stipulating that "a regular basis" means anything more than once per year.[85]

In the case of taxis, the government sent mixed political signals. In January 2016, the minister of transport, who had taken a hard line against Uber, was replaced with a minister who was seen as more conciliatory.[86] Taxi authorities continued to seize vehicles, and the new minister was loudly critical of Uber. Nevertheless, the government stopped short of shutting down Uber altogether. The government discussed measures that would truly have prevented Uber from functioning—such as suspending the *driver's* licences of Uber drivers—but never undertook such measures.[87] Uber continued to operate in Quebec, and remained popular.

Such mitigated responses show that the initial questions I have identified—whether or not to subject the new platforms and providers to existing regimes, and whether or not to dismantle the existing regimes—are not in fact all-or-nothing questions. Regulators may decide to compromise with regard to one, the other, or both. Such compromises may be achieved on a somewhat improvised basis, as in Quebec, or they may be more carefully planned. For example, regulators may decide to retain the existing licensing regime, but nevertheless set a threshold that allows some platform-based providers to legally operate without a licence. Alternatively, regulators may apply the same licensing requirements to everyone, but nevertheless lighten these requirements to accommodate platform-based providers. Finally, regulators may simultaneously lighten the licensing requirements and exempt some providers from their application. These possibilities suggest that the initial questions I identified might be reformulated as follows: first, *to what extent* should platform-based service providers be subject to the existing licensing regimes, and *to what extent* should they be exempt? Second, *to what extent* should existing licensing regimes be preserved, and *to what extent* should they be modified?

The answers to these questions will help to define the boundaries between different markets (or market segments) and to determine respective barriers to entry. They will inevitably have an impact on competition and market power. If a low threshold is established for the applicability of the licensing regime, or if the requirements associated with licensing remain high, this will work to the advantage of incumbents and may hinder the market entry of platforms and platform-based providers. If a high threshold is established for applicability or if the requirements associated with licensing are significantly lowered, this will weaken incumbents and make it easier for the platforms to launch.

The approaches I have discussed so far involve either subjecting incumbents and newcomers to the prevailing regime or exempting at least some newcomers from such a regime. However, legislators in some other jurisdictions have taken another track, creating new kinds of licences for platform-based service providers. Legislators in some jurisdictions have begun to regulate Airbnb hosts using the mechanism of licences, as with San Francisco's Short-Term Rental Registry[88] and Amsterdam's "Private Holiday Rental" law.[89] Some jurisdictions have required Uber drivers to obtain special licences, distinct from taxi licences.[90] The creation of separate licensing regimes for platform-based providers involves a departure from the "level playing field" idea, invoked both in defence of and as an attack on existing licensing regimes. It means treating platform-based services differently. Such licensing regimes also impose a degree of formality on platform-based services, in tension with the casual ethos the platforms have promoted. Nevertheless, under considerable public pressure, the platforms have accepted such requirements in many jurisdictions.

In the design of these new licensing regimes for platform-based providers, governments have generally eschewed quantity-limited, tradable licences, recognizing how such licences have the potential to disproportionately serve private interests.[91] Nevertheless, the new licensing regimes still impose barriers to entry. Indeed, in some cases, these regimes contain measures that seem designed to limit supply. One example of supply management can be seen in expensive licensing fees for platform-based providers.[92] Another example is found in the placing of limits, or ceilings, on providers' activity, such as weekly limits on Uber drivers' hours,[93] or annual limits on short-term rentals.[94]

Whether or not the effort to restrict supply is intentional, separate licensing regimes for platform-based providers have the effect of drawing boundaries between different market segments.[95] As with thresholds that exempt some providers from licensing requirements, the impact on competition and market power will depend on the details. Lax licensing regimes for providers will work to the advantage of the platforms. Restrictive licensing regimes, if enforced, may amount to bans.

Not only have some jurisdictions established separate licensing regimes for providers, some have established such regimes for the platforms themselves. California was a pioneer in this regard, with its 2013 certification of Uber and Lyft as "transportation network companies" (TNCs).[96] Such licensing regimes allow the state to control entry into the market for intermediation services. They also enable the state to delegate certain regulatory tasks to platforms, making the platforms responsible for ensuring that their drivers respect certain standards. As Katrina Wyman argues, there is little indication that such licensing regimes reflect evidence-based consideration of optimal regulatory design. In many cases, such regimes are the outcomes of negotiations between governments and platform companies, and there is evidence of regulatory capture: for example, through the requirement that the platforms pay significant licensing fees (sometimes in the hundreds of thousands of dollars), which will make it more difficult for new platforms to compete.[97]

In Quebec, the government has yet to create any novel licensing category for platforms or for providers in either the hotel or the taxi sectors. Instead, in each sector, it has nominally attempted to retain the notion of a level playing field and a single regulatory regime. Nevertheless, in the case of Uber drivers, it has created something akin to a separate licensing regime, at least on a temporary basis. In September 2016, the government agreed that, on an experimental basis for one year, Uber drivers could operate without traditional taxi owners' permits. In exchange, Uber would pay the government a per-ride fee, to be funnelled towards the modernization of the taxi industry.[98] This fee starts at 90 cents per ride, if Uber drivers in the province are collectively on the road for less than 50,000 hours in a given week; over 50,000 hours, the fee is $1.10 per ride; it goes up to $1.26 per ride if Uber drivers in the province are on the road for more than 100,000 hours in a given week. Uber must also pay the government an additional 7 cents per ride "to take into account the insurance costs incurred in the taxi industry." The agreement also requires Uber to set its minimum fare at $3.45, the same base fare established for taxis by the Commission des transports. Uber must also apply for a taxi intermediary's permit. In some respects, the agreement is akin to granting Uber a certain number of taxi owner's permits, albeit on per-hour rather than a per-vehicle basis. However, Uber drivers can only solicit passengers through the Uber smartphone application; unlike incumbent taxis, they may not pick up passengers who simply hail them on the street.[99]

The agreement between the government and Uber also imposes certain conditions on Uber drivers. Uber is responsible for carrying out background checks on its drivers and making sure that vehicles are properly registered, inspected, and insured. Uber drivers must hold commercial-grade drivers' licences. The *entente* between the government and Uber clearly provides some advantages to Uber drivers: it sets aside the greatest barrier to entry in the taxi market—the requirement of an owner's permit—and allows drivers to operate legally. But it also subjects them to new licensing requirements, negotiated between Uber and the government behind closed doors. And the enforcement of these requirements is in the hands of Uber, rather than those of a government agency.

The arrival of "sharing economy" platforms has therefore not necessarily led to the dismantling of licensing regimes. Nor, in their responses to these platforms, have policy makers necessarily established a "level playing field" for incumbents and newcomers. Instead, many government authorities have, through their design of licensing regimes, effectively, carved up the market between incumbents and newcomers. And in doing so, they have in some cases delegated a certain amount of regulatory authority to the platforms.

V. The Platforms as Private Licensing Regimes

For some commentators on the "sharing economy," peer platform markets provide an alternative to state licensing as a way of ensuring safety, privacy, and contractual fairness. The platforms are in a position to supervise the conduct of providers and to discipline them if they fail to meet certain standards. However, in carrying out these functions, platforms may function more or less like private licensing regimes. And as private licensing regimes, the platforms may reproduce the pathologies associated with publicly mandated licensing. They may place providers in a precarious position, and they are unlikely to operate in the public interest. These pathologies are only reinforced when the state formally delegates regulatory authority to the platforms through a public system of platform licensing.

Platforms such as Airbnb and Uber are generally considered private actors. In their original form, such platforms did not purport to exercise any regulatory authority delegated by the state. Instead, they developed software programs (protected by copyright law) and they used private law—contract law—to grant access to this intellectual property. Providers and consumers who use these platforms' software enter into licensing agreements, consenting to use the software according to the stipulated terms and conditions. However, the word "licence" is used here in a sense borrowed from property law, distinguishable from the administrative licensing regimes I have described. Because they rely on the mechanisms of private law, the platforms do not qualify as licensing regimes under the definition I have employed.

Nevertheless, such platforms operate in ways that mirror the operation of licensing regimes. In order to provide services through a platform, one must obtain the prior authorization of the platform company. Such authorization may be granted lightly, or it may be subject to tests, inspections, and background checks. Moreover, those who obtain this authorization are subject to ongoing monitoring. The platform collects data on every transaction; in the case of Uber, it can monitor the geographic location of its users. In some cases, providers may be subject to periodic inspections. In other cases, user ratings, reviews, and complaint mechanisms may perform a similar function. The platforms retain the discretion to banish providers who fail to meet their expectations.

In many respects, then, the platforms resemble private regulatory systems. Verifications and monitoring are used to ensure compliance with quality and safety standards. Uber sets a maximum age for its vehicles, and requires vehicles to undergo regular inspections. Uber once boasted that its drivers were subject to an "industry leading" system of background checks (a claim that it later renounced under the pressure of a class-action lawsuit).[100] Even more fundamentally, elements of the platforms' software make certain deceptive business practices less likely. These elements include the fact that payment *must* pass through the platform. In the case of Uber, they also include the standardization of fares (and the regulation of routes taken by drivers). Such mechanisms are praised by certain business authors for fostering the trust that encourages consumers to enter into online transactions.[101]

Of course, it is generally acknowledged that the platforms' regulatory regimes are not self-contained systems, and that they operate in tandem with state regulatory regimes. For example, the safety of an Airbnb rental depends in part on the application of building safety standards, which are not monitored by Airbnb but rather by other public and private actors. Uber requires its drivers to hold drivers' licences, issued by public authorities. Although Uber conducts its own driver background checks in some cities, in other places, public authorities have insisted on carrying out their own background checks on Uber drivers.[102] In some places, Uber has even agreed to make access to its platform conditional on the obtaining of a sector-specific licence issued by a state authority. For example, Uber initially operated with licensed limousines or other luxury vehicles, and this is still the case in some jurisdictions.[103] Moreover, as discussed in the previous section, the platforms have sometimes accepted the imposition of a distinct licensing regime for platform-based providers.

Of course, the platforms differ from public licensing regimes in certain respects as well. Most importantly, while the platforms control access to their own software, they do not necessarily control access to the industry or the economic sector in question. In principle, they may face competition from other platforms. One might therefore argue that it is possible for providers to enter the market without having access to the platforms.

However, the competition faced by the platforms may be more apparent than real. In practice, network effects may bar competing platforms from entering the market. Other factors may reinforce these dynamics as well. A platform's possession of data generated by millions of repeated uses may enable it to refine its algorithms in such a way that competitors will not be able to replicate.[104] Together, these effects may provide some platforms with an effective monopoly on intermediation services in a given sector, controlling entry for would-be providers—and functioning as an all but mandatory licensing regime.

In fact, with their recent legislative changes, some jurisdictions have formalized the platforms' role as licensing regimes, officially delegating to the platforms the power to issue a public licence. This is the case notably in the state of Massachusetts, where a statute legalizing TNCs was enacted in 2016.[105] The statute establishes a mandatory system of "transportation network driver certificates." The statute specifies the requirements for the issuance of these certificates (for example, the driver must be at least twenty-one years of age, have an appropriately registered vehicle and insurance, satisfy requirements related to criminal background and driving records, and so on). However, the TNC is responsible for issuing the certificate.[106] In Massachusetts, public authorities have effectively taken control of the private licensing regime, but then formally delegated control of this regime back to the platform, in a manner that parallels older systems of professional licensing.

But even in the absence of such formalization, the platforms, as private licensing regimes, may exhibit many of the pathologies typically associated with publicly mandated licensing regimes—and in some cases, they may be worse. Publicly mandated licensing regimes must at least maintain a pretence of operating in the public interest. The platforms have no such pressure.

The clearest way in which platforms may serve their own private interests at the expense of the public interest is through the extraction of rents—the exercise of market power.[107] Extraction of rents by the platforms may be masked by the fact that the platforms often provide low prices for consumers. However, such low prices do not necessarily mean that the platforms lack market power. It seems likely that, in keeping with a two-sided market strategy, the platforms are extracting rents from one group in order to subsidize participation by another group.[108] Acting as intermediaries, the platforms may charge high prices on one side of the market in order to offer low prices on the other side. While passengers may find Uber relatively cheap, Uber extracts a large portion of the fare—as high as 30 per cent in some places.[109] In effect, Uber extracts rents by charging drivers a high price for its intermediation service. To the extent that Uber faces competition (from taxis, or from other platform companies such as Lyft), it may have to keep fares low in order to attract passengers. But this dynamic certainly works to the detriment of drivers, and therefore raises distributive concerns.

The two-sided market dynamic also implies that rent-seeking need not be coupled with limits on supply. In effect, if platforms are competing for market share on one side of the market (passengers), it may be in their interest to increase supply on the other side of the market as much as possible (drivers). It is in Uber's interest to have more drivers on the road at any given time in order to reduce passenger wait times, whereas for drivers, such increased supply means more downtime spent waiting for rides.[110] Moreover, Uber's optimal number of drivers on the road may not correspond to the social optimum, when one takes into account externalities such as traffic congestion, accidents, and pollution. In short, supply management by platforms may be inefficient.

The tension between the platforms' private interests and the public interest has also been revealed through subtler issues in regulatory design. For example, should Uber drivers be required to submit to background checks by a public authority, or can Uber be relied upon to carry out its own background checks? Such background checks serve Uber's interests as well as the public interest. However, Uber may have an interest in carrying out such checks more strictly or more leniently than the public interest would warrant, depending on its profit-making objectives.[111]

The platforms' control of a private licensing regime may give rise to arbitrary exercises of power. The platforms retain the discretion to banish providers who fail to meet their standards. They may exercise this discretion fairly or unfairly. In the case of Uber drivers, there has been considerable scrutiny of the fact that drivers are banished when their star rating falls below a certain level.[112] Continued access to the platform therefore depends on customer satisfaction; however, it may also depend on customers' whims and prejudices. Just as importantly, providers have raised concerns about the platform companies' unilateral modifications of their terms and conditions, which can have an enormous impact on providers' work.[113]

Finally, the shift from public to private licensing regimes does not obviate concerns about regulatory capture. Indeed, by displacing public licensing regimes and purporting to exercise licensing functions themselves, the platforms may be understood as having devised a more effective form of regulatory capture. The fact that TNCs have accepted for themselves public licensing arrangements that will serve as bars to potential competitors add to these suspicions of regulatory capture.[114] The platforms must cooperate with public officials when necessary to head off political opposition. But the day-to-day operation of the system is entirely under their control.

In short, the platforms should not be seen as easy deregulatory substitutes for ossified licensing regimes. Instead, it must be recognized that the platforms operate as private licensing regimes. The platforms are able to reproduce some of the advantages of public licensing regimes, but they are also perfectly capable of reproducing these regimes' disadvantages. If state-imposed barriers to entry are eliminated, platform-imposed barriers may take their place. Eliminating or weakening existing licensing regimes so as to reduce barriers to entry does not necessarily eliminate the problem of barriers to entry. It may simply amount to a delegation of barriers to entry, shifting them from public into private hands.

The recognition that platforms may function as private licensing regimes makes it necessary to revisit the analysis, set out earlier, of the new public licensing regimes that have been designed for these platforms and their providers. It must be acknowledged that such arrangements effectively establish mixed public-private licensing regimes, in which private actors (the platforms) are asked to implement public interest goals, but in which these public requirements will conflict to some extent with their private interests. If providers are subject to distinct licensing regimes, this means that their entry into the market is subject to both public and private controls (those of the platform). If the platforms themselves are subject to licensing, this amounts to a formal delegation of regulatory authority to these platforms, albeit subject to public oversight.

But just as importantly, this recognition makes it clear that the *absence* of a public licensing regime for platforms or providers does not make it possible to avoid such issues as barriers to entry, market power, or arbitrariness. If the state eschews licensing, platform "self-regulation" may reproduce these same dynamics. The question is not whether to address these issues, but who should address them, when, where, and how.

VI. Conclusion

The arrival of peer platform markets has placed a harsh spotlight on publicly enacted licensing regimes. In this stark glare, the advantages as well as the disadvantages of such regimes have become even more apparent. Nevertheless, governments have found it impossible to dispense with licensing. Although some governments have modified licensing regimes in order to make way for the platforms, others have toughened or even multiplied these regimes, creating new licences for platform-based services. In addition, where governments have accepted the platforms' claims to be exempt from licensing, they have often done so because of the platforms' ability to mimic the functions of public licensing regimes. As private licensing regimes, however, the platforms not only reproduce the successes of public licensing regimes but also their many failures.

Licensing regimes need to be carefully examined, not only in order to determine whether they provide effective means of protecting consumers, but also to determine whether they respond effectively to concerns about efficiency, distribution, and power. As the foregoing analysis makes clear, however, the distinction between formal public licensing and ostensibly private, contractual arrangements will provide little guidance in this regard. Private entities are perfectly capable of generating modes of governance that resemble licensing regimes. Moreover, public regulation may end up modifying or simply reinforcing these arrangements. Regulatory responses to the "sharing economy" must take into account such interactions between public and private arrangements.

Notes

1. Assistant Professor, Faculty of Law, Université de Sherbrooke. I would like to thank the participants at the workshop as well as Geneviève Cartier, Katrina Wyman, and an anonymous reviewer for comments on previous drafts. Mistakes are mine.

2. I have chosen to place "sharing" in quotation marks when referring to Airbnb, Uber, and similar platforms, in recognition of the fact that these are profit-making enterprises. For an explanation of the distinction between markets and sharing as modes of economic organization, see Yochai Benkler, "Sharing Nicely: On Shareable Goods and the Emergence of Sharing as a Modality of Economic Production" (2004) 114 Yale LJ 273.

3. OECD, Committee on Consumer Policy, *Protecting Consumers in Peer Platform Markets: Exploring the Issues*, Background Report for Ministerial Panel 3.1, Doc No DSTI/CP(2015)4/FINAL (OECD, 2016), online: <http://www.oecd.org/officialdocuments/publicdisplaydocumentpdf/?cote=DSTI/CP(2015)4/FINAL&docLanguage=En> [OECD].

4. EC, Commission, *A European Agenda for the Collaborative Economy* (Brussels: EC, 2016), online: <http://ec.europa.eu/DocsRoom/documents/16881> [European Commission].

5. US, Federal Trade Commission, *The "Sharing" Economy: Issues Facing Platforms, Participants & Regulators* (A Federal Trade Commission Staff Report, 2016), online: <https://www.ftc.gov/system/files/documents/reports/sharing-economy-issues-facing-platforms-participants-regulators-federal-trade-commission-staff/p151200_ftc_staff_report_on_the_sharing_economy.pdf> [Federal Trade Commission].

6. European Commission, *supra* note 4.

7. The issue of whether Uber qualifies as an "information society service," immune from prior authorization requirements, subsequently came to the fore in the case of *Asociación Profesional Elite Taxi v Uber Systems*

Spain SL, before the European Court of Justice (ECJ). In May 2017, EU Advocate General Maciej Szpunar issued his opinion in the case, holding that Uber's electronic intermediation is inseparable from the transportation service offered by its drivers. Uber therefore constitutes a comprehensive transportation service and can be subject to national licensing regimes. See Opinion of Advocate General Szpunar, *Asociación Profesional Elite Taxi v Uber Systems Spain SL* (11 May 2017), Barcelona C-434/15, ECLI:EU:C:2017:364 (Comm Ct No 3, Barcelona, Spain), online: CVRIA <http://curia.europa.eu/juris/document/document.jsf?text=&docid=190593&pageIndex=0&doclang=EN&mode=req&dir=&occ=first&part=1&cid=611658>. At the time of writing, the ECJ had yet to render its judgment in the case.

8. Federal Trade Commission, *supra* note 5. The title page contains this disclaimer: "This staff report represents the views of the FTC staff and does not necessarily represent the views of the Commission or any individual Commissioner. The Commission, however, has voted to authorize the staff to issue this staff report."

9. See e.g. Karl Rettino-Parazelli, "Québec promet d'en «faire plus» pour encadrer Airbnb," *Le Devoir* (30 August 2017), online: <http://www.ledevoir.com/politique/quebec/506807/quebec-et-airbnb-s-entendent-sur-une-taxe-d-hebergement> (discussing Airbnb's agreement to begin collecting a 3.5 per cent lodging tax in Québec).

10. Shu-Yi Oei & Diane M Ring, "Can Sharing Be Taxed?" (2016) 93 Wash UL Rev 989.

11. Federal Trade Commission, *supra* note 5 at 89.

12. Arun Sundararajan, *The Sharing Economy: The End of Employment and the Rise of Crowd-Based Capitalism* (Cambridge, MA: The MIT Press, 2016).

13. See Brishen Rogers, "Employment Rights in the Platform Economy: Getting Back to Basics" (2016) 10 Harv L & Pol'y Rev 479.

14. See Michael L Katz & Carl Shapiro, "Systems Competition and Network Effects" (1994) 8:2 J Econ Perspect 93.

15. See K Sabeel Rahman, "Curbing the New Corporate Power," *Boston Review* (4 May 2015), online: <http://bostonreview.net/forum/k-sabeel-rahman-curbing-new-corporate-power>.

16. See Louis Kaplow, "Why (Ever) Define Markets?" (2010) 124 Harv L Rev 437.

17. See Federal Trade Commission, *supra* note 5.

18. See David S Evans, "The Antitrust Economics of Multi-Sided Platform Markets" (2003) 20 Yale J Reg 325; Julian Wright, "One-Sided Logic in Two-Sided Markets" (2004) 3:1 Rev Network Econ 44.

19. See e.g. Molly Cohen & Arun Sundararajan, "Self-Regulation and Innovation in the Peer-to-Peer Sharing Economy" (2015) 82 U Chicago L Rev Dialogue 116; Christopher Koopman, Matthew Mitchell & Adam

Thierer, "The Sharing Economy and Consumer Protection Regulation: The Case for Policy Change" (2015) 8 J Bus Entrepreneurship & L 529.

20. OECD, *supra* note 3 at 8.

21. See e.g. Glanville Williams, "Control by Licensing" (1967) 20:1 Curr Leg Probl 81.

22. See Anthony I Ogus, *Regulation: Legal Form and Economic Theory* (Oxford: Clarendon Press, 1994) at 214–42.

23. Pierre Issalys & Denis Lemieux, *L'action gouvernementale : Précis de droit des institutions administratives*, 3rd ed (Cowansville, QC: Éditions Yvon Blais, 2009) at 916.

24. *Ibid* at 215.

25. See e.g. *McInnes v Onslow Fane*, [1978] 1 WLR 1520, 3 All ER 211 (Ch).

26. Mariana Valverde, *Everyday Law on the Street: City Governance in an Age of Diversity* (Chicago: University of Chicago Press, 2012).

27. See Orly Lobel, "The Renew Deal: The Fall of Regulation and the Rise of Governance in Contemporary Legal Thought" (2004) 89 Minn L Rev 342.

28. For an extended treatment of this distinction, see Eric Bibert & JB Ruhl, "The Permit Power Revisited: The Theory and Practice of Regulatory Permits in the Administrative State" (2014) 64 Duke LJ 133 (distinguishing between "general" and "specific" permits, largely in the context of environmental regulation and land-use planning).

29. Some authors have distinguished licences, used to enforce standards, from public franchises, meant to restrict competition by imposing quantitative restrictions. See Ogus, *supra* note 22 at 214. I would argue that it is too difficult to draw a distinction between the two, and that there are many hybrid examples—as in the case of taxis. I therefore include public franchises within my definition of licences.

30. Jody Rosen, "The Knowledge, London's Legendary Taxi-Driver Test, Puts Up a Fight in the Age of GPS," *T: The New York Times Style Magazine* (10 November 2014), online: <https://www.nytimes.com/2014/11/10/t-magazine/london-taxi-test-knowledge.html?_r=0>.

31. See *Saulnier (Receiver of) v Saulnier*, 2008 SCC 58; see also Katrina Miriam Wyman, "Problematic Private Property: The Case of New York Taxicab Medallions" (2013) 30 Yale J Reg 125; Christopher Essert, "Property in Licences and the Law of Things" (2014) 59 McGill LJ 559.

32. See *Québec (Société de l'assurance automobile) v Cyr*, 2008 SCC 13.

33. Ian Ayres & John Braithwaite, *Responsive Regulation: Transcending the Deregulation Debate* (New York: Oxford University Press, 1992) at 35-36.

34. See Mariana Valverde, "Police Science, British Style: Pub Licensing and Knowledges of Urban Disorder" (2003) 32:2 Econ & Soc'y 234.

35. Compare Richard Posner, *Economic Analysis of Law*, 8th ed (Austin: Wolters Kluwer, 2011) at 489.

36. Charles A Reich, "The New Property" (1964) 73 Yale LJ 733.

37. *Roncarelli v Duplessis*, [1959] SCR 121, SCJ No 1.

38. See *Nicholson v Haldimand-Norfolk (Regional Municipality) Commissioners of Police*, [1979] 1 SCR 311, [1978] 3 ACWS 185; see also *Martineau v Matsqui Institution*, [1980] 1 SCR 602, [1979] SCJ No 121 at para 62.

39. See *Baker v Canada (Minister of Citizenship and Immigration)*, [1999] 2 SCR 817; SCJ No 39.

40. See *Act Respecting Administrative Justice*, CQLR c J-3, ss 5, 8.

41. See *Ocean Port Hotel Ltd v British Columbia (General Manager, Liquor Control and Licensing Branch)*, 2001 SCC 52.

42. Richard A Epstein, "The Permit Power Meets the Constitution" (1995) 81 Iowa L Rev 407.

43. *Ibid.*

44. See e.g. Thomas G Moore, "The Purposes of Licensing" (1961) 4 JL & Econ 93; Shirley Svorny, "Licensing, Market Entry Regulation" in Boudewijn Bouckaert & Gerrit De Geest, eds, *Encyclopedia of Law and Economics, Volume III: The Regulation of Contracts* (Cheltenham, UK: Edward Elgar, 2000) 296.

45. See Ogus, *supra* note 22 at 216–17.

46. See e.g. George J Stigler, "The Theory of Economic Regulation" (1971) 2:1 Bell J Econ & Manage Sci 3.

47. Epstein, *supra* note 42 at 407.

48. Ogus, *supra* note 22.

49. See Neil *Komesar, Imperfect Alternatives: Choosing Institutions in Law, Economics, and Public Policy* (Chicago: University of Chicago Press, 1994).

50. See Lon L Fuller, "Means and Ends" in Kenneth I Winston, ed, *The Principles of Social Order: Selected Essays of Lon L Fuller*, revised ed (Oxford: Hart Publishing, 2001) 61.

51. See Roderick A Macdonald, "The Swiss Army Knife of Governance" in Pearl Eliadis, Margaret M Hill & Michael Howlett, eds, *Designing Government: From Instruments to Governance* (Montreal: McGill-Queen's University Press, 2005) 203.

52. *Act Respecting Tourist Accommodation Establishments*, CQLR c E-14.2, s 1.

53. The statute expressly empowers the minister to delegate his or her powers with regard to the "issue, suspension or cancellation of classification certificates." See *ibid*, s 14.1.

54. Corporation de l'industrie touristique du Québec, "Frais annuels d'attestation," online: <http://citq.qc.ca/fr/fraisattestation.php>.

55. *Act Respecting Tourist Accommodation Establishments*, *supra* note 52, s 37(8).

56. *Act Respecting Transportation Services by Taxi*, CQLR c S-6.01, ss 4-23.

57. *Ibid*, ss 24-31.

58. *Ibid*, ss 32-34.

59. Until 2016, the Commission des transports also established the number of owner's permits for particular geographical areas; in 2016, the

government (e.g. the cabinet) assumed this power directly. See *ibid*, s 5.1.

60. *Ibid*, s 117.

61. *Ibid*, s 118.

62. See Tristan Péloquin, "La chute de la valeur des permis de taxi se confirme," *La Presse* (7 December 2016), online: <http://www.lapresse.ca/actualites/grand-montreal/201612/06/01-5048800-la-chute-de-la-valeur-des-permis-de-taxi-se-confirme.php>.

63. See Claude Turcotte, "L'industrie du taxi ne roule pas sur l'or, mais…," *Le Devoir* (30 August 2010), online: <http://www.ledevoir.com/economie/actualites-economiques/295262/l-industrie-du-taxi-ne-roule-pas-sur-l-or-mais>.

64. *Act Respecting Transportation Services by Taxi, supra* note 56, s 26(1).

65. *Ibid*, ss 26(2)–(4), 31.1-31.2; *Taxi Transportation Regulation*, CQLR c S-6.01, r 3, ss 4(5), 21.1–21.3.

66. *Taxi Transportation Regulation, supra* note 65, s 4(4).

67. *Act Respecting Transportation Services by Taxi, supra* note 56, s 27. See also City of Montréal, by-law No RCG 10-009, *Règlement sur le transport par taxi*, s 70 (Montréal requires new taxi drivers to undergo 150 hours of training).

68. *Act Respecting Tourist Accommodation Establishments, supra* note 52, s 6.1.

69. See e.g. Arrondissement Ville-Marie, by-law No 01-282, *Codification administrative du règlement d'urbanisme* (6 March 2017), s 136(8).

70. *Civil Code of Québec*, CQLR c CCQ-1991, art 1870.

71. See *9177-2541 Québec Inc c Li*, 2016 QCRDL 8129.

72. See *Côté c Pilon*, 2016 QCRDL 18913; *Ngo c Arakaki Inc*, 2016 QCRDL 21172. Moreover, 2015 legislative amendments make landlords liable for their tenants' regulatory offences, unless they can prove they exercised due diligence to avoid the offence. See *Act Respecting Tourist Accommodation Establishments, supra* note 52, s 41.1. In effect, landlords are obliged to ensure that their tenants are complying with the licensing regime.

73. *Taxi Transportation Regulation, supra* note 65, s 4(3).

74. Société de l'assurance automobile du Québec, "Obtenir un permis de conduire," online: <https://saaq.gouv.qc.ca/permis-de-conduire/obtenir-permis/taxi-limousine-classe-4c>.

75. Québec, National Assembly, *Bill 67: An Act Mainly to Improve the Regulation of Tourist Accommodation and to Define a New System of Governance as Regards International Promotion*, 41st Leg, 1st Sess, Vol 44, No 118 (first reading, 22 October 2015).

76. Québec, National Assembly, "Point de presse de Mme Dominique Vien, ministre du Tourisme" by Dominique Vien (2015), online: <http://www.assnat.qc.ca/fr/actualites-salle-presse/conferences-points-presse/ConferencePointPresse-25417.html> [Vien].

77. Pierre-André Normandin, "Le ministre Poëti veut freiner UberX," *La Presse+* (13 December 2014), online: <http://plus.lapresse.ca/screens/d5212508-29a5-469e-8a6e-701f05275812%7C_0.html>.

78. Tristan Péloquin, "Saisies de véhicules Uber: le Bureau du taxi 'perplexe' devant de nombreux cas," *La Presse* (25 February 2016), online: <http://www.lapresse.ca/actualites/201602/25/01-4954452-saisies-de-vehicules-uber-le-bureau-du-taxi-perplexe-devant-de-nombreux-cas.php>.

79. *Jean-Paul c Uber Technologies Inc*, 2017 QCCS 164.

80. *Uber Canada Inc c Québec (Agence du Revenu)*, 2016 QCCS 2158 [*Uber Canada Inc*].

81. See Marco Bélair-Cirino, "Uber défie Québec," *Le Devoir* (19 February 2016), online: <http://www.ledevoir.com/non-classe/463477/uber-defie-quebec>. Such a claim may have been plausible in some other jurisdictions. See e.g. *Toronto (City of) v Uber Canada Inc*, 2015 ONSC 3572. However, in Quebec, in the case of Uber, this claim was absurd: Uber drivers clearly fall within Quebec's legislative definition of "taxi." See *Act Respecting Transportation Services by Taxi*, *supra* note 56, s 2(3); see also *Uber Canada Inc*, *supra* note 80 at paras 193-204.

82. Françoise Bertrand, "L'industrie du taxi a un cadre réglementaire inadapté à notre époque," *Le Devoir* (22 February 2016), online: <http://www.ledevoir.com/politique/quebec/463595/uber-et-le-transport-de-personnes-l-industrie-du-taxi-a-un-cadre-reglementaire-inadapte-a-notre-epoque>.

83. Denis Lessard & Tristan Péloquin, "Tir groupé contre le système de permis," *La Presse+* (24 February 2016), online: <http://plus.lapresse.ca/screens/29e61708-1711-454b-ac4f-0f8e7e41c11a%7C_0.html>.

84. *Regulation Respecting Tourist Accommodation Establishments*, CQLR c E-14.2, r 1, s 1. Prior to 2015, tourist accommodation establishments that were only offered for rent "on an occasional basis" were exempt from Quebec's classification scheme. When it undertook its 2015 reform of the legislation, the government promised to clarify this rule. See Vien, *supra* note 76.

85. Québec, Tourisme Québec, "Guide d'interprétation de la loi et du règlement sur les établissements d'hébergement touristique," (Gouvernement du Québec, 2017), online: <http://www.tourisme.gouv.qc.ca/programmes-services/hebergement/guide-interpretation.html>. It was subsequently reported that enterprising Airbnb hosts had found that they could circumvent the classification scheme by *offering* their rooms and apartments only for periods of more than thirty-one days, then subsequently negotiating with potential guests for shorter stays. See Philippe Orfali, "La loi anti-Airbnb est aisément contournée," *Le Devoir* (17 August 2016), online: <http://www.ledevoir.com/societe/actualites-en-societe/477891/la-loi-anti-airbnb-est-aisement-contournee>.

86. Pierre Saint-Arnaud, "Robert Poëti n'avait pas la même vision d'Uber que le premier ministre," *La Presse Canadienne* (1 February 2016), online: <https://www.latribune.ca/actualites/robert-poeti-navait-pas-la-meme-vision-duber-que-le-premier-ministre-951ca1958cb04b49b3ec6db01565 62d7>.

87. See Simon Boivin, "Daoust envisage la suspension du permis des chauffeurs d'Uber," *Le Soleil* (23 February 2016), online: <https:// www.lesoleil.com/actualite/daoust-envisage-la-suspension-du-permis-des-chauffeurs-duber-b3179f7c8182a25c3f7f39 82f7039547>.

88. San Francisco, Office of Short-Term Rentals, "Office of Short-Term Rental Registry & FAQs," online: <http://sf-planning.org/office-short-term-rental-registry-faqs> [Short-Term Rental FAQs].

89. "Private Holiday Rental: What You Should Know," online: I Amsterdam <http://www.iamsterdam.com/en/visiting/plan-your-trip/where-to-stay/ private-holiday-rental> [Private Holiday Rental].

90. See e.g. City of Edmonton, by-law No 17400, *Vehicle for Hire* (27 June 2017), s 2(2)(n) ("private transportation provider"); Toronto, City Council, "Private Transportation Company (PTC) Drivers" (15 July 2016), online: <https://www1.toronto.ca/City%20Of%20Toronto/ Municipal%20Licensing%20&%20Standards/1-Files/PDFs/Taxireview/ ptc%20drivers%20fact%20sheet.pdf>.

91. See Katrina Wyman, "The Novelty of TNC Regulation" in Nestor Davidson, Michèle Finck & John Infranca, eds, *The Cambridge Handbook of the Law of the Sharing Economy* (Cambridge: Cambridge University Press) [forthcoming in 2018, draft on file with author].

92. See Annalise Klingbeil, "Uber Tells Calgary Drivers to Get a Class 4 Licence Ahead of Possible Relaunch," *Calgary Herald* (28 July 2016), online: <http://calgaryherald.com/news/local-news/uber-tells-calgary-drivers-to-get-a-class-4-licence-ahead-of-possible-relaunch>.

93. See e.g. Hara Associates Inc, "Framework for Choice: Discussion Paper to Inform and Support Vehicles-for-Hire Dialogue" (10 October 2015), online: City of Vancouver <http://vancouver.ca/files/cov/hara-report-framework-for-choice.pdf>.

94. Short-Term Rental FAQs, *supra* note 88; Private Holiday Rental, *supra* note 89. Although it does not belong to a licensing regime and thus falls outside the scope of this study, New York's requirement that Airbnb hosts be physically present performs a similar supply-limiting function. See New York State, "Multiple Dwelling Law," online: <https://www1. nyc.gov/assets/buildings/pdf/MultipleDwellingLaw.pdf>; see also James Dobbins, "How to Host on Airbnb Legally," *The New York Times* (7 April 2017), online: <https://www.nytimes.com/2017/04/07/realestate/how-to-host-on-airbnb-legally.html?_r=0>. The same is true of Berlin's restriction

of Airbnb rentals to *portions* of apartments. See Philip Oltermann, "Berlin Ban on Airbnb Short-Term Rentals Upheld by City Court," *The Guardian* (8 June 2016), online: <https://www.theguardian.com/technology/2016/jun/08/berlin-ban-airbnb-short-term-rentals-upheld-city-court>; Feargus O'Sullivan, "The City with the World's Toughest Anti-Airbnb Laws," *CityLab* (1 December 2016), online: <https://www.citylab.com/equity/2016/12/berlin-has-the-worlds-toughest-anti-airbnb-laws-are-they-working/509024>.

95. It is worth noting that the question of whether or not incumbents and newcomers should be subject to the same rules cannot be resolved simply by asking whether they participate in the same market. The answer to this question is bound to depend on how broadly or narrowly one defines the concept of "market"; it raises all of the market definition problems that are familiar from competition law. Moreover, attempting to answer the question in this way will give rise to a circularity. The extent to which incumbents and platforms belong to the same or different markets depends in part on the roles that the law assigns them.

96. State of California, Public Utilities Commission, "Transportation Network Companies," online: <http://www.cpuc.ca.gov/General.aspx?id=787>. Wyman notes that forty-eight American states now have equivalent legislation. See Wyman, *supra* note 91.

97. Wyman, *supra* note 91.

98. Louis-Samuel Perron, "Québec rend publique son entente avec Uber," *La Presse* (9 September 2016), online: <http://www.lapresse.ca/actualites/politique/politique-quebecoise/201609/09/01-5018739-quebec-rend-publique-son-entente-avec-uber.php>.

99. Québec, Ministre des Transports, de la Mobilité durable et de l'Électrification des transports, "Entente" (Québec, 2016), online: <https://www.transports.gouv.qc.ca/fr/salle-de-presse/nouvelles/Documents/2016-09-09/entente-uber.pdf>.

100. See Mike Isaac, "Uber Settles Suit Over Driver Background Checks," *The New York Times* (7 April 2016), online: <https://www.nytimes.com/2016/04/08/technology/uber-settles-suit-over-driver-background-checks.html>.

101. Sundararajan, *supra* note 12.

102. See Adam Vaccaro & Dan Adams, "Thousands of Current Uber, Lyft Drivers Fail New Background Checks," *The Boston Globe* (5 April 2017), online: <https://www.bostonglobe.com/business/2017/04/05/uber-lyft-ride-hailing-drivers-fail-new-background-checks/aX3pQy6QopJvbtKZKw9fON/story.html>.

103. See e.g. Jean-Baptiste Jacquin, "Le Conseil constitutionnel confirme l'illégalité du service Uberpop en France," *Le Monde* (22 September 2015), online: <www.lemonde.fr/economie/article/2015/09/22/

web-eco-uberpop-decision-conseil-constitutionnel_4767302_3234.
html#ohUqpBJ4Y2VCqY2K.99>.

104. See Cédric Argenton & Jens Prüfer, "Search Engine Competition with
Network Externalities" (2012) 8 J Comp L & Econ 73.

105. Code of Massachusetts Regulations, c 159A½, §3.

106. *Ibid*, §4.

107. The concept of market power comes from competition law, where it
refers to a monopolist's ability to raise prices above those that would
prevail under competitive conditions. See OECD, *Glossary of Industrial
Organisation Economics and Competition Law*, compiled by RS Khemani
& DM Shapiro, (1993), online: <http://www.oecd.org/regreform/sec-
tors/2376087.pdf>. In Canadian competition law, market power has
been defined as "the power to behave relatively independently of the
market." See *Canada v Nova Scotia (Pharmaceutical Society)*, [1992] 2 SCR
606, SCJ No 67.

108. In economics, a two-sided market is said to exist where an intermediary
facilitates transactions between two distinct groups, such as buyers and
sellers. In order to succeed, the intermediary must attract participants
on both sides of the market: buyers will only be interested if there are
enough sellers, and vice versa. Some have suggested the analogy of a
heterosexual nightclub or dating website, in which men will only be
attracted if there are sufficient women, and vice versa. See Wright, *supra*
note 18. While network effects work on both sides of the market, they may
be stronger on one side than the other. The platform may therefore be
able to extract greater revenue from one side of the market than the other;
indeed, it may find itself taking revenue from one side of the market to
subsidize participation on the other side. See Bernard Caillaud & Bruno
Jullien, "Chicken & Egg: Competition Among Intermediation Service
Providers" (2003) 34:2 Rand J Econ 309; Mark Armstrong, "Competition
in Two-Sided Markets" (2006) 37:3 Rand J Econ 668; Marc Rysman, "The
Economics of Two-Sided Markets" (2009) 23:3 J Econ Perspect 125.

109. Douglas MacMillan, "Uber Tests 30% Fee, Its Highest Yet," *The Wall
Street Journal* (18 May 2015), online: <https://www.wsj.com/articles/
uber-tests-30-fee-its-highest-yet-1431989126>.

110. See Noam Scheiber, "How Uber Uses Psychological Tricks to Push Its
Drivers' Buttons," *The New York Times* (2 April 2017), online: <https://
www.nytimes.com/interactive/2017/04/02/technology/uber-drivers-
psychological-tricks.html>.

111. See Vaccaro & Adams, *supra* note 102.

112. See Georgia Wilkins, "Dumped Uber Driver Pleads for Explanation,"
The Sydney Morning Herald (21 May 2016), online: <http://www.smh.com.
au/business/consumer-affairs/dumped-uber-driver-pleads-for-explan-
ation-20160519-gozodl.html>.

113. See Alan Feuer, "Uber Drivers Up Against the App," *The New York Times* (19 February 2016), online: <https://www.nytimes.com/2016/02/21/nyregion/uber-drivers-up-against-the-app.html>.

114. See Wyman, *supra* note 91.

CHAPTER II

The False Promise
of the Sharing Economy

Harry Arthurs[1]

I. Introduction: A Historical Perspective
on the Sharing Economy

Automation ended the drudgery of industrial production and heralded the advent of the "leisure society"; deregulation liberated us from markets distorted by entrenched, rent-seeking "special interests"; globalization freed us from the drag of protectionism and set in motion the beneficial forces of "natural advantage"; the shareholder society gave us all a stake in the success of finance capital; our *Charter of Rights and Freedoms* entrenched the principles of equality; the new public administration taught slimmed-down governments to govern "smarter"; and widespread adoption of social media enabled the "spontaneous" mobilization of grassroots social movements. But workers are working longer hours in less secure and less well-paid jobs; corporate economic and political power grows apace; offshore competition has stripped many jobs out of the economy; social and economic inequality are on the rise; businesses large and small violate financial, labour, and environmental regulations frequently and with apparent impunity; and citizens are subject to intrusive surveillance and sporadic abuse by spammers, scammers, and state security organizations. And now the sharing economy, which—we are told—will "empower" consumers, challenge corporate concentration, diminish the wasteful use of resources, and enable us to integrate our working and non-working lives, however, suits us best.

Will we never learn to look beyond the attractive packaging in which transformative or disruptive change often comes wrapped? To make a sensible calculation of whether such change can or will deliver the benefits its proponents and popularizers promise? To assess whether those benefits will likely outweigh the harms transformation and disruption are sure to cause?

The contemporary experiences briefly referenced above remind us that far-reaching changes in political economy, legal-institutional arrangements, and technology are almost certain to create losers as well as winners. Historical evidence points in the same direction. There was once a "sharing economy" worthy of the name, an economy in which resources actually were widely held and used in common. The result—inevitably, many economists and environmentalists contend[2]—was "the tragedy of the commons," the depletion of communally owned resources because no one owner was specifically responsible for their conservation. But the evidence points in a different direction. The actual experience of resource-based communities around the world demonstrates that common ownership does not lead to economic or environmental catastrophe.[3] Moreover, the "tragedy of the commons" thesis is wrenched out of its political context. As E. P. Thompson convincingly demonstrated, the rural economy of early-modern England was destroyed not because communities failed to take proper measures to conserve their shared resources, but because those resources were snatched away by the Whig magnates.[4] These powerful political operators seized common lands under cover of acts of Parliament, physically enclosed them to exclude the peasants who for generations had worked them, suppressed the "natural" or customary law that regulated the use of communal lands, and enlisted the criminal law and the state judiciary to effectively expunge "sharing" from the lexicon of England's eighteenth-century peasantry.

Nor is the tragedy of the commons, as described by Thompson, a long-ago wrong done to people in a faraway country of which we know nothing. It bears an uncanny resemblance to the sad history of Canada's Aboriginal peoples who were stripped of their communal lands and resources by the deployment of state law and state coercive power in aid of the private interests of non-Aboriginal settlers. And it is a cautionary tale for our own time, recently rehearsed by the rapacious post-Communist oligarchs who, aided by a corrupt state, appropriated what was once (at least in theory) "the people's common property."[5]

This is not to say that sharing is impossible in an advanced capitalist economy. The postwar corporatist welfare state was the sharing economy writ large: workers were implicitly offered a significant increase in employment benefits, social goods, and political power, in exchange for which they implicitly agreed to participate in the development of a mixed market economy.[6] Alas, the postwar welfare state reached its high-water mark in the 1960s and 1970s, and seems almost everywhere to be receding. By contrast, the highly successful worker-owned Mondragón cooperatives offer a model of the sharing economy writ small.[7] So too do other experiments in shared market organization and enterprise governance: credit unions, producer-run agricultural marketing schemes, and housing co-ops,[8] and so too does employee representation on corporate boards.[9] But these experiments are becoming less popular and less numerous, while those that survive are increasingly pressured to abandon their founding principles. None of them, ironically, has a place in the new sharing economy.

Of course, it would be impossible to persuade people of the attractions of our current sharing economy, if that economy never delivered on its promises, and if it produced no winners, only losers. Indeed, the sharing economy can boast of many successes.[10] New communications technologies and business strategies do actually—as promised—help people who need expensive tools or appliances to acquire them cheaply second-hand, facilitate the rental of holiday accommodation, enable cars and bicycles to be hired conveniently by sequential short-term users and, notoriously, permit urban travellers to book private automobile transportation between any two points online on short notice and at attractive rates.

So who wins and who loses in the sharing economy? The winners are largely the proprietors of the new technologies and architects of the new service models that characterize the sharing economy.[11] However, consumers have often gained as well, to the extent that they are provided with goods and services at lower prices as well as greater choice and convenience.[12] The losers are those whose interests are imbricated in long-established markets which have been destabilized by the advent of the sharing economy: participants in the supply chains that support those markets;[13] consumers who, though benefiting from lower prices, are often unsuspectingly exposed to new risks;[14] workers whose employment prospects in traditional enterprises have been radically diminished;[15] and a new cohort of operatives enrolled in the legally ambiguous and economically risky work relationships that make possible the consumer choice and lower prices delivered by the sharing economy.

Thus, the sharing economy presents problems in many markets, many domains of public policy, and many juridical fields. Attempts have been made, and others proposed, to resolve these problems by the creative interpretation, tweaking, or extension of existing laws or the enactment of new ones. These attempts, I will argue, may provide some relief to some "losers" some of the time; but they are unlikely to generate the breadth, depth, or durability of systemic reforms needed to ensure that our political economy is one in which fair "sharing" occurs, not the "shearing" of some of its members for the enrichment of others.

II. Labour Market Regulation in the Sharing Economy

Workers are often identified as one of the major "loser" groups under the new "sharing" dispensation. The usual riposte of labour lawyers is to categorize their plight as a "category problem,"[16] a mis-characterization of subordinate or dependent workers as independent contractors rather than as the employees of so-called platform providers of work opportunities who are in fact, and should be in law, employers.[17] In a closely linked approach, some have proposed the creation of a new designation that deems dependent contractors or autonomous workers to be employees or endows them with rights similar to those enjoyed by employees.[18] In either case, the new legal category would effectively provide most workers in the sharing economy with the right to bargain collectively, with protection under labour standards legislation and employment-based benefit schemes, and with access to the state-provided social safety net. Presumably, this category correction would also bring most sharing economy workers—though not technically employees at common law—within the protection of recent Supreme Court decisions requiring employers to adhere to standards of good faith and procedural fairness in their workplace relations.[19] Finally, it would also ensure that putative employers will be bound by the contractual undertakings of the workers who bear these new designations, made vicariously liable for their torts and held accountable for their regulatory transgressions.

Moreover, there are undoubted attractions to resolving work-place disputes and labour market controversies by characterizing them as a category problem. An authoritative court ruling that expanded the statutory or common law definition of "employment" to include the typically attenuated workplace relations of the sharing economy would resolve a difficult political controversy quickly and definitively. Indeed, a British employment tribunal has recently made such a ruling,[20] although it has yet to undergo scrutiny by a higher court. A legislative amendment could accomplish the same result, albeit with a greater expenditure of political capital and undiminished exposure to judicial revisionism. This latter approach has been used in Canada since the 1970s, when many jurisdictions amended their labour relations acts to provide access to collective bargaining for dependent contractors who would otherwise have been denied it.[21] If "dependent contractor" has acquired too settled and narrow a meaning, it might be replaced by a new term, such as "autonomous worker"[22] or "operative," to be defined as "anyone providing services to a client, customer or consumer directly or pursuant to a contract, custom or understanding with a labour market intermediary, or with the intervention or assistance of a labour market intermediary." A definition of "labour market intermediary" would clearly be necessary as well, but it would include the platform providers that play a central role in the sharing economy. However, my aim is not to advocate for any particular form of words but rather to demonstrate that it may be preferable (and technically possible) to create new categories of protected workers, rather than try to hammer the square peg of employment into the round hole of the sharing economy.

Both the judicial and the legislative resolution of the category problem have their advantages. Both would, in principle, not only benefit workers currently denied the protection of labour statutes but also relieve pressure on "true employees" whose rights and entitlements have been undercut by the "dis-employed" victims of the sharing economy. But both have their limitations as well. It is by no means clear that restoring dis-employed workers to employee status or its functional equivalent would have the desired effects in the long term.[23] Employment in general is not what it used to be. The standard employment relationship—and the edifice of protections and entitlements built upon it—is available to fewer and fewer workers.[24] Precarious, non-standard and self-employment are growing apace. The workplace has been "fissured" ("fracked" would be a better descriptor).[25] Large segments of the workforce can look forward only to gigs[26] or zero-hour contracts,[27] not to regularly scheduled work assignments around which they can organize their personal lives, and their financial and civic commitments.[28] Nor does even constitutionally guaranteed access to collective bargaining[29] automatically empower either employees or dis-employed workers.[30] Unionization has fallen to historically low levels for many reasons, including globalization, technological change, employer resistance, and antipathy or indifference to unions by the general public and/or workers themselves.[31] Nor does access to something approximating employment status ensure that workers will actually be protected by labour standards, workers' compensation, or unemployment insurance legislation: in some jurisdictions, coverage is contracting even for conventional employees,[32] benefits are being reduced,[33] and enforcement is faltering.[34] Nor, finally, does the one-size-fits-all nature of most labour legislation necessarily provide the kind of flexibility needed to respond to the myriad forms of workplace relations thrown up by the sharing economy.

III. Non-Labour Market Regulation

Workers are not the only potential losers in the sharing economy. Uber passengers may be at risk because drivers are poorly trained, insufficiently insured, or of bad character; tourists may experience loss because Airbnb accommodations are falsely advertised, harbour unsuspected health hazards, or facilitate antisocial behaviour by hosts; purchasers of tools acquired through an online sharing facility may find that they are stolen or not fit for purpose; Zipcar users may find that vehicles are less readily available than they are supposed to be. Of course, consumers confront similar risks in more conventional, non-sharing transactions, but at least they can seek recourse under well-established common law and statutory rules, in almost all cases against the real, ultimate and deep-pocketed corporate provider of defective goods or services.[35] Moreover, in many sectors of the economy, regulators pre-empt threats to consumer interests by establishing detailed standards to which vendors and service providers must conform, by restricting access to the market to licensed providers, by promoting fair, safe, and honest trade practices through educational programs and proactive audits, and by terminating the right of dishonest or incompetent providers to participate in the market.[36]

In technical terms, the issue for consumers may resemble that confronting workers: Are the new sharing economy abuses captured by the obsolete language of statutes or common law doctrines designed to protect consumers in more conventional, pre-sharing markets? If the answer is negative—if, say, renters of Airbnb accommodation are not eligible to recover from their host under existing legislation governing damage to the goods or person of hotel guests, or if Airbnb itself has no financial responsibility for such loss—an intense debate is likely to ensue. Should consumers be deprived of the benefits they admittedly enjoy in the sharing economy so that they can be protected by legislation that imposes costs on vendors and suppliers?

Nor are workers and consumers the only victims of predation. The well-documented Uber controversy reminds us that the sharing economy puts at risk conventional businesses and the investment and work opportunities they provide.[37] Taxi companies have heavy capital investments in the vehicles they own or lease. They must maintain their fleet, ensure that it meets municipal licensing standards, purchase licences, train, oversee and insure their drivers and meet other costs that Uber shifts onto its "non-employee" operatives. In some cities, worse yet, individual drivers (many of whom come from immigrant communities) own their own cars and licences, and operate through dispatch services provided by the major taxi companies. While arrangements for these owner-operator/micro-investors in many respects resemble those that subsist between Uber and its drivers, the latter do not have to bear the significant cost of a taxi licence, they do not have to comply with onerous municipal regulations, and they enjoy the benefits of Uber's innovative marketing strategies. In short, the interests of all participants in the conventional taxi industry—and in the communities dependent on it for sustenance or service—are put at risk by Uber. Similarly, Airbnb seems to be disrupting the hospitality industry, to the prejudice of established stakeholders including hotel owners and operators, hotel employees (some of whom are unionized), and suppliers of ancillary goods and services.[38] There is some suggestion that it is also affecting the real estate market, as investors turn vacant apartments and houses into year-round "sharing" accommodation, with noticeable consequences for the neighbourhoods in which they are located.[39]

And finally, the emergence of the sharing economy may undermine important public policies. I cite two examples. First, there is a real possibility (and some evidence)[40] that once organizations like Uber destroy their competitors and achieve dominance or monopoly in a particular market, they will lower the compensation paid to their operatives, raise their prices to consumers, and cease to provide innovative services. In short, they may engage in the kind of anti-social behaviour that competition laws are designed to prevent. However, it is by no means clear that competition laws, as presently drafted and administered, will prevent such behaviour. And second, a significant part of government revenue comes from conventional payroll and sales taxes that are efficiently levied at source; however, the altered character of many transactions in the sharing economy may mean that those transactions will have to be taxed by less efficient means, or that they will escape taxation altogether.

IV. Regulating the Sharing Economy

I have suggested several approaches to the resolution of the category problem, which would bring workers, consumers and others within the purview of existing regulatory schemes. However it is doubtful that this will suffice to counter the powerful array of technological, market, cultural, legal, and political strategies that are currently disempowering workers and putting consumers, businesses, and public interests at risk. To cite one example, the forms of relationship between autonomous workers or operatives and market intermediaries are as varied as the technology that functionally enables them, and are likely to have a similarly brief shelf life. Consequently, regulatory policies and the instruments designed to implement them should be not only custom-built but also easily reconfigured. Enabling the banking and portability of benefits, for example, becomes a policy priority given that many workers cannot expect to be employed in any given enterprise for extended periods of time. Employers who provide undertime as well as overtime premium pay to gig workers might be allowed to buy themselves flexibility under working time regulations. Fixing all labour market intermediaries with primary or exclusive responsibility for wages and working conditions may be a better strategy in some circumstances than designating temporary employment agencies as joint employers. Such a situation-, sector-, or enterprise-specific approach to labour standards would require effective vehicles for worker voice and regulatory oversight, neither of which currently exist in a format likely to work well in the sharing economy. Consequently, a flexible system would have to be constructed from the ground up.

History reminds us that such a project is technically feasible. The U.S. National Industrial Recovery Act (NIRA) of 1933[41]—the centrepiece of Roosevelt's New Deal—provided for consultative processes leading to the adoption of detailed industry-specific codes of conduct, which were to be given legal force and effect through executive orders, regulations, or binding agreements, all of which can be adopted initially and updated more rapidly than conventional legislation.[42] True, the NIRA was declared unconstitutional on the grounds that it violated the division and separation of powers,[43] a fate that might be avoided by more careful drafting and/or a shift in judicial thinking. Nonetheless, the NIRA's legacy has survived in the form of statutes that, eight decades later, continue to regulate work relations in America.[44] (Canada adopted its own version of the NIRA with approximately similar consequences.)[45] And not just work relations: the NIRA, and companion statutes, applied as well to a wide range of business practices, consumer transactions, agricultural markets, pipelines and public works, and provided a means of generating rapid, context-specific responses to perceived market failures and abuses. Conceivably, some such approach could be employed to deal with non-labour instantiations of the sharing economy. Indeed, there is a certain policy logic in treating work-related and non-work relationships in similar fashion, to the extent that they involve similar asymmetries of wealth and power.[46]

In sum, it is technically possible not only to solve the category problem but also to design flexible "pop-up" or "flash" regulatory regimes suitable for rapid deployment in the sharing economy. But what is technically feasible is unlikely to be politically achievable. The architects of the sharing economy own not only innovative software and efficient delivery systems, but financial capital, legal technology, and, especially, political influence. Or to put the matter differently, workers and consumers in the sharing economy have been stripped of their protections and entitlements intentionally, not by accident. Regulation in the sharing economy is thus ultimately a political issue, not a category issue or an issue of regulatory design.

V. Conclusion: The Political Economy of "Sharing"

What are the legitimate goals of public policy in structuring the market for goods and services, and what are the appropriate instruments by which to achieve them? Does the state have a responsibility to maintain existing market structures and the regulatory regimes that constitute them in order to protect the sunk investments and future prospects of existing market participants? Does the state have a responsibility to shape the emergence of new market institutions and processes, or to suppress them altogether, in order to ensure that those institutions do not subvert some higher-order version of the public good? If the state does have such responsibilities, does it have the capacity to discharge them? And if it has that capacity, what price are we prepared to pay in terms of foregone benefits or delayed "progress" in order to ensure that the new sharing economy serves society's values rather than undermines them?

These questions, I acknowledge, have an anachronistic ring to them. They assume that the aspirations of a polity may amount to something more than and different from the sum of the individual interests and desires of its citizens; and they imply that markets are neither decreed by nature nor the default instrument by which the public interest can be reliably addressed. Those assumptions—my assumptions—are less widely accepted than they used to be. Nonetheless, the questions that I have identified must be taken seriously.

Of course, they will be answered in different ways by people of different persuasions. Even ardent neoliberals generally accept that the state has a legitimate interest in suppressing practices that endanger capitalism itself or threaten the integrity of markets. Neoliberals of a somewhat more pragmatic inclination concede as well that governments must intervene in markets from time to time in order to regain or retain the confidence of outraged consumers (who are also potential outraged voters). Neoliberals of both persuasions, however, prefer that such interventions should be symbolic or at most reflexive, so that the state at best merely admonishes market actors or at worst mandates them to regulate themselves. Advocates of a more robust approach once favoured the deployment of regulatory strategies that were first introduced by states during the early years of the Industrial Revolution, that were famously adopted by administrative agencies during the New Deal and World War II eras, and that have been used more recently with good effect to enforce public safety, human rights, and environmental policies. Confidence in these strategies, however, has waned in the face of evidence that they often not only fail to deliver their promised outcomes, but sometimes turn out to be both costly and counterproductive. Alas, new approaches to regulation—"the renew deal," "smart regulation," "the new public administration," or "reflexive law"[47]—have turned out to be no more effective than the old regulatory technologies (and possibly less so), and the state's capacity to protect the public interest remains at a low ebb.[48] And there it is likely to remain for the near future for complex reasons.

The paradigmatic social structures and economic relationships on which existing regulatory schemes are based have been dissolving. The end of the "standard employment contract,"[49] the "fissuring" of workplaces,[50] the rise of the "precariat":[51] all of these are steps along the way to the so-called sharing or gig economy in which work relations are so fleeting, clouded in ambiguity, and often poorly paid that workers find it difficult to develop their skills, sustain family life, save for retirement, or find time or energy for civic or cultural activities. This transformation in work relations is clearly related—as both cause and effect—to the demise of labour as an industrial and political force, as a sociological descriptor, and as an important focus of public policy.[52] In place of labour (or workers) at the centre of our political economy, we now find consumers whose demand for cheap and easily accessible goods and services drives public policy decisions in fields as diverse as trade, fiscal policy, and transportation.

Further, this shift has produced a new political dynamic. Working-class voters have drifted away from progressive or social democratic parties to parties of the populist right that emphasize national, ethno-cultural, or taxpayer (rather than class) solidarity, such as the Front National and Alternative für Deutschland, the Trumpistas, and the UK Independence Party. Corporations have learned to pose as friends of the working class, or to persuade its erstwhile members that their primary identity is as consumers, rather than as producers. An astonishing example of this can be seen in a Walmart advertisement that ran in the progressive *New York Review of Books*, in 2005, claiming that the company's lower retail prices (made possible, the advertisement all but boasts, by keeping Walmart wages below union rates) demonstrate that it "acts as a bargaining agent for [middle- and lower-class] families—achieving on their behalf a negotiating power they would never have on their own."[53] Even authentic consumer advocates have largely succumbed to "globaliza-tion of the mind," a transnational consensus that free markets offer consumers better outcomes than well-regulated markets or public enterprise.[54]

Finally, a widespread conviction has developed—even among many who would rather think otherwise—that resistance to the sharing economy is futile, that technology will always trump regu-lation. Indeed, technology seems to generate its own imperatives. New techniques of production and service delivery, new modalities of communication and transportation, new means of data collection and decision-making by algorithm have transformed contemporary capitalism in many ways from the creation of global value chains to formulaic trading in capital markets to everyday tasks of human resources management. In principle, human agents still make deci-sions about whether and how to deploy new technologies; in prin-ciple, human agents are still subject to social controls; but in practice it seems to be the case that if technology can be harnessed to displace human agents or disrupt social controls, it will.

In short, there is at present neither an aroused political con-stituency nor a coherent intellectual movement that might mobilize support for the New Deal model of pop-up regulation that I have pro-posed as an antidote to the dislocation and distress being caused to workers and others by the sharing economy. What is likely to happen?

One possibility is that capitalism itself will falter or fail,[55] and with it the geo-political, financial, sociological and technological architecture that makes the sharing economy possible or (some say) inevitable. If so, if we find ourselves in what Daniel Rogers calls "the intellectual economy of catastrophe," we will be experiencing something like the profound social disjuncture that gave rise to the New Deal, the NIRA and other institutional innovations of the time.[56] In such circumstances, it may become possible to convince experts, policy-makers, voters, and governments that intensive regulation of labour and/or consumer markets is needed to save capitalism from itself. Or, in the alternative, after a period of uncertainty and experimentation, the sharing economy may deliver on its promises to both workers and consumers without being forced to do so by the state. Resilient new forms of work relations may emerge to replace those that have become sclerotic; new institutional architecture and industrial technologies may facilitate a better equilibrium between production and consumption such that people will somehow be able to maintain a decent standard of living even without standard jobs as we came to know them in the mid-twentieth century. In both cases, the catalyst is likely to be mobilization by the sharing economy's "losers": local Luddite-type workplace disruptions, appeals to public opinion and the forging of alliances with community groups, sporadic recourse to hard law remedies, soft law experiments in the democratization of workplace governance, as well as demands for state regulation of working conditions and for a renewed safety net for vulnerable workers and the unemployed. And in both scenarios, hopefully, the ultimate outcome will be the forging of a new social contract, formal in the first scenario, amorphous in the second, but fragile in both. There may be other scenarios, but no sensible person would wish to contemplate them.

Notes

1. University Professor Emeritus and President Emeritus, York University. I have received excellent research and editorial assistance from Michael Thorburn, JD candidate, York University, 2017.
2. See especially Garrett Hardin, "The Tragedy of the Commons" (1968) 162:3859 Science 1243.
3. Elinor Ostrom, *Governing the Commons: The Evolution of Institutions for Collective Action* (Cambridge, UK and New York, NY: Cambridge University Press, 1990); Thomas Dietz, Elinor Ostrom & Paul C Stern, "The Struggle to Govern the Commons" (2003) 302:5652 Science 1907.
4. See E P Thompson, *Whigs and Hunters* (London: Breviary Stuff Publications, 2013); E P Thompson, *Customs in Common* (London: Penguin Group, 1993).
5. "The land, its natural deposits, waters, forests, mills, factories, mines, rail, water and air transport, banks, post, telegraph and telephones […] as well as municipal enterprises and the bulk of the dwelling houses in the cities and industrial localities, are state property, that is, belong to the whole people." Bucknell University, "1936 Constitution of the USSR," online: <http://www.departments.bucknell.edu/russian/const/36cons01.html>.
6. Tony Judt, *Postwar: A History of Europe Since 1945* (New York: Penguin Group, 2006).
7. William Foote Whyte & Kathleen King Whyte, *Making Mondragón: The Growth and Dynamics of the Worker Cooperative* (Ithaca, NY: Cornell University Press, 1991); Anjel Mari Errasti et al, "The Internationalisation of Cooperatives: The Case of the Mondragon Cooperative Corporation" (2003) 74:4 Ann of Pub & Coop Econ 553.

8. Mark Goldblatt, "Canada's Nonprofit Co-operative Housing Sector: An Alternative That Works" in Brett Fairbairn, Ian MacPherson & Nora Russell, eds, *Canadian Co-operatives in the Year 2000: Memory, Mutual Aid and the Millennium* (Saskatoon, SK: Centre for the Study of Cooperatives, 2000) 143.

9. Gary Gorton & Frank A Schmid, "Capital, Labor, and the Firm: A Study of German Codetermination" (2004) 2:5 J Eur Econ Assn 863.

10. Arun Sundararajan, *The Sharing Economy: The End of Employment and the Rise of Crowd-Based Capitalism* (Cambridge, MA: MIT Press, 2016). Sundararajan has been described as a "technological utopian." See Christopher May, "Book Review: The Sharing Economy: The End of Employment and the Rise of Crowd-Based Capitalism by Arun Sundararajan" (31 May 2016), (blog), online: LSE Review of Books <http://blogs.lse.ac.uk/lsereviewofbooks/2016/05/31/book-review-the-sharing-economy-the-end-of-employment-and-the-rise-of-crowd-based-capitalism-by-arun-sundararajan/>.

11. Cristiano Codagnone, Federico Biagi & Fabienne Abadie, "The Passions and the Interests: Unpacking the 'Sharing Economy'" (Seville: Joint Research Centre, 2016), online: <http://publications.jrc.ec.europa.eu/repository/bitstream/JRC101279/jrc101279.pdf>.

12. Jeremiah Owyang & Alexandra Samuel, *The New Rules of the Collaborative Economy* (Vancouver: Vision Critical, 2015), online: <https://www.vision-critical.com/resources/new-rules-collaborative-economy/>. The report notes that "eighty-two percent of sharing transactions are at least partly motivated by price—making financial savings one of the top drivers of the collaborative economy" (*ibid* at 11).

13. Michael L Tushman, "The Existential Question Facing the Auto Industry" (12 April 2016), online: Harvard Business Review <https://hbr.org/2016/04/the-existential-question-facing-the-auto-industry>; Jeremy Green, "How the sharing economy is changing the face of the automotive industry" (2014) 193:3 Automotive Industries 6; ABI Research, "New Car Sharing Economy Disrupts Automotive Industry: ABI Research Predicts 400 Million People to Rely on Robotic Car Sharing by 2030" (14 March 2016), online: <https://www.abiresearch.com/press/new-car-sharing-economy-disrupts-automotive-indust>.

14. See e.g. Alexander B Traum, "Sharing Risk in the Sharing Economy: Insurance Regulation in the Age of Uber" (2016) 14 Cardozo Pub L, Pol'y & Ethics J 511; Molly Cohen & Corey Zehngebot, "What's Old Becomes New: Regulating the Sharing Economy" (2014) 58:2 Boston Bar J 34; Laura Geisser, "Risk, Reward, and Responsibility: A Call to Hold UberX, Lyft, and Other Transportation Network Companies Vicariously Liable for the Acts of Their Drivers" (2016) 89:2 S Cal L Rev 317.

15. Brishen Rogers, "The Social Costs of Uber" (2015) 82:1 U Chicago L Rev 85.

16. See e.g. Noah Zatz, "Does Work Law Have a Future if the Labor Market Does Not?" (2016) 91:3 Chicago-Kent L Rev 1081 at 1093-99; Megan Carboni, "A New Class of Worker for the Sharing Economy" (2016) 22:4 Rich LJ & Tech 11; Caleb Holloway, "Keeping Freedom in Freelance: It's Time for Gig Firms and Gig Workers to Update Their Relationship Status" (2016) 16:3 Wake Forest J Bus & Intell Prop L 298. But see Benjamin Sachs, "Do We Need an "Independent Worker" Category?" (8 December 2015), online: On Labor <https://onlabor.org/do-we-need-an-independent-worker-category/>; Valerio De Stefano, "The Rise of the "Just-in-Time Workforce": On-Demand Work, Crowdwork, and Labor Protection in the "Gig-Economy"" (2016) 37:3 Comp Lab & Pol'y J 471 at 494.

17. Jeremias Prassl & Martin Risak, "Uber, Taskrabbit, & Co: Platforms as employers? Rethinking the Legal Analysis of Crowdwork" (2016) 37:3 Comp Lab & Pol'y J 619; Jan Drahokoupil & Brian Fabo, *The Platform Economy and the Disruption of the Employment Relationship* (Brussels: European Trade Union Institute, 2016), online: <http://www.etui.org/Publications2/Policy-Briefs/European-Economic-Employment-and-Social-Policy/The-platform-economy-and-the-disruption-of-the-employment-relationship>.

18. See e.g. Miriam A Cherry & Antonio Alosi, ""Dependent Contractors" in the Gig Economy: A Comparative Approach" (2017) 66:3 Am U L Rev 635.

19. See *Bhasin v Hrynew*, 2014 SCC 71, [2014] 3 SCR 494; *Potter v New Brunswick Legal Aid Services Commission*, 2015 SCC 10, [2015] 1 SCR 500; *Wilson v Atomic Energy of Canada Ltd*, 2016 SCC 29, [2016] 1 SCR 770.

20. A recent UK tribunal decision declared Uber drivers to be "workers" (not independent contractors) and therefore entitled to the national minimum wage and to holiday pay: *Aslam v Uber BV* (2016), [2017] IRLR 4.

21. See e.g. Ontario's *Labour Relations Act, 1995*, SO 1995, c 1, s 9(5); *Canada Labour Code*, RSC 1985, c L-2, s 3(1). The term, derived from a Swedish precedent, was introduced to Canadian labour law in Harry Arthurs, "The Dependent Contractor: A Study of the Legal Problems of Countervailing Power" (1965) 16 UTLJ 89. See also Cherry & Alosi, *supra* note 18.

22. I proposed such a scheme in *Fairness at Work*. See Harry Arthurs, *Fairness at Work: Federal Labour Standards for the 21st Century* (Ottawa: Human Resources and Social Development Canada, 2006) [Arthurs, *Fairness at Work*].

23. See Alan Hyde, "Employment Law After the Death of Employment" (1998) 1:1 U Pa J Lab & Emp L 99.

24. Katherine Stone & Harry Arthurs, eds, *Rethinking Employment Regulation: Beyond the Standard Contract of Employment* (New York: Russell Sage Foundation, 2013).

25. See generally David Weil, *The Fissured Workplace: Why Work Became So Bad for So Many and What Can Be Done to Improve It* (Cambridge, MA: Harvard University Press, 2014).

26. See e.g. Sarah A Donovan, David H Bradley & Jon O Shimabukuro, *What Does the Gig Economy Mean for Workers?* (Washington, DC: Congressional Research Service, 2016), online: <https://fas.org/sgp/crs/misc/R44365.pdf>.

27. See e.g. Ian Brinkley, *Flexibility or Insecurity? Exploring the Rise in Zero Hours Contracts* (Lancaster, UK: The Work Foundation, 2013), online: <https://csgconsult.com/wp-content/uploads/2014/03/339_flexibility-or-insecurity-final.pdf>.

28. See e.g. Jill Rubery et al, "Working Time, Industrial Relations and the Employment Relationship" (2005) 14:1 Time & Soc'y 89; Gerald Friedman, "Workers Without Employers: Shadow Corporations and the Rise of the Gig Economy" (2014) 2 Rev of Keynesian Econ 171.

29. Harry Arthurs, "Of Sceptics and Idealists: Bernie and Me and the Right to Strike" (2016) 19:2 CLELJ 327.

30. It is unclear whether collective bargaining by persons who are neither "employees" nor "workers" ("workmen") might violate Canada's *Competition Act*, RSC, 1985, c C-34, s 4(1)(a). See Harry Arthurs, "The Dependent Contractor: A Study of the Legal Problems of Countervailing Power" (1965) 16 UTLJ 89.

31. See Joelle Sano & John B Williamson, "Union Decline in 18 OECD Countries and their Implications for Labor Movement Reform" (2008) 49:6 Int'l J Comp Soc 479; Graham Boone, "Welcome to the Jungle: Organized Labor in Decline" (2014) 137:11 Monthly Lab Rev 1.

32. Only 72 per cent of Ontario workplaces are covered by its Workplace Safety and Insurance scheme. Cover Me! WSIB, "Cover Me! WSIB Q&A," online: <https://covermewsib.ca/q-a/>.

33. See e.g. Marc Van Audenrode et al, *Employment Insurance in Canada and International Comparisons* (Gatineau, QC: Human Resources And Skills Development Canada, 2005), online: <http://web.hec.ca/scse/articles/Fournier.pdf>.

34. Prosecution is the prescribed method of enforcing the *Canada Labour Code*, Part III (employment standards). Between 1997 and 2006, no prosecutions were initiated. Between 2006 and 2016, one prosecution was begun. See Arthurs, *Fairness at Work, supra* note 22 at 220.

35. Sofia Ranchordás, "On Sharing and Quasi-Sharing: The Tension Between Sharing-Economy Practices, Public Policy and Regulation" in Pia A Albinsson & Yasanthi Perera, eds, *The Sharing Economy:*

Possibilities, Challenges, and the Way Forward (Santa Barbara, CA: Praeger Publishing, 2018) at 17, online: <https://papers.ssrn.com/sol3/papers.cfm?abstract_id=2851202>.

36. For example, the Financial Services Commission of Ontario employs all of these techniques in order to regulate cooperatives, credit unions, insurance brokers, trust companies, mortgage brokers and pension providers. See *Financial Services Commission of Ontario Act*, SO 1997, c 28.

37. Rogers, *supra* note 15.

38. See e.g. Daniel Guttentag, "Airbnb: Disruptive Innovation and the Rise of an Informal Tourism Accommodation Sector" (2015) 18:12 Current Iss Tour 1192; Brittany McNamara "Airbnb: A Not-So-Safe Resting Place" (2015) 13:1 Colo Tech L J 149; Steven Tufts, "The Gig Economy and Worker Classification" (8 August 2015) [unpublished, opening remarks delivered at the Centre for Labour Management Relations Conference at Ryerson University]. For a more positive view see Georgios Zervas, Davide Proserpio & John W Byers, "The Rise of the Sharing Economy: Estimating the Impact of Airbnb on the Hotel Industry" (2017) 54:5 J Mkg Res, 687–705, online: <http://journals.ama.org/doi/abs/10.1509/jmr.15.0204>.

39. See Barbara Nichols, "Airbnb Is Crashing the Neighborhood" (December 2015), online: Realtormag <http://realtormag.realtor.org/news-and-commentary/commentary/article/2015/12/airbnb-crashing-neighborhood>. Airbnb itself offers a site soliciting complaints from neighbours adversely affected by the operation of its listed properties. Airbnb, "Airbnb and Your Neighborhood" (2016), online: <https://www.airbnb.ca/neighbors>.

40. Jeremy Rifkin, *The Zero Marginal Cost Society: The Internet of Things, the Collaborative Commons, and the Eclipse of Capitalism* (New York: St. Martin's Press, 2014).

41. *National Industrial Recovery Act*, Pub L No 73-67, 48 Stat 195 (1933) (codified at 15 USC § 703 (1933)).

42. Jason Scott Smith, *A Concise History of the New Deal* (Cambridge, UK: Cambridge University Press, 2014); Bernard Beaudreau, *The National Industrial Recovery Act Redux: Technology and Transitions* (Bloomington, IN: iUniverse, 2005).

43. *ALA Schechter Poultry Corp v United States*, 295 US 495, 55 S Ct 837 (1935).

44. *Fair Labor Standards Act of 1938*, Pub L No 75-718, § 1, 52 Stat 1060; *National Labor Relations Act of 1935*, Pub L No 74-198, § 151–169, 49 Stat 449.

45. I have traced the history of the Canadian version of the NIRA in Harry Arthurs, "Labour Law as the Law of Economic Subordination and Resistance: A Thought Experiment" (2013) 34:3 Comp Lab L & Pol'y J 585 [Arthurs, "Thought Experiment"]. See also *Act Respecting Collective Agreement Decrees*, RSQ 1964, c D-2 (updated 2016); Jean-Guy Bergeron

& Diane Veilleux, "The Quebec Collective Agreement Decrees Act: A Unique Model of Collective Bargaining" (1996) 22 Queen's LJ 135. See also the *Industrial Standards Act*, RSO 1990 c I 6, as repealed by *Employment Standards Act, 2000*, SO 2000, c 41, ss 144(5), 145.

46. Arthurs, "Thought Experiment," *supra* note 45.

47. See e.g. Orly Lobel, "The Renew Deal: The Fall of Regulation and the Rise of Governance in Contemporary Legal Thought" (2004–2005) 89 Minn L Rev 342; Peter Van Gossum, Bas Arts & Kris Verheyen, "From "Smart Regulation" to "Regulatory Arrangements"" (2010) 43:3 Pol'y Sci 245; Donald J Savoie "What Is Wrong with the New Public Management?" (1995) 38:1 Can Pub Admin 112; Robert Howse, J Robert S Prichard & Michael J Trebilcock "Smaller or Smarter Government?" (1990) 40:3 UTLJ 498; Peer Zumbansen, "Law After the Welfare State: Formalism, Functionalism, and the Ironic Turn of Reflexive Law" (2008) 56:3 Am J Comp L 769.

48. Harry Arthurs, "The Administrative State Goes to Market—And Cries Wee, Wee, Wee All the Way Home" (2005) 55 UTLJ 797.

49. See e.g. Katherine Stone & Harry Arthurs, "The Transformation of Employment Regimes: A World-Wide Challenge" in Katherine Stone & Harry Arthurs, eds, *Rethinking Employment Regulation: Beyond the Standard Contract of Employment* (New York: Russell Sage Foundation, 2013) 1.

50. Weil, *supra* note 25.

51. Guy Standing, *The Precariat: The New Dangerous Class* (London: Bloomsbury Academic, 2014).

52. Harry Arthurs, "Labour Law After Labour" in Guy Davidov and Brian Langille, eds, *The Idea of Labour Law* (Oxford: Oxford University Press, 2011) 13 at 13.

53. Open letter from Lee Scott (7 April 2005), 52:6 NY Rev Books 6. In the letter/advertisement, running under the headline "An Open Letter to the Readers of *The New York Review of Books*," Wal-Mart CEO Lee Scott stated: "Wal-Mart's impact" is "a key moment in time for American capitalism."

54. Harry Arthurs, "Globalization of the Mind: Canadian Elites and the Restructuring of Legal Fields" (1997) 12:2 CJLS 219.

55. Wolfgang Streek, "How Will Capitalism End?" (2014) 87 New Left Rev 35.

56. Daniel T Rodgers, *Atlantic Crossings: Social Policy in a Progressive Age* (Cambridge, MA: Belknap Press of Harvard University Press, 1998) at 413–16.

CHAPTER III

The Fast to the Furious

Nofar Sheffi[1]

This is the story of my dear friend Jeanne, an ordinary traveller who was transformed overnight from an Airbnb guest into a bedbug host. Human beings, after all, are not the only creatures seeking accommodation. Fresh off the boat, after having spent only one night in the dream New York apartment she had booked through Airbnb, Jeanne woke up to a nightmare. Dreams, it dawned on her, can be fantastically good but also frighteningly bad. What would you have done in her place? Waking up in a foreign country, with what seems like an allergic reaction, no local phone number, neither family nor friends. Are these bed bug bites or not? Are such bites potentially dangerous? Are you experiencing an allergic reaction? Should you seek medical attention? Should you take any medication? Who else should you contact? How do you get rid of bed bugs? Should you confront your Airbnb host? Should you leave the property? What are the potential consequences of doing so? What are your options, and how much will each cost? Should you temporarily book a hotel room? Should you try to locate alternative accommodation for the duration of your planned stay? Would that even be possible on such short notice? Could you recover the cost of alternative accommodation? Could you recover the expense of dry cleaning all your belongings? Could you recover the cost of any new luggage you need to buy? Just put yourself in Jeanne's bedbug-infested shoes.

I. Law in Scrolls, Law in Emails

Our story takes place in a heteroglot universe governed by a multiplicity of jurisdictions. Yet, legal scholars would most likely make sense of, or ascribe legal meaning to our case, from an empire state of mind, from the vantage point of state jurisdiction, or by identifying—using traditional, state-centered legal principles and doctrines—the controlling law and appropriate fora. They would likely begin by studying the terms of the bilateral agreement signed between Jeanne and her "host," terms that were largely dictated by the home sharing platform. They would proceed to scroll down the lengthy Terms of Service agreement (the "ToS agreement" or "the Terms") that Jeanne (a resident of France) had entered with Airbnb Ireland.[2] Pursuant to section 21.3 of this contract of adhesion, they would likely note that all of the Terms should be interpreted in accordance with Irish law and the consumer protection regulations of France, Jeanne's country of residence, and that Jeanne agreed to submit any dispute between her and Airbnb to "the non-exclusive jurisdiction" of the Irish courts.[3] Referring to section 16, they may caution that Airbnb's service is provided without warranty of any kind, either expressed or implied. Referencing section 17, they would perhaps point out that, as Jeanne is a resident of the European Union, Airbnb is liable only under statutory provisions for intent and gross negligence, and for any negligent breaches of essential contractual obligations by the company, its "legal representatives, directors, or other vicarious agents." Citing section 17, they would note that "the same applies [...] in case of a culpable injury to life, limb, or health."

Few legal "scrollers"[4] would pay attention to the large but almost invisible dispute resolution mechanisms operated by Airbnb. Certainly, many would instruct Jeanne to contact Airbnb's Customer Service. However, how many of those who would recommend this course of action would conceive of this service as a mechanism of dispute resolution? Airbnb's role as a dispute processor has received very little legal or media attention.[5] Instead, citing the company's deafness or mishandling of a specific complaint as a ground for filing a claim with the relevant state institution, or sharing the story on social media,[6] critics have rather focused on Airbnb's obligations as a service provider. Although much attention has been directed at the alleged mass-circumvention of business-licensing regulation; bypassing of planning law; and tax evasion, avoidance, and shifting, very little consideration, if any, has been given to private law issues arising between Airbnb users.[7] In more recent years, following the increasing allegations of discrimination by Airbnb hosts, and the filing of a putative class-action suit against Airbnb under the *Civil Rights Act* and the *Fair Housing Act*, the arbitration clause, and class-action waiver, which are included in all agreements signed between Airbnb and residents of the United States, have received some attention. In late 2016, the United States District Court for the District of Columbia granted Airbnb's motion to compel arbitration and stay litigation, holding that the arbitration clause is applicable to discrimination suits and is enforceable.[8] This holding has opened the door to further debates over a variety of issues, such as the inclusion of arbitration provisions in online adhesion contracts and the submission of discrimination and civil rights claims to arbitration.[9]

Indeed, only a handful of private disputes (between Airbnb users and between Airbnb and its users) ever become public, let alone reach the courts. Moreover, hard data on the size and inner workings of the internal dispute resolution mechanisms operated by the private company are difficult to obtain. As of August 2017, on any given night, an average of two million people stayed in an Airbnb listing.[10] The platform currently has nearly five million listings, which span 81,000 cities across 191 countries. Most recently valued at $31 billion, the platform serviced around 100 million guests in 2017.[11] It is, however, worth considering how many of these interactions end on a sour note. How many disagreements or disputes arise between users? How many dissatisfied users turn to Airbnb for help? What kind of complaints do they lodge? How are complaints handled and by whom? In a 2016 interview, the global head of the Airbnb Customer Experience (CX) Department reported that, in any given week, her department alone deals with over 180,000 "customer interactions," and that during the summer months her agents' workload doubles in volume.[12] Despite the large share of "customer interactions" and "unmatched expectations,"[13] Airbnb continues to grow and, as recent surveys indicate, has strong favourability ratings by travelers.[14] More concretely, the Airbnb Engineering Department reports in its blog that intervention through customer support reduces the likelihood that guests who have encountered a "negative experience" will not use the service again from 26 per cent to less than 6 per cent.[15]

Yet where is the gate of Airbnb's domain? How can it be accessed? Which law governs the dispute between Jeanne and her host, and the way in which it would be processed? Only intrepid scrollers, who would scroll down the lengthy ToS agreement, would identify its most pertinent stipulations: section 9.5. "In certain circumstances," the section stipulates, "Airbnb may decide, in its sole discretion, that it is necessary to cancel a confirmed booking and make appropriate refund and payout decisions. This may be," it specifies, "for reasons set forth in Airbnb's Extenuating Circumstances Policy or (i) where Airbnb believes in good faith, while taking the legitimate interests of both parties into account, this is necessary to avoid significant harm to Airbnb, other Members, third parties or property, or (ii) for any of the reasons set out in these Terms." Section 9.6 further establishes that "[i]f a Guest suffers a Travel Issue pursuant to the Guest Refund Policy, Airbnb may determine, in its sole discretion, to refund the Guest part or all of the Total Fees in accordance with the Guest Refund Policy." Do any of these sections apply to Jeanne's case, our dedicated scrollers would likely wonder? What are the "Extenuating Circumstances Policy" and "Guest Refund Policy"? Where can they be found and what are their provisions? What is a "Travel Issue"? Would Jeanne be considered as "suffering" one? What is the procedure for submitting a request for a refund? Does Airbnb offer Jeanne any remedy other than a refund? A quick search would reveal that at least twelve additional terms and policies are "incorporated by reference" into the ToS agreement: the Payments Terms of Service (the "Payments Terms"), the Privacy Policy, the Copyright Policy, the Host Guarantee Terms and Conditions (the "Host Guarantee Terms"), the Gift Card Terms and Conditions, the Airbnb Experiences: Guest Release and Waiver, the Cookie Policy, the Nondiscrimination Policy, the Content Policy, the Extenuating Circumstances Policy, the Extortion Policy, and the most relevant—the Guest Refund Policy. A careful web search would additionally reveal that, only recently, Airbnb further announced the publication of its Standards and Expectations, a "single framework" gathering together the principles that guide the making of "enforcement decisions."[16] Reflecting what Airbnb hosts and guests "view as acceptable conduct and behavior,"[17] Airbnb explains, these "guidelines are an expression of the shared values of the Airbnb community."[18] Their publication is intended to help users, such as Jeanne's host, better understand what are Airbnb's expectations "from the people who are part of the Airbnb community."[19]

Overall, Airbnb's terms and policies provide users seeking redress with six types of recourse. A first type of procedure is initiated when a host or guest cancels a confirmed booking. When listing their property, hosts choose among three standardized cancellation policies (Flexible, Moderate, and Strict). The selected policy will apply to all reservations for less than twenty-eight nights; to all reservations of twenty-eight nights or more a fourth, fixed cancellation policy applies (Long Term).[20] In accordance with section 9.2 of the ToS agreement and in conjunction with section 10.2.1 of the Payments Terms, if a guest cancels a confirmed booking either prior to, or after arriving at the accommodation, Airbnb will immediately refund the guest the sums specified in the applicable cancellation policy (sums that are withheld by Airbnb for the first twenty-four hours after check-in) and initiate a "Payout" of any portion of the fees due to the host under it.[21] Pursuant to section 9.3 of the Terms and section 10.2.2 of the Payments Terms, if a host cancels a confirmed booking, Airbnb Payments will refund the total fees to the guest "within a commercially reasonable time of the cancellation."[22] It is important to clarify that, after a booking is cancelled, neither guests nor hosts are required to take any further actions; acting on behalf of both the host and the guest, Airbnb Payments immediately steps in, automatically initiating and effectuating all refunds and payouts due pursuant to the selected cancellation policy and the Terms. In case of host cancellation, Airbnb will also offer alternative accommodation suggestions to the guest. Hosts that cancel a confirmed booking may be subject to additional sanctions, including a cancellation fee, publication of an automated review on their listing informing other Airbnb users that they have withdrawn from a confirmed booking, and blocking their calendar for the dates of the cancelled booking, which prevents them from offering their space to other Airbnb users during this time.[23]

To hosts who suffer damage to their property, Airbnb offers two types of recourse. The first procedure is outlined in section 11 of the ToS agreement and section 12 of the Payments Terms. In accordance with section 7.2.2 of the Terms, Airbnb allows hosts to add a security deposit to their listing. Hosts can then claim all or part of the deposit to compensate for any damage done to their property. According to the Airbnb Help Center, such a claim must be submitted within fourteen days of a guest's check- out date or before the next guest checks in, whichever is earlier.[24] To submit a "Damage Claim," hosts must first contact their guest through the Airbnb Resolution Center. If the guest agrees to pay the requested amount, Airbnb Payments will collect the agreed-upon sum and send it to the host. According to the Airbnb Help Center, this takes between five to seven business days.[25] If the guest declines or does not respond within seventy-two hours, the host is given the opportunity to "escalate" the Damage Claim to Airbnb. After giving the guest an opportunity to respond, Airbnb will decide if the guest is responsible for the alleged damage, a decision made at Airbnb's sole discretion.[26] If the guest is found liable, Airbnb will collect the sum and transfer it to the host. According to Airbnb, the majority of security deposit claims are resolved within one week.[27] Another mode of redress for property damage is provided in the Host Guarantee Terms, which cover damage that exceeds the security deposit or when no security deposit is in place.[28] Before directly involving Airbnb, but via Airbnb's Resolution Center, a host must contact the guest with their complaint. If the parties are unable to reach an agreement within seventy-two hours,[29] the host may file an "Airbnb Host Guarantee Payment Request Form" (the "Form"). The process must be initiated either within fourteen days from the check-out date or before the next guest checks in, whichever is earlier, and the Form must be filed within thirty days after the loss was incurred. Airbnb "strive[s] to resolve most cases within a week of submission,"[30] and "will use commercially reasonable efforts to complete processing" of a Host Guarantee Payment Request Form within three months after receipt of all required documents and information.[31]

A fourth procedure is outlined in section 9.7 of the ToS agreement and section 9 of the Payments Terms. By facilitating the transfer of agreed-upon sums through its Resolution Center, Airbnb encourages users to "resolve issues on their own."[32] According to the Airbnb Help Center, the possibility of submitting a "Resolution Center Request" is available only in the first sixty days following a checkout, with the agreement of both parties.[33] In these cases, as established in section 9 of the Payments Terms, Airbnb acts merely as a "limited payment collection agent," transferring agreed-upon amounts. The section further establishes that, by agreeing to use the Center, both parties acknowledge that they, and not Airbnb, are responsible for performing their respective obligations, that Airbnb is not party to their agreements, and that Airbnb is immune from all liability arising from or related to use of its services.

A fifth approach is outlined in section 9.5 of the Terms, permitting Airbnb to cancel any reservation, override the cancellation policy selected by the host, make refund decisions, and waive the host cancellation penalties. "In certain circumstances," the section reads, "Airbnb may decide, in its sole discretion, that it is necessary to cancel a confirmed booking and make appropriate refund and payout decisions." "This may be," the section details, "for reasons set forth in Airbnb's Extenuating Circumstances Policy or (i) where Airbnb believes in good faith, while taking the legitimate interests of both parties into account, this is necessary to avoid significant harm to Airbnb, other Members, third parties or property, or (ii) for any of the reasons set out in these Terms." "Incorporated by reference" into the ToS agreement, the terms of Airbnb's Extenuating Circumstances Policy are not published alongside it. Anchoring Airbnb's sole discretion to override other policies (in cases of unexpected death, serious illness, significant natural disasters or weather incidents, urgent travel restrictions or severe security advisories, endemic diseases declared by a credible national or international authority, severe property damage or unforeseen maintenance issues, and the like), they are rather published in the Airbnb Help Center.[34] Claims under the Extenuating Circumstances Policy can only be considered after a reservation has been cancelled, and should "generally" be submitted no later than fourteen days from the original check-in date.[35]

Lastly, the Guest Refund Policy, which ostensibly covers Jeanne's situation, "help[s] protect guests from things like last-minute host cancellations, lock-outs, and listings that are misrepresented, unsanitary, or lacking in promised amenities or items."[36] The Policy's core provisions read as follows:

1. Travel Issue

A "Travel Issue" means any one of the following:

(a) the Host of the Accommodation (i) cancels a booking shortly before the scheduled start of the booking, or (ii) fails to provide the Guest with the reasonable ability to access the Accommodation (e.g. does not provide the keys and/or a security code).

(b) the Listing's description or depiction of the Accommodation is materially inaccurate with respect to:

- the size of the Accommodation (e.g., number and size of the bedroom, bathroom and/or kitchen or other rooms),

- whether the booking for the Accommodation is for an entire home, private room or shared room, and whether another party, including the Host, is staying at the Accommodation during the booking,

- special amenities or features represented in the Listing are not provided or do not function, such as decks, pools, hot tubs, bathrooms (toilet/shower/bathtub), kitchen (sink/stove/refrigerator or major other appliances), and electrical, heating or air condition systems, or

- the physical location of the Accommodation (proximity).

(c) at the start of the Guest's booking, the Accommodation: (i) is not generally clean and sanitary (ii) contains safety or health hazards that would be reasonably expected to adversely affect the Guest's stay at the Accommodation in Airbnb's judgment, (iii) does not contain clean bedding and bathroom towels available for the Guest's use, or (iv) has vermin or contains pets not disclosed in the Listing.

2. The Guest Refund Policy

If you are a Guest and suffer a Travel Issue, we agree, at our discretion, to either (i) reimburse you up to the amount paid by you through the Airbnb Platform ("Total Fees") depending on the nature of the Travel Issue suffered, or (ii) use our reasonable efforts to find and book you another Accommodation for any unused nights left in your booking which is reasonably comparable to the Accommodation described in your original booking in terms of size, rooms, features and quality. All determinations of Airbnb with respect to the Guest Refund Policy, including without limitation the size of any refund and the comparability of alternate Accommodations, shall be in Airbnb's discretion, and final and binding on the Guests and Hosts.

3. Conditions to Claim a Travel Issue

To submit a valid claim for a Travel Issue and receive the benefits with respect to your booking, you are required to meet each of the following conditions:

(a) you must be the Guest that booked the Accommodation;

(b) you must bring the Travel Issue to our attention in writing or via telephone and provide us with information (including photographs or other evidence) about the Accommodation and the circumstances of the Travel Issue within 24 hours after the later of (i) the start of your booking or (ii) you discover the existence of the Travel Issue, and must respond to any requests by us for additional information or cooperation on the Travel Issue;

(c) you must not have directly or indirectly caused the Travel Issue (through your action, omission or negligence); and

(d) unless Airbnb advises you that the Travel Issue cannot be remediated, you must have used reasonable efforts to try to remedy the circumstances of the Travel Issue with the Host prior to making a claim for a Travel Issue.

4. Minimum Quality Standards, Host Responsibilities and Reimbursement to Guest

4.1 If you are a Host, you are responsible for ensuring that the Accommodations you list on the Airbnb Platform meet minimum quality standards regarding access, adequacy of the Listing description, safety, cleanliness, and do not present a Guest with Travel Issues. During a Guest's stay at an Accommodation, Hosts should be available, or make a third party available, in order to try, in good faith, to resolve any Guest issues.

4.2 If you are a Host, and if (i) Airbnb determines that a Guest has suffered a Travel Issue related to an Accommodation listed by you and (ii) Airbnb either reimburses that Guest (up to their Total Fees) or provides an alternative Accommodation to the Guest, you agree to reimburse Airbnb up to the amount paid by Airbnb within 30 days of Airbnb's request. If the Guest is relocated to an alternative Accommodation, you also agree to reimburse Airbnb for reasonable additional costs incurred to relocate the Guest. You authorize Airbnb Payments to collect any amounts owed to Airbnb by reducing your Payout or as otherwise permitted pursuant to the Payments Terms.

4.3 As a Host, you understand that the rights of Guests under this Guest Refund Policy will supersede your selected cancellation policy. If you dispute the Travel Issue, you may notify us in writing or via telephone and provide us with information (including photographs or other evidence) disputing the claims regarding the Travel Issue, provided you must have used reasonable and good faith efforts to try to remedy the Travel Issue with the Guest prior to disputing the Travel Issue claim.[37]

From the perspective of the traditional private law scrollership, Jeanne's experience likely presents her with a "Travel Issue," as defined in section 1(c)(iv) of the Policy. Pursuant to sections 2 and 3 of the Policy, Jeanne could submit, within twenty-four hours from the start of her reservation, or after discovering that the accommodation is infested with bed bugs, a claim for a "Travel Issue" in writing or via telephone. This must, however, be only after using "reasonable efforts" to try to remedy the circumstances with her host. In her claim, Jeanne could request the service to refund the amount she paid her host through the platform, and to use its "reasonable efforts" to find and book her "reasonably comparable" accommodation for the remainder of her three-month stay.

Alas, which "reasonable efforts" to "try to remedy the circumstances" is Jeanne obliged to take prior to calling Airbnb? What efforts would Airbnb deem to be "reasonable"? What would constitute "reasonably comparable" "in terms of size, rooms, features and quality"? And for which of the "additional costs" incurred by Airbnb at its sole discretion to relocate Jeanne to the alternative accommodation could her host be found responsible? Scrolling the Airbnb terms and policies, the Airbnb law "in books"[38] would nonetheless only send us on a search for a more powerful system of laws by reference to which their meaning can be decoded. But where should our quest to reach this earlier, higher, universal, or more specific law, to discover the meaning of these texts, lead us? To the gate of which jurisdiction should we come praying for admittance?[39] In accordance with which "controlling law," to put the question in doctrinal terms, should our Policy be interpreted? In accordance with "Irish Law," as section 21.3 of the Policy directs us, or the Airbnb law "in action,"[40] as socio-legal scholars do? Taking a different path, this chapter considers a singular story as doorway to the law. It tells the story of one ordinary Airbnb user, who like Franz Kafka's "man from the country," found herself before the gates of the law.[41]

Why stories, you may ask, why *a* story? Airbnb's domain is heavily guarded, and very little concrete information about its architecture,
policies, protocols and processes is accessible. The only opening, the
only opportunity to catch a glimpse into the interior of the massive
dispute-processing mechanisms operated by Airbnb is afforded
momentarily to those for whom a gate was especially made, to ordinary end-users who, like our Jeanne, arrive before it to submit a claim
or be judged. Even those singular users who appear before Airbnb, as
will soon be revealed, are being barred from entering Airbnb's domain,
are being made to wait at its gate for a decision, a decision that is to be
made behind closed doors at Airbnb's sole discretion.[42] My telling of
Jeanne's story, however, is intended not to merely reveal the invisibility
of Airbnb's immense apparatus, its secretiveness and its inaccessibility. Just like Franz Kafka's "Before the Law," I would like to suggest,
Jeanne's story imposes on us, the guardians of the law, an interpretive
imperative to process and judge. Like Kafka's parable, Jeanne's story
summons us before the same law by reference to which we seek to
judge it, adjuring us to reflect on that which we so reverently represent.

II. JusToS Accused

The domain of Airbnb is unintelligible, inaccessible, and secretive.
Its architecture is enacted using incomprehensible programming
languages, jargons that an ordinary end-user cannot possibly grasp, a
secret that "a cast pretends to possess by delegation,"[43] a "secret that
has to be kept well, nothing either present or presentable."[44] Airbnb
users do not even have the *"right* to touch"[45] this cryptic text, a well-
kept trade secret to which very few, if any, have full or even limited
access to.[46] In accordance with section 14 of the ToS agreement,
"Members" agree not to "avoid, bypass, remove, deactivate, impair,
descramble, or otherwise attempt to circumvent any technological
measure" implemented by Airbnb to protect the platform. "Members"
further undertake the obligation not to "take any action that damages or adversely affects, or could damage or adversely affect the
performance or proper functioning of the Airbnb Platform," as well
as not to use "any robots, spider, crawler, scraper or other automated
means or processes to access, collect data or other content from or
otherwise interact with the Airbnb Platform."

To continue my invocation of Derrida's reading of Kafka's
"Before the Law," Airbnb's coded architecture, terms and policies,

and all other texts contained in the website are "original texts."[47] Despite their essential unreadability, their "form presents itself as a kind of personal identity entitled to absolute respect,"[48] and it is forbidden to change, disfigure, or touch them.[49] Pursuant to section 14, Airbnb has the "right to investigate and prosecute" violations of any of the Terms, including any infringement upon, violation of, or disfiguring of these texts, and "may take a range of actions" against any user who changes even one word or alters even one sentence of them. Section 14 prohibits any mirroring or framing of the source code forming the platform and any of the content published in the site. As part of it, users also undertake the contractual obligation not to "dilute, tarnish or otherwise harm the Airbnb brand in any way," as well as not to "attempt to decipher, decompile, disassemble or reverse engineer any of the software used to provide the Airbnb Platform."

The structure of the Airbnb apparatus, the architecture of its palaces, the design of its internal processes, and grounds for decision are all similarly inaccessible. Data on the internal structure of the organization is scarce, and the limited information that does exist must be painstakingly gathered from a multiplicity of non-traditional sources—LinkedIn profiles, technology blogs and podcasts, interviews, the Airbnb blog, and others. All interactions between "Members" and the law governing disputes between them are mediated via one of the over two hundred and fifty agents, "manning the phones and doing Chat and email,"[50] a member of the Airbnb Trust and Safety team or the CX department. Called "crewbies," members of the former are responsible "for all online and offline fraud and safety concerns, including but not limited to account security, property damage, safety concerns, and user trust."[51] Known as the "Aircorps," the latter is "responsible for escalated customer cases that begin online, but exist in the offline world," including "monetary and personality disputes, last minute cancellations, VIP rebookings, and 'outside the box' mediation for violations in Airbnb Terms of Use."[52] Airbnb "Members," to rephrase, are never in the presence of the law governing their disputes with others, and are never immediately before it, rather, they enter into relations "only with the law's representatives, its examples, its guardians."[53] All decisions are reached behind closed doors, and are transmitted to users in cryptic language by Airbnb representatives guarding the gate that the law made only for them. Dan Weber, the founder of AirbnbHell.com, a website dedicated to warning "potential hosts and guests about the dangers and risks associated with using the Airbnb service,"[54] recalls the story of his trial and judgment, the Kafkaesque experience that led him to launch the website:

> I had been a successful and enthusiastic Airbnb Host for almost a year when a young European couple in their mid 20's booked one of my rooms for a 6-month reservation, a very long stay by Airbnb standards. I welcomed them into my rental unit, and spent time with them socially on a few occasions during their stay as they were trying to learn their way around Los Angeles. My wife even sold them her used car well below blue-book value, just to help them out as they seemed like a nice young couple and they clearly didn't have a lot of money. Everything was going fine… until the couple left in the middle of the night without saying a word two nights before their 6-month reservation was scheduled to come to an end. I was surprised by that fact alone, but I was even more shocked when I received a notice from Airbnb saying that the couple had filed a complaint about me and they claimed there were mice in the condo! It should be noted that I had over 40 perfect reviews from previous guests at this point, and there most certainly were no mice anywhere on my property. According to Airbnb, their 'standard policy' when a guest claimed rodents were in the house was to refund 50 percent of the entire reservation, in this case almost $3,000 USD for 3 months of renting one of my bedrooms in Los Angeles, California.
>
> I immediately tried to contact Airbnb to dispute this obviously fraudulent claim, but I was passed around from one customer service agent to another, none of them able to give me any explanation better than 'this is our policy'. I was furious. After about 2 weeks of calling and emailing various Airbnb reps, I finally reached a 'manager' who provided me with a copy of the scammers' complaint including a photo of a mouse they had sent. My rebuttal included written testimony from another guest who was staying in the condo at the same time, stating that there were no mice or signs of any other pests in the house. Thanks to the wonders of google image search, I was even able to find the exact same mouse photo that the couple had used to file their complaint… it was originally posted on a blog TWO

> YEARS EARLIER! I sent all of this documentation to Airbnb and
> asked them to consider my many positive reviews, and that their
> 'policy' to refund 50% of a guest's entire reservation for a simple
> (obviously fraudulent) claim was crazy. Another week went by
> without my claim being addressed. Airbnb kept my last payment
> from the European scammers' reservation, as well as money
> from my next few guests, so in total I had lost almost $3,000.
> After about 3 weeks of this frustration I finally had enough.
> My last message to the manager at Airbnb was 'Go ahead and
> keep my money. I'm going to cost your company more money
> than you have cost me!' That was when I launched AirbnbHell.
> com – I felt that others needed to be warned.[55]

The law is silent, and of it nothing but its common name is said to
our very own Joseph K.[56] Guardian after guardian nevertheless
assures him that there is some "standard policy," which is not there
but which exists.[57] The singular and unique gate that Airbnb made
only for him remains open throughout and is never closed on him;
however, a final judgment never arrives. The doorkeepers that watch
over this "theater of the invisible"[58] adjourn, defer, evade, and divert
him. "What is delayed," as Derrida observes, "is not this or that
experience, the access to some enjoyment or to some supreme good,
the possession or penetration of something or somebody. What is
deferred forever till death is entry into the law itself, which is nothing other than that which dictates the delay."[59] What is deferred till
death is knowledge of the "standard policy"—deferred till social and
economic death. The story of our very own Joseph K ends with an act
of social and economic suicide, the deletion of his Airbnb account,
with a self-imposed exile from the lucrative "sharing economy."

The inaccessibility of Airbnb's domain, of its terms, policies,
palaces, codes, and processes is, to conclude, yet another instantiation
of what Derrida calls "the essentially inaccessible character of the
law, [... of] the fact that a 'first sight' of it is always refused."[60] The
law purports to apply universally and impartially to all, to be readily
accessible at all times and to everyone, to be known by everyone, to
be readable. Nevertheless, as Derrida suggests, to protect and preserve its autonomy and authority, the law must precisely frustrate
any narrated attempt to capture its meaning, to gain insight into its
essence, to tell its story; it must deny access to its domain, knowledge
of it and participation in it.[61] Doomed to be denied entrance, to be

discounted as "concerning only circumstances, events external to the law and, at best, the modes of its revelation,"[62] stories like those of Jeanne and AirbnbHell.com's founder (just as Kafka's parable) instead enact or expose the law's essential inaccessibility and structure of referentiality, the paradoxical logic of boundaries. The framing of each story creates an opening, an opportunity to access the law's essence, a portal into its domain. But, at the same time that it creates an opening, the unique door made by each story also serves as a barrier, drawing a line that cannot be crossed, protecting an essence that cannot be accessed. The framing of the door turns the law hidden behind it into a secret, something that remains inaccessible, an insight that cannot be gained.[63] By insisting that the law "should be accessible at all times and to everyone,"[64] on the law's generality and universality, it is the story itself that transforms the law into a secret, into that which will forever be obscured and inaccessible. It is the story itself that, by placing us in front of a portal that it itself comports, an internal boundary opening on nothing, reveals the law's essential structure of referentiality.[65]

In one of his lesser-known articles, socio-legal scholar Gunther Teubner invites us to imagine that Kafka's protagonist "is not the human individual who has been delivered up to the force of institutionalised legalism, [... rather] the individual legal procedure itself, or more generally the *decision-making practice of the legal process*, in all the confusion of life, that stands before its own law."[66] Modern law's claim of autonomy and universality, constant deployment of abstract categories, and inexorable compulsion to juridify all problems of the world are precisely, Teubner suggests, what sends it on a desperate search for an earlier, universal, higher or more specific law by which it can make its decisions.[67] The legal discourse that seeks to assure itself of its law is tormented by nightmares that are different from those experienced by an individual who, appearing before the judicial system, is exposed to its arbitrariness.[68] Precisely because it can only reflect on itself with the aid of the categories which it itself declared universal, the law becomes subjected to the torment of self-examination, and thus caught up in the paradoxes of self-reference. This, Teubner concludes, "is the fundamental paradox of the Law, which in response to the question as to its foundation does not get a clear yes or a clear no, but an almost mocking interchange between positive and negative value of a viable justification."[69]

It is the paradox inherent in the law's sense of "justice," of what makes a dispute resolution mechanism "just" or "fair," of what makes one institutional design better or worse than others, that this chapter attempts to gain insight into. Would Jeanne's situation be any different had she woken up with bed bugs in a traditional hotel room? If so, how? Would she have benefited from a procedurally and more substantively "just" institutional design had she lodged elsewhere, outside of Airbnb's domain? Would that alternative jurisdiction have offered her a "fairer" legal procedure? Would that procedure have produced a "better" outcome? What makes the Airbnb dispute resolution mechanism either "superior" or "inferior" to the mechanisms offered by the "controlling law"? What would allow us to judge that Jeanne's "Before the Law" is a story of either "justice" or "injustice"?

Before returning to Jeanne's story, it is important to note that this chapter leaves aside the eternal question: What is law? It goes beyond investigating the legal quality of this invisible and inaccessible dispute resolution mechanism, searching for that which makes laws of its terms, policies, and decisions, the being-law of these. It is further important to highlight that the goal of this chapter transcends merely exposing Airbnb's "law in action," the inner workings of the sophisticated *dispositif* operated by the home sharing service, its ideological dimensions, and the distributive implications of the various decisions conveyed by the guardians stationed before it. Furthermore, the aim is neither to evaluate by reference to one or another pre-existing private law system or a certain ideal Airbnb dispute resolution mechanism, nor place it on one or another point along some spectrum. Any such endeavour would, necessarily, require a subscription to, or focus on, a specific idea or ideal by reference to which a binary distinction—between "fair" and "unfair," "legitimate" and "illegitimate," "just" and "unjust," "good" and "bad," "better" or "worse," or "more" or "less"—could be drawn. In this respect, this chapter also avoids arguing for institutional reforms, making any policy recommendation, or producing a definitive conclusion as to who should process private disputes, and how such mechanisms should be designed. It neither commends nor condemns Airbnb's mechanism of dispute processing. It does not call upon traditional jurisdictions—state, municipalities, or transnational bodies—to intervene or regulate. It does not suggest the introduction of a new transnational regulator. Rather, the following telling of Jeanne's story is intended to incite a reflection on the intuitions and assumptions with which we approach "law stories"[70] and the principles by which we judge mechanisms of dispute processing.

III. Before the Law

Before the law, "on the front lines,"[71] stands Jason from the Airbnb Trust and Safety department. To this "crisis manager"[72] there comes an end-user praying for admittance to the law. "Hello!" she cries on the other side of the phone line. "Is there anybody in there?" "Come on now," he replies soothingly. "I hear you're feeling down." And after listening to her plea, he assures her, "Well, I can ease your pain and get you on your feet again." "Relax," he continues, "I'll need some information first." "Just the basic facts," he reassures her. "Can you show me where it hurts?" After receiving pictures of the alleged bedbug bites, he writes her with a medical diagnosis, a written confirmation of his promise to reimburse her for up to $30 for a meal, and a short explanation of the crux of their phone conversation—his ruling.

> Hello [Jeanne],
> This is Jason from Airbnb again.
> This email is just a quick follow up from our phone conversation earlier.
> I have received the photos of [… your] bites and I can confirm that these are from bed bugs. I will be canceling this reservation on the hosts behalf and will be refunding you in full. As we discussed the original payment will be held in Airbnb's system initially and will be transferred directly to a new reservation. As the original reservation was for 3 months I will be looking for a shorter reservation at first and then we can attempt to rebook you for the rest of the reservation later.
> For now I have promised to reimburse you for up to $30 USD for a meal while I begin to reach out to other hosts in NYC.
> Thank you for your call and I will be in touch.
> Best regards,
> Jason[73]

Throughout their phone conversations, Jason gives Jeanne advice on how to get rid of bed bugs. Not only is the first time that she has ever had to deal with an infestation, nor does she know of anyone who ever has. Hell, up until that very morning, she was not even aware that she is allergic to bed bugs. In shock, she follows Jason's instructions, one after the other. Two hours pass by and Jason, who is still searching for alternative accommodation for the next three months, books Jeanne a hotel room for the night. "Hello Jeanne," he writes with an update, "This is Jason from Airbnb again." "I have booked you for one night into The Aloft Harlem as the Astor unfortunately no longer had availability by the time I actually tried to book you into it. As I said previously if you need to take a cab to the Hotel I will gladly reimburse for the cost."

After giving her the hotel's address and phone number, he again reassures her: "I will continue to reach out to other hosts in the area tonight, so just rest easy Jeanne!" After settling into the hotel room he booked for her, she sends him an email, just to update him and to thank him for being there for her during her long and trying day.

> Dear Jason,
> You are great. I am in the hotel, so I am fine. I threw to the garbage all my belongings that have been in contact with the bed of bedbugs. I will go tomorrow to the laundry for all my other clothes, that I packed for now in a new bag (I also threw my suitcase). Do you have other advices? I hope my clothes will not be contaminated by bedbugs. Maybe we should wait a bit more and keep me in the hotel before risking to contaminate another place? This is really terrible, in only one night my body is covered with bites. Hopefully I took my medicines against my allergies and it's a bit better now, but still, I am all red.
> Again, you have been extremely helpful and reactive, I am very, very grateful.
> Best,
> [Jeanne]

It is 1:00 a.m. in New York, 10:00 p.m. in San Francisco. Jason's shift is coming to an end, and he sends Jeanne an email, in English and French, just to let her know, "I want to make sure you feel supported here," he explains. "[P]lease know," he reassures her, "that a colleague will be in touch very shortly!" "In the meantime, if there's any other information you'd like to make sure we have, you can reply here and let us know."

Five hours pass. It is slightly after 6:00 a.m. in New York, and 3:00 a.m. in San Francisco. Jeanne receives a long message; it's in French and from Hakima, a member of the Airbnb CX department, the "keepers of a magical customer experience."[74]

> *Bonjour [Jeanne],*
> *J'espère que vous allez bien. Je m'appelle Hakima et je suis une responsable faisant partie de l'équipe Trip Experience à Airbnb. Je viens de prendre connaissance de votre dossier et je suis sincèrement désolée de la situation que vous avez rencontrée après avoir passée une première nuit chez [Lily]. J'imagine qu'avoir un réveil de la sorte n'a pas du [sic] être agréable."**

After expressing her sympathy, Hakima proceeds to explain to Jeanne that her three-month reservation has been modified to last only the one night.

> *"[E]n effet,"* she notes, *"je constate que vous avez quitté le logement la nuit après votre arrivée et il était bien sure [sic] hors de question que vous y restiez dans ces conditions."***

> *"Même si officiellement maintenant la réservation ne dure qu'une nuit,"* she clarifies, *"nous vous avons entièrement remboursé [sic], même pour la nuit passé [sic] dans le logement."****

---

*   The cited message was sent in French. On the necessity and impossibility of translation, see Jacques Derrida, "Des tours de Babel" in Peggy Kamuf & Elizabeth Rottenberg, eds, *Psyche: Inventions of the Other Volume I* (Stanford, CA: Stanford University Press, 2007) 191. [Hello Jeanne, I hope you are doing well. My name is Hakima and I am a member of the Trip Experience team at Airbnb. I have just reviewed your file and I am truly sorry for the situation that you encountered after your first night at [Lily's]. I imagine that it was an unpleasant way to wake up.] All the translations are from the author.

**   [Indeed, I see that you left the night after your arrival and it was evidently out of the question for you to stay under such conditions.]

***   [Though the reservation is now officially for just one night, we fully reimbursed you, even for the night that you spent in the accommodation.]

After providing Jeanne with the details of the reimbursement already in place by Airbnb, she proceeds to explain why, for the time being, Jeanne cannot be relocated to alternative accommodation. *"[N]'aurons* [sic] *pas confirmation que vos affaires ayant pu être en contact avec les punaises de lit soit nettoyées,"***** she apologizes. "After you receive the invoice for the dry cleaning," she requests, "please send it to me by email, and I will take care of your reimbursement." Hakima concludes her long message with an adjournment, a cryptic prolongation of Jeanne's forced stay in a hotel, a deferral of her relocation to an alternative accommodation:

> *Concernant le séjour à l'hôtel, il semble que le paiement est* [sic] *été validé par Airbnb pour la nuit passée, si vous décidez de rester à l'hôte* [sic] *ce soir ou les jours suivants, nous ne pourrons malheureusement prendre en charge le coup* [sic] *de la réservation à l'hôtel.******

Jeanne wakes up to find Hakima's message in her email inbox. Although slightly confused by the vague wording of the last paragraph, she understands that Airbnb will neither book her accommodation nor reimburse her for her prolonged stay in the hotel, a stay that was booked by Airbnb only the day before, and that cannot end until Airbnb itself decides so. In desperate search of a lifeline, she attempts to contact the only person she can think of, the guardian with the human, friendly face, the person that "had her back"[75] the day before, the doorkeeper to whom she has already formed an attachment. Replying to the only email address she has, response@airbnb.com, she writes:

> Dear Jason,
> Thank you for your answer. Again, you've been amazing, you are the best crisis-manager ever!
> I had a rather worrying answer from Hakima France. She said that Airbnb cannot find me a solution/a place to stay for tonight.

**** [Until we have confirmation that any belongings that may have been in contact with the bedbugs have been cleaned.

***** With regard to your stay at the hotel, it looks like the payment has been validated by Airbnb for last night. If you decide to stay at the hotel tonight or the following days, unfortunately, we won't be able to take care of the costs of the hotel reservation.

I will go to the laundry today to wash my stuff and buy new clothes, I can send you the receipt. Is it possible to stay another night in the hotel, or to find a airbnb?

I have to stress that I just arrived in New York and I don't know anybody here. Plus I am a student, so I don't have a lot of money. I cannot afford to pay by myself another night to the hotel. I already had to pay to buy new clothes as I threw up all clothes that have been in contact with the infected bed.

I also have to stress that it is a very disturbing situation for me: I am allergic, so I am covered by red bites, even in my face!!!!!!!! I couldn't sleep last night because I was so stressed, and because all the bites were itching. Hopefully I had my medicines from France, but still. I really need you to help me find a sustainable and durable solution to my problem: I need a place to sleep for tonight!

Thanks again for your help,

[Jeanne]

The phone-a-friend lifeline, Jeanne soon realizes, can be used only once. These are the rules of the game.[76] How naïve of her to think that Jason was real, a friend, a human friend. For although he was the face of Airbnb, Jason had no human face; his voice and words touched her, but it was not a human touch.[77] He is but one of many, and for him she was only one of many. Jason was stationed on the border between her and the law, but it was not her that he was there to guard. Even though he too was standing outside the domain of the law, he was not on her side. Even though he stood with his back to the law, facing her, it was the law that he had guarded all along, it is from her that he guarded it.

One short hour after Jeanne had written to Jason, she received an email from Hakima, "the case manager on this case for now," writing to teach her this valuable lesson, explaining to her "the way it's going to work." "I'm going to write you in English as this seems to be your preferred way of written communication," she sarcastically begins, as if in acknowledgement of the limits of language, of its self-referentiality. "I'm sorry that Jason promised you something we couldn't guarantee," she continues, stepping into her role as an empathetic guardian, the new "Jason." Her message not only delays Jeanne's relocation to a reasonably comparable accommodation, but once again obstructs entry to the law itself:

Hello [Jeanne],

I'm going to write you in English as this seems to be your preferred way of written communication.

I'm sorry that Jason promised you something we couldn't guarantee.

Because it's bed bugs we can't risk any contamination for safety reason, that is why for the moment we can't assist you to rebook a listing on Airbnb, however when you are able to provide clear documentation that all your belongings have been treated for bed bugs we can start the process to assist you, and I'll be more than happy to assist you myself as I'm the case manager on this case for now.

So right now, I want to confirm that exceptionally, I'll offer a refund of an hotel stay of up to 150$ for tonight.

The way it's going to work is that you can book the hotel of your choosing on your own, and then send me the receipt by replying to this email.

As soon as I receive it, I'll refund you of up to 150$, as mentioned above.

To process to this hotel refund, you will need to add a payout method, you can add it by clicking on the link: https://www.airbnb.com/users/payout_preferences/3029474.

Then as soon as I received documentation from you confirming that all your belongings have been cleaned, I'll refund you up to 100$ on the laundry cost.

As for the rebooking, just to clarify, we are more than willing to assist you, but we have to receive documentation confirming your belongings are free of bed bugs.

I know and understand that you don't have a lot of money on your that is why I'm offering you those courtesy refund on Airbnb's behalf and that those refund will be sent to you as soon as we have documentation and that you have added a payout method.

Also I want to confirm once again that the payment of the reservation with [… Lily] was fully refunded to you.

I hope this is more clear, but if I wasn't feel free to let me know and I'll be getting back to you as soon as possible.

Thanks [sic] you.

Hakima

After receiving a much-needed clarification and a much more detailed explanation, Jeanne replies to Hakima that she will stay in the same hotel. Otherwise, she explains, she will not have time to get her remaining belongings dry-cleaned, buy new clothes and luggage, and go to the university to meet professors and complete all administrative requirements. "I am waiting for the dry cleaner to be open, and I get back to you as soon as I have the receipt," she promises before thanking Hakima "again" for her help. Hakima replies promptly. "Hi Jeanne, I'll keep an eye on your case and will be awaiting for your documentation," she reassures her. "I wish you well this afternoon for your trip to your new University. :)"

Before long, Jeanne realizes that Airbnb probably did not pay the full rate for her hotel room, which is actually $250 per night. Being a student, she obviously cannot afford paying the $100 difference. It also dawns on her that finding a hotel room in New York for under $150 a night is an almost impossible task. In distress, she writes to Hakima again, requesting help finding a hotel room close to her university. Hakima denies her request, without ever citing the basis for her refusal. "I'm sorry for the situation you are in," she apologizes, "however, we won't be able to book a night in the hotel for you." "We did it as a courtesy yesterday," she explains, "but it won't be possible again for today." "As I explained to you earlier," she reiterates for the third time, "if you book a hotel for tonight I am more than happy to refund you up to 150$ when you send us the receipt." "I know this is not the best situation and we are here to help," she concedes, "but in this situation there's unfortunately a limit to what we can do."

What precisely is this "situation," Jeanne is left to figure out. What is this "limit" of which Hakima speaks, how it was defined, and by whom, she will never know. Which law dictated the decision conveyed by Hakima? Jeanne is left to wonder. "Let me know if you have any question," Hakima defers almost mockingly, leaving our distressed and mystified Jeanne with more questions than answers, sending her, and us as the readers of her story, on a journey to the origin of the law by which Hakima made her decision.

Hours pass by—how time flies when you are having a hell of a time! Eventually, Jeanne has all the documentation to send to Hakima, proof that she no longer poses a health and safety threat to the Airbnb community. She, like the bed bugs that failed to make her their home, relocates to an alternative accommodation, to the home of a new and, hopefully, more accommodating host.

IV. Revolving Doors

How would jurists react to and evaluate Jeanne's story? With which common intuitions would the members of the epistemic community of the law approach it? How quick would they be to judge? Would they take the side of the stodgy civil justice system, or would they be dazzled by the swiftness, efficiency, and responsiveness of this alternative to state institutions? Would they resort to the idea of "access to justice," the notion of "procedural transparency,"[78] or the "law of standing"?[79] Would they frame the story through the lens of civil procedure, or as a market regulation issue? What would be their ruling?

The most striking aspect of Airbnb's processing of Jeanne's dispute with her host is its swiftness. How would jurists consider it? Is time on Airbnb's side, or is it on the side of the traditional state court system? Is it of the essence, or is the administration of justice through law—just as the abstract norms that purport to guide the law's ostensibly autonomous and objective processes—largely unaffected by it? To what extent is time of the essence, and of what essence is it? "Justice delayed is justice denied" goes the common legal adage, whose originator is a secret of the past. The contradiction inherent in this recited maxim is exposed through Jeanne's story. Contemplating the role of time in the context of her story, it must be considered whether it is even possible to deliver immediate justice, and what constitutes a "delay"? Can justice through law be obtained without delay? Is some degree of delay therefore desirable? The paradoxicality of this celebrated maxim is beautifully exposed through Martin Luther King's inspiring and inciting "Letter from a Birmingham Jail." In response to claims that his actions were "untimely," and suggestions that he should have given the new city administration of Birmingham time to act, he writes:

> [f]or years now I have heard the word "Wait!" It rings in the ear of every Negro with piercing familiarity. This "Wait" has almost always meant "'Never." We must come to see, with one of our distinguished jurists, that "justice too long delayed is justice denied."[80]

The last two sentences of King's reply confront two opposing positions on the relation between justice and time. In the first, King restates the conventional formulation of the adage, which suggests that to delay is to deny access to justice. The ensuing sentence positions itself as opposition to the previous: "[w]e must come to see," King subtly reformulates the maxim, that "justice *too long* delayed is justice denied."[81] Writing from jail the story of his trial and judgment by the law, by his adversaries and by his friends, King does not turn his back on this revered principle; rather, he insists on its universality and *precisely* on its timelessness. However, while writing on its timelessness, his narrative works to penetrate justice's atemporal realm, to introduce a dimension of time into it. Justice should be considered denied, King's letter suggests, only when it is served with excessive delay. The accessibility of the Airbnb dispute resolution processes and of the state civil justice system should be assessed not by reference to time alone, but by reference to the reasonable or optimal length of a dispute resolution procedure. Was the swiftness of Jeanne's process reasonable? Is speed necessarily optimal? Would state courts have processed Jeanne's dispute within a (more) reasonable period of time, had she turned to them? Paradoxically, this claim and the questions it elicits are themselves a form of an adjournment; they send us on a quest for a higher law, a law of delay, a criterion against which we could judge a "delay" as "excessive" or "reasonable."

The swiftness with which Airbnb carries out its processes further raises the traditional jurisprudential problem of discretion. What is the scope of Jason and Hakima's discretionary power? What effect does a tight time limit have on discretion? Does pressure to make a quick decision result in a more mechanical application of rules or overreliance on intuition? Is it more or less likely to produce "accurate" determinations? Is it more or less likely to yield "just" outcomes? What would be an optimal timeframe to exercise judgment?[82] Given the type of disputes processed by Airbnb, is the swiftness of its procedures less of a concern? Given the commercial context, is it more of a concern? The problem of discretion subsequently evokes the question of what makes state-employed judges more impartial or qualified decision-makers than Jason and Hakima? And who are Jason and Hakima, we may ask, and what are their credentials? Who should be given the authority to interpret the law, to determine the meaning of a legal text? Who should be authorized to judge the actions of Jeanne's host as either "acceptable" or "unacceptable," "reasonable" or "unreasonable"? Alas, we hit yet another roadblock, delayed once again.

It is not just a question of time, others would likely stress. Other concerns, should also be taken into account when assessing Airbnb's processes in the context of Jeanne's story. A quicker procedure, they would caution, is not necessarily a more accessible one. To be considered accessible, a dispute resolution mechanism should provide more than a quick response. It must also produce just results and fair treatment. It must be easily understood by its users, responsive to their needs, adequately resourced, and well-organized.[83] Does the Airbnb dispute resolution apparatus meet these criteria? Do any of the traditional civil justice systems, to which the Airbnb customer support service is being compared, satisfy them? Is it possible to achieve all of these objectives simultaneously? Which of these systems under consideration comes closest to meeting these goals? Do the millstones of the state civil justice system grind more finely, precisely because they turn more slowly? Alas, we arrive before yet another gate, of another law, deferred, struggling to compose a conclusive list of criteria that is additionally prioritized by the relative value of each item.

Time is money, many would likely point out in an attempt to get the discussion back on track. Much like the cases that reach small-claims courts, disputes between Airbnb users are relatively straightforward, and generally do not involve large sums of money. Airbnb users are not given a separate charge for services provided by the Airbnb dispute processing apparatus; rather, as is explained by the Airbnb Help Center, these costs are covered by service fees charged to guests on booking confirmation.[84] As they are not represented, neither do users pay attorneys' fees. Procedures are simplified, arbiter-led (as opposed to adversarial), and informal. Decisions are reached and enforced quickly, and all communication is in simple language devoid of legal jargon. Moreover, it is not necessary for Airbnb users to wait until the end of their vacation to make a claim. Airbnb's customer service is available 24/7, providing instant guidance and relief. Speedy and responsive justice, the argument goes, is a more certain justice. In this process, Jeanne was not subjected to the prolonged apprehension typically suffered while anticipating a future court ruling. Airbnb immediately notified her that her booking had been cancelled and instructed her to leave the infested accommodation. Jeanne did not have to assess which of her options a court might find "reasonable" to mitigate her damages, or for which of the expenses she incurred she might later be compensated. She was immediately sent to a hotel, although temporarily, helped to find comparable alternative accommodation, instructed to throw away all of her belongings that had been in direct contact with bed bugs, requested to have all of her remaining clothing dry cleaned, and encouraged to take a taxi to her hotel. The substantial cost of all each of these actions was borne by Airbnb, and when incurred by Jeanne, she was quickly reimbursed. However, as suggested by both critical evaluations of the relationship between access to justice and small claims courts and critical race theory's challenge to the assumption that informal dispute resolution mechanisms are more accessible than formal ones,[85] swift, less-costly, simplified, and more informal procedures led by a fact-finding, activist adjudicator do not necessarily enhance access to either courts or "justice." A conclusion that is reinforced, as some might observe, by Airbnb's efforts to divert (discrimination) claims from state courts to arbitration, and by recurring claims by hosts that Airbnb's decisions systematically favour guests over hosts.[86] Alas, we are summoned to appear before another law, sent on a journey to find its origin: What is "justice"? What is meant by "access"? And to what extent does "access" relate to "justice"?

Moreover, as the Ontario Ministry of the Attorney General explains, a favourable judgment does not guarantee payment. "Some people," the ministry observes, "think that when the trial is over and the judge's decision is made or a default judgment is obtained, the successful party [...] will automatically be paid [...] and that is the end of the case. Obtaining a judgment," they caution, "is sometimes just the beginning for both parties."[87] Indeed, often costly and time-consuming steps are required to collect a favourable judgment, especially a foreign one. Moreover, in many jurisdictions, to request enforcement of a foreign judgment, a writ of execution or garnishment, an additional legal process is required. Airbnb users are fortunate to bypass this added delay and barrier to justice. Although Jeanne was charged in full the moment her host confirmed her booking, payment was held by Airbnb until twenty-four hours after check-in. This hold, as Airbnb explains, gives both parties "time to make sure that everything is as expected."[88] Within hours of receiving Jeanne's claim for a "Travel Issue," Airbnb accepted her claim and effectuated her refund. Jeanne's story is not exceptional. The ToS agreement and Payments Terms grant Airbnb extensive authority to enforce its judgments; refunds and reimbursements are effectuated immediately and in many cases automatically.

The relative ease and speed of judgment and enforcement, some would likely remind us, do come at a price. What's done is done, they might caution, referring to the Kafkaesque experience of AirbnbHell.com's founder. Once judgments are made and enforced it becomes much more complicated to review, and even more so, reverse them. Given the disincentive to reverse decisions and order the return of sums that have already been paid, does not the passage of time reduce the probability of judicial mistakes, guaranteeing better outcomes? In this context, the "in books" finality of Airbnb's decisions and the speed of their enforcement further raises concerns about the lack of a formal, internal appellate procedure. In practice, however, as the story of AirbnbHell.com's founder reveals, Airbnb's door remains forever open, and its representatives never turn dissatisfied users away, rather inviting them to submit decisions for review or to talk to a "manager."[89] Moreover, as a resident of France, Jeanne could have challenged any of Airbnb's decisions in an Irish court or any court of competent jurisdiction. As a resident of the Unites States, her host could have initiated arbitration, which would have been conducted in the location of her choice; she could have also elected to participate by phone, video conference, or, for claims under $25,000, by the submission of documents.[90] Alas, we arrive before yet another law, appealing for admittance, desiring knowledge of the essence and the scope of the "right of appeal." Is the possibility of taking one state court's decision to another state court for review more consistent with the right of appeal than the possibility of referring a dispute to arbitration by a third party? What is the value of that right and how essential is it? The past, some might retort, should be left in the past, and the sooner it is left there the better. Whether favourable or not, a swift and final decision can enable disputants to close the door on their trying episode and start a new chapter. Are the psychological costs of a swift process, experienced as Kafkaesque, necessarily lower than those of a long process with favourable outcomes? Would the founder of AirbnbHell.com have been more satisfied had he been subjected to a lengthier and more formal process, regardless of the outcome?

State law, some would likely conclude, offers disputants like Jeanne too little, too late. Considering the financial costs of obtaining a lawyer, litigating and collecting, considering also Jeanne's limited resources, the nature of her dispute and the prospects of a lengthy multinational litigation against a wealthier party, and considering the international context, questions of jurisdiction, and the potential need to prove and litigate under Irish law, would Jeanne have even bothered to ask for legal advice or to take her case to court? Indeed, it should be considered whether the disputes arbitrated by Airbnb are the kinds of disputes that reach state courts, including small-claims courts. How many of the disputes arbitrated by Airbnb might have entered formal legal institutions, had the Airbnb Resolution Center not been available to them? Moreover, as the recent decision to compel arbitration of discrimination claims suggests, what does the state civil justice system even offer disputants such as Jeanne? Are its procedures "fairer" or more "efficient," and in what sense? Do they produce more "just" or "efficient" outcomes, and in what sense? Does, to conclude, access to courts necessarily enhance access to justice?

Rivalry between the hotel industry and Airbnb is often depicted as a conflict between a stodgy incumbent and a disruptive newcomer. The relation between Airbnb and the state can also be framed in the same way. Would jurists be quick to adopt this neoliberal rhetoric of competition? Are we indeed facing a confrontation between two "competing sovereigns,"[91] an appearance of two laws before each other? If so, in accordance with which law should we resolve the dispute? Before the gate of which jurisdiction should we summon both to make a determination? Alternatively, might the gate to Airbnb's domain be merely the first of two doors, a passageway towards the gate of another, more powerful law, that of state jurisdiction? By positioning state jurisdiction above that of Airbnb, the juridical rhetoric of hierarchy could give rise to a different set of questions and another series of delays. Taking the perspective of the state and assuming their traditional position as guardians, legal scrollers would likely read Jeanne's story as a summoning of Airbnb's legal personality before state law. Some would perhaps examine Airbnb's compliance with existing regulation, embarking on an impossible quest to determine the controlling law and discover its meaning. Others might adopt a "centrifugal perspective,"[92] setting Jeanne's story "in the shadow" of state law,[93] studying both the "bargaining chips"[94] and "regulatory endowments"[95] that the state had conferred on her and on Airbnb. Highlighting the distributive or economic implications of existing regulations, their likely conclusion would send them on a desperate search for a higher law, a principle of social justice by which the existing economic conditions could be judged, and an argument for reform made. Considering Jeanne's story from the perspective of the state, it might further be read as a narrative of accessibility and the growing movement towards alternative dispute resolution (ADR). Providing a quicker, cheaper, flexible and specialized redress for a large number of otherwise unresolved minor disputes, does this alternative to the traditional process render civil justice more accessible? Should the state embrace it for its potential to divert minor cases from overburdened state courts, thus avoiding costly trials at the public's expense, and ultimately reducing public expenditure? Can, however, existing models of ADR or online dispute resolution (ODR) be used to describe and analyze the immense apparatus operated by Airbnb and similar platform owners?[96] Airbnb's exclusive jurisdiction as the dispute processor is established not by an agreement between Jeanne and her host, but in the separate agreements that each signed with Airbnb. In accordance with section 22.3 of the Terms, these agreements do not confer rights or remedies on third parties. Can we say that Jeanne's dispute was resolved through "arbitration" or "mediation"? Should Airbnb's dispute processing mechanism be conceptualized or recognized as a new method of ADR or ODR? Would such a move enhance or restrict access to "justice?" Is "justice" ever really accessible?

V. Conclusion

It is with many questions that I would like to close the door on this investigation. Although imposing a series of delays upon our attempt to make legal sense of the story of Jeanne, Airbnb and the "sharing economy," I have hopefully incited deeper reflection on our most basic intuitions and presuppositions on the possibility of "justice through law." Indeed, as any process of reflective examination, the search for a law by which we can judge Jeanne's story is bound to impose many delays. From its place of hiding, the law for which we search is destined to obscure, defer, and adjourn, rendering evermore irresistible the attempt to uncover its essence and meaning. What is the value of embarking on a never-ending quest towards the non-existent? Perhaps it is Kafka himself, an insurance clerk, who spent his days as the doorkeeper to the law, protecting the non-existent, who his protagonist, a man from the country, had been observing all along. Perhaps "Before the Law" is not the story of a man from the country, but of the doorkeeper who spends his days with his back to the law, never turning to look through the open gate he himself guards, never seeking admittance to the law. Perhaps it is not the story of a man delayed entrance, but of a doorkeeper using a man from the country as a mirror, observing a reflection of himself and of what lies hidden behind him. Perhaps it is to us, his fellow guardians of the law, that Kafka was writing to, adjuring us to examine ourselves through the eyes of the man from the country, to reflect ourselves on the questions he frames, on what it is that we so reverently guard, to conclude with a question in place of a statement.

Notes

1. In dedication to Gunther Teubner. Thank you for teaching me the value of "productive misreading," and thank you for encouraging me to embark on a journey in search of my own law.

2. In accordance with the preamble to the ToS agreement, residents of the United States enter into agreement with Airbnb, Inc; residents of the People's Republic of China who use the service to book or list accommodation in China contract with Airbnb Internet (Beijing) Co, Ltd (Airbnb China); and all other users enter into agreement with Airbnb Ireland UC (Airbnb Ireland).

3. Section 21.1 of the Terms stipulates that all contracts signed with Airbnb Inc will be interpreted in accordance with the laws of the State of California and the United States; section 21.2 establishes that contracts with Airbnb China will be governed by the laws of China; and section 21.3 stipulates that all agreements made with Airbnb Ireland will be interpreted in accordance with Irish law and the consumer protection regulations of the user's country of residence. Section 19 of the Terms contains an arbitration clause and class-action waiver that applies to all disputes with Airbnb Inc and any action brought against Airbnb in the United States. As part of section 21.2, parties to agreement with Airbnb Inc consent (unless otherwise agreed upon by both parties) to bring all claims excluded from the Arbitration Agreement in section 19 in state or federal court in San Francisco, California. In accordance with section 21.2, residents of China agree to submit any dispute with Airbnb China to the China International Economic and Trade Arbitration Commission for arbitration in Beijing. Lastly, as part of section 21.3, consumers agree to submit disputes with Airbnb Ireland to the non-exclusive jurisdiction of the Irish courts; businesses agree to submit to their exclusive jurisdiction. Consumers further agree to bring judicial proceedings against Airbnb Ireland only in a court located in Ireland or a court with jurisdiction in their place of residence. As part of section 21.3, Airbnb Ireland agrees to enforce any of its rights against consumers (as opposed to businesses) only in the courts of the jurisdiction in which they reside.

4. Blending the words "scroll" and "scholar," the *portmanteau* word "scroller" is intended to allude to both the process of scrolling down a lengthy text—whether a ToS agreement published electronically or an ancient scroll—and the deductive logic employed by many jurists and scholars.

5. Some of the extreme cases that have reached the media include the complete trashing of apartments; a man's death at an Airbnb rental in Texas; an alleged unlawful imprisonment and sexual assault by a transsexual host in Madrid; and multiple claims of sexual-orientation and racial discrimination. See e.g. Ruth Halkon & Gemma Mullin, "First Picture from Inside Airbnb Flat Shows Destruction Caused by Revellers," *Mirror* (6 January 2016), online: <http://www.mirror.co.uk/news/uk-news/first-picture-inside-trashed-airbnb-7122497>; Ron Lieber, "Death in Airbnb Rental Raises Liability Questions," *The New York Times* (13 November 2015), online: <http://www.nytimes.com/2015/11/14/your-money/death-in-airbnb-rental-raises-liability-questions.html>; Ron Lieber, "Airbnb Horror Story Points to Need for Precautions," *The New York Times* (14 August 2015), online: <http://www.nytimes.com/2015/08/15/your-money/airbnb-horror-story-points-to-need-for-precautions.html>; Caroline O'Donovan, "Airbnb Removes Host Who Denied a Trans Woman a Place to Stay," *BuzzFeed News* (6 June 2016), online: <https://www.buzzfeed.com/carolineodonovan/host-who-denied-a-trans-woman-a-place-to-stay-removed-from-a>. (6 June 2016)

6. See e.g. Erik Larson & Andrew M Harris, "Airbnb Sued, Accused of Ignoring Hosts' Race Discrimination," *Bloomberg* (18 May 2016), online: <https://www.bloomberg.com/news/articles/2016-05-18/airbnb-sued-over-host-s-alleged-discrimination-against-black-man>; Alexander Howard, "A Man Died at an Airbnb Rental. Here's How the Company Responded," *The Huffington Post* (10 November 2015), online: <http://www.huffingtonpost.com/entry/a-death-at-an-airbnb-rental-puts-the-tech-company-in-the-hot-seat_us_5640db66e4b0b24aee4b18f7>.(18 May 2016).

7. Several recent articles consider mostly liability issues, applying the traditional conceptual framework of state law or calling for the introduction of new state or municipal regulation. See e.g. Chad Marzen et al., "The New Sharing Economy: The Role of Property, Tort, and Contract Law for Managing the Airbnb Model" (2016–2017) 13 NYU J L & Bus 295; Talia G. Loucks, "Travelers Beware: Tort Liability in the Sharing Economy" (2014–2015) 10 Wash J L Tech & Arts 329. In the law and technology literature, some attention has been directed to disputes between members of "virtual worlds." See e.g. Mia Consalvo, *Cheating: Gaining Advantage in Videogames* (Cambridge, MA: MIT Press, 2009) at 142; F Gregory Lastowka, *Virtual Justice* (New Haven: Yale University Press, 2010) at 97–100. In this context, several virtual-worlds scholars

have studied the dispute processing mechanisms (as well as property and contract systems) developed by the members themselves. See especially Jennifer L Mnookin, "Virtual(ly) Law: The Emergence of Law in LambdaMOO" in Peter Ludlow, ed, *Crypto Anarchy, Cyberstates, and Pirate Utopias* (Cambridge, MA: MIT Press, 2001) 245 at 256–57. Others have debated whether or not state law should recognize virtual worlds as separate, foreign, self-governing jurisdictions, applying the rules of private international law to disputes between virtual worlds' members. See e.g. Mnookin, *supra* at 272–84; Lastowka, *supra* at 88. Another strand of literature has been debating the applicability of "real world" private law to disputes arising in virtual worlds, questioning whether in-game property rights should be recognized as a basis for claims in contract and tort law, whether terms of service agreements create enforceable obligations between users, and whether users could be recognized as third-party beneficiaries. See e.g. Michael Risch, "Virtual Third Parties" (2008) 25 Santa Clara Comp & High Tech LJ 415; Joshua Fairfield, "Anti-Social Contracts: The Contractual Governance of Virtual Worlds" (2008) 53 McGill LJ 427; Farnaz Alemi, "An Avatar's Day in Court: A Proposal for Obtaining Relief and Resolving Disputes in Virtual World Games" (2007) 11 UCLA JL & T 6; Lastowka, *supra* at 95. Lastly, the growing body of literature on online dispute resolution (ODR), a new approach to dispute resolution that advocates for the use of digital technology to assist in resolving disputes, also deserves mention. eBay's collaboration with SquareTrade, an external mediation service, is commonly given as a successful example of technology-assisted dispute processing. See e.g. Ethan Katsh & Orna Rabinovich-Einy, *Digital Justice: Technology and the Internet of Disputes* (Oxford: Oxford University Press, 2017); Ethan Katsh, "Bringing Online Dispute Resolution to Virtual Worlds: Creating Processes through Code" (2004) 49 NYL Sch L Rev 271.

8. See *supra* note 3; *Selden v Airbnb Inc*, 2016 WL 6476934 (DC Dist Ct) [*Selden*]. On February 2, 2017, the Court of Appeals for the District of Columbia Circuit ruled that the district court's order compelling arbitration and staying litigation pending arbitration is not appealable. See *Selden v. Airbnb, Inc.*, 2017 16-7139 (D.C. Circuit).

9. See *Selden, supra* note 8.

10. "Airbnb is Global and Growing" (10 August 2017), online: Airbnb Citizen <https://www.airbnbcitizen.com/airbnb-is-global-and-growing/>.

11. Rani Molla, "Airbnb Is on Track to Rack Up More than 100 Million Stays This Year — And That's Only the Beginning of Its Threat to the Hotel Industry" (19 July 2017), online: Recode <https://www.recode.net/2017/7/19/15949782/airbnb-100-million-stays-2017-threat-business-hotel-industry>.

12. Jeanne Lombardo Bliss, "How Airbnb Scales Culture and Customer Experience" (7 June 2016) at 00h:25m:00s, online: CustomerBliss <http://www.customerbliss.com/airbnb-scales-culture-customer-experience-aisling-hassell-cb008>.

13. *Ibid* at 00h:23m:00s.

14. See Kia Kokalitcheva, "More People Who Use Airbnb Don't Want to Go Back to Hotels," *Fortune* (16 February 2016), online: <http://fortune.com/2016/02/16/airbnb-hotels-survey>; "Goldman Sachs: More and More People Who Use Airbnb Don't Want to Go Back to Hotels," *The Business Times* (16 February 2016), online: <http://www.businesstimes.com.sg/consumer/goldman-sachs-more-and-more-people-who-use-airbnb-dont-want-to-go-back-to-hotels>.

15. Riley Newman & Judd Antin, "Building for Trust: Insights from Our Efforts to Distill the Fuel for the Sharing Economy" (14 March 2016), *Airbnb Engineering & Data Science* (blog), online: <https://medium.com/airbnb-engineering/building-for-trust-503e9872bbbb>.

16. "What Are Airbnb's Standards and Expectations?," online: Airbnb Help Center <https://www.airbnb.com/help/article/1199/what-are-airbnb-s-standards-and-expectations>.

17. "New Developments" (29 March 2016), *At Airbnb* (blog), online: <http://blog.airbnb.com/newdevelopments>.

18. *Ibid.*

19. *Ibid.*

20. "Cancellation Policies," online: Airbnb <https://www.airbnb.com/home/cancellation_policies>.

21. "Payments Terms of Service," s 10.2.2, online: Airbnb Terms <https://www.airbnb.ca/terms/payments_terms>.

22. *Ibid.*

23. See "I'm a Host. What Penalties Apply if I Need to Cancel a Reservation?," online: Airbnb Help Center <https://www.airbnb.com/help/article/990/i-m-a-host--what-penalties-apply-if-i-need-to-cancel-a-reservation>.

24. "How Does Airbnb Handle Security Deposits?," online: Airbnb Help Center <https://www.airbnb.com/help/article/140/how-does-airbnb-handle-security-deposits?topic=226>.

25. "What Do I Do if My Guest Breaks Something in My Place?," online: Airbnb Help Center <https://www.airbnb.com/help/article/264/what-do-i-do-if-my-guest-breaks-something-in-my-place>.

26. In various sections of the website, Airbnb assures its users that it will ensure that both parties "are represented fairly," will gather any details and documentation needed to reach a resolution, and will review this information before making a final decision. See "What Is the Resolution Center?," online: Airbnb Help Center <https://www.airbnb.com/help/

article/767/what-is-the-resolution-center?topic=226>; "What Happens if a Host Makes a Claim on My Security Deposit?," online: Airbnb Help Center <https://www.airbnb.com/help/article/352/what-happens-if-a-host-makes-a-claim-on-my-security-deposit?topic=226>.

27. "What Do I Do if My Guest Breaks Something in My Place?," *supra* note 25.

28. "What is the Airbnb Host Guarantee?," online: Airbnb Help Center <https://www.airbnb.com/help/article/279/what-is-the-airbnb-host-guarantee>.

29. "What Do I Do if My Guest Breaks Something in My Place?," *supra* note 25.

30. "The $1,000,000 Host Guarantee," online: Airbnb <https://www.airbnb.com/guarantee>.

31. "*Host Guarantee Terms and Conditions*," s V, online: Airbnb Terms <https://www.airbnb.com/terms/host_guarantee>.

32. "How Do I Submit a Host Guarantee Payment Request?," online: Airbnb Help Center <https://www.airbnb.com/help/article/361/how-do-i-submit-a-host-guarantee-payment-request>."

34. "What Is Airbnb's Extenuating Circumstances Policy?," online: Airbnb Help Center <https://www.airbnb.com/help/article/1320/what-is-airbnb-s-extenuating-circumstances-policy>. While some of the additional Terms and Policies incorporated by reference into the ToS agreement (for example, the Guest Refund Policy) are published alongside it, others, such as the Extenuating Circumstances Policy and the Extortion Policy, are rather published in the Help Section of the website.

35. *Ibid.*

36. "Do I Have to Refund My Guests when They Make a Complaint?," online: Airbnb Help Center <https://www.airbnb.com/help/article/326/do-i-have-to-refund-my-guests-when-they-make-a-complaint>.

37. "Airbnb Guest Refund Policy," online: Airbnb Terms <https://www.airbnb.ca/terms/guest_refund_policy>.

38. The allusion here is, of course, to Roscoe Pound's seminal distinction between "law in books" and "law in action." See Roscoe Pound, "Law in Books and Law in Action" (1910) 44 Am L Rev 12.

39. See Jacques Derrida, "Before the Law" in Derek Attridge, ed, *Acts of Literature* (New York: Routledge, 1992) 181 at 214–15; Cornelia Vismann, *Files: Law and Media Technology* (Stanford, CA: Stanford University Press, 2008) at 23–24 (construing the "unalterable" status of scripture as a barrier and questions of interpretation as questions of access). See also Mariana Valverde, *Chronotopes of Law: Jurisdiction, Scale and Governance* (Abingdon, UK: Routledge, 2015) at 83 (claiming that, for lawyers, "jurisdiction is the law of law").

40. By "law in action" I mean to refer to the study of statistical data, behavioural patterns, regularities, commercial usage or practice, informal norms and sanctions, rules of conduct, and decision rules.

41. Franz Kafka, "Before the Law," cited in Derrida, *supra* note 39 at 183–84.

42. See Marc Galanter, "Justice in Many Rooms: Courts, Private Ordering, and Indigenous Law" (1981) 19 J Leg Pluralism 1; see accompanying text on ODR, *supra* note 7.

43. Derrida, *supra* note 39 at 205.

44. *Ibid.*

45. *Ibid* at 211.

46. On the "lenticular logic" of computer systems, see Tara McPherson, "U.S. Operating Systems at Mid-Century" in Lisa Nakamura & Peter Chow-White, eds, *Race after the Internet* (Abingdon, UK: Routledge, 2011) 21.2013

47. Derrida, *supra* note 39 at 211.

48. *Ibid.*

49. *Ibid.*

50. See Steve Portigal, "Judd Antin of Airbnb" (19 January 2016) (podcast), online: Portigal <http://www.portigal.com/podcast/7-judd-antin-of-airbnb>.

51. "Director, Trust and Safety," online: Careers at Airbnb <https://www.airbnb.com/careers/departments/position/515516>. The Trust and Safety team is referred to as the "Aircorps" in job listings published by Airbnb. See e.g. "Customer Experience Specialist (French)," online: Careers at Airbnb, <https://www.airbnb.com/careers/departments/position/254235>.

52. "Customer Experience," online: Careers at Airbnb <https://www.airbnb.com/careers/departments/customer-experience>. On the term "crewbies," see Portigal, *supra* note 50.

53. Derrida, *supra* note 39 at 202-03.

54. Dan Weber, "Why AirbnbHell Exists—From the Founder," online: AirbnbHell <http://www.airbnbhell.com/why-airbnbhell-exists>.

55. *Ibid.*

56. See Derrida, *supra* note 39 at 208.

57. *Ibid* at 205.

58. *Ibid* at 207.

59. *Ibid* at 205.

60. *Ibid* at 196.

61. *Ibid* ("[t]he law, intolerant of its own history, intervenes as an absolutely emergent order, absolute and detached from any origin. It appears as something that does not appear as such in the course of a history. At all events, it cannot be constituted by some history that might give rise to any story. If there were any history, it would be neither presentable nor relatable: the history of that which never took place" at 194).

62. *Ibid* at 191. See also William LF Felstiner, Richard L Abel & Austin Sarat, "The Emergence and Transformation of Disputes: Naming, Blaming, Claiming..." (1980–81) 15:3/4 Law & Soc'y Rev 631 (claiming that by reducing cases to records, legal institutions reify cases and "embody disputes in a concrete form that can be studied retrospectively" as factual and socially situated events that are external to the examination, at 631).

63. See Vismann, *supra* note 39 at 15.

64. Kafka, *supra* note 41.

65. *Ibid* at 212–13.

66. Gunther Teubner, "The Law before Its Law: Franz Kafka on the (Im) possibility of Law's Self-Reflection" (2013) 14:2 German LJ 405 at 406.

67. *Ibid* at 407.

68. *Ibid*.

69. *Ibid* at 409.

70. See Peter Brooks, "Clues, Evidence, Detection: Law Stories" (2017) 25:1 Narrative 1.

71. "Customer Experience Specialist (German)," job posting from airbnb. com, on file with the author.

72. Jason's job title was given to Jeanne only over the phone and is not mentioned in writing anywhere in their written correspondence. In effect, the only explicit mentioning of the position on the entire Airbnb website is provided—and even there, only for limited periods of time—in jobs listings published in its careers section.

73. All communications cited in this section are original and were forwarded to me by "Jeanne" herself; they are used with her explicit permission. The names of Jeanne and her host were modified to preserve their privacy. The names of the Airbnb representatives, acting in official capacity, were not modified.

74. See "Customer Experience Lead, Japan," online: Careers at Airbnb <https://www.airbnb.com/careers/ departments/position/461115>.

75. The global head of CX at Airbnb explains, in an interview, that "global customer experience at Airbnb is about [...] we call it 'having your back.'" See Bliss, *supra* note 12 at 00h:19m:27s.

76. The game show rhetoric is borrowed from the global head of CX at Airbnb. She explains: "we want it to be like [...] you know those quiz games where you can dial a friend? Right? We want it to feel like if you are stuck at any moment calling Airbnb or having to contact us is like that dial a friend moment where you know your friend is going to be there [...] well sometimes a friend doesn't have all the answers but you know that regardless you are going to get an empathetic response from someone who's on your side in terms of trying to help you with whatever your problem is." See *ibid* at 00h:09m:44s.

77. *Ibid* at 00h:10m:12s.
78. David M Trubek, "The Handmaiden's Revenge: On Reading and Using the Newer Sociology of Civil Procedure" (1988) 51:4 Law & Contemp Probs 111 at 114-15.
79. Louise Trubek & David Trubek, "Civic Justice through Civil Justice: A New Approach to Public Interest Advocacy in the United States" in Mauro Cappelletti, ed, *Access to Justice and the Welfare State* (Amsterdam: Luitingh-Sijthoff, 1981) 119 at 119.
80. Letter from Martin Luther King, Jr to Clergymen (16 April 1963), cited in "Letter from a Birmingham Jail [King, Jr]," online: African Studies Center, University of Pennsylvania <https://www.africa.upenn.edu/Articles_Gen/Letter_Birmingham.html>.
81. *Ibid* [emphasis added].
82. On the potential negative implications of swiftness on the quality and accuracy of judicial determinations, see e.g. H Lee Sarokin, "Justice Rushed is Justice Ruined" (1986) 38 Rutgers L Rev 431; Alex Whiting, "In International Criminal Prosecutions, Justice Delayed Can Be Justice Delivered" (2009) 50:2 Harv Intl LJ 323; Chris Guthrie, Jeffrey J Rachlinski & Andrew J Wistrich, "Blinking on the Bench: How Judges Decide Cases" (2007) 93:1 Cornell L Rev 1 at 35–36.
83. See Roderick A Macdonald, "Access to Justice in Canada Today: Scope, Scale and Ambitions" in Julia H Bass, William A Bogart & Frederick H Zemans, eds, *Access to Justice for a New Century: The Way Forward* (Toronto: Law Society of Upper Canada, 2005) 19 at 23–24.
84. Guest service fees are only refundable in cases of host cancelation. See "What are Guest Service Fees?," online: Airbnb Help Center <https://www.airbnb.com/help/article/104/what-are-guest-service-fees>. According to the Help Center, the host service fees cover only the cost of processing payments. See "What Are Host Service Fees?," online: Airbnb Help Center <https://www.airbnb.com/help/article/63/what-are-host-service-fees>. As aforementioned, hosts may nevertheless be found responsible for the costs incurred by Airbnb to relocate their guests to an alternative accommodation, or obliged to pay a cancellation fee.
85. On small claims courts, see Seana C McGuire & Roderick A MacDonald, "Small Claims Court Cant" (1996) 34:3 Osgoode Hall LJ 509. For critical race theory's defense of formality, see e.g. Richard Delgado et al, "Fairness and Formality: Minimizing the Risk of Prejudice in Alternative Dispute Resolution" (1985) 1985:6 Wis L Rev 1359; Patricia J Williams, "Alchemical Notes: Reconstructing Ideals from Deconstructed Rights" (1987) 22 Harv CR-CLL Rev 401.
86. See e.g. "Appeal to Airbnb's Final Decision" (7 December 2015), online: Airbnb Community Center, Hosting <https://community.airbnb.com/t5/Hosts/Appeal-to-Airbnb-s-final-decision/m-p/6490#M1049>.

87. Ontario, Ministry of the Attorney General, "After Judgment—Guide to Getting Results", (Toronto: Queen's Printer for Ontario, 2016).

88. "When Am I Charged for a Reservation?," online: Airbnb Help Center <https://www.airbnb.com/help/article/92/when-am-i-charged-for-a-reservation?topic=220>.

89. "Our enforcement teams are made up of dedicated professionals, but they're still human," explains one of the sections of the Airbnb Help Center. "So, in rare cases, enforcement decisions may be incorrect. If you disagree with a decision we've made, you can contact us and we'll re-review the decision carefully." See "What Are Airbnb's Standards and Expectations?," *supra* note 16.

90. Section 19 of the Terms. Section 19 caps the initial filing fee for the consumer at $200. As part of the section, Airbnb also waives all rights it may have to recover attorney fees and expenses if it prevails in arbitration.

91. Lawrence Lessig, *Code: And Other Laws of Cyberspace* (New York: Basic Books, 1999) ch 14–15.

92. Galanter, *supra* note 42.

93. See Robert H Mnookin & Lewis Kornhauser, "Bargaining in the Shadow of the Law: The Case of Divorce" (1979) 88:5 Yale LJ 950.

94. *Ibid* at 968.

95. Galanter, *supra* note 42 at 9.

96. See accompanying text on ODR, *supra* note 7.

PART II

REGULATING TECHNOLOGY

CHAPTER IV

The Normative Ecology
of Disruptive Technology

Vincent Gautrais[1]

I. Introduction

Technological Neutrality: Hogwash! This brief chapter will not elaborate on the nature of disruptive technology. Neither will it express an opinion on its merits,[2] or on issues of disruption that arise when faced with controlled markets, where organized and protected monopolies have been profoundly affected.[3] Instead, it will deal with the normative environment within which this innovation is currently developing—an environment that is necessarily shaped not only by the technology itself, but also by the sheer speed of its evolution. More precisely, it will take for granted that technology has a major impact on our way of operating. Technology—let us make no bones about it—is not neutral.[4] It infiltrates our lives with myriad effects on power relations. Such issues are therefore worthy of consideration and integration into the controls that the law, conceived globally as formal and informal norms, seeks to implement. Thus, law is a tool for the management of power relations. In keeping with the image of scales, the law weighs; it weighs in. But technology, due to the changes that it brings, far too frequently creates an extraordinary opportunity for calling into question the very principles and scales that have taken centuries to crystallize.

Disruptive Technology. Implicit in the notion of the "sharing economy" is a minor anodyne dimension, as well as a major dimension that is just as untrue. As concerns the former, it is anodyne because sharing is seen as a good thing. Like apple pie, one cannot possibly be against it. And as concerns the latter, there is also a fundamental falsehood that certain of these companies "share," when, in fact, they operate through a formidable unilateral retention of information. To be precise, they retain the information shared by others, about others. In fact, this notion of sharing as understood in the context of projects of limited size, such as those which happily flourish in municipalities everywhere,[5] is incompatible with megastructures such as Uber and Airbnb. On the contrary, the latter companies are the poster children of retention. Such issues of retention first surface in the contract, which emphasizes the ownership of data,[6] and this in spite of the natural suspicion that should arise when faced with such an appropriation of personal information. A lack of transparency is also at play in the manner in which the algorithms are programmed, despite the degree of accountability that is increasingly required in this respect.[7]

Revolution/Evolution. This equilibrium is all the more difficult to attain where technology becomes infused with emotion; when faced with the "technomagic"[8] frequently associated with technology—frequently perceived as either eminently dangerous or highly lifesaving—it is important to take a calm look at the "revolution"[9] that we face. For while we certainly observe a "factual" revolution, with technology creating technological and economic upheaval,[10] it is met by a normative "toolbox" that has both merit and tradition. Strongly creative, the law remains a marvellous means: capable of evolution, of adaptation. When faced with this technological revolution, the law may perhaps simply give rise to an evolution in terms of which traditional tools are considered to be sufficiently effective. This is a debate as old as the law, as old as the Internet itself. Since its very beginnings, the Internet has given rise to questions regarding the best way of managing this new reality.[11]

Normative Porosity. But to return to the sharing economy: many consider that because of its technological upheavals the sharing economy has created a legal vacuum without precedent. This is incorrect. It often is the case that those who invoke the notion of a legal vacuum are the ones who consider that the law only works against them.[12] Quite to the contrary, there is not only a broad variety of applicable laws but also an increased need for them. Hence norms should not be considered through the narrow lens of formal norms that (directly or indirectly) derive from the state; normativity should be grasped pluralistically, with frequent interactions between the various levels of normativity. Apart from formal texts, this also obviously includes a contractual structure with its own set of particularities, but also that which I like to call individual normativity,[13] namely internal company documentation that details a certain level of requirements. Yet neither contracts nor internal company documentation entail real control. Essentially, few contracts have been analyzed by the courts—and even this jurisprudence has difficulties in assessing such (frequently technical) commercial texts.

   Normative Pervasiveness. Contrary to popular thought, we therefore have a broad range of normative tools. Among them, four contribute to the development of an ecosystem of norms—an overlapping, intersecting ecology. The Kelsinian pyramid has reached its limits; a more plural, more global, vision is needed. But beyond this so-called ecosystem that needs to be described in quantitative terms, it is also important that it be evaluated, as several of these norms are not truly effective. Indeed, while certain formal norms manage, in spite of their flaws, to harness the activities that are linked to the sharing economy (section II), other contractual or individual norms have some limitations, meaning that they are not always able to control the activities of Uber, Airbnb, and the other platforms that form the subject matter of this study (section III). Accordingly, it is an overview of these legal tools that will be presented below.

II. Formal Norms under Oversight

It is a natural reflex: when technology raises new problems, let us pass a law! Paradoxically, issues relating to the sharing economy are quite easily dealt with by judges applying existing law. The law in its traditional guise applies even though specific features are absent.

i. The Relative Effectiveness of Laws

Much can be said about the numerous[14] laws that come into play in the regulation of the sharing economy. With regard to the situation in Quebec, there is, of course, the issue relating to the specific and temporal law that was imposed on Uber. A law that is not quite one: this text, called an "agreement," does not have the generality that is typically associated with the law.[15] Nonetheless, originating from a government institution, this text created quite a stir in September 2016, and was made public, meaning that it could be subjected to analysis. The same goes for the texts relating to short-term accommodation.[16]

1. Law and Technology: Limits

The Law Questioned. Naturally, laws raise questions far beyond the power relations that they introduce, in terms of which some actors receive rights while the rights of others are limited. It is often the case that those who are faced with new laws are not content to see their rights trampled upon nor their prerogatives threatened. This is not where the question arises for present purposes, as it is beyond my field of expertise. Instead, the legal enquiry envisaged relates to the two following elements.

First, governments all too often adopt "communication" laws which have as a core objective to demonstrate to the population that the government acts and that it performs its sovereign role of distributing interests. Thus, as Professor Atias emphasizes, the *Act* is a communication tool to which "the name of a discoverer might be attached."[17] As it happens, this objective of the law is manifest in the Quebec agreement relating to Uber where the text establishes general principles with which the company must comply. Thus, in addition to clearly identified obligations, the text also details extremely vague objectives such as transparency, innovation, and privacy. While the *Act* is prescriptive, it is therefore also somewhat idealistic in that it deems itself able to effect profound changes in power relations. What conceit. The same goes for the *Act Respecting Tourist Accommodation Establishments*,[18] which, while identifying some specific obligations to be met, does not appear to place great value on the controls exercised by the administrative authorities.[19]

Partial Laws. Second, immense areas are completely left by the wayside. Still speaking of Uber, the text essentially targets two kinds of power relations: on the one hand, the relation "Uber/Quebec State"; on the other, that of "Uber/Taxi Industry." With regards to the former, the monetary aspects have been developed with great precision. A fiscal agreement is appended to the text, which provides for fees in similar detail.[20] Some public safety and public interest considerations are also present; [21] not much more. Concerning the latter, as far as the relation to the taxi industry is concerned, a dividing up of the respective territories is proposed, with a heavy reliance on technology: telephonic services and the streets are taxis' domain—Uber is limited to online solicitation.[22] That being said, many shortcomings and issues remain outside the ambit of the text. Admittedly, there are other laws and multiple legal texts that will likely apply to Uber.

Nonetheless, the following matters remain opaque: What about the right to privacy?[23] What about the risks of discrimination inherent in the choice of clients or of drivers? The law of the platform[24] asserts itself; individual normativity should not only be envisaged but should above all give rise to real control.[25] None of these norms are considered in the slightest in the agreement with Uber.

  2. *Law and Technology: Mastering the Limits*

The Law and Its Ability to Act. The above being said, while one may criticize the law, the fact remains that it works. Contrary to many an Internet service, the sharing economy frequently—and specifically in the case of the ones that are best known (UberX; Airbnb)—is very much a physical reality. In the case of these frequent examples, it must be underlined that they amount to a real service of physical transport, and to a real service of physical accommodation. Hence, this is not an instance of the eternal non-application of the law brought about by the international dimensions of relations. In fact, it is indeed Uber Canada that is the contracting party to agreements initiated by the government, both with regards to operating modalities[26] and fiscal compliance,[27] which enhances the "domestic" nature of the *Act.* Similarly, insofar as Airbnb in its various forms is concerned, the *Act Respecting Tourist Accommodation Establishments,*[28] like the *Regulations Respecting Tourist Accommodation Establishments*[29] applies to the whole of Quebec. The governmental response is especially specific, constituting proof that the authorities have tackled the "Airbnb issue" head-on, the Ministère du Tourisme having gone so far as to furnish the public with an interpretative guide.[30] In these two cases the government has elected to authorize. The use of these platforms is accordingly allowed, subject to compliance with conditions that do not appear—when compared to other jurisdictions[31]— particularly onerous.

ii. The Effectiveness of Jurisprudence
Jurisprudence and Adapting to New Developments. While new laws could apply to new developments, they nevertheless have some shortcomings that I believe are important to identify.[32] In certain respects the old law is sometimes more effective than the new,[33] and the legislative reflex is often to hold back in relation to new issues.[34] As one author puts it, "it is urgent to wait."[35] Indeed, this is what the Airbnb

litigation has demonstrated.[36] This balancing, therefore, involves recourse to a judge.

Interpretation. In Canada, the interpretation of legislation is taught as a mandatory course in the majority of law faculties. Far be it for me to try and summarize this complex subject matter in a few lines. Simply put, and beyond the three interpretative approaches that are generally identified (formerly "literal, teleological, contextual"[37] and nowadays, rather, "text, context and subject"),[38] it seems likely that some are by nature more applicable than others, depending on the circumstances. Depending on the situation, and linked to the digital environment, I have previously drawn distinctions[39] based on the hypotheses[40] that, on the one hand, the law under interpretation plays a more "mechanical"[41] role, or, on the other hand, that it carries out a further evaluation of the issues at hand, which requires a higher level of complexity.[42] Divided along these lines, I believe it is possible to identify that the teleological approach is prevalent in the first instance and the contextual approach in the second. By way of illustration, it seems likely that the jurisprudence in the Airbnb dispute has relatively straightforward objectives, the transposition of which into the digital world seems relatively easy to effectuate.[43]

It is impossible to produce a comprehensive account of all the jurisprudence that finds application in this context. This is because the courts already have a sustained response, despite the relative newness of the economic models. Hence this chapter is restricted to two hypotheses. The first is that a local response emerging from the province of Quebec is concerned with the jurisprudential reaction to the phenomenon of Airbnb-type accommodations. The second is more global, as it analyzes the general contractual disqualification by the courts that gives rise to the fact that Uber drivers might fall within the domain of labour law.

1. *The Effectiveness of Jurisprudence in the Airbnb Dispute*

Airbnb vis-à-vis the Régie de logement. With the emergence of shared accommodation, a series of cases have illustrated the great capacity of jurisprudence to adapt. While it is possible to locate disputes in Quebec regarding the relationship between the state and these "renters,"[44] several, in fact, concern landlords and tenants, since this subletting of short duration effectively changes the deal made in the original contract. Without entering unduly into this, one realizes that judicial interpretation can easily take place by applying the old texts to these new situations. In essence, the tenant who sublets his apartment through Airbnb is obliged to advise his landlord of this fact and to obtain the landlord's consent.[45] Hence, a landlord may repudiate the contract when a tenant has contravened article 1870 of the Quebec Civil Code (CCQ) that requires the landlord's consent to an act of subletting.[46] In addition, the landlord will be able to repudiate on the basis that the tenant has changed the destination of the leased property by subletting it to a third party, and will be entitled to compensation for damages.[47] Once again, in many respects the "old texts" such as the CCQ are easier to interpret than the new ones such as the *Act Respecting Tourist Accommodation Establishments*, which poses difficulties both in relation to its interpretation[48] and its application.[49]

2. The Effectiveness of Jurisprudence in the Uber Dispute

Uber and the Status of Drivers. A further illustration of the relative effectiveness of the traditional rules is to be found in the application of labour law to this multinational entity. First, an extensive debate has occurred in several jurisdictions over whether the drivers can be considered as employees in spite of contractual stipulations that clearly set out their status as independent contractors. More often than not, the judicial response has been to set aside the contract—as was the case, for instance, in California,[50] London,[51] and in Switzerland.[52] Second, several courts have modified the contractual qualification that the multinational is not considered to be a taxi company but rather a software company.[53] Therefore, contractual attempts to extract themselves from intensely regulated domains have not functioned very well in many instances.

Interpretation. It thus appears that the legal complacency of which some complain, [54] in light of the development of disruptive technology, has by no means been established. Of course, by nature the law is slow to react, and it takes time before the rules will be plainly applicable. Quite simply, whether through qualification or through the creation of new categories of workers,[55] jurisprudence constitutes a marvellous tool for adapting the facts to the law—as indeed the Airbnb example demonstrates.

II. Norms in Search of Oversight

Traditional normative tools work. They have their deficiencies, especially in the case of statutes, but they work. That said, they are often insufficient. For reasons of complexity, laws cannot specify certain types of obligations in too much detail. Being general and impersonal, they cannot always define with the necessary finesse what exactly the parties in question should respect. Among the normative tools that can sometimes go further, there are contracts and what I like to call "individual normativity." Contracts naturally include those of adhesion (standard form contracts) that the platforms impose on their users. In order to limit the scope of the analysis, the focus here is on contracts between Uber and its drivers and passengers, as well as those between the landlords and tenants of Airbnb. But then there are the norms that the platforms self-proclaim: these establish their level of diligence in relation to privacy rights, security, and the choice of algorithms that occasionally are loaded with discrimination and bias.[56] These rules, much like the contracts, do not give rise to meaningful legal oversight. Due to their technicality, a significant degree of laissez-faire, their newness, and the changing nature of the data, legal interpreters are not very prompt in their analysis of these tools. Here we have a real normative gap[57]—certainly not a vacuum, but a zone that passes under the radar. And yet these norms are quite real, even though they operate in relative autonomy. This autonomy must be subjected to oversight.[58] Each of these categories of (i.) individual norms and contracts (ii.) will now be considered more closely.

i. The Quest to Oversee Individual Normativity

In one of his works, the philosopher Bernard Stiegler advances that, in the digital sphere, data poses at once the problem and the solution, the disease and the remedy. Similar to Pharmakon in Greek thought,[59] this normative production that originates from the actors themselves disposes, on one hand, a real capacity to regulate, but on the other, these rules do not lead in practice to any oversight. Hence, individual normativity is essentially the solution that has almost unanimously been proposed in multiple domains of law and technology, particularly in several legal texts; however, this approach gives rise to very weak legal oversight. It is expected that such oversight will become more rigorous in years to come.

1. Delegated Individual Normativity

Generalization of Individual Normativity. This increase is undoubtedly linked to the fact that contemporary society gives rise to ever more complexity. To put it in ancient law terms: in order to manage this complexity, it is preferable to consider the law as a process, as presented by Plato, rather than a substantial principle, proposed by Aristotle in his writings. Indeed, the quest for legal objectification can no longer simply proceed through general substantive principles such as "adequate" security, "reasonable" management, and so on, but increasingly requires that the law be proceduralized, which may lead to an *a posteriori* assessment. This could be undertaken in isolation by judges who would accordingly evaluate whether the documents in question are based on "rational justifications," as Jacques Lenoble puts it.[60]

Documentation. When faced with the complexity of factual situations, one often sees laws requiring actors to document their practices. Whether this is in the domain of privacy[61] (where the notion of accountability has made incredible strides since the beginning of 2010) or in the domain of security[62] (where the same process is evident), it is clear that this is an olive branch for the actors themselves. They accordingly should develop the documentation in question by basing themselves directly on either formal norms (laws or regulations) or (most likely) on "community" norms derived from commercial associations or national and international standardization bodies. Thus, sharing economy companies are expected to demonstrate more transparency when it comes to their use of the data that is at the core of their business model. This calls for management with oversight: a standard should be proposed and an oversight entity identified. Moreover, many of the older digital companies have followed this approach: for instance, in 2011 Facebook negotiated an agreement with the United States Federal Trade Commission under which the company undertook to open up its books.[63] This generalized form of oversight is operationalized by the implementation of an audit procedure.

Audit of Activities. We are therefore witnessing the generalization of a process-based approach in every shape and form,[64] and that takes shape in Michael Power's world-famous book, *The Audit Society: Ritual of Verification*, in which he documents a significant increase of this practice.[65] Despite the lack of a definition,[66] the models vary over time; originally conceived of as a means of detecting fraud, in the twentieth century the audit was focussed more on getting an overview of the state of play.[67] However, while the public still sees this role as a protective one, this is not the case in practice,[68] where auditors are apprehensive that this will give rise to too extensive liability.[69] Audit therefore has an inherently dark side in spite of the alleged quest for objectification. Auditors sometimes recognize the lack of clarity, even the doubts, that arise with regards to effectiveness, even more so given the fact that big investments are often the order of the day. They acknowledge being the bearers of "comfort"[70] rather than of evidence. In sum, as Power argues, internal audits will soon eclipse external audits, and the distinction between them will become extremely vague. Internal auditors will play a role in matters of regulation and internal oversight will be outsourced to external agencies.[71]

Specific Cases in the Sharing Economy. Insofar as the sharing economy is concerned, there are multiple hypotheses wherein this normative solution would appear to be unavoidable. First, we know that companies abuse consumer data that they source ubiquitously. Admittedly, privacy laws apply, but these only indicate a general duty of "responsibility,"[72] of accountability. Hence—and this goes beyond data that is forwarded due to state mandates[73]—we need to know more about the use to which such data is put by the company itself, whether the data derives from drivers or clients, landlords or lodgers. Second, the same goes for the scant oversight that exists in respect of the calculations effected by algorithms and their impacts in terms of discrimination. Here, again, there is not a legal vacuum at play but rather ignorance of the way in which to apply general principles as recognized by human rights legislation. In both instances, the problems appear by accident, because of an inquest, or due to a leak by a former employee.

2. *Individual Normativity in Search of Oversight*

Two Kinds of Individual Normativity. In order to address these shortcomings, and to ensure the improved oversight of such activities, it is important to illustrate how such individual normativity might occur. Two main hypotheses may be made in this regard. The first concerns the internal documents with which the company directs in sufficient detail that which the law cannot do directly. In fact, such commercial structures are characterized by a plurality of policies and procedures, and there is no doubt that these can bring about a high level of turnaround in the conduct of the actors involved (be they drivers or landlords). Second, and even more insidiously, the increased use of algorithmic calculation methods points to the likelihood of neutrality and of a level of technicality that greatly reduces or eliminates the need for judicial oversight. However, nothing could be further from the truth.

Documentary Normativity. Initially I did not take an *a priori* negative view regarding the drafting of documents based on informal benchmarks, frequently originating either from commercial associations or from associations where the industry has a say. In fact, there undoubtedly is no other way. But the fact remains that it is necessary to press for a thorough thinking-through of both the document's drafting process and the benchmarks on which it will be based. And a multitude of voices are challenging this firm but very little thought-through tendency of norm imposition.[74] The important observation to be made here is that we are unfortunately at present very far from it, as much due to the "industry of norms" as to the "norms of industry"[75] themselves.

Deficient Normativity. To begin with, deficiencies arise in respect of the financial context within which such norms are drafted. All too often the norms "flourish," in the words of Thibault Daudigeos, creating a multiplicity that is characterized by confusion.[76] We are faced with a veritable "bazaar" of norms[77] where, on the one hand, it is not known when and why government requires recourse to such norms,[78] and, on the other, it is in the interests of certain organizations to "sell" theirs. This excessive profusion that needs to be analyzed is all the more problematic because certification and advice services are directly dependent on the norms in question.

Normativity at a Cost. In the second instance, in addition to this normative multiplicity, there is an openness that is inherent to law, in that there is the need for law to be accessible and available to all who wish to navigate it. This seems very remote to someone who has had to pay 150 Swiss francs for a set of ISO norms. It is problematic, to say the least, that one cannot dispose of such "norms" freely, when legal doctrine acknowledges beyond a shadow of a doubt the "values" that are of importance, and instructs to take them seriously.[79] Such norms are thus "techniques," but they are not only that; they also constitute norms with a real political reach that are aimed at both things and persons.[80] This is all the more so in the case of copyright laws, which are completely ridiculous and where the online sale process is very far removed from the best practices that these laws are supposed to uphold.[81]

Algorithmic Normativity. The second hypothesis mentioned above relates to the choices effected by the industry itself, both in terms of complex algorithmic calculations as well as strictly commercial decisions. Thus, by way of example, it has been observed that Uber's rate-fixing system is flexible and can be adjusted in terms of neighbourhood and the relationship between supply and demand. Hence, there are peak times (surge pricing)[82] that provide drivers with a higher rate of remuneration.[83] On the one hand, the drivers do not always have access to all the information that the company has at its disposal, and, on the other hand, the company sometimes transmits messages to drivers that encourage them to work during specific time periods, while the forecasted traffic volumes are not necessarily very reliable. A real information symmetry is accordingly needed. The same goes for the rating system for drivers whose apparent "neutrality" still needs to be considered. In essence, the calculation methods remain nebulous for the main persons involved.[84]

Zone of Tolerance. In spite of this reflex, which first made its appearance at the beginning of the digital era,[85] the purported "legal vacuum" was soon discarded.[86] To the contrary, we instead see an explosion of law, with new rules being added to the old. Yet, while I consider the use of the "vacuum" expression to be erroneous, it cannot be ignored that some areas of normativity remain under the half-hearted oversight of the law. Of this what I call "individual normativity" is a good example. In fact, whereas this mode of regulation remains fundamentally new, because the mode of regulation has become generalized, I have not yet sufficiently evaluated the extent of the change and jurists have not yet sufficiently considered the domain that needs to be overseen. Although they bear different titles, the same propositions can be found with regards to the quest for improved transparency of algorithmic calculations,[87] for a decrease in informational asymmetry,[88] for greater accountability,[89] in the need for more diligent processes,[90] as well as in the notion of "platform loyalty."[91] While there thus is relative unanimity on the need for greater oversight—in fact, there has been for a long,[92] long,[93] time—what form should such oversight take? What means could be put into place to ensure that lack of transparency loses ground?

Development of Tools for Oversight. Insofar as this issue is concerned, the tools are well known. They are documentary, technological, and legal. First, in managerial contexts, as previously discussed, both an explosion of individual documents and of oversight by skilled persons (via internal or external audits) can be observed. Despite the previous generalization, such solutions are not a cure-all. Documentation certainly contains clearer objectives, thanks to technical norms that detail the obligations to be respected. In fact, audits, aside from their cost, are limited in terms of effectiveness. Documentary deficiencies have been measured in financial security matters,[94] as well as in the particular instance of electronic voting.[95] Second, there is a completely natural reflex towards a more technological solution. In this context, authors propose a range of solutions for purposes of ensuring oversight if desired. One that stands out is software testing, which makes it possible to measure potential biases associated with particular algorithms. Another is cryptologic captures that freeze the informatics tools under analysis in time.[96] In all of these cases such means nevertheless contain deficiencies. One of them, of a politico-economic nature, is that the testing is generally done by an agency, a "certification body." This means that although the managerial solution rests on the shoulders of the company, the technological approach appears rather to require the intervention of an entity that closes in on a function usually fulfilled by the state.[97] This is no innocent distinction: oversight takes on a different centre of gravity. And this brings us to a third pathway: judicial oversight. In view of the area's newness and its inherent complexity, there has not yet been a real appropriation of this oversight, if not by the law, then at least by the judiciary. Thus, there still is scope for improvement in the courts' reception of this normativity. While jurisprudence has the marvellous ability to adapt itself to the circumstances, judges are hindered by the inherent complexity of the subject matter, the references to technical norms,[98] and the frequent interventions by expert witnesses. There is a discrepancy at work. The ties between law and technique need strengthening. We will have no other choice but to promote a new *lex electronica;*[99] a new *lex informatica.*[100]

ii. The Quest to Control Contractual Normativity

The contract, a pillar of commerce, is a very flexible legal tool. With a few exceptions, it takes no specific form, with consent sufficing to conclude one.[101] Bolstered by this flexibility, Canadian jurisprudence has given a generous interpretation to contractual performance in the digital context, and laws—especially those pertaining to consumers—have established procedures that are easy to comply with.[102] This decrease in legal oversight has led industry to adopt contractual practices that would appear to be contestable. These are practices that deserve more stringent legal oversight that is more attuned to the first principles that prevail in contract law.

1. Contractual Normativity as Pervasive and Deficient

Drafting Difficulties. The "standard" contracts that are currently flourishing on Internet platforms, such as those used in the sharing economy, present another example of normative omnipresence in this context. Once again, claims are made of a legal vacuum when, in effect, it is overfull. This is a contractual pathology[103] if ever there was one. A simple look at the Uber and Airbnb contracts induces amazement and hand-wringing because of their undue length, the contracts being respectively sixteen[104] and seventy-five[105] pages in length. In addition to being long, they are vague[106] and too often subject to interpretation. Moreover, the texts are crammed full of hypertext links—which serves to further increase their length.[107] We are therefore witnessing true contractual pathologies, both with regard to the usage conditions and the protection of personal information. This means that there is a "cost"[108] for the members-consumers that largely outweighs the potential advantages.[109] This is a cost that even diligent consumers who read the clauses do not manage to reduce in practice.[110]

Difficulties in Indicating Consent. But that is not all: such deficiencies appear not only in the drafting of the contract but also in the way in which the parties indicate their consent. Various behaviour patterns have been developed, and several among them have been interpreted by the courts. Thus "click wraps" (clicking on an icon) are generally deemed to provide more protection to the member than "browse wrap" (entering into a contract by reason of the mere presence of a contract on the site that engages the user). This certainly is better, but how very little. Indeed, an American author demonstrates that the fact that the user is given the opportunity to click on such an icon basically changes nothing in terms of awareness of the contractual content.[111] The entire process is designed to be quick, and the consumers do not read, nor do they want to read.

General Acknowledgement of the Deficient Form of Electronic Contracts. In spite of the aforementioned pathologies, a fairly lax judicial tendency can be observed when it comes to admitting them. In Canada, the flagship case is undoubtedly *Dell Computer*,[112] where the Supreme Court, in July 2007, refused to consider a long and verbose contract as being incomprehensible[113] or otherwise abusive.[114] More specifically, the judges ruled that such violations had not been demonstrated. Even though the respondents' reasoning was essentially quite weak, the court did not dare take the leap towards increased oversight of online contracts. The free-for-all approach that globally characterizes contractual practice was therefore condoned. The "old" American case that modified the cases preceding it,[115] *ProCD v Zeidenberg*,[116] was followed. Consent in contract, once mythologized, thus became decorative.[117] And what a pity![118] The effect of this condonation has been to extol the status quo. No need to improve contracts; the debate on the notion of "plain English"[119] that took place in the 1970s was buried, although the jurisprudence occasionally sees rare instances of reminiscence.[120]

Conceptual Difficulties Relating to the Status of "Consent." There is thus a jurisprudential tendency to weaken the place of "consent" within contracts. In fact, while the principle of consent remains one of the conditions for entering into a valid contract,[121] consent is now relatively easy to demonstrate—even if this is known to be completely illusory in practice. In North America, autonomy of will, without being formally challenged, is diluted on two levels. As we have previously seen, this flexible understanding is confirmed both in the communication of the contractual information and in the way in which consent is manifested. Condemning this practice, and this change of an important paradigm, Mark Lemley observes that "[t]oday, by contrast, more and more courts and commentators seem willing to accept the idea that if a business writes a document and calls it a contract, courts will enforce it as a contract even if no one agrees to it."[122] An erosion can thus be observed: "The idea of voluntary willingness first decayed into consent, then into assent, then into the mere possibility or opportunity for assent, then to merely fictional assent, then to mere efficient rearrangement of entitlements without any consent or assent."[123] This erosion is all the more contradictory when one considers that these contracts continue to repeat that the member has read and understood the incomprehensible provisions.[124]

2. *Contractual Normativity in Search of Oversight*

When it comes to potential pathways for increased oversight of the contracts under discussion, they present themselves in two dimensions: form and substance.

Potential Pathways to Overseeing the Contractual Form. In contracts put forward by disruptive technology companies, as is the case with the rest of electronic commerce, it appears imperative that a real "contractual marketing"[125] be put forward. It is therefore important to draft the contract's content bearing in mind that it will not be read by the consumer if it keeps being presented in standard format. Drafting efforts that may have been suggested in the past, based on the use of colours or distinct characters,[126] are poor stopgaps, a Band-Aid on a wooden leg. Rather, a complete redraft needs to be considered. Apart from their length, the contracts should be integrated in the purchase process, meaning that they are part of it in the same way as the choice of product. It is an astonishing fact that on Internet sites it is only contracts that are designed with the objective of not informing. Everywhere else the objective is to retain the customer's interest; when it comes to online contracts, the position is the opposite. In this informational context, and because of the fact that consent is being reconsidered, the possibility for increasing consumer understanding of contracts is limited only by the creativity of the lawyers. A first step might be to insert images, such as pictograms, each of which represents a different clause.[127] Next, why not render the contract accessible in audio format? In an era where the number of functional illiterates approaches 50 per cent, it is not inconceivable to vocally "translate" the contract. The digital environment makes this process possible, and there is no doubt that such a solution would of itself affect the length, the majority of current contracts not being capable of being read in a reasonable time. Then, there is scope for categorizing contracts: they could differ on the basis of the products sold, the profile of the purchaser, the consumer's geographical location, and so on. Finally, and without claiming to be exhaustive, the reinforcement of consent could also manifest itself through the individualization of the contract: the names of the parties could be inserted into the contract. The idea behind this is that the consumer would feel more involved if he or she saw his or her name appear, and would therefore consider the contractual obligations to be more closely associated to his or her person.

Administrative Oversight. That said, we saw that judicial over-sight—especially in the *Dell* matter—has been minimalist. This is why alternative solutions in the form of contractual oversight practises have been suggested in the literature. One of the most commonly proposed solutions is to ensure that a dedicated government agency could, at an early stage, sift out "unconscionable"[128] clauses. While this solution works in the United States in other domains, strongly flavoured as being a public policy measure—for instance concerning mortgage loans—I consider it too complex to extend to an economic sector of such a cross-cutting nature as disruptive technology. In fact, digital technology constitutes a tool and the electronic contract cannot be confined to a sector. This renders it difficult to bundle prac-tices. As well, this is a matter of culture, and the integration of state agencies is not a common reflex in North America. Hence, notwith-standing their undeniable benefits and their real achievements,[129] the French[130] or Israeli[131] solutions would not appear to be easily transposable onto other continents.

Potential Pathways to Overseeing Contractual Substance. But beyond the form of these digital contracts, it would seem that salvation is likely to lie in oversight of substance rather than form. Llewellyn, the great architect of the United States codification around 1960, claimed that the judicial system fulfills this contractual oversight function in circumstances where it is practically impossible to consent to clauses:

> Instead of thinking about "assent" to boiler-plate clauses, we can recognize that so far as concerns the specific, *there is no assent at all.* What has in fact been assented to, specifically, are the few dickered terms, and the broad type of the transaction, and but one thing more. *That one thing more is a blanket assent (not a spe-cific assent) to any not unreasonable or indecent terms the seller may have on his form,* which do not alter or eviscerate the reasonable meaning of the dickered terms.[132]

This solution has, moreover, been integrated in certain statutory texts.[133] But beyond the wisdom inherent in this formula, it should be noted that this traditional mode of oversight does not operate in an optimal manner. In fact, as we have seen, there are few decisions that sanction contractual practices. In Canada, the *Dell Computer* decision has served to illustrate the judges' refusal to perform this oversight role,[134] legal security being given preference over consumer interests.[135] Neither has this oversight role been emphasized in the new legislative provisions pertaining to electronic consumer contracts that nevertheless aimed to strengthen the need for contractual information.[136]

Jurisprudential Hope? Still, despite this somewhat despondent discourse, the question arises whether there is not perhaps reason for hope. Indeed, on 23 June 2017, the Supreme Court of Canada rendered an important decision that has tempered contractual omnipotence, *Douez v Facebook.*[137] In an admittedly divided decision, the majority went in an unexpected direction in ruling that there were substantial grounds for not upholding a choice of forum clause in favour of Californian law with the District Court of Santa Clara as the court of competent jurisdiction.[138] Thus the majority considered that while such clauses are usually valid, a series of arguments weighed in favour of a reversal. Among them there was first and foremost the fact that this was in a consumer context.[139] This justification is remarkable, for there is no discussion on this point: it is self-evident and the decision notes that a consumer context is involved,[140] even though the Facebook contract is offered free of charge. The lack of discussion is intriguing, although this position appears to be completely justified. It remains novel, in the sense that some older decisions have suggested the converse.[141] The consequence is that this relationship comprises an inherent fragility, one that is emphasized and multiplied by the development of the Internet[142] but also by the fact that the users are not really in a situation where they have the freedom to choose something else.[143] This is therefore a major decision in the sense that it introduces a case with an individualistic approach to contracts, even if this is limited to a specific question pertaining to choice of forum. It is an approach that Justice Abella would undoubtedly be keen to extend beyond the present question.[144]

Notes

1. Vincent Gautrais is the Director of the Centre de recherche en droit public (CRDP), Full Professor at the Faculty of Law of the Université de Montréal, and L R Wilson Chair in E-Commerce Law. He can be found at the following addresses: www.gautrais.com (personal website) / vincent.gautrais@umontreal.ca (institutional email address) / @gautrais (Twitter). Text translated by Elizabeth Steyn. Unless otherwise indicated, all translations of legislation and of judgements are unofficial.

2. Ryan Calo & Alex Rosenblat, "The Taking Economy: Uber, Information, and Power" (2017) 117:6 Colum L Rev, online: <http://columbialawreview.org/content/the-taking-economy-uber-information-and-power/>. See especially Part 1 entitled, "The Story of the Sharing Economy." See also Edith Ramirez, Maureen K Ohlhausen & Terrell P McSweeny, *The "Sharing" Economy: Issues Facing Platforms, Participants, and Regulators* (November 2016), online: Federal Trade Commission <https://www.ftc.gov/system/files/documents/reports/sharing-economy-issues-facing-platforms-participants-regulators-federal-trade-commission-staff/p151200_ftc_staff_report_on_the_sharing_economy.pdf>.

3. Brishen Rogers, "The Social Costs of Uber" (2015) 82 U Chicago L Rev Dialogue 85.

4. Vincent Gautrais, *Neutralité technologique: Rédaction et interprétation des lois face aux changements technologiques* (Montreal: Éditions Thémis, 2012) at 54ff [Vincent Gautrais, *Neutralité technologique*].

5. A mapping of collaborative initiatives in Quebec can be found at OuiShare Québec, *Cartographie des initiatives collaboratives du Québec*, online: <http://ouishare.net/fr/projects/cartographie-des-initiatives-collaboratives-du-quebec>.

6. See Section ii., below, entitled, "The Quest to Control Contractual Normativity".

7. See Section i., below, entitled, "The Quest to Control Individual Normativity".

8. Vincenzo Susca, "Technomagie: La nature de la mutation anthropologique" (2008) 16:2 Logos 29.

9. Michel Serres, *Les nouvelles technologies: révolution culturelle et cognitive* (20 December 2007), online: Interstices <http://interstices.info/jcms/c_33030/les-nouvelles-technologies-revolution-culturelle-et-cognitive>.

10. Orly Lobel, "The Law of the Platform" (2016) 101:1 Minn L Rev 87 at 87: "A leading critic of what is termed 'the gig economy,' economist Robert Reich argues that the rise of platform companies is making work life unpredictable, insecure, and, ironically, not even profitable."

11. This specifically refers to the "old" debate between Lessig and Easterbrook as to whether the regulation of cyberspace "differs" from traditional spheres. Frank H Easterbrook, "Cyberspace and the Law of the Horse" (1996) 1996 U Chicago Legal F 207; Lawrence Lessig, "The Law of the Horse: What Cyberlaw Might Teach" (1999) 113 Harv L Rev 501.

12. André Lucas, "La réception des nouvelles techniques dans la loi: l'exemple de la propriété intellectuelle" in Ysolde Gendreau, ed, *Le lisible et l'illisible* (Montreal: Éditions Thémis, 2003) 125 at 134: "There is a real fantasy of the legal gap, one that is relayed by the media and frequently also by politicians. The trust is that pressure groups call existing rules that do not please them, 'legal gaps.' Clamouring for legislation with

every new technological advance means leaping into a headlong rush that could only bring about legal insecurity."

13. Vincent Gautrais, "Normativité et droit du technique" in Stéphane Rousseau, ed, *Juriste sans frontières – Mélanges Ejan Mackaay* (Montreal: Éditions Thémis, 2015) 311 at 311–40.

14. Alison Griswold, "Uber Pulled Off a Spectacular Political Coup and Hardly Anyone Noticed" *Quartz* (21 January 2016), online: <http://qz.com/589041/uber-pulled-off-a-spectacular-political-coup-and-hardly-anyone-noticed/>, cited by Michael Geist elsewhere in this collection.

15. *Agreement between the Ministère des transports, de la mobilité durable et de l'électrification des transports and Uber Canada Inc* (9 September 2016), online: <https://www.transports.gouv.qc.ca/fr/salle-de-presse/nouvelles/Documents/2016-09-09/entente-uber.pdf>; *Entente relative aux exigences de conformité fiscale au Québec à l'égard des chauffeurs utilisant les plateformes « uberX », « uberXL » ou « uberSELECT », between the Ministère des finances du Québec and Uber Canada Inc* (15 August 2016) [Agreement between the *Ministère des finances du Québec* and Uber Canada Inc].

16. *Act Respecting Tourist Accommodation Establishments*, CQLR c E-14.2 and *Regulation Respecting Tourist Accommodation Establishments*, CQLR c E-14.2, r 1.

17. Christian Atias, "Tendance d'un temps ou inexorable loi du droit? De l'obligation au droit" (2010) Recueil Dalloz 2536.

18. *Act Respecting Tourist Accommodation Establishments, supra* note 16. S 6 reads as follows: "The operation of a tourist accommodation establishment is subject to the issue of a classification certificate. The application for a classification certificate must be filed with the Minister under the conditions prescribed by regulation of the Government."

19. See II.ii.1, below.

20. *Agreement between the Ministère des finances du Québec and Uber Canada Inc*, supra note 15. The same applies to the *Entente de conformité fiscale relative à la taxe sur l'hébergement à l'égard des hôtes utilisant la plateforme « Airbnb » between the Ministère des finances du Québec and Airbnb Ireland* (21 July 2017), online: <http://www.revenuquebec.ca/documents/entente-airbnb.PDF>.

21. In that respect, a revision request was lodged with the Commission des transports by the taxi industry on the express basis that the public interest should be considered. This request was rejected in view of the fact that the public interest does not constitute a revision criterion for the agreement in question. The Commission des transports stated that "in any event, because of the Decreet the Commission need not consider the public interest in the present matter. It only needs to apply the Decreet": *Comité provincial de concertation et de développement de l'industrie du taxi v Uber*, 2017 QCCTQ 0224 at para 185.

22. Agreement between the *Ministère des transports, de la mobilité durable et de l'électrification des transports* and Uber Canada Inc, *supra* note 15, s 2.12.

23. *Ibid.* The preamble of this agreement merely alludes to this.

24. Lobel, *supra* note 10.

25. See III.i., below.

26. Agreement between the *Ministère des transports, de la mobilité durable et de l'électrification des transports* and Uber Canada Inc, *supra* note 15.

27. *Agreement between the Ministère des finances du Québec and Uber Canada Inc, supra* note 15.

28. *Act Respecting Tourist Accommodation Establishments, supra* note 16.

29. *Regulation Respecting Tourist Accommodation Establishments, supra* note 16. S 1 reads as follows: "Any establishment in which at least 1 accommodation unit is offered for rent to tourists, in return for payment, *for a period not exceeding 31 days,* on a regular basis in the same calendar year and the availability of which is made public is a tourist accommodation establishment." [my emphasis].

30. Tourisme Québec, *Guide d'interprétation de la Loi et du Règlement sur les établissements d'hébergement touristique,* (19 October 2016), online: <http://www.tourisme.gouv.qc.ca/publications/media/document/ services/hebergement-guide-interpretation-campagne.pdf>.

31. See the obligation envisaged by a recent French decree, in terms of which lessors located in cities of more than 200,000 inhabitants are obliged to register at the town hall: *Décret n° 2017-678 du 28 avril 2017 relatif à la déclaration prévue au II de l'article L. 324-1-1 du code du tourisme et modifiant les articles D. 324-1 et D. 324-1-1 du même code,* JO, 30 April 2017. This rule will specifically apply in Paris, Bordeaux and Nice with effect from December 2017.

32. See II.i.2., above,. entitled "Law and Technology: Mastering the Limits."

33. Vincent Gautrais, *Neutralité technologique, supra* note 4 at 131ff.

34. Thus, many consider in respect of block chains that this field should not be regulated too fast: see Éric A Caprioli, "Les enjeux juridiques et sécurité des blockchains" (2017) 3 C de D entr 54.

35. Isabelle Renard, "Régulation de la Blockchain : Il est urgent d'attendre" (2016) 414 Expertises 215 at 215–18.

36. See II.ii.1., below, entitled "The Effectiveness of Jurisprudence in the Airbnb Dispute."

37. Stéphane Beaulac & Pierre-André Côté, "Driedger's 'Modern Principle' at the Supreme Court of Canada: Interpretation, Justification, Legitimization," (2006) 40 RJT 131 at 142: "It [the modern principle] suggests that a proper interpretation shall take into account the object of the enactment (Mischief Rule), the words with which it is expressed (Literal Rule) and the harmony among its provisions and other statutes

(Golden Rule); not one of them, or two of them, but all three aspects may be relevant and be taken into account."

38. Stéphane Beaulac, *Précis d'interprétation législative – Méthodologie générale, Charte canadienne et droit international* (Montreal: LexisNexis, 2008) at 49.

39. Vincent Gautrais, *Neutralité technologique, supra* note 4 at 220ff.

40. In terms of the dichotomy suggested by Clare Dalton: Clare Dalton, "An Essay in the Deconstruction of Contract Doctrine" (1985) 94:5 Yale LJ 997.

41. For example, in contracts evidence law, the interpretation of a signature or of a hypertext link.

42. For example, in privacy law the distinction between individual and commercial interests; and in copyright law, conflicts between rights holders and users.

43. See the paragraph entitled "The Effectiveness of Jurisprudence in the Airbnb Dispute," below.

44. Even if the sanctions are dissuasive in nature (section 37 of the *Act Respecting Tourist Accommodation Establishments* mentions sanctions ranging from $2,500 to $25,000), it has not been possible to locate cases where such penalties have been invoked. There is one solitary decision fining an individual ($ 20,000) for contempt of court for failing to comply with an injunction under the new provisions of the *Act Respecting Tourist Accommodation Establishments*: *Chabot c Leblanc*, 2016 Qc Sup Ct 3825.

45. See *9177-2541 Québec Inc v Li*, 2016 QCRDL 8129. The effect of this condition is to severely restrict such a sub-letting capacity.

46. *Rouleau v Bilodeau*, RDL 2016 QCRDL 1486.

47. *St-Germain v Levasseur*, 2016 QCRDL 2804; *Ngo v Arakaki Inc*, 2016 QCRDL 21172; *Côté c Pilon*, 2016 QCRDL 18913.

48. It is claimed that "'Where the advertisement on Airbnb constitutes an offer in excess of 31 days, but the actual lease period is shorter than 31 days, there is no infraction. *The law contains a loophole, in that it focuses on the offer to let rather than on the physical act of letting.* In addition, it speaks of a public offer, meaning that people who privately come to an agreement among themselves do not commit an infraction either.' The law furthermore determines that the rental offer be made 'on a regular basis' before it is considered as being illegal, a term that is 'very broad, very vague', according to Me Fauchon. [...] The *Ministère du Tourisme* acknowledges that it is well aware of the situation. Airbnb users and the users of other websites for accommodation rentals 'who advertise rentals in excess of 31 days are not in contravention of the law,' says spokesman Dominique Bouchard" [my emphasis]: Philippe Orfali, "La loi anti-Airbnb est aisément contournée" *Le Devoir* (17 August 2016), online: <http://www.ledevoir.com/societe/actualites-en-societe/477891/la-loi-anti-airbnb-est-aisement-contournee>.

49. Philippe Orfali, "La loi anti-Airbnb pratiquement pas utilisée" *Le Devoir* (30 July 2016), online: <http://www.ledevoir.com/economie/actualites-economiques/476700/hebergement-la-loi-anti-airbnb-pratiquement-pas-utilisee>: "[...] up until now, *Tourisme Québec* has issued a total of three Notices of Violation to users of websites such as Airbnb and chaletalouer.com. [...] As for the sum collected from the guilty parties, it amounts to ... $0.00. 'The Notice of Violation is not linked to a fine. It amounts to a letter informing the receiving party that he or she is carrying on the activities of a tourist accommodation establishment without the requisite classification certificate in contravention of article 6 of the *Act Respecting Tourist Accommodation Establishments*. The Notice also provides information on how the receiving party could comply with the Act, in order to prevent further prosecution,' explains the spokesman for *Tourisme Québec*, Guy Simard."

50. Orly Lobel, "The Law of the Platform" (2016) 101:1 Minn L Rev 87 at 133: "While both Uber and Lyft have been firm in classifying their drivers as independent contractors, others have viewed the arrangement differently. Recent class-action suits brought against both companies by drivers claiming misclassification stress the degree of control and direction the companies exercise. [...] In preliminary hearings in one such lawsuit, Judge Edward Chen stated, 'The idea that Uber is simply a software platform, I don't find that a very persuasive argument.' Chen found that the fact that 'Uber sets the rates by which drivers are paid, screens them ... and can terminate them' weighs in favor of finding them to be employees. In a parallel case against Lyft, the court stated, '[P]eople who do the kinds of things that Lyft drivers do here are employees.' In June 2015, the California Labor Commissioner, citing the high degree of control Uber exercises over its drivers, ruled in an individual hearing that at least one driver of Uber was an employee" [footnotes have been omitted].

51. See particularly the following decision referred to in this article: Rob Price, "The Bombshell Uber Driver Ruling Could Affect Almost Half a Million 'Self-Employed' Brits" *Business Insider UK* (28 October 2016), online: <http://uk.businessinsider.com/uber-driver-employee-ruling-could-affect-460000-self-employed-brits-rights-citizens-advice-2016-10>. While I have been unable to trace the decision, several extracts are to be found in Shane Hichey, "Uber Tribunal Judges Criticise 'Fictions' and 'Twisted Language'" *The Guardian* (28 October 2016), online: <https://www.theguardian.com/technology/2016/oct/28/uber-tribunal-judges-fictions-twisted-language-appeal>: "Any organisation ... resorting in its documentation to fictions, twisted language and even brand new terminology, merits, we think, a degree of scepticism."; "Ms Bertram [Uber's regional general manager for the UK] spoke of Uber assisting

the drivers to 'grow' their businesses, but no driver is in a position to do anything of the kind, unless growing his business simply means spending more hours at the wheel."; "We are satisfied that the supposed driver/passenger contract is a pure fiction which bears no relation to the real dealings and relationships between the parties."

52. In Switzerland, diametrically opposed positions are found in two reports put forward by labour law specialists. On the one hand, Professor Kurt Pärli published on 10 July 2016 a study in terms of which the employee was in a dominant position, mainly based on the fact that a situation of *de facto* dependency existed between the driver and Uber: Philip Thomas, *Résumé de l'expertise du Prof. Kurt Pärli concernant les "Questions de droit du travail et des assurances sociales dans le cas des chauffeuses et chauffeurs de taxis Uber"* (10 July 2016) at 5, online: <https://www.unia.ch/uploads/tx_news/2016-08-29-r%C3%A9sum%C3%A9-expertise-droit-du-travail-assurances-sociales-chauffeuses-chauffeurs-taxi-Uber-professeur-Kurt-P%C3%A4rli_01.pdf>. In particular, this Report states that "Uber drivers are not obliged to accept the requests that they receive via the Uber application. As well, they are not obliged to offer their services during predetermined periods or for a specified period. Such circumstances demonstrate the absence of a subordination relationship from the company's point of view. However, it would appear that the Uber application excludes those who regularly refuse to accept rides from consideration for further rides—which amounts to the *de facto* equivalent of an obligation to accept rides. Moreover, the operating agreement provides for automatic termination in the event that no ride is undertaken for a period of 90 days." On the other hand, a very recent study conducted in June 2017 at the behest of Uber finds that "criteria qualifying this activity as independent are largely predominant". For further information, see "Le statut des conducteurs d'Uber: un casse-tête" *Tribune de Genève* (5 July 2017), online: <http://www.tdg.ch/suisse/Le-statut-des-conducteurs-d-Uber-un-cassetete/story/31508990>.

53. Note in particular the position in Taiwan, where the authorities denied such status. Further references are available in Michael Geist's contribution in this collection.

54. "Much of [Uber's] spectacular growth has been fueled by outdated regulation," says Rafi Mohammed: Rafi Mohammed, "Regulation Is Hurting Cabs and Helping Uber" *Harvard Business Review* (9 July 2014), online: <https://hbr.org/2014/07/regulation-is-hurting-cabs-and-helping-uber>.

55. Professor Arthurs, in this collection, notably claims that the second route is preferable: "my aim is not to advocate for any particular form of words but rather to demonstrate that it may be preferable (and technically possible) to create new categories of protected workers, rather

than try to hammer the square peg of employment into the round hole of the sharing economy."

56. Yanbo Ge, Christopher R Knittel, Don Mackenzie & Stephen Zoepf, *Racial and Gender Discrimination in Transportation Network Companies* (October 2016), online: National Bureau of Economic Research <http://www.nber.org/papers/w22776>. This study specifically demonstrates that the waiting time and the cancellation percentage is higher among Black Americans and that women pay more on average.

57. To quote Calo & Rosenblat, *supra* note 2, who state: "A central aim of this Essay is to address this gap and put forward a positive vision of how consumer protection law should engage with the sharing economy."

58. This notion of technological autonomy brings to mind the work of Jacques Ellul, *Ellul par lui-même: Entretiens avec Willem H. Vanderburg* (Paris: Éditions de La Table Ronde, 2008) at 100: "To begin with, as a system technology follows its own laws, its own logic. Technology is autonomous, it is wrapped up in itself. [...] The difficulty is that, like any system, technology should have its own regulation, its own feedback. But we are not there. I note that there is zero self-regulation of the technology system."

59. Bernard Stiegler, "Pharmacologie des métadonnées" in Bernard Stiegler, Alain Giffard & Christian Fauré, *Pour en finir avec la mécroissance: quelques réflexions d'Ars Industrialis* (Paris: Flammarion, 2009) 87 at 89: "Any technical object is pharmacological: it simultaneously comprises poison and remedy. The pharmakon is at once that which allows for care to be taken and that in respect of which care must be taken, in the sense that one should pay attention to it: it is a healing power where proportional, and where inproportional, it is a destructive power."

60. Jacques Lenoble, *Droit et communication. La transformation du droit contemporain* (Paris: Éditions du Cerf, 1994).

61. Documentation is expressly stated in legal texts, both in Canada (in the *Personal Information Protection and Electronic Documents Act*, RSC 2000, c 5 [PIPEDA], specifically in Annex 1 thereto, in which there are close to 25 references to terms such as "policy," "documentation," "procedure," etc. Although less explicit, the same principle is to be found in Quebec laws such as the *Act Respecting the Protection of Personal Information in the Private Sector*, CQLR c P-39.1 and the *Act Respecting Access to Documents Held by Public Bodies and the Protection of Personal Information*, CQLR c A-2.1) and in Europe (see especially Jan Philipp Albrecht, *Report on the Proposal for a Regulation of the European Parliament and of the Council on the Protection of Individuals with Regard to the Processing of Personal Data and on the Free Movement of Such Data (General Data Protection Regulation)* (22 November 2013), online: <http://www.europarl.europa.eu/sides/getDoc.do?pubRef=-%2F%2FEP%2F%2FTEXT%2BREPORT%2BA7-2013-

0402%2B0%2BDOC%2BXML%2BV0%2F%2FEN&language=EN> [Albrecht Amendment], and more specifically arts 40ff.

62. For instance, the documentation concept has grown strongly in several recent statutes in the field of law of evidence. The *Act to Establish a Legal Framework for Information Technology* (CQLR c C-1.1 and specifically arts 17, 20, 31, 34, etc.) entails such a requirement in several instances. Implicitly, the position is the same insofar as the federal evidence law is concerned (*Canada Evidence Act*, RSC 1985, c C-5, s 31.1). Such references are even more obvious in texts of a technical, or community nature: whether these are from the International Organization for Standardization (ISO), American National Standards Institute (ANSI), Association of Records Managers and Administrators (ARMA), Modular requirements for records systems (MoReq), etc., such organizations draft texts that systematically require procedures to be put in place.

63. A very American procedure that applies to various legal domains holds that it is possible to obtain judicial recognition of particular agreements entered into between a governmental institution and a private company. In addition, on 29 November 2011, Facebook undertook to be more transparent insofar as the utilization of its members' personal information is concerned. For further information, see US, Federal Trade Commission, *Agreement Containing Consent Order—In the Matter of Facebook, Inc., a Corporation* (092 3184) (2011), online: <http://www.ftc.gov/sites/default/files/documents/cases/2011/11/111129facebookagree.pdf>.

64. Daniel Mockle, "Gouverner sans le droit? Mutation des normes et nouveaux modes de régulation" (2002) 43 :2 C de D 143 at 202ff.

65. Michael Power, *The Audit Society: Rituals of Verification* (Oxford: Oxford University Press, 1999) at 31–2.

66. Sasha Courville, Christine Parker & Helen Watchirs, "Introduction: Auditing in Regulatory Perspective" (2003) 25:3 Law & Pol'y 179 at 179: "audit has a series of overlapping definitions. Power [...] suggests that 'definitions are attempts to fix a practice within a particular set of norms or ideals.' In other words, the use of the word *audit* (and its definition) is itself often an attempt to claim a particular mission, social status, or policy objective for a practice of accountability and control."

67. Power, *supra* note 65 at 58.

68. *Ibid* at 60.

69. *Ibid* at 65.

70. Brian Pentland, "Getting Comfortable with the Numbers: Auditing and the Microproduction of Macro-order" (1993) 18:7/8 Account Organ Soc 605. This notion of "comfort" has been taken up in several other pieces that followed. See e.g. Jagdish Pathak & Mary R Lind, "Audit Risk, Complex Technology, and Auditing Processes" (March 2003) 31:5 EDPACS 1 at 3: "For an auditor to offer an opinion on the material

correctness of a corporation's financial statements, he or she must rely heavily on the company's business practices and internal controls in order to gain comfort in the reported numbers."

71. Power, *supra* note 65 at 267.

72. See especially Principle 1 of Annex 1 of the PIPEDA, *supra* note 61.

73. See especially the points made by Professor Scassa in this collection.

74. Roland Gori, *De l'extension sociale de la norme à la servitude de la norme*, online: Appel des appels <http://www.appeldesappels.org/interventions-de-la-journee-du-22-mars-2009/de-l-extension-sociale-de-la-norme-a-la-servitude-volontaire--762.htm>. The author argues that "the first act of resistance comprises analyzing and deconstructing the functioning of our standardization devices. It is there that the tyranny of contemporary power is to be found."

75. This distinction was suggested by Nicolas W Vermeys, *Responsabilité civile et sécurité informationnelle* (Cowansville, QC: Éditions Yvon Blais, 2010) at 103.

76. Thibault Daudigeos, "Des instituts de normalisation en quête de profit et de légitimité. Étude comparée de la production de normes de développement durable en France et en Angleterre" in Corinne Gendron, Jean-Guy Vaillancourt & René Audet, eds, *Développement durable et responsabilité sociale : De la mobilisation à l'institutionnalisation* (Montreal: Presses internationales Polytechnique, 2010) 175 at 175.

77. Stacy Baird, "The Government at the Standards Bazaar" (2007) 18 Stan L & Pol'y Rev 35.

78. *Ibid* at 37: "However, to date there has been no objective analysis by which the need for and nature of government action may be determined. It is up to government policymakers to determine the best course in the public interest."

79. Benoît Frydman, "Prendre les standards et les indicateurs au sérieux" in Benoît Frydman & Arnaud van Waeyenberge, eds, *Gouverner par les standards et les indicateurs : De Hume aux rankings* (Brussels: Bruylant, 2014) 5.

80. Karim Benyekhlef, "Une introduction au droit global" in Karim Benyekhlef, ed, *Vers un droit global?* (Montreal: Éditions Thémis, 2016) 1 at 21, citing Frydman, *ibid* at 55.

81. For instance, it is very expensive to purchase ISO norms (between 1,000 and 2,000 Swiss francs) and, in addition, several of these norms give rise to a contractual process where the contractual information is only available after payment has been effected by credit card (and the copyright licenses in particular are excessively stringent). This very approach is contrary to best practices.

82. This practice has even been prohibited in Delhi, India. See in this context the piece by Michael Geist in this collection.

83. Alex Rosenblat & Luke Stark, "Algorithmic Labor and Information Asymmetries: A Case Study of Uber's Drivers" (2016) 10 Int J Commun 3758 at 3772: "Through surge pricing's appeal to the concept of algorithms and automated management, Uber can generate and coordinate clusters of labor in response to dynamic market conditions [...] without explaining the reliability of its cluster incentives or guaranteeing the validity, accuracy, or error rates of its labor deployments."

84. *Ibid* at 3775.

85. The infamous 1996 cyberspace declaration of independence comes to mind: John Perry Barlow, *A Declaration of the Independence of Cyberspace* (1996), online: Electronic Frontier Foundation <https://projects.eff. org/~barlow/Declaration-Final.html>.

86. See para 11, above.

87. Frank Pasquale, *The Black Box Society: The Secret Algorithms that Control Money and Information* (Cambridge, MA: Harvard University Press, 2015).

88. Calo & Rosenblat, *supra* note 2.

89. Joshua A Kroll et al, "Accountable Algorithms" (2017) 165 U Penn L Rev 633 at 636: "Many observers have argued that our current frameworks are not well-adapted for situations in which a potentially incorrect, unjustified, or unfair outcome emerges from a computer. Citizens, and society as a whole, have an interest in making these processes more accountable. If these new inventions are to be made governable, this gap must be bridged."

90. Danielle Keats Citron, "Technological Due Process" (2008) 85:6 Wash U L Rev 1249.

91. See especially s 3, *"Loyauté des plateformes et information des consommateurs"* of the *Loi n° 2016-1321 du 7 octobre 2016 pour une République numérique,* JO, 8 October 2016, even though this very vague text only serves for consumer protection purposes.

92. Paul Schwartz, "Data Processing and Government Administration: The Failure of the American Legal Response to the Computer" (1992) 43 Hastings LJ 1321 at 1323–25: "So long as government bureaucracy relies on the technical treatment of personal information, the law must pay attention to the structure of data processing [...]. There are three essential elements to this response: structuring transparent data processing systems; granting limited procedural and substantive rights [...] and creating independent governmental monitoring of data processing systems." Cited by Kroll, *supra* note 89 at 668.

93. See in particular the SABRE airline reservation system that in the 1950s led to a better indexing of specific airline companies, notably American Airlines. This company was obliged to prove the transparency of its system through the passing of a specific anti-competition law. For more on this, see Christian Sandvig et al, *Auditing Algorithms: Research Methods*

for Detecting Discrimination on Internet Platforms (2014), online: <https://perma.cc/DS5D-3JYS >.

94. A good example is the excessive documentary requirements that were imposed pursuant to the financial scandals that marked the early 2000s and that led to the adoption of the *Sarbanes-Oxley Act*. See especially Henry N Butler & Larry E Ribstein, *The Sarbanes-Oxley Debacle: What We've Learned; How to Fix It* (Washington, DC: AEI Press, 2006); Vincent Gautrais, "La gestion électronique de l'information financière: illustration de l'acculturation du droit des affaires électroniques" in Jean-Louis Navarro & Guy Lefebvre, eds, *L'acculturation en droit des affaires* (Montreal: Éditions Thémis, 2007) 379.

95. Kroll, *supra* note 89 at 661.

96. *Ibid* at 662–74 under the subtitle "Technical Tools for Procedural Regularity."

97. *Ibid* at 667: "This means a government agency or other organization can commit to the assertions that (1) the particular decision policy was used and (2) the particular data were used as input to the decision policy (or that a particular outcome from the policy was computed from the input data). The agency can prove the assertions by taking its secret source code, the private input data, and the private computed decision outcome and computing a commitment and opening key (or a separate commitment and opening key for each policy version, input, or decision). The company or agency making an automated decision would then publish the commitment or commitments publicly and in a way that establishes a reliable publication date, perhaps in a venue such as a newspaper or the Federal Register. Later, the agency could prove that it had the source code, input data, or computed results at the time of commitment by revealing the source code and the opening key to an oversight body such as a court."

98. Vincent Gautrais, "Preuve et développement durable: objectivation du droit par la normativité individuelle" in Vincent Gautrais & Mustapha Mekki, eds, *Preuve et développement durable* (Montreal: Éditions Thémis, 2016) 43.

99. Vincent Gautrais, *Le contrat électronique international* (Brussels: Bruylant, 2002) at 220.

100. Joel R Reidenberg, "Lex Informatica: The Formulation of Information Policy Rules through Technology" (1997) 76 Tex L Rev 553.

101. Art 1386 CCQ.

102. For instance, arts 54.1ff of the *Consumer Protection Act*, CQLR c P-40.1.

103. Vincent Gautrais, "Contrat 2.0: les 2 couleurs du contrat électronique" in Benoît Moore & Générosa Bras Miranda, eds, *Mélanges Adrian Popovici—Les couleurs du droit* (Montreal: Éditions Thémis, 2010) 241 at 256 [Gautrais, Contrat 2.0].

104. Uber, *US Terms of Use*, online: <https://www.uber.com/fr/legal/terms/us/>; Uber, *Privacy Policy*, online: <https://www.uber.com/legal/privacy/users/en/>.

105. Airbnb, *Terms of Service*, online: <https://www.airbnb.com/terms>.

106. For instance, analyses undertaken regarding privacy policies reveal that they are almost systematically imprecise. Joel R Reidenberg et al, "Ambiguity in Privacy Policies and the Impact of Regulation" (2016) 42:S2 J Leg Stud S163.

107. Vincent Gautrais, "Les contrats de cyberconsommation sont presque tous illégaux!" (2005) 106 R du N 617 [Gautrais, Les contrats de cyberconsommation].

108. Aleecia M Mcdonald & Lorrie Faith Cranor, "The Cost of Reading Privacy Policies" (2008) 4:3 I/S: JL & Pol'y for Info Soc'y 543.

109. Omri Ben-Shahar & Carl E Schneider, "The Failure of Mandated Disclosure" (2011) 159 U Pa L Rev 647.

110. Tess Wilkinson-Ryan, "Contracts Without Terms" (2016) U of Penn Inst for Law and Econ Working Paper No 16-5.

111. Florencia Marotta-Wurgler, "Will Increased Disclosure Help? Evaluating the Recommendations of the ALI's 'Principles of the Law of Software Contracts'" (2011) 78 U Chicago L Rev 165.

112. *Dell Computer Corp v Union des consommateurs*, 2007 SCC 34, [2007] 2 SCR 801.

113. Art 1436 CCQ.

114. Art 1437 CCQ.

115. The pertinent trilogy is: *Step-Saver Data System, Inc v Wyse Technology*, 939 F (2d) 91 (3rd Cir 1991); *Vault Corporation v Quaid Software Limited*, 847 F (2d) 255 (5th Cir 1988); *Arizona Retail Systems, Inc. v The Software Link, Inc.*, 831 F Supp 759 (D Ariz 1993).

116. *ProCD, Inc v Zeidenberg*, 86 F (3d) 1447 (7th Cir 1996).

117. Mark A Lemley, "Terms of Use" (2006) 91 Minn L Rev 459. With regards to the period 1996–2006, the author makes the following points, at 459: "Electronic contracting has experienced a sea change in the last decade. Ten years ago, courts required affirmative evidence of agreement to form a contract [...]."

118. Vincent Gautrais, "Le vouloir électronique selon l'affaire *Dell Computer*: dommage!" (2007) 37:2 RGD 407 at 420.

119. See Ruth Sullivan, "The Promise of Plain Language Drafting" (2001) 47 McGill LJ 97; Carl Felsenfeld & Alan Siegel, *Writing Contracts in Plain English* (St Paul, Minn: West, 1981); Jeffrey Davis, "Protecting Consumers from Overdisclosure and Gobbledygook: An Empirical Look at the Simplification of Consumer-Credit Contracts" (1977) 63:6 Va L Rev 841; Robert C Dick, "Plain English in Legal Drafting" (1980) 18 Alta L Rev 509; Carl Felsenfeld, "The Plain English Movement in the United

States" (1981) 6 Can Bus LJ 408; David M Laprairie, "Taking the 'Plain Language' Movement Too Far: The Michigan Legislature's Unnecessary Application of the Plain Language Doctrine to Consumer Contracts" (2000) 45 Wayne L Rev 1927. See also Melvin Aron Eisenberg, "The Limits of Cognition and the Limits of Contract" (1995) 47 Stan L Rev 211; Melvin Aron Eisenberg, "Text Anxiety" (1986) 59 S Cal L Rev 305.

120. This notably brings to mind the decision in *Mofo Moko c Ebay Canada Ltd.*, 2013 Qc Sup Ct 856.

121. Catherine Thibierge-Guelfucci, "Libres propos sur la transformation du droit des contrats" (1997) RTD civ 357 at 375: "Will, in order to be effective in this hierarchical relationship, must take the form of a consent whose expression, agreement and effects must be consistent with this superior ideal."

122. Lemley, *supra* note 117 at 459.

123. Margaret Jane Radin, "Boilerplate Today: The Rise of Modularity and the Waning of Consent" (2006) 104:5 Mich L Rev 1231.

124. By way of example, the Airbnb contract mentions twenty-six times that the member understands ("you understand ...") the contractual content. In the same way, the member is invited to read a particular clause nine times.

125. Gautrais, Contrat 2.0, *supra* note 103 at 256.

126. Gautrais, Les contrats de cyberconsommation, *supra* note 107.

127. The solution was envisaged in an earlier draft of the European Privacy Regulations where pictograms were proposed, notably in order to better describe the kind of processing that a site effects: Albrecht Amendment, *supra* note 61. However, a similar approach is definitely in effect in the six distinct licences envisaged by *Creative Commons*. For further information in this regard, see *Creative Commons*, online: <https://creativecommons.org/>.

128. Arthur A Leff, "Unconscionability and the Code: The Emperor's New Clause" (1967) 115:4 U Pa L Rev 485; W David Slawson, "Standard Form Contracts and Democratic Control of Lawmaking Power" (1971) 84:3 Harv L Rev 529, cited by Ian Ayres & Alan Schwartz, "The No-Reading Problem in Consumer Contract Law" (2014) 66 Stan L Rev 545.

129. This brings to mind in particular the French Commission des clauses abusives that listed a series of clauses in contracts for the supply of Internet access services and automobile rentals. This grading function has since been taken over by jurisprudence.

130. With the Commission des clauses abusives.

131. Sinai Deutch, "Controlling Standard Contracts—The Israeli Version" (1985) 30 McGill LJ 458.

132. Karl Llewellyn, *The Common Law Tradition: Deciding Appeals* (Boston: Little, Brown & Co, 1960) at 370, cited by Ayres & Schwartz, *supra* note 129 at 556 [my emphasis].

133. Restatement (Second) of Contracts, § 237: "Although customers typically adhere to standardized agreements and are bound by them without even appearing to know the standard terms in detail, they are not bound to unknown terms which are beyond the range of reasonable expectation," cited in William J O'Connor, Jr, "Plain English" (1979) 34:3 Bus Lawyer 1453 at 1453.

134. *Dell Computer Corp v Union des consommateurs, supra* note 112. See especially paras 101–3 on illegible or otherwise abusive clauses.

135. Alain Prujiner, "L'opposabilité d'une clause d'arbitrage accessible par hyperlien dans un contrat de consommation et l'exigence d'extranéité en droit international privé québécois, note sous Cour suprême du Canada, 13 juillet 2007" (2007) 3 Rev arb 567 at 606: "the restrictive interpretation given to the external clause in adhesion contracts in cyberspace signifies a strong tendency from the Court in favour of legal security for the drafters of the contract rather than a preoccupation for the protection of the adherent."

136. Insofar as the Quebec example is concerned, the amendments introducing the obligation to draft contracts so as to "present information prominently and in a comprehensible manner and bring it expressly to the consumer's attention" (*Consumer Protection Act, supra* note 102 s 54.4ff), have in ten years not given rise to a single decision.

137. *Douez v Facebook, Inc, supra* note 142.

138. *Ibid*. This appears in para 8.

139. *Ibid*. See especially at para 33: "And as one of the interveners argues, instead of supporting certainty and security, forum selection clauses in consumer contracts may do 'the opposite for the millions of ordinary people who would not foresee or expect its implications and cannot be deemed to have undertaken sophisticated analysis of foreign legal systems prior to opening an online account' (Samuelson-Glushko Canadian Internet Policy and Public Interest Clinic Factum, at para. 7)."

140. From the first paragraph, the matter is classed as falling into a consumer context: "[1] Forum selection clauses purport to oust the jurisdiction of otherwise competent courts in favour of a foreign jurisdiction. To balance contractual freedom with the public good in having local courts adjudicate certain claims, courts have developed a test to determine whether such clauses should be enforced. *This test has mostly been applied in commercial contexts*, where forum selection clauses are generally enforced to hold sophisticated parties to their bargain, absent exceptional circumstances. *This appeal requires the Court to apply this test in a consumer context*" [my emphasis].

141. See especially the decision *St-Arnaud c Facebook*, 2011 Qc Sup Ct 1506, where para 19 states, "Facebook does not have a consumer relationship with its Users."

142. *Douez v Facebook, Inc*, 2017 SCC 33, particularly at para 36: "Such a development is especially important since online consumer contracts are ubiquitous, and the global reach of the Internet allows for instantaneous cross-border consumer transactions." See the points made by Justice Abella among similar lines at para 99.

143. *Ibid* at para 56: "In particular, unlike a standard retail transaction, there are few comparable alternatives to Facebook, a social networking platform with extensive reach. British Columbians who wish to participate in the many online communities that interact through Facebook must accept that company's terms or choose not to participate in its ubiquitous social network. As the intervener the Canadian Civil Liberties Association emphasizes, 'access to Facebook and social media platforms, including the online communities they make possible, has become increasingly important for the exercise of free speech, freedom of association and for full participation in democracy' (I.F., at para. 16). Having the choice to remain 'offline' may not be a real choice in the Internet era."

144. *Ibid* at para 104: "In general, then, when online consumer contracts of adhesion contain terms that unduly impede the ability of consumers to vindicate their rights in domestic courts, particularly their quasi-constitutional or constitutional rights, in my view, public policy concerns outweigh those favouring enforceability of a forum selection clause."

CHAPTER V

Information Law in the Platform Economy: Ownership, Control, and Reuse of Platform Data

Teresa Scassa[1]

I. Introduction

The platform (or sharing) economy business model is defined by Katz as having "(A) an online intermediary that (B) acts as a market for P2P services and (C) facilitates exchanges by lowering transaction costs."[2] Scholars such as Lobel talk about the platforms "transforming the service economy, allowing greater access to offline exchanges for lower prices."[3] Although the platform economy has already generated considerable scholarly interest, much of the legal literature to this point has focused upon regulatory issues,[4] taxation,[5] and issues relating to employment law,[6] consumer protection,[7] and discrimination.[8]

This chapter considers platform economy companies in terms of the data they collect and generate. The data that are the stock-in-trade of these companies is considered—both by the companies and under current legal regimes, to be proprietary to them. Under a proprietary model, the companies can control who can access and use the data, and for what purposes.[9] As Kitchin notes, companies can also control what subsets of data they make available when they choose to do so.[10] Yet digital data cannot be so easily owned or controlled—nor should it necessarily be. As this chapter will demonstrate, publicly accessible platform data is of significant interest to a broad range of both commercial and non-commercial users, including government, civil-society actors, researchers and other businesses. The data, therefore, have both private and public dimensions.

This chapter uses Airbnb as a case study in order to explore the application of existing information law frameworks to publicly accessible data in the platform economy and to identify areas where courts must take into account its public interest dimensions. Unlike some platform companies, Airbnb must necessarily make a considerable amount of its data accessible on its website in order to facilitate the desired transactions between hosts and guests for short-term rental accommodation.[11] These data are commercially valuable to Airbnb; they are also of use or value to a range of different actors. This chapter begins by developing a legal typology for the kinds of Airbnb data that are contributed by users and generated through use of the platform. In section III, it considers the data "ecosystem" that has evolved around Airbnb data. It looks at different categories of users of both publicly accessible and confidential Airbnb data. While these two sections consider both the data and actors in broad terms, the remainder of the chapter focuses more narrowly on the category of publicly accessible Airbnb data and on the actors who engage in "scraping" this data. Section IV considers Airbnb's Terms of Service to explore the claims made by the company with respect to ownership, use, and control of its data. Section V examines the legal frameworks that protect data, and that protect the public interest with respect to publicly available private sector data. While the main focus of this section is on copyright law, the law relating to confidential information, contracts, and trespass to chattels is also discussed.

The consideration of these various issues in the context of the platform economy suggests that there is something particular about this context. Many of the issues are not exclusive to the platform economy. Nevertheless, the size of platforms such as Airbnb, their global reach and local dominance make this context of particular interest. Platform companies such as Airbnb can have significant local and public impacts, affecting incumbent industries, municipal regulation, public tax revenues, and even urban quality of life. Their reliance on huge volumes of data and the relevance of this data to understanding and addressing the public impacts of such companies create interesting tensions around access to and control over this data. Thus, while some of the legal issues considered in this chapter arise in other contexts as well, the focus here is upon data ecosystems within the platform economy and the particular public policy challenges they present for the interpretation and application of laws as they pertain to data.

II. A Legal Typology of Airbnb Data

Airbnb is a platform that allows the pairing of those seeking to rent short-term accommodation with those who have available space to rent. It does so on a global level. According to Airbnb, it operates in over 191 countries and over 65,000 cities. It claims to offer over three million listings worldwide, and to having provided accommodation for over 150 million travellers.[12] As Sabrina Tremblay-Huet explains in her chapter in this volume, while the "myth" of Airbnb is that it allows ordinary individuals to monetize extra space in their homes, the reality is that Airbnb's hosts are increasingly commercially oriented, and a growing number offer whole units instead of shared accommodation.

The large volume of data collected or generated by Airbnb can be categorized in a number of different ways. Such categorizations are useful in that they can point to differences in how data may be treated under law; they are not mutually exclusive. For example, personal information can be either confidential data or public data, depending on how it is treated by the company. Similarly, not all personal information is collected directly from the individual; much personal information can be collected through the tracking of individual activities on the site.

The first dichotomy distinguishes between confidential and public data. As noted earlier, in order to operate its service, Airbnb must make a considerable amount of information publicly accessible via its website. This is its "public data." Airbnb relies on this data to connect those who have short-term accommodation to rent (hosts) and those who are seeking short-term accommodation (guests). Its platform offers hosts and guests the opportunity to share information about themselves and about available rental units in order to facilitate rental agreements. A host, for example, will provide a description of the property, typically with photographs, as well as availability, location, price, and any relevant features or limitations. Hosts also provide some information about themselves. Guests must create profiles through the Airbnb registration process and can include photographs and other personal information. Profiles may also be linked to Facebook or Google accounts. Guests also provide content in the form of comments and reviews of rented accommodations, and hosts may review guests. These reviews are part of the "trust system" that enables a company like Airbnb to achieve the volume of business that it does.[13] While a great deal of the public-facing content is provided by users, this information and the manner in which it is shared are shaped by the policies and templates used by Airbnb. In addition, some public-facing content may be provided in conjunction with Airbnb. For example, Airbnb offers a "verified photographs" service through which hosts can have their properties photographed by Airbnb representatives. These photos are then presented in the listings as having been verified by Airbnb.[14] The process is designed to increase user trust that the accommodations offered for rent are as they appear in the photographs.

In addition to its public data, Airbnb also collects and generates a considerable amount of confidential commercial information. This includes some of the data contributed (both directly and indirectly)[15] by Airbnb users, as well as data collected, derived or generated from the company's operations.[16] For example, at the time of registration, Airbnb asks for scanned identification documents for the purposes of verifying user identities as part of their Verified ID program.[17] It also collects information about users' activities on the site, including what units they make available to rent as well as the dates and frequency of activities. It collects transaction-related data. Airbnb will also collect data from social networking sites to which a user has provided access. In addition to data provided to Airbnb by its members, Airbnb collects data through the tracking of usage of its site through logs and cookies. It also amasses a variety of personal and other data from users of its mobile app, including location information.[18] Airbnb collects data from its other contacts with users, including service or assistance requests, complaints, and disputes regarding rented accommodations.[19] Where an Airbnb user links his or her account to Facebook or Google Plus, Airbnb will have access to some of the information contained in user accounts on those social networking sites.[20] Any of this information that is not published on the website is treated as confidential information.[21]

The second dichotomy divides the data collected by Airbnb into the categories of personal and non-personal information. The distinction is relevant in the context of privacy or data protection laws. Data protection laws impose obligations on companies to protect that which is defined as "personal information."[22] Information that is non-personal falls outside of the scope of such laws. Typically, personal information is defined as information about *identifiable* individuals.[23] This includes specific data such as names and other unique identifiers. However, information about identifiable individuals includes any information that can lead to their identification, even if no unique identifier makes this connection plain at the outset.[24] An age linked to a postal code, for example, can lead to the identification of a specific individual.[25] In combination, this would constitute information about an identifiable individual.

The Airbnb website collects a significant amount of personal information from individuals, whether directly or indirectly. This includes the type of personal information needed for registration and transaction purposes, as well as information about rental properties, vacation times or preferences, and profile information. It may also include information shared by the user from other linked social media sites, and includes tracking and profiling data. Personal information also includes users' reviews of properties and ratings for hosts and renters.

Airbnb also deals in aggregate and de-identified data about its users. These latter categories, so long as reidentification is not possible, constitute non-personal information. Non-personal information includes data derived from Airbnb site usage and can include information about markets, prices, occupancy, peak travel periods and destinations, and so on. As Airbnb notes in its privacy policy, it may "share aggregated information (information about our users that we combine together so that it no longer identifies or references an individual user) and non-personally identifiable information for industry and market analysis, demographic profiling, marketing and advertising and other business purposes."[26]

The third dichotomy distinguishes between raw and processed data. Raw data is simply data that has been collected through some means, and that has yet to be processed. Processed data is that which has been sorted, analyzed, compiled, or categorized in some way. As will be seen in the discussion of the Airbnb data "ecosystem," a significant proportion of users of Airbnb data are interested in raw data extracted from the site in bulk for the purposes of analytics—whether commercial or non-commercial. The distinction between raw and processed data is important from an intellectual property point of view. Copyright law does not protect raw, unprocessed data. These data are considered to be in the public domain,[27] although copyright law will protect an original compilation of data. There are interesting questions around whether some processed data (especially where the output is not strictly factual, as is the case with predictive or profiling data) may themselves be considered original works and not simply compilations.[28] The more processed the data, the greater the likelihood that it can be protected under copyright law. The distinction between raw and processed data may therefore also be significant in a copyright fair dealing analysis, since data extracted in bulk for the purposes of analytics will also eventually become processed data— something that may be recognized as a new and independent work.

III. The Airbnb Data Ecosystem

The data collected by Airbnb are enormous in quantity and variety. These data are of interest and value to a significant number of different users. In this part of the chapter, these users, their means of accessing the data, and the uses to which they put the data are described. Table I below provides an overview of what is referred to as the Airbnb data "ecosystem." The variety of users, uses and means of accessing the data are extremely interesting in an evolving data society. While Airbnb considers its data to be proprietary, the discussion of the ecosystem reveals significant private and public interests in the data.

Table I: Airbnb Data "Ecosystem"

Data Users	Uses
Public Data	
Airbnb hosts and guests	Sharing/renting short-term accommodations
Civil-society organizations	Supporting activism through data collection and analysis
Researchers	Carrying out research on Airbnb, its activities, and impacts
Journalists	Investigating/reporting on Airbnb, its activities, and its impacts
Opportunistic businesses	Performing data analytics services to clients, investigative services
Confidential Data	
Regulators	Carrying out regulatory activities (taxation, health and safety, urban planning)
Law enforcement	Criminal investigations, national security

i. Public Data

The public portions of Airbnb's website contain a trove of data that is of interest to a broad range of users. These users access data from the site in a number of different ways. One of these is simply through browsing the site and examining the information on public display. Others extract data from Airbnb's website by copying it on a small scale (downloads or printouts of particular pages, or screen shots). Still others use software tools to "scrape" large quantities of data from the site. Scraping has been described as "using computer software to 'crawl' an online data source to identify data of interest and then extract data from that source."[29] Other users may generate new data through research methods that involve interactions with hosts or guests.[30] The categories of users are discussed below, with examples provided of some of the uses to which they put Airbnb data.

Airbnb hosts and guests are the primary audience for the Airbnb platform. In fact, the platform is designed to enable those seeking rentals to find suitable available accommodations at their target destination. Hosts and guests register with the site, and they are permitted to browse the site and to use it to reserve accommodation or to leave feedback. Hosts and guests generally have no particular interest in extracting data from the site. They have accounts, and the data relevant to their renting activities is stored in their accounts or communicated to them by other means as part of the operation of the platform.

Civil-society organizations, particularly those with an interest in affordable housing and shortages in long-term accommodation, have been known to scrape Airbnb data. For example, advocate Tom Slee openly discusses scraping Airbnb data on his website, and provides a link to his code.[31] He scrapes Airbnb data in order to produce reports that he makes available for use in public policy discussions. He also provides visualizations (charts, tables, and maps) of Airbnb listings around the world.[32] Slee also makes his code used for scraping data publicly available. Slee states on his website that "[t]he listings are provided as a contribution to the debates that surround Airbnb and its effects on the places where it operates."[33] Another civil-society website, InsideAirbnb.com, operated by Murray Cox, offers Airbnb data, commentary, and analysis. Cox states that "[b]y analyzing publicly available information about a city's Airbnb's listings, Inside Airbnb provides filters and key metrics so you can see how Airbnb is being used to compete with the residential housing market."[34] Issues of interest to civil-society actors include the availability of affordable housing, and the impact on neighborhoods of widespread, extended short-term rentals.[35]

Researchers also have an interest in Airbnb data, again for a wide range of reasons, including those that relate to research for urban planning, social justice, and the sharing economy more generally. Researchers may scrape their own data, or they may use data scraped by others. For example, graduate student Iain Majoribanks used scraped Airbnb data from Inside Airbnb to conduct a study of the impact of the service on the Vancouver market for long-term rental accommodation.[36] Another graduate student, Karen Sawatzky, scraped Airbnb data in order to carry out similar research on the Vancouver rental market.[37] Other researchers have used Airbnb data to study the incidence of discrimination in the renting of Airbnb units.[38] In this latter example, the researchers used the website to gather their own data; they signed in as users, researched available properties, and made contact with potential hosts with inquiries about rentals.[39] This is an example of a combination of making use of available Airbnb data about hosts and properties and creating new data (research data) through interactions with hosts using the platform.

Journalists may also scrape data in order to better understand the activities or impacts of Airbnb. For example, the *San Francisco Chronicle* has used scraped data in a story on Airbnb's impact.[40] The travel industry news site Skift also used scraped data in a study of the impact of Airbnb in New York City.[41] Journalists may also use data scraped by others, such as the civil-society groups noted above, or data made available in published studies commissioned by others. They may also engage directly in data scraping. Data scraping by journalists is described as a way to gather large amounts of data for newspaper stories.[42] From a journalist's perspective, the data is already publicly available and thus open for investigation and inquiry. Scraping merely facilitates that process.[43]

"Opportunistic" businesses also make use of data that they extract from Airbnb's website. These businesses rely upon the existence of Airbnb and offer services that are directly or indirectly related to it. Note that this category does not include any companies that use Airbnb data to compete directly with Airbnb; rather, these companies offer a range of services that are distinct from or complementary to those offered by Airbnb. In some cases, these businesses provide services that may undermine Airbnb (such as services that detect illegal hosts); in other cases, they may use data in ways that adversely impact Airbnb (such as, for example, demonstrating negative impacts of Airbnb rentals on urban housing situations).

Perhaps the best-known opportunistic company is Airdna. Airdna, which operates through a website at airdna.co, offers a broad range of "data services." According to their site, "Airdna presents market reports and other data products that feature occupancy rates, seasonal demand, and revenue generated by short-term rentals. This information—once only available to corporate hotel chains—is now accessible to the everyday homeowner and real estate investor."[44] The company provides "market summary reports," a "pricing co-pilot" tool to provide supply and demand data on short-term rental accommodations in particular markets, market intelligence reports, and property performance data. Its clients include lodging analysts, tourism agencies, academics, realtors, Airbnb hosts and potential hosts.[45] The data used by Airdna to drive its analysis is sourced from Airbnb's website. The company states that "Airdna analytics and reports are based on Airbnb data gathered from information publicly available on the Airbnb website."[46] This claim implies that the data is legally obtained, although the terms of use of Airbnb prohibit the scraping of data, its extraction by any technological means, and its use for any commercial purposes.[47] Airdna is also linked to the spinoff company Rentingyourplace.com,[48] which offers consulting services for prospective Airbnb hosts.

Other businesses that draw on Airbnb data include Beyond Pricing.[49] This company offers Airbnb hosts services that assist them in managing the pricing of multiple Airbnb listings. They claim: "Our pricing algorithm updates your rates every day according to real-time demand, so we'll automatically post the best rate for your weekends."[50] They also make recommendations as to other fees such as cleaning charges and fees for extra guests. The service requires hosts to allow Beyond Pricing to have access to their Airbnb accounts "to collect real-time information about your listing and to automatically update prices on your calendar every day."[51] Beyond Pricing does not state as explicitly as Airdna that it relies upon Airbnb data, but this reliance can be inferred from numerous references to its algorithms on its website. These algorithms, designed to predict periods of peak demand in order to drive pricing, take into account a great deal of data from different sources, but one of these sources is definitely Airbnb.[52] Similar companies include SmartHost,[53] (which provides a range of analytics services to hosts on Airbnb, VRBO, and similar sites), Everbooked[54] (which offers similar services and explicitly indicates that it uses Airbnb data in its analytics), and PriceLabs[55] (which also offers data analytics in support of short-term rental pricing, although it is not explicit about whether it relies upon Airbnb data).

A related category of businesses that may use scraped data from Airbnb includes consulting companies that may work for clients with various interests in Airbnb data. For example, in order to better understand the impact of Airbnb in Vancouver, the City of Vancouver hired a consulting company that scraped data in order to produce its report.[56] Newspapers have commissioned consulting companies to scrape data for their stories on Airbnb.[57]

Another category of businesses that relies upon Airbnb data are those that offer services to condominium boards or the owners of rental buildings who wish to identify residents or tenants who may be renting their units as short-term accommodation in violation of their condominium agreements or leases. These may be private detectives whose services include determining when units have been illegally rented.[58] Their data-gathering methods may be as simple as browsing the site for leads on which they follow up. Other businesses are emerging that offer detection services tailored specifically to the sharing economy. These include Building Snitch,[59] a company that uses automated search tools (robots) to trawl listings to detect illegal rentals.[60]

ii. Confidential Data

Gaining access to Airbnb's confidential data or confidential commercial information is much more difficult than accessing public data, and indeed, legal access is limited to those outsiders who are able to obtain a subpoena or court order. Court orders can be used by governments and private litigants to gain access to Airbnb data for a variety of purposes. Court orders may be used to obtain either public or private Airbnb data (or both). For example, if data is needed for the purposes of law enforcement, scraped data may be inadequate as it is necessary to link rental information to individuals and their contact information. The questionable legality of data scraping may also make scraped data unsuitable for law enforcement purposes. Where some or all of the data sought from Airbnb is confidential, a court order is essential to access the data.

In the case of governments, the data may be relevant for purposes that include the enforcement of provincial/national laws or regulations, or the pursuit of criminal or national security investigations involving Airbnb hosts or guests. Following criticism by the Electronic Frontier Foundation for its failure to provide transparency reports,[61] Airbnb released its first such report in September 2016.[62] The report reveals that in the first six months of 2016, Airbnb received 188 law enforcement requests and provided data in response to eighty-two of these.[63]

Government officials and regulators may also be interested in data for the purposes of urban planning, to address or understand housing market issues, to regulate or decide how to regulate short-term accommodation rentals, or to impose or enforce the collection of hotel taxes and income taxes. While the data that is most likely to be of interest to regulators is confidential data that is not part of the public-facing content, scraped public-facing data may also be of some use—particularly for broader planning purposes, and for the purposes of understanding Airbnb impacts. Governments do not necessarily scrape their own data. Some may rely on data scraped by civil-society groups. Others contract with consultants for studies of the local impact of Airbnb. As noted above, these consultants may in turn scrape data from Airbnb's website.[64] Scraped data may also be useful to governments in attempting to identify where subpoenaed data might be necessary, or as a point of comparison to assess the quality of data obtained under subpoenas or other releases.[65]

Table II: How Airbnb Data Are Accessed

Methods of Access	Hosts and guests	Civil-society groups	Researchers	Journalists	Opportunistic businesses	Governments
Browsing the site	✓	✓	✓	✓	✓	✓
Scraping		✓	✓	✓	✓	?
Court orders						✓
Regulatory requirements		?	?	?		✓
Interaction	✓		✓		✓	
Request to Airbnb		✓	✓	✓		✓

Table II provides an overview of the different ways in which different participants in the Airbnb data ecosystem access the data that they use. The question mark for "regulatory" requirements is used in the case of researchers, journalists, and civil-society groups. These groups would almost certainly access data that are submitted to governments as part of regulatory and permitting requirements if such data were available either through access to information requests or as open data. However, where Airbnb operates outside of the regulatory frameworks for short-term rental accommodation, data are not available through these avenues. For these groups, such data are primarily available through scraping activities.

IV. Airbnb's Terms of Service

It is commonplace now for commercial websites to provide links to their Terms of Service (TOS). The role of such terms is to set the parameters of what is considered to be acceptable use of the website. Courts have shown considerable deference to these TOS, and increasingly they are found to be binding on users of such sites. This section examines Airbnb's TOS, while the following section considers some of the legal issues raised by data scraping activities.

Although it is possible to search Airbnb's listings without registering as a host or guest, it is impossible to book accommodations without having registered. However, anyone who uses the site (not just hosts and guests) is considered by Airbnb to be bound by the TOS.[66] A link to Airbnb's TOS is found at the bottom right-hand corner of the home page and in the same location on every other page on the site. Hosts and guests are also provided with links to the TOS and other policies at the point of registration, with notice being provided in the following terms: "By signing up, I agree to Airbnb's Terms of Service, Nondiscrimination Policy, Payments Terms of Service, Privacy Policy, Guest Refund Policy, and Host Guarantee Terms." Hyperlinks are provided to each of the relevant policies.

The Airbnb user agreement addresses only the publicly accessible data that can be found on its site, and it describes this data as content. Airbnb's TOS distinguish between three types of content:

> 5.1 Airbnb may, at its sole discretion, enable Members to (i) create, upload, post, send, receive and store content, such as text, photos, audio, video, or other materials and information

on or through the Airbnb Platform ("**Member Content**");
and (ii) access and view Member Content and any content
that Airbnb itself makes available on or through the Airbnb
Platform, including proprietary Airbnb content and any content
licensed or authorized for use by or through Airbnb from a third
party ("**Airbnb Content**" and together with Member Content,
"**Collective Content**").[67]

Airbnb asserts copyright in Airbnb content.[68] Although Airbnb does
not claim copyright in content contributed by members,[69] nor asks
for an assignment of copyright in this material, Airbnb does acquire
a perpetual, non-exclusive worldwide licence to use and disseminate
this content.[70]

Airbnb offers a limited, non-exclusive, non-transferable licence
to its members, and to any other visitors to the site, to access and
view Airbnb Content, as well as any Member Content to which a
user has been granted access. The licence is solely for personal and
non-commercial purposes.[71] Permitted uses of the data are therefore
extremely limited. In fact, the TOS specifically deny permission to a
broad range of potential uses of the site's content. For example, users
may not "copy, adapt, modify, prepare derivative works of, distribute,
license, sell, transfer, publicly display, publicly perform, transmit,
broadcast or otherwise exploit the Airbnb Platform or Collective
Content [...]."[72]

Airbnb uses its TOS to impose additional restrictions on the
extraction of its content.[73] The TOS specifically address (and prohibit)
the scraping and harvesting of data from the website.[74] Manual or
automated scraping is prohibited.[75] Further, it is prohibited to "use,
copy, adapt, modify, prepare derivative works of, distribute, license,
sell, transfer, publicly display, publicly perform, transmit, broadcast
or otherwise exploit the Airbnb Platform or Collective Content [...]."[76]
In case this is not sufficiently clear, the TOS specifically provide that
a user will not "use the Airbnb Platform or Collective Content for
any commercial or other purposes that are not expressly permitted
by these Terms."[77] The TOS also provide that there is to be no circumvention of any technological protection measures that are put in
place to protect Airbnb or member content. Article 14.1 specifically
states that users shall not "avoid, bypass, remove, deactivate, impair,
descramble, or otherwise attempt to circumvent any technological
measure implemented by Airbnb or any of Airbnb's providers or any

other third party to protect the Airbnb Platform."[78] Airbnb retains a number of different options for responding to violations of its TOS. For example, breach of the terms entitles Airbnb to deactivate user accounts or to ban users from the site.[79] Airbnb also reserves the right to take legal action against those who engage in unauthorized activities. As will be discussed in section V below, there are a number of different legal recourses that may be available to Airbnb to protect the rights it asserts in its data.

Table III: Data and Airbnb Terms of Service

Terms of Service
Copyright is asserted in Airbnb "collective" content
No scraping or harvesting of data from the site is permitted whether manually or by automated means
No right to copy, access, or use data for purposes not expressly permitted; permitted purposes are to "access" and "view"
No circumvention of technological protection measures
No creation of derivative works, no distribution, licensing, or sale of content

Airbnb essentially has three versions of its TOS, depending upon the place of residence of the contracting users. The versions are substantively similar, but each includes a choice of law clause, and a forum selection clause. For United States residents, the TOS are to be interpreted according to the laws of California.[80] Airbnb has established a binding arbitration process for any disputes arising out of the TOS and involving United States residents.[81] This would seem to encompass disputes regarding the improper use of data on the site, including copyright infringement actions and actions related to breach of the terms around scraping data, although Airbnb also reserves the right to apply to the courts for injunctions to prevent the infringement of intellectual property (IP) rights.[82] In addition, the parties have the right to seek injunctive relief in the specified courts in order to prevent ongoing or future violations of their IP rights.[83] Disputes governed by Chinese law are subject to mandatory binding arbitration by the China International Economic and Trade Arbitration Commission in Beijing. However, this does not limit the right of Airbnb to apply for injunctive relief to any court of competent jurisdiction.[84] For disputes between Airbnb and residents of countries other than China or the United States, the law governing the TOS is Irish law, and disputes are subject to the jurisdiction of the Irish courts. Nevertheless, Airbnb, in bringing an action against a user of its site may choose between the Irish courts and the courts of the country in which the defendant is resident.[85] This is pragmatic enough; an Irish court might not wish to take jurisdiction over a defendant located in a foreign country in relation to acts he or she carried out while resident of that country. Further, even though the law of the contract is Irish law, a defendant located in another country who has, for example, allegedly breached Airbnb's copyright could be sued for breach of contract (governed by Irish law) as well as breach of copyright (governed by the laws of the jurisdiction in which the infringement took place). Disputes relating to other bodies of law including privacy or torts are similarly complex in terms of choice of law issues.

As has been noted above, the scraping of data from Airbnb's website is carried out by many different actors for many different purposes, both commercial and non-commercial. There is no record of Airbnb's enforcement of its rights in this regard under its TOS,[86] although this does not mean it does not take place.[87] Article 22.5 of the TOS provides that "[t]he failure of Airbnb to enforce any right or provision of these Terms will not constitute a waiver of future enforcement of that right or provision."

V. Legal Framework

As the overview of the Airbnb data ecosystem makes clear, there are a broad range of users of Airbnb's publicly accessible data, and many of the users of these data are either not directly competing or are non-commercial actors. Yet, as seen in section III, Airbnb's TOS place significant contractual restrictions on the use of its publicly available data, asserting extremely broad rights of control. The result is that private control over publicly accessible data may not serve the public interest. As Kitchin notes, "[t]he fact that socially and culturally rich big data are largely in the hands of private interests means that, at present, computational social science and digital humanities research is not necessarily easy to do in practice."[88]

In this part of the chapter, we consider the legal frameworks or infrastructure that provides support to the claims asserted in the TOS. We also consider the extent to which the legal framework is adapted to take into consideration the public interest in access to and use of these data.

Airbnb's TOS constitute a contract, and breach of the contract is actionable as described in the TOS and outlined above. In addition, copyright law provides independent and/or complementary protection for Airbnb data. Copyright law has also expanded in recent years to provide protection against the circumvention of technological protection measures. These areas of law and the challenges with their application to Airbnb data are discussed below.

As noted earlier, the international nature of the Airbnb platform as well as its complex corporate structure make choice of law issues complex and raise interesting and debatable issues around the appropriate and applicable law. The focus in this chapter is on Canadian law, although many of the legal principles are similar in the United States. Indeed, United States law is also discussed where relevant, as there is often relatively little case law on some of the novel and emerging technology law issues that are relevant here. The goal of this section is to provide an overview of the elements of the legal framework that can be invoked by Airbnb to protect its rights in its data.

i. Contract Law

Airbnb's TOS constitute a contract that is meant to bind users of its site. In considering the enforceability of Internet TOS, courts have distinguished between so-called browse-wrap contracts (where a user is considered bound where they continue to use a website after being given notice of TOS)[89] and click-wrap contracts (where a user must click to indicate their agreement with the TOS).[90] Not surprisingly, click-wrap contracts are on more solid legal footing, but even browse-wrap contracts have been upheld by the courts.

A key issue for the enforceability of online TOS is whether users have been given appropriate notice of the terms and whether there is clear assent.[91] Users of the Airbnb website who become members (hosts or guests) are presented with specific notice of the TOS and other policies at the point of registration, and are asked to click to indicate their awareness of these and their agreement to be bound. This is almost certainly sufficient notice.[92] While there may be separate issues as to whether particular terms are enforceable in specific jurisdictions, where notice of terms is provided in this way, the contract will bind the parties. Other visitors to the site—for example, users who have not registered—do not click to agree to the TOS. For this category of users, the TOS are part of a browse-wrap agreement.

Whether a user of the Airbnb website who is not required to click to agree to the TOS is still bound by them may depend on the surrounding circumstances. In *Century 21*, the court summarized the relevant considerations in browse-wrap cases in these terms:

> the law of contract requires that the offer and its terms be brought to the attention of the user, be available for review and be in some manner accepted by the user. Such an analysis turns on the prominence the site gives to the proposed Terms of Use and the notice that the user has respecting what they are agreeing to once they have accepted the offer. To establish a binding contract consideration will also be given to whether the user is an individual consumer or a commercial entity and in addition a one-time user or a frequent user of the site.[93]

On the issue of notice, a relevant consideration is how easy it is for users to locate the TOS. For example, in the United States case of *Cvent v. Eventbrite*[94] the court dismissed a breach of contract argument regarding the TOS because it found that the TOS for the Cvent site were difficult to find, and did not require users to click their acceptance of the terms at any point, or to indicate that they had read or agreed to the terms.[95] The ease with which the terms may be located, and their presence, for example, at the bottom of each page of the site visited, may be factors that support a finding that the user had effective notice of the terms.[96]

A finding that there has been acceptance of TOS in browse-wrap cases is made more complicated since there is no obvious clicking of a button to indicate agreement. Courts have ruled that assent can be found in a website visitor's decision to continue past the home page to view the deeper pages within the site. In *Century 21*, the court stated: "The act of browsing past the initial page of the website or searching the site is conduct indicating agreement with the Terms of Use if those terms are provided with sufficient notice, are available for review prior to acceptance, and clearly state that proceeding further is acceptance of the terms."[97]

Another relevant consideration in terms of the enforceability of particular terms or the enforceability of browse-wrap or even click-wrap contracts is the sophistication, status, or experience of the user.[98] A business competitor may be presumed to know that companies in the same field use terms of service, and so may be considered to be aware of not only the existence of the TOS on a competitor's website but of their likely content.[99] If the user is an ordinary consumer, courts may be less inclined to find that a browse-wrap agreement is enforceable if it is not properly brought to the consumer's attention.[100] However, ordinary online consumers are now more experienced than they were in the early days of the Internet, and courts may be prepared to assume that Internet users expect that the websites they visit will have TOS. This may lead courts to consider site website users to be bound by those terms.

Those seeking to scrape Airbnb do not need to become members, and the robots do not scrape behind a login interface. However, scrapers will have needed to visit and browse the site in order to program their robots, raising the issue of whether the browse-wrap agreement is engaged. A court might well consider a web scraper to be both technologically savvy and familiar with the layout of the targeted website. Thus, in such cases, the scraper is more likely to be considered bound by the TOS.[101]

Typically, an action for breach of contract requires damages to be established, although an injunction may also be available where ongoing breaches are possible.[102] Although in cases where non-commercial scraping is at issue, it may seem that the plaintiff will have suffered no commercial losses, but damages may still be available for the costs incurred in trying to prevent the scraping activity, including the costs of staff time.[103] In addition, a court may award nominal damages where other proof of damage is limited.[104] While it is likely that the non-commercial nature of some scraping activities may be a factor in a court's assessment of damages for breach of TOS, the risk of litigation expenses, an award of costs, and even modest damages may be a sufficient deterrent for those who scrape data for non-commercial purposes that serve the public interest. It is important to remember as well that differences in economic power can make non-commercial users easily deterred by cease-and-desist letters.[105]

The question of whether a user is bound by website TOS is relevant not just to determining whether there is recourse for breach of contract. As will be seen in the discussion in the next section, whether a user is bound by TOS may be a factor in assessing fair dealing as a defence to copyright infringement.

ii. Copyright Law

Copyright law protects original works of authorship. In order to succeed in a claim for copyright infringement, a plaintiff will first have to show that she has a valid copyright in the work. This will involve establishing that the work in question qualifies as a work under the *Copyright Act*, that it is original, and that the plaintiff holds the rights to the work.[106] The plaintiff will also have to show that the defendant exercised one of the exclusive rights of the copyright holder without consent or justification.[107] The exclusive rights include the right to reproduce all or a substantial part of a work, to create adaptations, as well as the right to communicate the work to the public by telecommunications, and the right to authorize these activities, among other rights.[108]

Copyright law protects literary, dramatic, musical, and artistic works.[109] Compilations, whether of data or of a combination of other works, are also capable of protection as works in their own right.[110] The Airbnb website as a whole is likely a multimedia work—a compilation consisting of literary works (text) and artistic works (photos, graphic design, and the like), as well as data. Some of the elements of the compilation are also independently protectable as works. These would include photographs, text, drawings, logos, graphic design, and so on. The Airbnb TOS provide that hosts and guests retain copyright in those works that they upload to the site. However, Airbnb would be the owner of the copyright in the compilation as a whole.

Works must also be "original" for copyright to subsist.[111] While the threshold for originality may vary slightly from one jurisdiction to another, for the most part it is a relatively low threshold. Originality in copyright law does not have a qualitative dimension—there is no assessment of the work's original contribution to the state of knowledge or literature.[112] Originality typically means that the work has not been copied, and that it displays some manifestation of human intellect. In the United States this is referred to as a "spark" of creativity; in Canada this is an "exercise of skill and judgment."[113] In either case, the threshold is low. Airbnb's website as a multimedia work reflects original choices in terms of the selection and arrangement of its elements.

Airbnb asserts intellectual property rights over "Airbnb Content" although its claim is more ambiguous in relation to what it calls "Collective Content."[114] The "Collective Content" is a compilation composed of a variety of elements, some of which are considered proprietary to Airbnb, and some of which may be the intellectual property of their contributors. This Collective Content may also include data that are considered to be in the public domain. The Airbnb Content is similarly a compilation, although it is more likely to be a combination of elements contributed by Airbnb itself.

Some things cannot be protected under copyright law. For example, copyright law does not protect ideas in the abstract, only original expressions of ideas.[115] Copyright law also does not protect facts. As a result, facts are considered to be in the public domain.[116] The rationale for this may vary somewhat. Some courts consider facts to be incapable of authorship, as they are copied from the world around us.[117] Others raise public policy considerations.[118] Copyright law is meant to support and encourage innovation; providing a monopoly to a party over factual material is more likely to hinder than to stimulate innovation. Of course, issues around facts are not straightforward. It has been argued that some facts are authored (for example, facts about characters or events in literary works or television shows).[119] Issues have also been raised regarding the extent to which data that is the output of analytics, such as predictions or profiling data, are authored as well.[120] Nevertheless, even if facts cannot be protected on their own, they can be protected in compiled form. In *Geophysical Services Inc. v. Encana Corp.*,[121] the court found that compilations of both raw and processed data are capable of copyright protection. In the case of processed data, there may be substantial skill and judgment in the processing.[122] The court acknowledged that depending upon the skill and judgment of the person or persons involved in the processing, the processing of the same data or similar purposes might lead to different outputs.

Because the authorship in a compilation consists of selecting and arranging those elements which form part of the compilation, the originality of a compilation is assessed in terms of the skill or judgment that goes into the selection or arrangement, and not the originality of the underlying elements.[123] Thus, in a compilation of data, the data themselves are considered to be in the public domain; what is protected is any original selection or arrangement of the data.[124] Where what is extracted from the Airbnb site is data, there is only an infringement of copyright if what has been extracted is a substantial part of an original selection or arrangement of those data.[125]

As noted above, the concept of originality draws on the notion of authorship, as the spark of creativity or skill and judgment required to create the work must come from a human author. In the case of compilations of data, the spark, or skill and judgment, may be found in the choices around what data to select and include and how to arrange or present it.[126] Where data is scraped, its presentation (or arrangement) is rarely copied (scraping extracts the content rather than creating a visual facsimile). Nevertheless, it might be possible to argue that scraping still extracts a substantial part of the original *selection* of Airbnb content, to the extent that the presence of those data on the site reflects Airbnb's choices as to what to include in its compilation.[127]

Where the data extracted through scraping includes other parts of the multimedia compilation that are copyright protected works in their own right, there can be a breach of copyright in the individual works, notwithstanding the outcome of any dispute over infringement of the compilation itself.[128] Thus, for example, scraping that includes photographs from the website might violate individual copyrights in photographs owned by those who uploaded them to the site.[129]

Although copyright law offers some basis for protection for Airbnb's website and their contents, it is a relatively porous protection. Only a substantial taking is copyright infringement; thus, the extraction of an insignificant quantity of the selection or arrangement of the factual material would not be infringing. Someone who reproduced all of the data on Airbnb's website would have copied the entire selection of data, but scraping tools are typically configured to scrape only certain categories of data, thus creating their own selections of the underlying data.[130] These selections of data reflect, in their own right, independent exercise of skill and judgment.

The above discussion raises the possibility that a platform company such as Airbnb could argue that its copyright in its original selection of data on its website is infringed by scraping activities. Yet it would be equally possible to find that there is no substantial taking of that selection, particularly where scraping takes only a subset of data. Unfortunately for scrapers, substantial taking generally requires a case-by-case assessment. Thus, while it might be possible to contest either the existence or the scope of Airbnb's copyright interests in its compiled data/information, this would likely be an uphill battle against a well-resourced and motivated party.

1. Fair Dealing/Fair Use

While copyright law provides a means for Airbnb to assert control over its data, copyright law also contains important users' rights, such as fair dealing (or, in the United States, fair use). Where the fair dealing or fair use defence applies, uses of the work which would otherwise be infringing are considered justified. The scope of fair dealing or fair use is therefore important here, as such rights may actually permit a variety of different uses of Airbnb data.

In Canada, fair dealing must be for one of the purposes set out in the *Copyright Act*. These include research or private study, education, parody or satire, news reporting, and criticism or commentary.[131] In the United States, by contrast, fair use purposes are open-ended.[132] In addition to being for a permitted purpose, the dealing must also be "fair." In *CCH Canadian v. Law Society of Upper Canada*, the Supreme Court of Canada identified six criteria that can be used in assessing the fairness of any dealing with a work. These are: the purpose of the dealing, the character of the dealing, the amount of the dealing, alternatives to the dealing, the nature of the work, and the effect of the dealing on the work.[133] In the United States, four criteria for assessing fair use are set out in the legislation: the purpose and character of the use; the nature of the copyrighted work; the amount and substantiality of the portion taken; and the effect of the use upon the potential market for the original.[134] There is therefore a considerable amount of overlap between the concepts of fair use and fair dealing, although United States courts have been more open to recognizing the freedom of expression values embedded in the fair use exception.[135]

Although the purpose of the dealing must fit within one of the statutory categories of fair dealing in Canada, courts will also consider other dimensions of "purpose" in assessing whether the dealing was fair. Thus, for example, it may be relevant to consider whether the dealing with a work was to create a new work or to transform the original. Where this is the case, it may support a finding of fair use in the United States. The situation is less clear in Canada, where the courts have yet to build a strong link between transformative uses and fair dealing. Nevertheless, transformation may still be a relevant consideration.[136] The degree of transformation may also be significant.[137] However, simple repackaging or republication of content from the original work is less likely to be fair.[138] Whether a use is for commercial or non-commercial purposes is also a relative consideration; non-commercial uses are more likely to be considered fair,[139] although the commercial/non-commercial distinction is not determinative.[140] It is also the case that "a use that generates value for the 'broader public interest' weighs in favor of fair use."[141]

In the United States *Meltwater* case, data scraped from the plaintiff's site were essentially repackaged and sold. It was news content that was provided to Meltwater's subscribers. The fact that the plaintiffs and defendants were in competition—at least to some extent—proved relevant to the analysis. The court noted that Meltwater did not add its own commentary or insight to the material it circulated to its subscribers. It characterized Meltwater as intending "to serve as a substitute for AP's [Associated Press] news service."[142] In *Meltwater*, the content scraped from the AP websites was considered "the fruit of AP's labor," which was extracted for Meltwater's profit and used in a manner that competed directly with AP's business (which included licensing access to its database to news aggregators).[143]

Unlike the situation in *Meltwater*, Airbnb's data is a by-product of its main operations. There is no competition from the scrapers discussed in this chapter with Airbnb's main business (short-term rental accommodation). Some of the opportunistic businesses that scrape Airbnb data do not compete with Airbnb. Some offer analytic services to their customers[144] that actually support or encourage their customers to continue using Airbnb. However, in some cases, these analytics services may compete with Airbnb's own analytic services. Further, there is a potential market for Airbnb in licensing its data to analytics companies. Thus, it is not entirely clear that there is no impact from these activities on Airbnb's ability to economically exploit its compilation of public data. As for the researchers and civil-society groups that scrape Airbnb data, they principally do so for non-commercial purposes, and they may provide value-added analytics or commentary. In some cases, they may also provide scraped data to other users.[145] Such uses are more likely to be considered fair, as they are non-commercial, non-competing, and transformative. They are also a form of critical speech.

The second fair dealing criterion identified by the Supreme Court of Canada is the character of the dealing. This involves considering how the work is dealt with by the defendant. It may take into account how many copies are made, how widely they are disseminated, whether they are destroyed once their purpose has been served, or whether the dealing is consistent with accepted standards.[146] In theory, the "character of the dealing" may also take into account whether the access to the work was legitimate or not. For example, whether data is scraped from a website that uses the robot exclusion standard[147] might be relevant to the character of the dealing. This has been found to be a relevant consideration in the fair use balance in the United States in a few cases.[148] Nevertheless, making a copyright owner's consent relevant to a fair dealing analysis is clearly problematic. In the Canadian *Century 21* case, it was argued that the defendant's refusal to comply with the robot exclusion standard was a relevant consideration in assessing fair dealing. The court cautioned against making a copyright owner's consent to fair dealing a consideration, noting that it is the nature of fair dealing that it often takes place in contexts where copyright owners might otherwise refuse to permit uses of their works.[149]

The amount and substantiality of what has been copied is a further consideration in the fair dealing analysis. Courts will consider this from both quantitative and qualitative perspectives.[150] Essentially, a use will be fair when the defendant takes no more than what they need to take.[151] There is no magic formula from a quantitative perspective. In some circumstances it may be fair dealing to copy the entire work; in others circumstances taking a relatively small portion may not be fair use, particularly if that small portion is qualitatively central to the work.[152] In the case of transformative works such as parody, it may be essential to capture a significant portion of the copyright protected work.[153] Where the work at issue is a compilation of data, it is important to keep the focus on that part which is capable of copyright protection: the expression in such a compilation is found in the selection or arrangement of the data.[154] Taking a quantitatively significant amount of data may not be infringing at all, if there is no substantial taking of the original selection or arrangement of the data. Even if there is some taking of the original selection or arrangement, it is the substantiality of the taking of the selection or arrangement that must be assessed for the purposes of fair use, and not the volume of data taken. In *Century 21*, in considering the amount of the dealing, the court also took into account the fact that the defendant's robots made repeat visits to the site to extract updated data.

The fair dealing analysis also requires a consideration of alternatives to the dealing. Thus, for example, it may be relevant to consider whether there is "a non-copyrighted equivalent of the work that could have been used instead of the copyrighted work."[155] If Airbnb made some of its data available—for example, by providing downloadable datasets—it might be argued that data scraping would be much less likely to be considered fair dealing. However, such an approach must be considered with caution. There might still be reasons to scrape data, including to acquire data with different parameters, or to verify the accuracy of the data being provided. In *Century 21*, the court found that since the real-estate companies whose content was scraped by the defendant company already made their content available to the public over the Internet, it was not fair dealing for the defendant to scrape this data in order to produce its competing website. In other words, legitimately visiting the realtor's website to view the data was a reasonable alternative to scraping. However, where Airbnb data is scraped for the purposes of data analytics, the scrapers are, for the most part, creating content, products, or services that are distinct from those available on the Airbnb website.[156]

The nature of the copyright protected work is also a key consideration in a fair use analysis. The Supreme Court of Canada has identified whether a work is published or unpublished as a relevant consideration.[157] The fact that scraped Airbnb data is publicly accessible may therefore be a factor supporting a finding of fair dealing, although such an argument might be counterbalanced by the fact that a human being could not easily reproduce the level of data extraction carried out by technologically assisted scraping. In other words, the data is made publicly accessible to humans, not to machines. This is supported by the site's TOS, which specifically prohibit scraping. In the United States, in considering the nature of the work, the court may also take into account whether the copyright protected work is expressive or creative, or whether it is predominantly factual. The latter category of works is further from the core of what is meant to be protected under copyright law.[158] A compilation of data is further from the core of copyright protection, because the data themselves are in the public domain. Their selection and arrangement can be very easily transformed by those who use the data for other purposes. For example, a selection and arrangement that aims to facilitate short-term rentals is different from a selection and arrangement that attempts to understand the impact of Airbnb on the market for long-term accommodation. As a result, the reuse of data in these contexts may be more conducive to a fair dealing defence.

The final criterion in both a fair dealing and a fair use analysis is the effect of the use of the work by the defendant on the potential market for or value of the work. Use of a work to compete with the plaintiff's work is less likely to be fair.[159] If, for example, Airbnb is in the practice of licensing its data for use by others in analytics or for research, then it becomes much more difficult to argue that scraping data for these purposes is fair dealing.[160] On the other hand, courts in both the United States and Canada have cautioned that the possibility of paying for a licence to access a work does not automatically preclude a fair dealing/fair use argument.[161] In addition, it might be that even if Airbnb provided options to license data or to download some datasets for free, some users might still feel a need to scrape data if they wished to verify or challenge the data being provided. Such a use might still be considered fair. Courts are more likely to find transformative uses to be fair,[162] whereas uses that create a substitute for the original are less likely to be considered fair.[163]

The disclaimers on the Inside Airbnb website state: "This site claims 'fair use' of any information compiled in producing a non-commercial derivation to allow public analysis, discussion and community benefit."[164] If Inside Airbnb is based in the United States, its fair use claims may well be supportable. In any event, in the United States there might be a finding that there is no copyright infringement. Only data is scraped, not other protected copyright expression. It is scraped according to Inside Airbnb's own selection, and it is processed by Inside Airbnb to produce its own datasets and analyses. Arguably Inside Airbnb has taken nothing that is protected by copyright. Even if the contrary is found, Inside Airbnb's use of the scraped material is transformative, non-commercial, and in the public interest. This would seem to be an entirely appropriate result.

The situation in Canada might be more precarious, although there is absolutely no public policy reason why it should be. There is relatively little case law on copyright infringement of compilations of facts, but what little there is reveals a tendency to favour the initial compiler. Assuming that a court found that the scraping of Airbnb data was substantial taking from Airbnb's original compilation, a fair dealing defence would be more challenging to make out. This is because Canadian fair dealing law does not recognize transformative uses as an independent basis for finding fair dealing. While Airbnb's scraping of data could be considered to be for the purpose of research or private study, there is uncertainty as to whether Canadian courts would find that a dealing that required the breach of TOS could be fair. For example, in *1395804 Ontario Ltd. (c.o.b. Blacklock's Reporter) v. Canadian Vintners' Association*,[165] the court stated: "it is patently clear that unless you have obtained the material legally, you cannot avail yourself of the defence of fair dealing for the purpose of education, criticism or review."[166] While this is a small claims court decision and should be given relatively little weight, it does reveal a tendency that could be problematic.

These issues highlight a need for a robust and principled approach when it comes to issues of copyright infringement and fair dealing involving the scraping of data from publicly accessible websites. Where the use is non-commercial and serves the public interest—particularly when it engages freedom of expression values such as critical speech—copyright law should not pose a barrier.

What is more challenging is the situation of the so-called opportunistic businesses. This element of the Airbnb data ecosystem is an interesting one. In many cases, the businesses do not compete directly with Airbnb, and they build new business models based on data analytics that combine publicly accessible and open data from a variety of sources. These are arguably transformative uses of the data, and although commercial, they are not directly competing. The question is whether copyright law should accommodate such uses. To do so is arguably to adapt to the emerging dynamics of a big data economy. How and under what terms and conditions companies should be allowed to limit access to and use of their publicly accessible data is an interesting question; it may be that copyright law does not provide the best framework for managing these issues.

2. *Technological Protection Measures/Rights Management Information*

Section 41.1(1) of the Canadian *Copyright Act*, added by amendments in 2012, provides that "No person shall (a) circumvent a technological protection measure within the meaning of paragraph (a) of the definition **technological protection measure** in section 41." The definition of a technological protection measure is

> any effective technology, device or component that, in the ordinary course of its operation,

(a) controls access to a work, to a performer's performance fixed in a sound recording or to a sound recording and whose use is authorized by the copyright owner; or

(b) restricts the doing — with respect to a work, to a performer's performance fixed in a sound recording or to a sound recording — of any act referred to in section 3, 15 or 18 and any act for which remuneration is payable under section 19.

According to this provision technological protection measures (TPMs) may either control access to works or may restrict certain uses of the works. The equivalent provision in the United States *Copyright Act* states that "[n]o person shall circumvent a technological measure that effectively controls access to a work protected under this title."[167] While the United States legislation makes some provision to allow for research activities or other forms of fair use to take place with respect to works protected by digital locks,[168] the Canadian *Copyright Act* contains no such exception, and the definition of an "effective technological protection measure" has recently been given an extremely broad interpretation. In *Nintendo of America Inc. v. King*,[169] one of the few cases thus far to interpret Canada's new anti-circumvention provisions, the court stated: "The open-ended language of this definition reflects Parliament's intention to empower copyright owners to protect their business models with any technological tool at their disposal."[170] The court found that in the case of TPMs that provide access control, these "do not need to employ any barrier to copying in order to be 'effective.'"[171] In other words, where there are access controls, it is not necessary for a TPM to "encrypt [...], scrambl[e] or [accomplish] some 'other transformation of the work.'"[172] In the United States, courts have interpreted the anti-circumvention provisions with a bit more nuance, perhaps because of the wording of the statute, which expressly addresses concerns over fair use by providing that "Nothing in this section shall affect rights, remedies, limitations, or defenses to copyright infringement, including fair use, under this title."[173] This is interesting because it suggests that the fact that a TPM has been circumvented would not factor into a fair use analysis.[174] By contrast, in Canada, it might well be that a court would consider the circumvention of a TPM to militate against a finding of fair dealing.[175]

The anti-circumvention provisions are breached where there has been circumvention of an effective technological protection measure. The concept of "circumvention" is therefore also relevant. In one of the few Canadian cases interpreting the anti-circumvention provisions, the court found that when the defendant asked a subscriber to a paywalled service to send them a copy of an article, this amounted to circumvention of the paywall by the defendant.[176] In *Nintendo*, the court found that the definition of "circumvent" can include "anything else that otherwise avoids, bypasses, removes, deactivates, or impairs the technological protection measure."[177]

Scraping cases therefore raise the question of whether the robot exclusion standard can constitute an "effective technological protection measure." If it can, then presumably scraping a website that uses this standard will likely constitute circumvention. Entities that do not wish to have their websites searched by mechanical agents (robots, crawlers, spiders, and the like) can use the "robot exclusion header," or robots.txt file, to indicate that they do not wish this to take place. In *eBay v. Bidder's Edge*[178] the court described a "robot exclusion header" as "a message, sent to computers programmed to detect and respond to such headers, that eBay does not permit unauthorized robotic activity."[179] In *Meltwater*, the court stated:

> Robots.txt protocol, also known as the Robot Exclusion Standard, was designed by industry groups to instruct cooperating web crawlers not to access all or part of a website that is publicly viewable. If a website owner uses the robots.txt file to give instructions about its site to web crawlers, and a crawler honors the instruction, then the crawler should not visit any pages on the website.[180]

For the exclusion to work, the programmer of the robot must have coded the robot to read the robots.txt data file, and to comply with its directives.

The actual robots.txt file is described as "a simple text file placed in the root directory of the server that one wants to protect."[181] The file can be coded so as to stop all robots, or it can be coded to permit certain ones. It can block indexing of all content or only of certain categories of content. It has been described as a method that "offers an opportunity to control access to information and control server load."[182] The robots exclusion protocol, although widely used, is not a formal standard.

It is as yet unclear whether the "robot exclusion header" constitutes a TPM the circumvention of which would independently constitute a violation of copyright law. As noted by Lundblad, if it were considered to be a TPM, "it follows that disobeying the robots. txt file would constitute illegal circumvention."[183] Lundblad is undecided on the issue. While acknowledging the possibility that it might be considered a TPM, he also notes that "the robots exclusion standard seeks to prevent acts relating not to a specified set of works, but rather to a repository of works (if the Web site is not seen as a unitary work)."[184] Where a website is seen as a unitary work— a multimedia work, or a compilation—the issue of circumvention remains. Lundblad suggests that the robots.txt file is more like a "no trespassing" sign than it is like a lock on a door.[185]

In a rare case considering this issue, a United States court stated:

> No court has found that a robots.txt file universally constitutes a "technological measure effectively controll[ing] access" under the DMCA. The protocol by itself is not analogous to digital password protection or encryption. However, in this case, when all systems involved in processing requests via the Wayback Machine are operating properly, the placement of a correct robots.txt file on Healthcare Advocates' current website does work to block users from accessing archived screenshots of its website. (Pl's Mot. Partial Summ. J. Ex. F, Expert Report of Edward Felton at 10). The only way to gain access would be for Healthcare Advocates to remove the robots.txt file from its website, and only the website owner can remove the robots. txt file. Thus, in this situation, the robots.txt file qualifies as a technological measure effectively controlling access to the archived copyrighted images of Healthcare Advocates. This finding should not be interpreted as a finding that a robots.txt file universally qualifies as a technological measure that controls access to copyrighted works under the DMCA.[186]

In this case, the files in question were stored in the Wayback Machine. Because the plaintiff's website was protected by a robots. txt protocol, the policy of the Wayback Machine was to block public access to the archived images. However, at the date of the defendant's access request, the Wayback Machine systems, which normally checked for the robots.txt file and blocked access, were down, and the defendant was able to gain access to the documents. The facts are therefore quite specific to this case. In this instance, the presence of the robots.txt protocol combined with the functioning of the Wayback Machine should have operated in combination to effectively block access to the content. This case cannot, therefore, be interpreted as finding that the robots.txt protocol, on its own, is an effective TPM under United States law. However, it does suggest that it is at least arguable that it meets those criteria in some cases.

A secondary question might be whether the robot exclusion standard constitutes an *effective* TPM.[187] After all, it is easily bypassed. In fact, a programmer has to take affirmative steps to program his or her bots to recognize and read robots.txt file before the measure can be effective. As Jasiewicz notes, the use of the robots exclusion protocol does not physically prevent robots from accessing and crawling a site.[188] The robots.txt file simply serves to "notify the robot of the site owner's wishes."[189]

In addition to making the circumvention of TPM actionable, the *Copyright Act* also provides that it is actionable to make available or to disseminate the means to circumvent TPM. It should be noted that some of those who scrape data in the public interest share their code for scraping data so that others can either learn from this code or use it to scrape their own data. Civil-society actor Tom Slee does this for the code he uses to scrape Airbnb data. There is clearly a public interest in this type of exchange of information and tools to assist in the carrying out of research using publicly accessible data. Overall, the potential ramifications for the public interest of finding that the robots exclusion standard is a TPM are such that courts should steer well away from such a finding.

iii. Trespass to Chattels

Copyright law addresses data scraping in terms of the protection of rights in the underlying compilation of data. Yet the mechanical extraction of data from a website can also impact the stability and performance of the server on which the data is hosted. This is so whether the data is extracted through an authorized application programming interface[190] or through unauthorized scraping practices. Whether there are such impacts may depend on the number of different robots engaged in extracting data at any given time; the volume of data scraped by these robots; and the capacity of the servers on which the data is hosted.

A few cases, predominantly from the United States, have considered whether data scraping may constitute a form of trespass to chattels. The tort of trespass to chattels involves improperly interfering with the lawful possession of the server, and not the data itself.[191] In this sense, therefore, the trespass to chattels action is not directly linked to protecting the data, and any trespass is not to the data itself. Nevertheless, by making actionable the activity of scraping because of its impact on the server on which the data is stored, the recourse could be used as a means of shielding the data from extraction. Such arguments focus on the impact on the server.

Trespass to chattels requires an interference with the plaintiff's possession of a chattel, in this case a server or servers.[192] Such actions have had limited success in the United States and even less in Canada. In the first place, for the action to succeed, the plaintiff must demonstrate that they were in possession of the chattel (the server) at the time of the trespass. In *Century 21*, the court found that the plaintiff paid for hosting space on servers owned by another company. Thus it could not assert trespass to chattels because it lacked physical possession of the servers. The reasoning in this case highlights some of the challenges with relying on this tort action.

In addition to the issue of possession, a court must be willing to find that data scraping is a trespass. In *Century 21*, the court observed that it was "not at all clear" that electronic access to a computer server was sufficiently "physical" to amount to a trespass. It may be that access without impact will lack the physical element required. Thus, for example, if the scraping activity has no discernible impact on the proper functioning of the servers, it may simply not be actionable.[193]

Early cases in the United States breathed some life into the tort as it applied in the digital context. For example, in *eBay v. Bidder's Edge*[194] a United States court found scraping activities to constitute trespass to chattels. In doing so, it rejected the argument that there could be no trespass since the plaintiff's website was publicly accessible. The court noted that "eBay's servers are private property, conditional access to which eBay grants the public. eBay does not generally permit the type of automated access made by BE [Bidder's Edge, Inc.]."[195] The trespass was to the private servers; the publicly accessible character of the data was not material. The decision has had relatively little traction, however, and trespass to chattels has not become mainstream, nor has it been embraced in Canada.

If the digital trespass paradigm is accepted, the use of the robots exclusion standard might reinforce the idea that data scraping is a trespass.[196] In other words, the robots.txt file conveys acceptable use conditions digitally to robots programmed by others and that visit the site. In this sense, it is like a no-trespassing sign—or perhaps more accurately, a set of instructions provided to those who come to the metaphorical gate. If the robot ignores the robots.txt file, it has breached these digital terms of use, and its entry is a trespass.

One of the problems with an action in trespass to chattels is that it relies on a fairly absolutist notion of property rights. If there is a trespass—an interference with the possessory right—then there is liability. It does not depend on the trespass being on such a scale that harm is caused. In a context where the scraping of publicly accessible data can be carried out in the public interest, trespass to chattels risks prioritizing private rights over that public interest. If trespass to chattels is to be accepted as a recourse that offers some protection against excessive use of a server, there must also be exceptions for access to and extraction of publicly accessible data where there is no discernable adverse impact. Alternatively, recourse might only be available for reckless or malicious acts. The public interest dimensions and the competing considerations suggest that if any legal recourse is required, this is an area better left to the legislature.

VI. Conclusion

Platform companies such as Airbnb host a significant amount of data on publicly accessible websites. While this data is necessary for the operation of their service, it has interest and importance for other users as well. Perhaps most importantly, because of the hugely disruptive effects of Airbnb in some cities, the data has significant public interest for those seeking to document, understand, and address these impacts.

While companies often frame data issues in terms of private property rights (whether rights in tangible or intangible property), this chapter has questioned the appropriateness of this paradigm, or, has argued for, at the very least, an approach that creates robust space for uses in the public interest. Thus, the protection afforded to compilations of data under copyright law should not be interpreted so broadly as to overly extend rights in data, and copyright exceptions such as fair dealing should create a robust space for uses in the public interest broadly defined. At the same time, TPM provisions in copyright law should not be interpreted in such a way as to create unnecessary barriers to using publicly accessible data. Finally, recourses such as trespass to chattels in the digital context should be strictly limited so as not to create unnecessary and even detrimental barriers to access to and use of publicly accessible data.

The public interest is easy to identify in some contexts. For example, the use of data for research or advocacy purposes is generally considered to serve the public interest. However, in our rapidly evolving big data society, the public interest should also be considered broadly. This chapter has shown how there may be a rich array of opportunistic commercial users of publicly accessible data. And, while such uses may raise their own public policy challenges, the fact remains that strict property rights-based approaches to publicly available data might have impacts that adversely affect the public interest in innovation and competition. This is particularly the case in the evolving big data environment.

Notes

1. Canada Research Chair in Information Law and Policy, Faculty of Law, University of Ottawa. I gratefully acknowledge the support of the Canada Research Chairs program and of the Social Sciences and Humanities Research Council of Canada through the Geothink project of which this research is a part. Many thanks to Mistrale Goudreau, Florian Martin-Bariteau, and Pamela Robinson for their willingness to discuss different issues with me. Thanks also to James McKinney, Jean-Noé Landry, Karen Sawatzky, and Murray Cox for helping me understand technological issues. I am grateful to Wei Jiang for his research assistance. Many thanks to Charles Sanders for his insightful comments on an earlier draft. All errors and inaccuracies are my own.

2. Vanessa Katz, "Regulating the Sharing Economy" (2015) 30:4 BTLJ 1067 at 1070.

3. Orly Lobel, "The Law of the Platform" (2016) 101:1 Minn L Rev 87 at 96.

4. *Ibid*; Daniel E Rauch & David Schleicher, "Like Uber, But for Local Governmental Policy: The Future of Local Regulation of the 'Sharing Economy'" (2015) George Mason University Law and Economics Working Paper No 15-01, online: <https://papers.ssrn.com/sol3/papers.cfm?abstract_id=2549919>; Sofia Rancordas, "Does Sharing Mean Caring? Regulating Innovation in the Sharing Economy" (2015) 16:1 Minn J L Sci & Tech 413; Stephen R Miller, "First Principles for Regulating the Sharing Economy" (2016) 53 Harv J on Legis 147.

5. Shu-yi Oei & Diane M Ring, "Can Sharing Be Taxed?" (2016) 93 Wash ULaw Rev 989; Caroline Bruckner, "Shortchanged: The Tax Compliance Challenges of Small Business Operators Driving the On-Demand Platform Economy" (23 May 2016), online: Kogod School of Business <http://www.american.edu/kogod/news/ Shortchanged.cfm>.

6. Antonio Aloisi, "Commoditized Workers. Case Study Research on Labour Law Issues Arising from a Set of 'On-Demand/Gig Economy' Platforms" (2016) 37:3 Comp Lab L & Pol'y J 653; Deepas Das Acevedo, "Regulating Employment Relationships in the Sharing Economy" (2016) 20:1 Employee Rts & Employment Pol'y 1.

7. Christopher Koopman, Matthew Mitchell & Adam Thierer, "The Sharing Economy and Consumer Protection Regulation: The Case for Policy Change" (2015) 8:2 JBEL 529.

8. Benjamin Edelman, Michael Luca & Dan Svirsky, "Racial Discrimination in the Sharing Economy: Evidence from a Field Experiment" (2017) 9:2 Am Econ J Appl Econ 1.

9. Rob Kitchin, *The Data Revolution: Big Data, Open Data, Data Infrastructures & Their Consequences* (London: Sage Publications, 2014) at 152.

10. *Ibid*. Note that this is also the case with Airbnb. In some instances where it has chosen to release data about its operations in certain cities, civil-society actors and researchers who scrape data have challenged the accuracy of the data provided by Airbnb. See e.g. Murray Cox & Tom Slee, "How Airbnb's Data Hid the Facts in New York City" (10 February 2016), online: Tom Slee <http://tomslee.net/2016/02/how-airbnbs-data-hid-the-facts-in-new-york-city.html>.

11. The terms "Hosts" and "Guests" are those used by Airbnb for people who make accommodation available for rental and those who book rental accommodation respectively. See Airbnb, *Terms of Service* (19 June 2017) at art 1.1, online: <https://www.airbnb.ca/terms/>.

12. Airbnb, *About Us*, online: <https://www.airbnb.ca/about/about-us>.

13. Daniel Guttentag, "Airbnb: Disruptive Innovation and the Rise of an Informal Tourism Accommodation System" (2015) 18:12 Curr Issues Tour 1192 at 1195.

14. Airbnb, *Terms of Service, supra* note 11, art 5.6.

15. Data is collected indirectly from users by, *inter alia*, the use of cookies and other digital devices to track their activities over the platform.

16. Airbnb, for example, will perform analytics on its own stores of data with a view to developing a better understanding of its users, its markets, and so on.

17. Airbnb, "How Does Providing Identification on Airbnb Work?," online: <https://www.airbnb.ca/help/ article/1237/how-does-providing-identification-on-airbnb-work>.

18. Airbnb, *Airbnb Privacy Policy* (19 June 2017) at art 1.2, online: <https://www.airbnb.ca/terms/privacy_policy>.

19. For a discussion on formal and informal dispute resolution on the Airbnb platform, see the chapter by Nofar Sheffi in this volume.

20. Airbnb, *Privacy Policy, supra* note 18. Article 1.3 provides that where the Airbnb account is linked to a third-party account such as Facebook, "the third party service may send us information such as your registration and profile information from that service. This information varies and is controlled by that service or as authorized by you via your privacy settings at that service."

21. The distinction between public and confidential data is legally significant in that public data cannot be protected by the body of law that protects confidential commercial information.

22. See e.g. *Personal Information Protection and Electronic Documents Act*, SC 2000, c 5, s 2(1).

23. *Ibid.*

24. See e.g. Teresa Scassa, "Geographic Information as Personal Information" (2010) 10:2 OUCLJ 185.

25. On the issue of ease of reidentification, see Paul Ohm, "Broken Promises of Privacy: Responding to the Surprising Failure of Anonymization" (2010) 57 UCLA L Rev 1701; Latanya Sweeney, "k-Anonymity: A Model for Protecting Privacy" (2002) 10:5 Intl J Uncertain Fuzz 557.

26. Airbnb, *Airbnb Privacy Policy, supra* note 18 at art 3.14.

27. See the discussion of this issue in V.ii. below.

28. For a discussion of the copyright status of predictive data, see Larry W Thomas, *Legal Research Digest 37: Legal Arrangements for Use and Control of Real-Time Data* (Washington, D.C.: Transportation Research Board of the National Academies, 2011), online: <http://www.trb.org/Publications/Blurbs/165626.aspx>.

29. *Trader Corporation v CarGurus, Inc.* 2017 ONSC 1841 at para 5. In *Century 21 Canada Ltd. Partnership v Rogers Communications Inc.*, 2011 BCSC 1196, [2011] BCJ No 1679 at para 10, the court described scraping as: "A form of indexing that looks for specific information located in known positions on selected web pages with known layouts."

30. See e.g. the study by Edelman, Luca & Svirsky, *supra* note 8.

31. Tom Slee, *Airbnb Data Collection: City Maps*, online: <http://tomslee.net/airbnb-data>.

32. Tom Slee, *Airbnb Data Collection*, online: <http://tomslee.net/category/airbnb-data>.

33. Tom Slee, *Request Airbnb Data for a City*, online: <http://tomslee.net/request-airbnb-data-for-a-city>.

34. Murray Cox, *About Inside Airbnb*, online: <http://insideairbnb.com/about.html>.
35. Note that the data scraped by civil-society organizations is typically made available to others to use in various ways. For example, the Canadian Centre for Policy Alternatives, a think tank, used scraped data provided by Tom Slee in its research on the impacts of Airbnb in Toronto. See Zohra Jamasi & Trish Hennessy, *Nobody's Business: Airbnb in Toronto* (Ottawa: Canadian Centre for Policy Alternatives, 2016), online: <https://www.policyalternatives.ca/airbnb>.
36. Ian Majoribanks, "Airbnb in Vancouver and its Impacts on Affordable Housing" (1 June 2016) at 5, online: <https://affordablevancouver.files.wordpress.com/2016/07/airbnb-vancouver-report-iain-marjoribanks.pdf>.
37. Karen Sawatzky, *Short-Term Consequences: Investigating the Extent, Nature and Rental Housing Implications of Airbnb Rentals in Vancouver* (M Urb Thesis, Simon Fraser University, 2016) [unpublished], online: <http://summit.sfu.ca/item/16841#310>.
38. Edelman, Luca & Svirsky, *supra* note 8.
39. Majoribanks, *supra* note 36, used interviews with Airbnb hosts as part of his research methodology.
40. Carolyn Said, "The Airbnb Effect" *San Francisco Chronicle* (12 July 2015), online: <http://www.sfchronicle.com/airbnb-impact-san-francisco-2015/#1>. For this study, the newspaper retained two "data extraction companies" to scrape Airbnb data.
41. Jason Clampet, "Airbnb in NYC: The Real Numbers Behind the Sharing Story" *Skift* (13 February 2014), online: <https://skift.com/2014/02/13/airbnb-in-nyc-the-real-numbers-behind-the-sharing-story/>. The author of this study also relied upon data from the data extraction company Connotate Inc.
42. Quite apart from the legalities of web scraping, it does raise interesting issues of journalistic ethics. Nael Shiab, "On the Ethics of Web Scraping and Data Journalism" *J-Source* (22 June 2015), online: <http://www.j-source.ca/article/ethics-web-scraping-and-data-journalism>.
43. *Ibid*. Ethical issues raised by such practices include respect for privacy law. Journalists also debate whether they have a duty to inform the target of the scraping activities, and whether they have an obligation to reveal their code (which can help in understanding their methodology and any flaws it may incorporate).
44. Airdna, *About Airdna*, online: <https://www.airdna.co/about>.
45. Airdna, *Airdna Data Services*, online: <https://www.airdna.co/services/datafeed>.
46. Airdna, *Airdna Data Methodology*, online: <https://www.airdna.co/methodology>.

47. Airbnb, *Terms of Service, supra* note 11, art 14. Note that the TOS also prohibit the registration and/or use of the term Airbnb or any derivative term in "domain names, trade names, trademarks or other source identifiers" (art 14). It is possible that Airdna has entered into a non-public agreement with Airbnb to access and use its data.

48. *Renting Your Place,* online: <http://rentingyourplace.com/>.

49. *Beyond Pricing,* online: <https://beyondpricing.com/>.

50. Beyond Pricing, *FAQ – I have weekly, monthly, and weekend prices on my listing. Can I still use Beyond Pricing?,* online: <https://beyondpricing.com/faq#i-have-weekly,-monthly,-and-weekend-prices-on-my-listing-can-i-still-use-beyond-pricing>.

51. Beyond Pricing, "FAQ—Why Do I Have to Connect My Airbnb Account?," online: <https://beyondpricing.com/faq#why-do-i-have-to-connect-my-airbnb-account>.

52. David Kelso, "Predicting Peaks in Local Demand" (18 May 2014), *Beyond Pricing* (blog), online: <https://blog.beyondpricing.com/predicting-peaks-in-demand>.

53. *Smart Host,* online: <http://smarthost.co.uk/>.

54. *Everbooked,* online: <https://www.everbooked.com/>.

55. *PriceLabs,* online: <https://www.pricelabs.co/>.

56. Host Compliance LLC, *City of Vancouver: Short-Term Rental Market Overview* (San Francisco: Host Compliance LLC, 2016), online: <http://vancouver.ca/files/cov/overview-vancouver-short-term-rental-market.pdf>.

57. See Said, *supra* note 40, and Clampet, *supra* note 41.

58. See e.g. CondoLegal.com, *Airbnb: The Plateau Counter Attack* (17 August 2016), online: <http://en.condolegal.com/syndicate/news/2074-Airbnb:%20%20the%20Plateau%20Counter%20attack>; Jessica Dailey, "Landlord Hires Private Detective Over Illegal Short Term Rental" *Curbed New York* (22 July 2012), online: <http://ny.curbed.com/2013/7/22/10217500/landlord-hires-private-detective-over-illegal-short-term-rental>; Airconcierge.net, *New York's Undercover Apartment Detective* (21 April 2014), online: <http://www.airconcierge.net/blog/2014/4/21/new-yorks-undercover-apartment-detective>.

59. *Building Snitch,* online: <http://www.buildingsnitch.com/>; Adi Gaskell, *New Site Aims to Hunt Down Illegally Sublet Rooms on Airbnb* (9 October 2015), online: The Horizons Tracker <http://adigaskell.org/2015/10/09/new-site-aims-to-hunt-down-illegally-sublet-rooms-on-airbnb/>.

60. The use of robots is specifically contrary to the terms of use of Airbnb's site. See Airbnb, *Terms of Service, supra* note 11, art 14.

61. Nate Cardozo, Kurt Opsahl & Rainey Reitman, *Who Has Your Back? Protecting Your Data from Government Requests: Sharing Economy Edition*

(San Francisco: Electronic Frontier Foundation, 2015), online: <https://www.eff.org/fr/who-has-your-back-2016>.

62. Airbnb, *Airbnb Law Enforcement Transparency Report* (2 September 2016), online: <http://transparency.airbnb.com/>.

63. *Ibid.*

64. See e.g. the City of Vancouver's use of a consulting company to produce a report on the city's short-term rental market: HostCompliance LLC, *supra* note 56.

65. See e.g. Cox & Slee, *supra* note 10.

66. Airbnb, *Terms of Service, supra* note 11, provides in the preamble that: "By accessing or using the Airbnb Platform, you agree to comply with and be bound by these Terms of Service."

67. *Ibid*, art 5.1.

68. Airbnb, *Terms of Service, supra* note 11, art 5.2.

69. *Ibid*, art 5.5.

70. *Ibid.*

71. *Ibid*, art 5.4.

72. *Ibid*, art 5.3.

73. See e.g. *ibid*, art 14.1.

74. For example, article 14.1 of the *Terms of Service, ibid*, provides that users will not "use any robots, spider, crawler, scraper or other automated means or processes to access, collect data or other content from or otherwise interact with the Airbnb Platform for any purpose." In case this provision is not sufficiently explicit, article 14 also requires users to not "use, display, mirror or frame the Airbnb Platform or Collective Content, or any individual element within the Airbnb Platform [...]."

75. *Ibid*, art 14.1.

76. *Ibid*, art 5.3.

77. *Ibid*, art 14.1.

78. *Ibid.*

79. *Ibid*, art 15.5.

80. *Ibid*, art 21. Disputes involving residents of China who use Airbnb are to be resolved by a separate arbitration process, but may also be heard by any court of competent jurisdiction (art 21.2). Residents of all other countries are subject to the non-exclusive jurisdiction of the Irish courts (art 21.3).

81. *Ibid*, art 19.

82. *Ibid*, art 19.5.

83. *Ibid.*

84. *Ibid*, art 21.2.

85. *Ibid*, art 21.3.

86. Although there is no record of legal enforcement, Airbnb does take technological steps to limit scraping. For example, in a comment on his website, Tom Slee notes that: "Airbnb is getting more aggressive about

blocking scrapes." See Tom Slee (16 Aug 2015 at 11:15 am), comment on: Tom Slee, *Airbnb Data Collection: Methodology and Accuracy*, online: <http://tomslee.net/airbnb-data-collection-methodology-and-accuracy>.

87. For example, there is no public record of any cease and desist letters that Airbnb may have sent to scrapers of its data. It may be also that some issues regarding use of the site have been raised in confidential arbitration proceedings under Airbnb's TOS.

88. Kitchin, *supra* note 9 at 152.

89. *Century 21, supra* note 29 at para 92.

90. Teresa Scassa & Michael Deturbide, *Electronic Commerce and Internet Law in Canada*, 2nd ed (Toronto: Wolters Kluwer, 2012) at 19.

91. *Century 21, supra* note 29; *Specht v Netscape*, 150 F Supp (2d) 585 (SDNY 2002), aff'd 306 F (3d) 17 (2nd Cir 2002). In *Cvent v. Eventbrite*, 2010 US Dist Lexis 96354 (ED Va), the court noted that in browse-wrap cases, most courts have found that "the website user must have had actual or constructive knowledge of the site's terms and conditions, and have manifested assent to them."

92. Scassa & Deturbide, *supra* note 90 at 15; *Rudder v Microsoft Corporation* (1999), 106 OTC 381 at paras 16–7, 2 CPR (4th) 474 (Ont SCt).

93. *Century 21, supra* note 29 at para 107.

94. *Supra* note 91.

95. In *Specht, supra* note 91, the fact that it was necessary to scroll to the bottom of the website to find the terms but that a user could download the offered software without scrolling to the bottom of the page meant that there was insufficient notice of the terms.

96. *Dell Computer Corporation v Union des consommateurs*, 2007 SCC 34 at paras 100–01. See also: *Ticketmaster Corp. v Tickets.com, Inc.*, 2003 US Dist Lexis 6483 at para 6 (CD Cal).

97. *Century 21, supra* note 29 at para 119.

98. Scassa & Deturbide, *supra* note 90 at 21. In *Century 21, supra* note 29 at para 77, the court stated: "expectations change as does the sophistication of the user." See also para 107 of the same case.

99. *Century 21, supra* note 29; *Canadian Real Estate Association v Sutton (Quebec) Real Estate Service Inc.*, [2003] JQ No 3606, 2003 CanLII 22519 at para 44 (QCS). In both *Century 21* and *Sutton*, the fact that the defendants also had similar terms of service on their own websites contributed to the courts finding both notice and acceptance.

100. Note, however, that the court in *Century 21, supra* note 29, finds user expectations to be relevant but not determinative.

101. *Century 21, supra* note 29 at para 108. In *Register.com Inc. v Verio, Inc.*, 126 F Supp 238 (Dist Court SDNY 2000), aff'd 356 F (3d) 393 (2nd Cir NY 2004), the court also found a repeat visitor to a database with browse-wrap terms of service had notice due to the frequency of the visits.

102. In *Century 21, supra* note 29 at para 375, the court granted an injunction for the breach of the TOS because of "the difficulty of assessing damages, Zoocasa's past conduct and their apparent view that with the consent of Century 21 brokers they can access the Century 21 Website in violation of the Terms of Use."

103. See e.g. *Century 21, supra* note 29 at para 390.

104. *Ibid* at para 395. Note that in *Century 21, ibid,* in the absence of specific proof of losses and expenses, nominal damages for scraping carried out in breach of the website's TOS were set at $1,000.

105. Examples of the use of cease and desist letters in scraping cases where there is at least some public interest dimension are provided in Teresa Scassa, "Police Service Crime Mapping as Civic Technology: A Critical Assessment" (2016) 5:3 IJEPR 13; Teresa Scassa, "Public Transit Data Through an Intellectual Property Lens: Lessons About Open Data" (2015) 41:5 Fordham Urb LJ 1759.

106. *Copyright Act*, RSC 1985, c C-42, s 5 refers to copyright subsisting in "every *original* literary, dramatic, musical and artistic work" (emphasis added).

107. *Ibid,* ss 3(1), 27.

108. *Ibid,* s 3(1).

109. *Ibid,* s 5.

110. *Ibid,* s 2, definition of "compilation."

111. *Ibid,* s 5(1).

112. David Vaver, *Intellectual Property Law: Copyright, Patents, Trade-Marks,* 2nd ed (Toronto: Irwin Law, 2011) at 100.

113. *CCH Canadian Limited v Law Society of Upper Canada,* 2004 SCC 13 at para 16, [2004] 1 SCR 339 [*CCH Canadian*]. In the United States, the threshold is a "spark" of creativity. See *Feist Publications Inc. v Rural Telephone Service Co.,* 499 US 340 at 348 (1991) [*Feist*].

114. Airbnb, *Terms of Service, supra* note 11, art 5.2.

115. Vaver, *supra* note 112 at 158.

116. *Feist, supra* note 113, quoting from *Miller v Universal City Studios Inc.,* 650 F (2d) 1365 at 1369 (5th Cir 1981). In Canada, it is also the case that facts are in the public domain. See e.g. *CCH Canadian, supra* note 113 at para 22.

117. *Feist, supra* note 113 at 347. In *Nihon Keizai Shimbun, Inc. v Comline Business Data, Inc.,* 166 F (3d) 65 at 70 (2nd Cir 1999), the court stated that facts are "never original to an author."

118. See discussion in Teresa Scassa, "Copyright Reform and Fact-Based Works" in Michael Geist, ed, *From "Radical Extremism" to "Balanced Copyright": Canadian Copyright and the Digital Agenda* (Toronto: Irwin Law, 2010) 571.

119. See e.g. *Castle Rock Entertainment, Inc. v Carol Publishing Group, Inc.*, 150 F (3d) 132 (2nd Cir 1998); *Warner Bros. Entertainment Inc. v RDR Books*, 575 F Supp (2d) 513 (SDNY 2008). See also Justin Hughes, "Created Facts and the Flawed Ontology of Copyright Law" (2007) 83:1 Notre Dame L Rev 43.

120. See e.g. Thomas, *supra* note 28, who considers the issue of whether predictive data might be "authored."

121. 2016 ABQB 230 [*Geophysical*].

122. *Ibid* at para 3.

123. *Robertson v Thomson Corp.*, 2006 SCC 43 at para 37; *Tele-Direct (Publications) Inc. v American Business Information Inc.*, (1996), 74 CPR (3d) 72 (FCTD), aff'd (1997), [1998] 2 FCR 22, 76 CPR (3d) 296 (FCA), leave to appeal to SCC refused, [1998] 1 SCR xv [*Tele-Direct*].

124. *Geophyiscal, supra* note 121; *Tele-Direct, supra* note 123.

125. For example, in *Century 21, supra* note 29 at para 268, the court found that the copying of "basic information" from real estate listings was not copyright infringement, even if copying someone's written description of a property was.

126. *Geophysical, supra* note 121 at 80-1, 83. Note that the court in *Geophysical* did not find it necessary to identify a specific human author; instead, it recognized that with data the processing could be a team effort.

127. Of course, to reflect an original selection of data, Airbnb's data requirements must not be routine, banal, or the industry standard.

128. *Century 21, supra* note 29; *Trader, supra* note 29.

129. The scraping of photographs with different owners is at issue in both *Century 21, supra* note 29; and *Trader, supra* note 29. Of course, it is also possible that the scraping activity extracts data from the photos (for example, the use of facial recognition software to identify persons in photos). In such cases, the analysis might get really complicated. Are photographs artistic works from one perspective, and compilations of fact from another? In *Geophysical, supra* note 121 at para 76, the court found: "I find the seismic sections, i.e. the squiggly or zebra lines, fit within the definition of an artistic work, similar to a map, plan or chart, or a compilation of an artistic work since the product is the result of selection or arrangement of the data, or sound recordings, from the geology of the subsurface." The fact that Justice Eidsvik found that the seismic sections were either artistic works such as maps or charts *or* compilations that resulted from a selection or arrangement of data illustrates how the line between the two can blur.

130. See e.g. Tom Slee's discussion of his methodology for scraping Airbnb data: Tom Slee, *Airbnb Data Collection: Methodology and Accuracy, supra* note 86.

131. *Copyright Act, supra* note 106, ss 29, 29.1, 29.2.

132. *Copyrights*, 17 USC §§101 et seq (2011).

133. *CCH Canadian, supra* note 113 at para 53.

134. *Copyrights, supra* note 132, §107.

135. In the United States, for example, "transformative uses" are more likely to be considered fair use. In *Century 21, supra* note 29 at para 234, the court noted: "What may be transformative, and as a result fair use in the US, may still be copyright infringement in Canada."

136. Note, however, that the Supreme Court of Canada in *SOCAN v Bell Canada*, 2012 SCC 36 at para 21, expressly rejected the idea that it was necessary, for a finding of fair dealing for the purposes of research, to find that the research resulted in a new work.

137. See e.g. *Associated Press v Meltwater U.S. Holdings Inc.*, 931 F Supp (2d) 537 at 551–552 (SDNY 2013) [*Meltwater*]; *Campbell v Acuff Rose* 510 US 569 at 579 (1994) [*Campbell*].

138. *Infinity Broadcast Corp. v Kirkwood*, 150 F (3d) 104 at 108 (2nd Cir 1998) [*Infinity*].

139. See e.g. *CCH Canadian, supra* note 113 at para 54. Similarly, in *Century 21, supra* note 29 at para 222, the court noted that "[w]hen the intended use of copyrighted material is to generate revenue in competition to the copyright holder the use may be less fair." A similar view is found in United States jurisprudence. For example, the United States Supreme Court has observed that "whether the user stands to profit from exploitation of the copyrighted material without paying the customary price" is a key consideration. *Harper & Row Publishers, Inc. v Nation Enterprises*, 471 US 539 at 562 (1985) [*Harper & Row*].

140. *SOCAN v Bell Canada, supra* note 136 at para 36.

141. *Meltwater, supra* note 137; *Blanch v. Koons*, 467 F (3d) 244 at 253 (2nd Cir 2006). In *Century 21, supra* note 29 at para 222, the court stated that "if the purpose produces a value to the public interest that may be more fair."

142. *Meltwater, supra* note 137 at 552.

143. The court noted that "permitting Meltwater to avoid paying licensing fees gives it an unwarranted advantage over its competitors who do pay licensing fees" (*Ibid* at 553.)

144. They do so without providing the customers with the underlying data that they have scraped from Airbnb. This too may be a relevant factor in the fair use analysis. For example, in *Meltwater, supra* note 137, the court set aside consideration of whether the analytics provided by Meltwater were fair use because this was not attacked by the plaintiff. Rather, the plaintiff's objection was to the communication of the scraped news content to Meltwater subscribers.

145. For example, both Tom Slee and Inside Airbnb provide data sets composed of scraped data. It should be noted that in both cases, the data

are scraped according to a particular selection and are "cleaned up" or processed before being made available. There is therefore more to the activity than simple bulk copying.

146. *CCH Canadian, supra* note 113 at para 55.

147. This is referred to in *Century 21, supra* note 29 at para 239, as a "kind of *de facto* standard" that "governs relations between websites and automated processes."

148. See e.g. *Field v Google Inc.*, 412 F Supp (2nd) 1106 (D Nev 2006); *Parker v Yahoo!, Inc.*, 2008 US Dist Lexis 74512 (ED Pa 2008).

149. *Century 21, supra* note 29 at para 252.

150. For example, in *Warman v Fournier*, 2012 FC 803 at para 33, [2012] FCJ No 851, the court found that the taking of excerpts from the plaintiff's work that totalled almost half the length of the work were nonetheless a "very limited" dealing with the work, as the court considered these excerpts to be *qualitatively* insignificant.

151. See e.g. *CCH Canadian, supra* note 113 at para 56; *Century 21, supra* note 29 at para 265.

152. *CCH Canadian, supra* note 113 at para 56.

153. *Campbell, supra* note 137.

154. Although *Warman v Fournier, supra* note 150 is not a case involving a compilation of data, the court nonetheless found that the taking of large portions of a literary work that were predominantly factual in nature was qualitatively not significant.

155. *CCH Canadian, supra* note 113 at para 57.

156. Snell and Care specifically identify big data analytics as a phenomenon that may change how courts approach scraping issues. See Jim Snell & Derek Care, "Use of Online Data in the Big Data Era: Legal Issues Raised by the Use of Web Crawling and Scraping Tools for Analytics Purposes" *Bloomberg Law* (28 August 2013), online: <https://www.bna.com/legal-issues-raised-by-the-use-of-web-crawling-and-scraping-tools-for-analytics-purposes>.

157. *CCH Canadian, supra* note 113 at paras 47, 58. *Century 21, supra* note 29 at para 272.

158. *Meltwater, supra* note 137 at 557; *Infinity, supra* note 138 at 109.

159. *CCH Canadian, supra* note 113 at para 59.

160. *Meltwater, supra* note 137 at 559; *Castle Rock, supra* note 119 at 145; *Harper & Row, supra* note 139 at 566.

161. *CCH Canadian, supra* note 113 at para 70; *American Geophysical Union v Texaco Inc.*, 60 F (3d) 913 at 930–31 (2nd Cir 1994).

162. *Meltwater, supra* note 137 at 560–61; *Campbell, supra* note 137 at 592–93.

163. *Meltwater, supra* note 137.

164. Inside Airbnb, *Disclaimers*, online: <http://insideairbnb.com/about.html#disclaimers>.

165. 2015 CanLII 65885 (ON SCSM) [*Blacklock's*].

166. *Ibid* at para 54. This decision should be treated with caution as it is a Small Claims Court decision and is not binding on other courts. Further, there are reasons to question the correctness of some of the legal conclusions. There is, for example, no basis in the *Copyright Act* to find that legally acquiring a copy of the copied material is necessary for a fair dealing defence. The fact that legal acquisition is an express precondition for the exception for the making of copies for private use in s 80 of the *Copyright Act* suggests that its omission from the fair dealing exceptions is meaningful.

167. *Copyrights, supra* note 132, §1201(a)(1)(A).

168. *Ibid*, §1201(c).

169. 2017 FC 246 [*Nintendo*].

170. *Ibid* at para 73.

171. *Ibid* at para 84.

172. *Ibid* at para 80.

173. *Copyrights, supra* note 132, §1201(c)(1).

174. Note that the networking website LinkedIn has commenced legal action in the United States against opportunistic businesses that scrape its public data (see *LinkedIn v Doe, Complaint*, Case No 5:16-cv-4463 (ND Cal 2016), online: <http://digitalcommons.law.scu.edu/cgi/viewcontent.cgi?article=2261&context=historical>). The suit alleges violations of the *Computer Fraud and Abuse Act*, 18 USC §§ 1030 et seq (1986) and the *Digital Millennium Copyright Act*, 17 USC §§ 1201 et seq (1998) [DMCA]. The DMCA claims are based on the circumvention of technological protection measures to protect the underlying copyright protected materials. In response to actions being taken by LinkedIn, one company, hiQ Labs, has sought a declaratory relief, arguing that its scraping activities are legal. See *hiQ Labs, Inc. v LinkedIn*, Case 3:17-cv-03301-EMC (ND Cal 2017), online: <https://static.reuters.com/resources/media/editorial/20170620/hiqvlinkedin--complaint.pdf>.

175. See e.g. *Blacklock's, supra* note 165.

176. *Ibid*.

177. *Nintendo, supra* note 169 at para 82.

178. *eBay v Bidder's Edge Inc.*, 100 F Supp (2d) 1058 (ND Cal 2000).

179. *Ibid* at 1061.

180. *Meltwater, supra* note 137 at 563. See also *eBay v Bidder's Edge, Inc., supra* note 178 at 1161, cited in *Century 21, supra* note 29 at para 242.

181. Niklas Lundblad, "e-Exclusion and Bot Rights: Legal Aspects of the Robots Exclusion Standard for Public Agencies and Other Public Sector Bodies with Swedish Examples" (2007) 12:8 First Monday, online: <http://firstmonday.org/ojs/index.php/fm/article/view/1974/1849>.

182. *Ibid* at 2.2. This dual function is interesting: one relates to the protection of content from scraping or indexing; the other relates to the protection of the server from being overloaded, as the activities of indexing and scraping can place a burden on server capacity.

183. *Ibid* at 6.3.1.

184. *Ibid.*

185. *Ibid.*

186. *Healthcare Advocates v Harding, Earley, Follmer,* 497 F Supp (2d) 627 at 643 (ED Pa 2007).

187. Lundblad, *supra* note 181, also raises this issue.

188. Monika Isia Jasiewicz, "Copyright Protection in an Opt-Out World: Implied License Doctrine and News Aggregators" (2012) 122 Yale LJ 837 at 844.

189. *Ibid.*

190. See e.g. Teresa Scassa & Alexandra Diebel, "Open or Closed? Open Licensing of Real-Time Public Sector Transit Data" (2016) 8:2 J eDem 1, in which the authors consider a context where some providers of open real-time data and associated APIs place limits on the number of calls that can be made on the server in order to manage the demand on the server.

191. In *Intel Corp. v Hamidi,* 30 Cal (4th) 1342 (2003), the court found trespass to chattels in the repeated sending of unsolicited emails. It stated: "It is undisputed that plaintiff has a possessory interest in its computer systems" (at para 35). Further, the court found that electronic signals were sufficiently tangible to support a finding of trespass. Scraping of data does place a demand on the servers where the data is hosted. In this sense, trespass harm can arise from the consumption of excessive bandwidth in a manner that diminishes the quality or value of the plaintiff's computer systems.

192. *Century 21, supra* note 29 at para 285.

193 See e.g. Snell & Care, *supra* note 156.

194 *eBay Inc. v Bidder's Edge, Inc., supra* note 178.

195 *Ibid* at 1070.

196 Lundblad, *supra* note 181 at 2.4.1.

PART III

THE SPACE OF REGULATION— LOCAL TO GLOBAL

Urban Cowboy E-Capitalism Meets Dysfunctional Municipal Policy-Making: What the Uber Story Tells Us about Canadian Local Governance

Mariana Valverde[1]

I. Introduction

M unicipal officials' struggles to develop workable and fair policies to regulate Airbnb and Uber, in Canada and elsewhere, show that local regulatory systems and, just as important, customary regulatory approaches have been stretched to the breaking point by what I here call "urban cowboy e-capitalism." That e-capitalism poses regulatory difficulties for many domains and levels of government is well known. But this chapter focuses on the conflicts, and the eventual policies to manage those conflicts, that have arisen in Canada as one particularly aggressive, cowboy-like, e-capitalist firm, Uber, suddenly disrupted a regulatory field traditionally governed by cities under their business licensing powers.

Uber is considered by many as a corporate outlier due to its extreme unwillingness to accept regulation or work collaboratively with governments. But as I will show, even if Uber's civic behaviour is unusual, cities' regulatory dilemmas in regard to Uber clearly expose the underlying systemic weaknesses of regulatory approaches that municipalities have long taken for granted. These approaches are not well known or well researched; the fact that the urban is a scale and a jurisdiction with distinct governance traditions and peculiarities, as I have shown in detail elsewhere, is not widely appreciated.[2]

An economist might not want to single out e-corporations occupying a traditionally urban regulatory space from those operating

at other scales. But socio-legal scholarship finds it useful to differentiate companies such as Facebook, which have contributed to the
creation of *new* social and legal spaces, from companies that operate in a venerable jurisdictional space that has plenty of rules and
norms, but is characterized by structural weaknesses: the municipal
regulatory space.[3] And as Eric Tucker's contribution in this volume
shows, commercial/passenger driving has been central to municipal
business regulation for a very long time.

After briefly recounting some highlights of Uber's defiant law-
breaking career, focusing mainly though not exclusively on Canada,
I will then describe a range of regulatory regimes—or ongoing
regulatory efforts that may or may not evolve into settled regimes.
Comparing Toronto, Edmonton, and Ottawa to the situation in British
Columbia and Quebec, we will see that if provinces wholly vacate the
regulatory space, municipalities face grave difficulties in devising
regulatory measures to minimize the risks posed by urban cowboy
e-capitalism. In other words, Uber's story reveals much about the
structural fractures and limitations of local governance.

II. Preliminaries: Defining the Object of Regulation

Much confusion has been generated by the phrase "the sharing
economy." Electronic platforms and applications can indeed enable
peer-to-peer transactions—horizontal transactions previously confined to newspaper want ads and notes posted on local (physical)
bulletin boards. As a recent study by the Canadian Centre for Policy
Alternatives (CCPA) shows, those horizontal, typically one-off
transactions, which have always existed but can now benefit from
electronic tools, do constitute a "sharing economy," one that is not
new but is expanding in size and visibility due to developments in
cyberspace.[4]

Sharing economies, electronically mediated or not, have often
operated on the margins of the law, and local as well as provincial
authorities have long tolerated activities such as informal handyman
work and unlicensed babysitting. Regulators have sometimes tried to
draw a legal line above which an activity ought to be regulated and/
or taxed, for example, by differentiating babysitting from daycare
services, or defining where carpooling ends and where commercial
driving for others begins.[5] It is not always possible or advisable to
try to provide hard-and-fast legal definitions that separate the legal

from the illegal (or from the perhaps larger category of the a-legal or semi-legal)—as practical experience with any number of municipal policy areas, for example, around basement apartments and rooming houses, shows.[6]

The CCPA cogently argues that it is very important to distinguish the sharing economy that has always existed but is now growing in size and efficiency from a rather different economy whose logic is actually the opposite of sharing—what they call "the on-demand service economy."[7] In this realm, corporations, often quite large, capitalize on today's ample pools of precarious labour by developing electronic platforms so that consumers can access on-demand services provided by workers (typically not formal employees) who are linked to customers only through the proprietary business application, not directly, and who usually provide their own capital (for example, an apartment for Airbnb, or a car for Uber). For instance, Kijiji is a platform that enables two people who don't know one another to engage in peer-to-peer exchanges that do not provide regular employment income; and Kijiji does not set prices for goods, nor does it develop a continuing, hierarchical relationship with people who use the application. By contrast, Uber sets prices in advance, and it exercises extensive and continuous surveillance over both clients and workers, sometimes forcing drivers or customers off the platform. Uber transactions are thus not peer-to-peer (as a number of international court decisions, most recently by an advocate general at the Court of Justice of the European Union, have found).[8] The labour and employment dimensions of this type of corporation are explored in this volume by Harry Arthurs and Eric Tucker; here, I focus on regulatory and especially licensing rules, since my expertise lies in local governance and municipal bylaws.

Focusing on what the Uber story can teach us about municipal governance is best done by drawing comparisons with regulatory efforts at other scales. While Uber's law-breaking acts across jurisdictions are similar, as explained in the following section, regulatory responses have been rather different, and here jurisdiction plays a key role. Beginning with a brief look at the Canadian provinces that have taken responsibility for the problems caused by Uber (British Columbia and Quebec)—however unsuccessfully at least as of this writing—we will then take a detour through Europe, where nation-states have played a much larger role than in North America. Only then will we return to Canadian cities.

The conclusion will use the Uber legalization story to reflect on the importance of scale and jurisdiction in regulatory policy work, business licensing in particular. In Canada, where unlike in most of Europe the federal government would not and could not wade into any matters traditionally regarded as local and municipal, for constitutional reasons of long standing, it has become crystal clear, I will argue, that only provinces can develop and enforce proper regulations governing Uber and similar transportation companies. Or, in the alternative, provinces need to support municipal governments that want and need policy muscle. The fact that the policy process appears, in mid-2017, to be stalled in both British Columbia and Quebec is perhaps not a great advertisement for provincial jurisdiction in this area; but, in the long run, only provincial governments have the regulatory capacity, the fiscal tools, and the data-gathering resources that are required. Cities are currently sadly lacking in all three departments.

The on-demand service economy poses regulatory challenges at all levels; but cities are peculiarly unsuited to meeting these challenges, especially when urban spaces are suddenly invaded by very large, deep-pocketed transnational corporations wielding sophisticated databases and applications, and enjoying worldwide name recognition and top-notch public relations expertise.

III. Law-Breaking on a Grand Scale

Showing an odd disregard for legality, the majority of scholarly articles on Uber and similar businesses are written as if Uber had found a juridical *terra nullius* and built a business on it, John Locke–like. Law and economics professors who write about "the platform economy" and "the gig economy" tend to assume the point of view of a convenience-seeking consumer—rather than the standpoint of public policy—and proceed to document, for instance, the relative efficiency of Uber versus taxis, waxing enthusiasm about innovation and suggesting regulations that amount to industry capture.[9]

Neoliberal perspectives, which only consider individual consumer convenience and/or overall market efficiency, excluding not only worker standpoints but also public policy logics, are not limited to law and economics publications. In Toronto, the city staff's own detailed and thoughtful reports on Uber legalization weighed all perspectives carefully; but instead of relying on these, an external consultant report was commissioned and produced for the City of Toronto by the MaRS Solutions Lab. That a chapter in the MaRS report is entitled "Sharing in Transportation"[10] is the first clue about its bias; the second clue is the glowing praise lavished on "today's entrepreneurs."[11] After listing a variety of regulatory challenges posed by commercial platforms providing services without the use of employment contracts, the authors exclaim, "[e]nter entrepreneurs!"[12]—as if entrepreneurs were not responsible for the very problems to which solutions are being sought. Remarkably, despite being commissioned by the City of Toronto, the report re-describes Uber's systematic and defiant law-breaking as "opportunities to reduce unnecessary regulatory burdens."[13]

In keeping with this pro-business bias, Uber's notorious cowboy practices have been frequently attributed to the personality of its founder and, until his resignation in June 2017, CEO, Travis Kalanick—rather than to the nature of corporations in general or even this corporation in particular.

On its part, media coverage—which tends to be produced by the largely white, well-educated, younger Canadians who are the heaviest users of Uber and similar applications (as the CCPA report cited above documents)—has occasionally exposed Uber's exploitation of its drivers and the heavy lobbying of politicians; but Uber's long career of law-breaking is often presented as an understandable response by entrepreneurs frustrated by an antiquated and inflexible system of taxi licensing. By contrast, taxi drivers, who in Canadian cities are overwhelmingly racialized men, often recent immigrants, have had great difficulty obtaining positive and informed media coverage.

Uber has also managed to generate biased Google search results. Typing "Uber + Vancouver" into Google in early 2017, several times over several days, consistently produced a list headed by five or six Uber websites, including one recruiting drivers—even though the company was banned in Vancouver at that time. To find more neutral information, not to mention blog posts by Uber drivers documenting exploitation, one would have had to scroll down very far. This is replicated for other cities, where Google users see, at the top of the search, not only the usual corporate website, but a number of other items that look as if they are not corporate communications but turn out to be (such as explanations as to how to become an Uber driver, not marked as "sponsored content").

Uber likes to attribute its success to innovation, although whether its algorithms and applications are in fact technically innovative (compared to similar tools developed by others) cannot be known, given the corporate blanket of secrecy, as described by Teresa Scassa in her contribution to this volume. In any case, technical wizardry, while probably necessary, is not a sufficient condition of corporate success, as the dot.com crash amply showed. The fact is that, in city after city, Uber actually achieved rapid success (and in fact achieved a near-total monopoly) by entering the market without even a nod to the rule of law, openly ignoring all local business licensing rules and municipal as well as provincial and federal tax law,[14] while simultaneously manipulating both prices and driver incentives to drive out any competitors. Lyft provides competition to Uber in many American cities, but Lyft does not operate in Canada. Hailo was an application developed in Toronto in order to speed up and rationalize taxi services, but it seems to have been driven into the ground by Uber. Illegal businesses do exist in most sectors, often persisting for a long period, but achieving monopoly status while remaining wholly illegal is extremely unusual, if not unique.

How was this open and continued law-breaking possible? Comparing Uber with comparable forms of illegality may be helpful. A lone marginal entrepreneur using his vehicle as an illegal taxi might be able to make a living by illegally picking up passengers at airports and train stations, but he has no access to marketing and advertising resources—so he cannot change public perceptions of what he does, even in jurisdictions where the public may well be unhappy with existing taxi provisions (as has long been the case in the Vancouver area). By contrast, by virtue of size, elaborate marketing, and lobbying on an unprecedented scale, Uber's cowboy e-capitalists worked both social media and mainstream media to develop a fan base that could be quickly mobilized to secure a positive on-line presence. In Toronto, the chief lobbyist for Uber was none other than David Plouffe, who successfully ran Obama's re-election campaign, and City Hall journalists reported upwards of one hundred Uber lobbyists working during 2014–2016.[15]

The unusual volume and sophistication of Uber's lobbying was noted in Toronto and in other cities by City Hall press gallery members and councillors who opposed Uber; but, in Toronto and Edmonton in particular, some councillors, and to an extent Toronto Mayor John Tory, turned a blind eye or even condoned Uber's law-breaking. The day Uber obtained legalization in Toronto, on extremely favourable terms, Mayor John Tory, instead of speaking the language of public policy and regulation, declared that "[t]he public wants to have choices, and they should have choices."[16]

In Toronto and Ottawa, mayors and councillors reported getting hundreds or thousands of emails asking for Uber to be legalized. It is impossible to tell if these were actual emails sent by individual satisfied customers or fake, automated emails—a distinct possibility given Uber's command of algorithms—but local politicians treated the emails as genuine. Uber then used its marketplace profile to push for either no regulation at all or for extremely favourable regulatory terms.

Against all precedent, Uber continued to operate in breach of the law, even when favourable rules were in the offing. In a story with parallels around the country, Calgary Mayor Naheed Nenshi said: "I'm a bit baffled that they [Uber] launched when the insurance product is just a few months away [...]. Our friends at Uber have known for many, many months that they've got an insurance problem [...]."[17]

Meanwhile, in Ottawa, where the city council showed a bit more backbone, an enforcement blitz aimed at fining unlicensed Uber drivers gave rise to an Uber corporate response—cited by CBC *News* as a legitimate comment—to the effect that "[c]ostly [municipal] sting operations, [...] seek to protect a monopoly [...]."[18] This kind of comment underlines the weak legitimacy of traditional city rules about taxis and vehicles for hire. If a booze can had been raided and fined, it is doubtful CBC *News* would have given the bootlegger's views on breaking provincial liquor law such respect.

Similarly in Alberta, when after a long period of law-breaking Uber was, without any penalty, rewarded by municipal legalization, on condition Uber drivers obtain commercial driving licences (at their own expense), the Uber representative complained that legalization would result in "less flexible earning opportunities [...]."[19] Again, if transposed to a provincially regulated domain, such as beer and wine sales, environmental rules, or drivers licences, the claim that businesses are entitled to the "flexible earning opportunities" associated with an absence of regulation would not go very far.

Uber's law-breaking has gone far beyond operating commercial vehicles in breach of taxi rules. A group of disgruntled employees revealed to the *New York Times* that Uber had used its algorithm expertise to build a special software program specifically designed to fool and foil any municipal inspectors (anywhere) that might be trying to identify and fine illegally operating vehicles. This program, known as "Greyball," enabled the corporation to send real-looking but actually false data to the Uber application of anyone suspected of being a municipal employee. The very tools of law enforcement (city workers' smartphones) were thus hacked by the suspect (Uber). Uber's Greyball program was even able to cancel any ride requests made by such users— "essentially Greyballing them as city officials."[20]

Claiming that municipal inspectors were the law breakers, not the law enforcers, because they were "misusing" the application in contravention of the private law unilaterally set out in its terms of service, Uber initially said: "[t]his program [Greyball] denies ride requests to users who are violating our terms of service [... by colluding] with officials on secret 'stings' meant to entrap drivers."[21] More recently, Uber appears to be softening its stance, at least in public; but the corporate belief that a private terms of service agreement trumps public policy rules may remain (especially given parallel developments in private law-making, as Nofar Sheffi's chapter in this volume documents in regard to Airbnb).

Throughout Uber's epic law-breaking campaign, the rhetoric of the "sharing economy" had to do heavy lifting, since illegality this blatant, and at such a scale, is unprecedented. As mentioned at the outset, cities in the advanced capitalist world as well as in the Global South have always had an underground, illegal economy, especially in personal or home services. But the illegal informal economy is generally kept within certain boundaries—as in the established distinction between neighbourhood babysitters and daycare centres—or else it is limited in time—as in the bootlegging that came to an abrupt end with the repeal of Prohibition. To my knowledge, Canadian legal history does not furnish any historical equivalent to the *ex post facto* legalization, without any consequences or sanctions of Uber.

IV. Municipal Jurisdiction in Business Licensing: A Primer

The most important feature of municipal business licensing in Canada, and to a large extent also in the United States and the United Kingdom, is the fact that major corporations are almost completely exempt from local regulation and local taxes. Ontario is perhaps at the extreme in this regard: unlike in the United States and some parts of Canada, Ontario cities cannot levy a hotel room tax, although this will likely change as an indirect result of Toronto's rather feeble efforts to put limits on Airbnb short-term rentals. Similarly, Ontario cities cannot in any way tax or regulate the trucking firms whose heavy-duty vehicles wear out their roads and create congestion. Along the same lines, the bank buildings that dominate the downtown Toronto skyline are only counted and regulated as buildings, not as businesses. The height and density of the buildings need municipal permission, as do any illuminated signs placed on them, and the owners do pay property tax; but the banking business provides no direct revenue and is indeed invisible, legally, to the city.

While Ontario cities may be at the low-end of the spectrum of local legal powers, there is no doubt that, in the present as in the past, cities' business-regulation energies are devoted almost completely to the micromanagement of small entrepreneurs: food-truck operators, shop owners, restaurant owners, street vendors, and last but not least, taxi drivers. And it is taxi drivers—not the taxi plate (medallion) owners or the owners of brokerages and dispatching firms—who bear the brunt of regulation. Until 2017, would-be Toronto taxi drivers had to pay for a seventeen-day training course and had to comply with onerous and expensive rules (for example, frequent vehicle inspections at city garages); and as in other cities, fares were fixed by the city, with no discounts or "surge prices" allowed, and no allowance for changing gasoline prices. About half of Toronto's drivers own their vehicles, but the other half (about 5,000, though the numbers are probably dropping as a result of Uber) have to work for several hours each day to pay rent on the vehicle, as well as gas and insurance, before they can start to make any money. The situation is similar in other cities: it is common for a handful of people, often ex-drivers, to accumulate a few taxi plates, and live as rentiers on the proceeds of renting the plates to working drivers.[22]

Limiting the number of taxi plates has long been the centerpiece of municipal taxi licensing systems, in Toronto as in other North American cities. Until the arrival of Uber, the cap on plates meant that the market value of plates could be as high as several hundred thousand dollars—though some cities, including Toronto, were making efforts to encourage owner-driven taxis and discourage rentier taxi capitalism.[23] At other scales, businesses are certainly regulated in a variety of ways (zoning restrictions and building codes, for example), but putting caps on numbers is not a common technique in contemporary economic policy.

The cap on plate numbers suggests that municipal taxi licensing may have more in common with ancient guild regulations, designed to prevent too many labourers and apprentices from becoming masters and business owners, than with contemporary capitalism. While the arrival of Uber made taxi drivers around the country, and indeed the world, suddenly rise to defend municipal licensing against cowboy challenges, the irony is that, prior to Uber, taxi drivers were the most severe critics of the system—one that had long provided them with lower than minimum wage incomes and subjected them to a great deal of surveillance and discipline from municipal inspectors.

To put the Uber question in its proper legal context, it needs to be noted that while taxi licensing may well be the most extreme example of municipal micromanagement of micro-entrepreneurs, it is not completely unique. Food-truck operators and hot-dog vendors have been micromanaged, often right out of business, by the same city officials and in the same manner. In general, one can say that municipal business licensing—which has deep historical roots in the detailed "police regulations" that in pre-capitalist cities sought to control access to trades and limit market exchanges—has never undergone a modernist overhaul.[24] Today, in many sectors and in many cities, consumer demand for variety and for new types of goods and services goes unmet (as Toronto's minuscule food-truck economy demonstrates); licensing is often seen as a privilege, not a right; onerous conditions are attached to the licence; and municipal inspectors often enforce old-fashioned and not particularly rational rules just because they are there, not because any harm is being done.

In addition, municipal licensing, as a branch of local government, does not draw the well-educated civil servants who populate departments such as economic development, planning, public health, and transit. And at the political level, licensing ranks pretty low on council's hierarchy. Even in Canada's largest city, business licensing issues have long been neglected by politicians, with policy often monopolized by a single councillor with deep connections to a particular group of small-time owner/capitalists. Rational risk management and flexible regulation have transformed other areas of municipal jurisdiction (such as public health and, in some instances, planning), but remain largely foreign to municipal licensing and standards departments.

In sum, then: while municipal business licensing is undoubtedly at the pre-modern extreme of the spectrum of modes of governing urban risks, the logics by which such regulations have long functioned are unlikely to be easily reformed, since they are deeply rooted in a long history of local business micromanagement—the governing tradition known in the United States as "the police power of the state."[25] And while other areas of municipal governance have become more evidence-based and more attuned to governing risks rather than enforcing coercive rules, business licensing generally remains unmodernized.

V. Provincial Interventions: British Columbia and Quebec

The Lower Mainland, British Columbia's most urbanized area, is not politically organized in a way that would support sensible municipal regulation of commercial driving: the City of Vancouver is a small legal island in a sea of suburban municipalities. Since the 2010 Vancouver Olympics, a few light rail lines—built with federal and provincial funds—have revolutionized life for some localities; but reliance on private cars remains a key feature of life in the Lower Mainland. The conditions were thus ripe for Uber to set up shop there.

Initially, around 2012, the Vancouver City Council banned Uber,[26] on the grounds that it was in breach of city taxi rules. Uber then mounted an expensive public relations campaign. The campaign did not target the Vancouver City Council alone, however, since Uber managers knew that a very large market existed outside city limits, in the vast areas not well served by public transit. Very soon this campaign became part of the larger political battle pitting the then ruling Liberals (more akin to Conservatives elsewhere in Canada) against the opposition social democratic party (the NDP). Transposing the fight about Uber regulation to the provincial arena—in contrast to Ontario, where the province has studiously avoided entering the fray—and doing so in the lead-up to an election campaign, completely changed the stakes.

Aware of the jurisdictional specificity of Canadian provincial governments, Uber was able to hire, as their chief British Columbia lobbyist, well-known Canadian Conservative public relations strategist Dimitri Pantazopoulos, who had previously worked for none other than British Columbia Liberal Premier Christy Clark.[27]

Choosing to make Uber legalization into an election issue, provincial Transport Minister Peter Fassbender took the problem away from municipalities like Vancouver and used the province's power to override and trump local bylaws and issue a proposed set of rules.[28] The rules imposed a few requirements—but as in the rest of Canada, these requirements mainly fall on Uber drivers, not on the company. It is drivers who (if the rules continue to be implemented) will need to acquire a commercial driving licence, pass a safe driving record check, pay for a criminal record check, and have their vehicles regularly inspected. If these or similar rules prevail in British Columbia's politically uncertain times, Uber drivers would thus have to incur new costs—but they would not have to turn over a few cents per ride to the city, as is the case in many other cities.

In the Lower Mainland, the number of taxi licences had long been capped despite surging demand—a manoeuvre that taxi drivers felt was designed precisely to create a market for Uber even while it remained banned. During the spring 2017 election campaign, the Liberals promised to "[address] the provincial taxi shortage,"[29] intimating that Uber was the solution.

The NDP has been siding with licensed taxi drivers—mainly racialized men, South Asian for the most part, living in the key suburban ridings around Vancouver. An NDP government, if it succeeds in holding on to provincial power in the wake of a June 2017 election that created no clear majority but did bring the Liberals down (at least temporarily), will likely support existing taxi drivers. However, Uber may ultimately be legalized as well—though there is little doubt it would be subject to regulation, and probably regulations that are more driver-friendly rather than corporate-friendly, and that impose some kind of fee on Uber rides.

Whatever happens in British Columbia, it is important to recall, more generally, that in the Canadian system provinces can always take back any of the powers that are traditionally delegated to municipalities, including business licensing and taxi licensing. Provincial powers have also been used in Quebec, and so it is to this province we now turn.

In Quebec, Uber first appeared as a market player posing regulatory problems in the City of Montreal. But as was the case in British Columbia, the issue was quickly shifted to the scale of the province, in regard to policy, though municipalities remained in control of enforcement—with Montreal setting a Canadian precedent by impounding hundreds of Uber cars. Uber's public relations talent managed to find a silver lining in this rather dire situation. However, as management chose to pay the fees required to release the cars, the corporation then disseminated numerous stories featuring drivers expressing deep gratitude for having been "rescued" by the company. Clearly, Uber had concluded that continuing to provide illegal services was important enough, in terms of sustaining and increasing its market, to justify spending corporate money paying the drivers' fines. Indeed, at the time, Uber sent messages to all the people who had signed up to drive for it, stating that "[f]or the moment, you can continue driving as an Uber Quebec partner-driver as usual"[30]—even though a provincial law had specifically banned services like Uber.

Eventually Quebec developed province-wide rules to legalize Uber, though only by way of a one-year pilot project. Quebec's regulatory traditions, which are more social democratic and pro-labour than is the case in other Canadian provinces, were clearly visible in the proposed new rules. Quebec Uber drivers will need to acquire a commercial driving licence; Uber's surge pricing is controlled in emergency situations; and fees amounting to about a dollar per ride have to be paid, with the proceeds being used to improve the taxi industry. In general, Uber has not been forced to provide accessible vehicles for disabled passengers, unlike taxi companies, so perhaps the funds will be used to transform or buy accessible taxis. Other Canadian cities have also imposed a per-ride fee, but this ranges between six to thirty cents, not around one dollar as in Quebec. However, a key point is that while more onerous than other regimes, what the Quebec pilot project has in common with the rules developed municipally and in British Columbia is that the new regulations are mainly burdens on drivers and would-be drivers—not on the highly profitable company.

However, the regulatory process in Quebec is unsettled in two ways. First, as already mentioned, Quebec's regulatory scheme was not enacted as permanent rules, as is the case elsewhere, but rather as a pilot project valid only for a year and subject to review. Second, legalizing Uber went hand in hand (as was the case in Toronto, for example) with loosening the rules previously governing taxi drivers and taxi driver licences. But in June 2017, the taxi industry walked out of the ongoing talks to "modernize" the taxi licensing rules. It would be logical to foresee that this boycott of the policy process by the taxi industry will have an effect on the political scene when the one-year Uber pilot project concludes, but what effect exactly, one cannot say.

Whatever happens, what is clear from events thus far, and from what Canadian political scientists have long documented about provincial jurisdiction generally, is that provinces have more than sufficient legal powers and enforcement tools to exercise considerable pressure on cowboy capitalism in the service sector, whether they choose to use these powers or not.

This means, in my view, that provincial rather than municipal governments are the appropriate site for devising regulations for sectors that present new technical or economic features and that, perhaps most importantly, feature extremely powerful foreign corporations, transnational behemoths that have little or no precedent in the long history of municipal business regulation. It is not a coincidence that in the United States the best example of Uber regulations that are not unfair to taxi drivers is found not in a municipality but in the state of California, where the state-wide utilities commission has taken responsibility for regulating transportation network companies, demanding not only vehicle inspections and driver training but also commercial insurance.[31] The brief discussion of Ottawa, Edmonton, and Toronto that concludes the chapter will provide further evidence for this claim about the right scale/jurisdiction for transnational e-capitalism, especially its cowboy variety. But first we will take a brief detour through legal proceedings that could have a major impact on regulatory strategies across many borders—future policies as well as existing ones.

VI. Defining the Nature of Uber

An appeal by Uber to the European Court of Justice, challenging a Barcelona business tribunal's decision to the effect that Uber was illegally breaching municipal taxi rules, may have a far-reaching impact. The reason is that this case, instead of being fought on administrative law technicalities, as one might have expected given the forum and the type of law, revolves around a key substantive question. Is Uber, as it claims, merely a platform, an electronic entity that should be allowed to innovate and spread across borders with the help of the European Union's information technology policy? Or is Uber a transportation company, whose real business is rides provided on a commercial basis?[32]

European Union member states are divided. The Netherlands is siding with Uber—since it is the jurisdiction where Uber has its base for all non-American business (though few Canadian customers appear to have noticed that the terms and conditions they must accept include having to go to Dutch courts if they want to sue Uber). Ireland is on Uber's side as well, not surprisingly since it is the European home of Google, Twitter, Facebook, and Airbnb. However, the Spanish government (which generally opposes anything that the City of Barcelona does, for ideological reasons) weighed in to support the regulated taxi industry against Uber—as did several other European countries including Italy, France, Belgium, and Denmark. In France, the situation is compounded by the fact that Uber drivers have organized against the company to demand better pay and working hours that more closely resemble the French standard of thirty-five hours per week.

On May 11, 2017, EU Advocate General Maciej Szpunar released a preliminary opinion that represents a major defeat for Uber's claim to be an electronic platform and not a transportation company.[33] The fact that Uber sets the price for each ride, unlike how prices are set in e-Bay and similar platforms, was highlighted, as was the total dependence of the drivers on the company—a point that may have impact on employment law forums. The key point, however, was that the advocate general concluded that Uber provides transportation services; using privately owned cars to do so rather than its own fleets does not exclude it from the realm of transportation.

Advocate general preliminary decisions are usually confirmed by the actual court; if this is indeed the case, the court decision will likely have an impact even in jurisdictions outside the European Union. As seen earlier in relation to Quebec and British Columbia, the Uber issue has become highly politicized in most, if not all, of the Canadian jurisdictions that are involved, as well as in other countries. If an authoritative judicial body such as the European Court of Justice confirms the advocate general's conclusion that Uber is in fact mainly a transportation company (because customers pay for rides, not for the application, among other reasons), this will be influential, especially among lawyers. At the level of popular opinion rather than law, the decision may perhaps help to undermine the prestige of the hi-tech, information-society, "innovation" discourse that Uber has so successfully mobilized to justify its blatant law-breaking. And it is the theme of law-breaking that takes us into the final section of this chapter, covering the situation in three major Canadian cities.

VII. Regulatory Capture at the Municipal Level

As mentioned above, Vancouver and Montreal have seen municipal authorities using strong measures against Uber, from prohibition to impounding vehicles to large fines; but in both cities the regulatory lead has shifted to their respective provincial governments. The major cities that have been left on their own to address the Uber challenge are Ottawa, Toronto, and Edmonton.

Uber started operating illegally in both Edmonton and Calgary between 2012 and 2013. Taking the initial regulatory lead—at that time no Canadian jurisdiction had a policy on Uber—a Calgary City report warned that drivers who regularly drive others for money need to get commercial insurance and should also have a commercial driver's licence. Since Uber drivers had neither, the City of Calgary obtained a court injunction to stop Uber drivers from working. Incidentally, the City of Toronto also tried to get an injunction, in the early days, but the Ontario court refused.[34] Edmonton seems to have followed Calgary's lead, with commercial driver's licences and proper insurance being made conditions for granting a special non-taxi licence to Uber. The insurance industry, however, in Alberta as in Ontario, took its time devising an appropriate product, and in the meantime Uber drivers continued to ply their trade in both main Albertan cities.

Edmonton beat other Canadian cities in devising some minimum regulations—rules falling mainly on drivers.[35] A key point here is that, as in other Canadian cities, the Edmonton City Council was officially designing and passing a bylaw governing vehicles for hire in general—though in fact Uber had a monopoly, as far as the news coverage reveals. Throughout, it was Uber spokespeople and lobbyists who were pushing the city and making claims such as the opinion that commercial insurance for their drivers was "unrealistic," as if the taxi industry had not managed to obtain and pay for such insurance. Whether similar but less cowboy-like corporations, such as Lyft or Hailo, would have made less outrageous comments is of course impossible to tell. But the important point here is that in all Canadian cities, the regulatory process legalizing application-enabled for-hire vehicles took the unusual form of disputes between the city and a single company, not between the city and an industry or even an oligopoly.[36]

Be that as it may, the corporation is now obliged to pay a $50,000 annual fee to the city, plus $20,000 to help provide accessible transportation (far less, of course, than it would cost them to comply with the rules about accessible vehicles that have long been imposed on the taxi industry throughout Canada). And the city gets six cents per trip by way of a fee. The rest of the rules fall on drivers: they have to obtain commercial driving licences, pay for criminal record checks, and prove that their vehicles have had annual inspections. Uber customers have to pay a minimum of $3.25, like taxi passengers, but Uber can charge whatever it wants over that minimum. In general, Uber gives a prospective customer a non-negotiable price as they book the ride, and the algorithm by which the price is generated is not shared with drivers. Whether per-ride fees being charged by cities will come out of the drivers' share or the corporation's is not specified in the bylaws; one suspects, however, that since Uber has continuously moved to increase its profit margin, by upping their share of the fare from 20 per cent to 25 per cent or 29 per cent, while greatly lowering fares in less competitive markets such as Detroit, it will be drivers who end up paying the city fee.

Foreshadowing what would happen later elsewhere, as the Edmonton City Council moved to legalize "transportation network companies" as a separate, non-taxi category, it simultaneously lowered the regulatory requirements that had long governed the taxi industry. All taxi driver training was eliminated and English proficiency and defensive-driving course requirements were also removed. And Edmonton taxi drivers can now work for less money than the standard fare because brokerages (not individual drivers) are allowed to offer discounts. The harmonization is only in the downward direction, however: neither taxi owners nor drivers can make up for lost revenue during busy times by charging the "surge prices" for which Uber is notorious.

The Alberta insurance uncertainties continued (and as seen above, Uber, in Edmonton as elsewhere, was not interested in either proactively paying for commercial insurance for their drivers or asking drivers to obtain proper insurance themselves). The insurance issue meant that Uber was not operating legally even after the new licensing rules were passed by the city council—thus, Edmonton issued 159 tickets to Uber drivers during a six-month period in 2016.

Eventually a commercial driving insurance product for Uber drivers was developed, and legality ensued. But legalization took place on terms highly favourable to the Uber corporation, as just described. Taxi drivers, for their part, are no longer trained, which saves them time and money but has problematic consequences for the public. And the taxi brokerages were "freed" to race Uber drivers to the bottom during non-peak times, by discounting fares when demand is low.

The Toronto City Council followed a similar approach a short time later, in the wake of extremely heated anti-Uber protests by taxi drivers, similar to those in Edmonton.[37] To make a long and tortuous story short,[38] the rules eventually passed by council in May 2016 are as follows:

- Uber cars' basic (minimum) fare was raised from $2.50 to $3.25.
- Uber drivers—unlike in Alberta—need only an ordinary, non-commercial driver's licence, although both drivers and corporations have to obtain a permit from the city.
- Uber drivers have to pay for criminal record checks.
- Each Uber driver must pay for commercial insurance coverage up to $2 million. The company, in comparison, needs only $5 million in insurance coverage.
- The company is to pay the city an application fee of $20,000 (for a business claiming 45,000 rides per year) as well as an annual fee of $15 per driver and 30 cents per ride.

No limits are imposed by the city either on the number of Uber cars or on the prices charged.

As if these conditions did not already presage financial disaster for taxi drivers, not to mention continuing exploitation for Uber's own drivers, who cannot increase their fares to compensate for new costs such as commercial insurance, the Toronto City Council followed Edmonton's lead in rolling major changes in taxi licensing rules into the Uber policy process. The changes affecting taxis are as follows:

- Taxi brokerages (not individual drivers) can offer prices that differ from the standard fare if rides are booked through an application—although one of the largest Toronto taxi brokerages, Beck, has already said they will not attempt surge pricing (no doubt to maintain some semblance of competitive advantage).

- The seventeen-day compulsory training for taxi drivers is eliminated; so are the requirements of a CPR course and knowing English.
- Application and licence fees for accessible taxicabs are to be waived (a change whose financial implications worried city staff, but not council)—with the taxi industry being still compelled to offer accessible vehicles, while Uber is not so obliged.
- The decades-old policy by which the city had fostered owner-driven cars and capped the number of "standard" plates (which allow plate owners to collect rent from drivers) was reversed, eliminating the owner-driven "ambassador" taxi licence category altogether.
- Taxis continue to be subject to semi-annual city vehicle inspections, whereas Uber cars can obtain certification of inspection in any garage, and only once a year.
- Taxis can now stay on the road longer, with maximum vehicle age raised from five to seven years.

Toronto city councillor Gord Perks summarized the city's policy change as follows: "[y]es, there's a more level playing field between the millionaires [taxi plate owners] and the billionaires [Uber], but for the consumer, the level playing field goes down. The drivers lose, the public lose, the billionaires and the millionaires win."[39]

Finally, the City of Ottawa, which had engaged in aggressive bylaw enforcement in the early days of Uber, eventually passed a legalization bylaw that is very similar to the Edmonton and Toronto ones just discussed.[40] A telling detail is that while in Montreal Uber has to pay ninety cents, roughly, to the city per ride, in Ottawa the per-ride fee is less than eleven cents.

And as in the other cities, Ottawa taxi companies, while unsuccessful in their demand that Uber be subject to the same financial and regulatory rules applying to them, obtained some loosening of the rules, including greatly lowered prices for both driver and taxi plate yearly licence fees. Ottawa's taxi industry is a near monopoly, which no doubt affected the policy process; in Toronto, by contrast, Uber operates as a *de facto* monopoly, but the taxi industry is not unified, with several large brokerages operating alongside a few thousand individual operators.

Municipal politicians and staff members who have negative views either about the on-demand service economy in general or about Uber in particular may at some point attempt to change the rules implemented during 2016 in cities including Edmonton, Toronto, and Ottawa, so that they are not such blatant examples of regulatory capture. But given the "unmodernized" state of municipal business licensing in general,[41] mentioned above, what may be a much better option is to question whether trying to incorporate Uber and similar corporate behemoths into the straitjacket of existing rules for municipal business licensing is the best approach. Shifting responsibility for this new type of business regulation to a level of government that has both more legal powers and more research and policy capacity, namely provinces (or even nation-states, as in the European story briefly covered above), is more likely to provide real solutions. The issue of scale and jurisdiction in regulatory work brings us to the conclusions.

VIII. Conclusion: Scale and Jurisdiction in Business Regulation

A comprehensive review of policy options that would not prohibit the platform-enabled "on demand service economy" but would seriously regulate it, authored by the Ontario transit authority, Metrolinx, helpfully points out that municipalities have long had licensing responsibilities in regard to many types of business, but have been unable—both for legal reasons, for organizational behaviour reasons, and for capacity reasons—to engage in proactive, evidence-based policy planning. The report's careful attention to the difference between the traditional, backward-looking licensing of local businesses, on the one hand, and evidence-based policy covering potential future events on the other hand, notes that while the City of Toronto will now get data from Uber about Uber cars, "the data will be used for licensing purposes; it will not provide the information needed to manage an efficient urban mobility system."[42] Carefully worded to avoid offending municipal politicians, this remark goes to the heart of the issue. A less diplomatic way of putting the problem would be to note that licensing hot-dog carts and street vendors and taxis has not provided municipalities with the kind of collective experience that would allow them to now begin regulating transnational giants that operate without brick-and-mortar store fronts and have top tech experts and top public relations experts, paid help that municipal corporations could only dream about.

One original suggestion made in the Metrolinx report is worth mentioning, because instead of merely complaining about city governance habits, it turns the tables and points out that Uber would be most useful where it does not operate, that is, in outlying areas that are close to cities but are not well served either by transit or by taxis. The report suggests that companies such as Uber should be encouraged to start operating not in downtown areas already well served by public transit as well as taxis but rather in low-density and semi-rural areas, where people who do not drive or do not have cars have severe mobility limitations.[43]

But of course, only a provincial government could use its powers to demand, perhaps as a condition of operating in certain preferred markets, that companies also provide service elsewhere—as is routinely done through utilities regulation, which is mainly provincial in Canada and is state-based in the United States. Indeed, the semi-rural municipality of Innisfil, north of Toronto, has apparently already approached Uber, offering an annual subsidy for a certain minimum level of service that would cost the municipality far less than operating a bus service, but would meet citizens' needs.[44] It is unlikely that given current law, Canadian provinces could redefine Uber (and any future competitors that might arise) as what United States law calls "common carriers," a classification that would subject them to utilities regulations, including mandatory coverage of a whole geographic area. But some provincial policy tools could no doubt be brought to bear, if there was political will, especially in Ontario and Alberta, to stop leaving city councils and city staffs to fend for themselves, as is now being done with Airbnb as well as Uber.

Provincial governments are of course highly politicized too, and do not always proceed on the basis of evidence. But recent history shows that strong measures to protect farm land, minimize sprawl, and ensure "greenbelts" can only come from the province, for political, legal, and capacity reasons. In general, provinces have not hesitated to seize jurisdiction in regard to urban planning from municipalities, through a variety of measures. Agricultural land cannot be protected by municipalities competing with one another for development projects and new housing; only by the province. And so too, if the issue of taxi and taxi-like transportation were rescaled at the level of the province, perhaps more creative and fairer policies might evolve.

The policy process is as of this writing stalled in both Quebec and British Columbia, for different reasons; but these two provinces have taken some responsibility for governance in regard to Uber, and so far these provinces have not seen the blatant regulatory capture that Uber legalization has wrought in Edmonton and Toronto. Meanwhile, Ontario's Metrolinx report reminds us that the people who could really use a service like Uber may be those who have thus far been neglected by the corporation, as well as by politicians, because they do not live within the limits of the big cities that are Uber's profit centres. Therefore, this is an excellent time for Canadians, in city and provincial governments and outside of them, to begin thinking seriously about which types of businesses, and which types of risk, should still be managed municipally as opposed to provincially.

Notes

1. Professor, Centre for Criminology and Sociolegal Studies, University of Toronto.
2. See Mariana Valverde, "Police Science, British Style: Pub Licensing and Knowledges of Urban Disorder" (2003) 32:2 Economy & Society 234 [Valverde, "Police Science"]; Mariana Valverde, "Authorizing the Production of Urban Moral Order: Appellate Courts and Their Knowledge Games" (2005) 39:2 Law & Soc'y Rev 419; Mariana Valverde, "Jurisdiction and Scale: Legal 'Technicalities' as Resources for Theory" (2009) 18:2 Soc & Leg Stud 139.
3. Elsewhere I have developed a series of arguments about the specificity of urban governance, both as a jurisdiction and as a particular bundle of governing habits. See *ibid*; Mariana Valverde, "Seeing Like a City: The Dialectic of Modern and Premodern Ways of Seeing in Urban Governance" (2011) 45:2 Law & Soc'y Rev 277 [Valverde, "Seeing Like a City"]; Mariana Valverde, *Everyday Law on the Street: City Governance in an Age of Diversity* (Chicago: University of Chicago Press, 2012) [Valverde, *Everyday Law on the Street*].
4. See Sheila Block & Trish Hennessy, "'Sharing Economy' or On-Demand Service Economy? A Survey of Workers and Consumers in the Greater

Toronto Area" (2017) CCPA 1, online: <http://metcalffoundation.com/ wp-content/uploads/2017/04/CCPA-ON-sharing-economy-in-the-GTA. pdf>.

5. See WSP Group & Metrolinx, "New Mobility Background Paper: Technical Paper 4 to Support the Discussion Paper for the *Next Regional Transportation Plan*" (July 2016), online: Metrolinx <http://www.metrolinx.com/en/regionalplanning/rtp/technical/04_New_Mobility_ Report_EN.pdf>.

6. See Valverde, *Everyday Law on the Street, supra* note 3 ch 5.

7. Block & Hennessy, *supra* note 4 at 1.

8. Court of Justice of the European Union, Press Release, 50/17, "According to Advocate General Szpunar, the Uber Electronic Platform, Whilst Innovative, Falls Within the Field of Transport: Uber Can Thus Be Required to Obtain the Necessary Licences and Authorisations Under National Law" (11 May 2017), online: CVRIA <https://curia.europa.eu/ jcms/upload/docs/application/pdf/2017-05/cp170050en.pdf>.

9. See Judd Cramer & Alan B Krueger, "Disruptive Change in the Taxi Business: The Case of Uber" (2016) National Bureau of Economic Research Working Paper No 22083; Hannah A Posen, "Ridesharing in the Sharing Economy: Should Regulators Impose Über Regulations on Uber?" (2015) 101:1 Iowa L Rev 405; A Alexander DeMasi, "Uber: Europe's Backseat Driver for the Sharing Economy" (2016) 7:1 Creighton Int'l & Comp LJ 73.

10. Joeri van den Steenhoven et al, "Shifting Perspectives: Redesigning Regulation for the Sharing Economy" (2016) MaRS Solutions Lab Sharing Economy Public Design Report, online: <https://www.marsdd. com/wp-content/uploads/2016/04/MSL-Sharing-Economy-Public-Design-Report.pdf>.

11. *Ibid* at 59.

12. *Ibid*.

13. *Ibid* at 64.

14. During 2017 some provinces began to work on methods to charge Uber the usual provincial sales tax, while the federal spring 2017 budget promised that federal sales tax would also be charged (though it is not clear how this would work, in practice).

15. I have put in a request to Toronto's city clerk to see the lobbyist registry for the relevant period, in order to identify not only the number of Uber lobbyists but also their identities; but at the time of writing I had not yet obtained this information. Extensive local press coverage, too extensive to cite in detail, did report both David Plouffe's presence in Toronto and the fact that about one hundred lobbyists were operating (an unprecedented number not seen even in regard to large development projects, where a handful of lobbyists would be a normal number).

16. Oliver Moore, "UberX Will Be Allowed to Operate Legally in Toronto, City Council Decides," *The Globe and Mail* (3 May 2016), online: <http://www.theglobeandmail.com/news/toronto/divided-toronto-council-seeks-middle-ground-as-uber-debate-begins/article29835110>.

17. Trevor Scott Howell, "Council Opens Door for Uber; Company Will Continue to Defy Bylaw While Changes in Works." *Calgary Herald* (17 November 2015), online: <http://calgaryherald.com/news/local-news/calgary-approves-regulatory-framework-that-opens-the-door-for-uber>.

18. "Uber Says It's Standing by Drivers after 2 of Them Fined by City," *CBC News* (6 October 2014), online: <http://www.cbc.ca/news/canada/ottawa/uber-says-it-s-standing-by-drivers-after-2-of-them-fined-by-city-1.2788605>.

19. "Uber Back in Business in Edmonton," *CBC News* (30 June 2016), online <http://www.cbc.ca/news/canada/edmonton/uber-back-in-business-in-edmonton-1.3659878>.

20. Mike Isaac, "How Uber Deceives the Authorities Worldwide," *The New York Times* (3 March 2017), online: <https://www.nytimes.com/2017/03/03/technology/uber-greyball-program-evade-authorities.html>.

21. *Ibid.*

22. See Valverde, *Everyday Law on the Street, supra* note 3 ch 7.

23. See the chapter by Eric Tucker in this volume, "Uber, and the Unmaking and Remaking of Taxi Capitalisms: Technology, Law and Resistance in Historical Perspective" [ed.].

24. See Valverde, "Police Science," *supra* note 2.

25. For more on the persistence of pre-modern forms of knowledge and of regulation in contemporary cities, see Valverde, "Seeing Like a City." *supra* note 3.

26. In 2014, the Vancouver City Council imposed a temporary moratorium on new taxi licenses and requested that staff study the impact of new ride-sharing services, such as Uber, on industry standards. See Vancouver, Standing Committee of Council on Planning, Transportation and Environment, "Report to Council," (Vancouver: City Council, 1 October 2014), online: <http://council.vancouver.ca/20141001/documents/ptec20141001min.pdf>.

27. Joanne Lee-Young & Rob Shaw, "Uber Vancouver: B.C. Government Announces Support for Ride-Hailing Services," *Vancouver Sun* (7 March 2017), online: <http://vancouversun.com/news/local-news/uber-vancouver-bc-government-announces-support-for-ride-sharing>.

28. See *ibid*; Rhianna Schmunk, "Uber is Coming to B.C., Province Announces," *CBC News* (7 March 2017), online: <www.cbc.ca/news/canada/british-columbia/bc-taxi-1.4013315>. Note that these new rules are proposals only, and their fate is uncertain given that the provincial

Liberals failed to win a majority government in the spring 2017 election. Presently, any vehicle for hire in British Columbia must be licensed by the province and any ride-hailing service must be approved by the provincial Passenger Transportation Board pursuant to the *Passenger Transportation Act*, SBC 2004, c 39. Uber has yet to be approved by the Passenger Transportation Board.

29. Schmunk, *supra* note 28.

30. Jonathan Montpetit, "Uber Paying Its Drivers to Flout Quebec Law," *CBC News* (4 October 2016), online: <www.cbc.ca/news/canada/montreal/uber-paying-its-drivers-to-flout-quebec-law-1.3789784>.

31. The state of Maryland has also subjected Uber to rules governing vehicles for hire, through its powers to regulate "common carriers"; but in this as in other fields, it is California whose regulations will have an impact well beyond its borders.

32. See Leonid Bershidsky, "EU Court Will Resolve Uber's Identity Crisis," *Bloomberg View* (30 November 2016), online: <https://www.bloomberg.com/view/articles/2016-11-30/taxi-or-tech-eu-court-will-rule-on-uber-s-identity>. American court decisions, in Maryland and elsewhere, classifying Uber as a "common carrier" have some similarities with this opinion; but the European Union advocate general more directly and forcefully addresses Uber's claim that it is an e-company or pure technology corporation by using the European Union's divide between information and technology services—governed by the European Union free-trade, no-border rules—from taxi and similar transportation services, which are firmly left where they have always been, within local (usually municipal) jurisdiction.

33. Court of Justice of the European Union, *supra* note 8.

34. *Toronto (City of) v Uber Canada Inc*, 2015 ONSC 3572.

35. City of Edmonton, by-law No 17400, *Vehicle for Hire Bylaw* (27 June 2017, in force as of 1 March 2016).

36. See Elise Stolte & Gordon Kent, "Uber: The Ins and Outs of What Edmonton City Council Passed for It and the Taxi Industry," *Edmonton Journal* (28 January 2016), online: <http://edmontonjournal.com/news/local-news/the-ins-and-outs-of-what-council-passed-for-uber-and-the-taxi-industry>.

37. See City of Toronto, by-law No 546, *Licensing of Vehicles-for-Hire* (7 October 2016, in force as of 15 July 2016).

38. Toronto, Municipal Licensing and Standards, *Staff Report: A New Vehicle-for-Hire Bylaw to Regulate Toronto's Ground Transportation Industry*, Reference No P:\2016\Cluster B\MLS\LS16003 (Toronto: Municipal Licensing and Standards, 31 March 2016), online: <http://www.toronto.ca/legdocs/mmis/2016/ls/bgrd/backgroundfile-91911.pdf>.

39. Moore, *supra* note 16.

40. City of Ottawa, by-law No 2016-272, *Vehicle for Hire* (30 September 2016).

41. See *supra* note 2.

42. WSP Group & Metrolinx, *supra* note 5 at 29.

43. *Ibid* at 32.

44. "Innisfil, Ont., Chooses Uber Over Buses in Canadian First," *CTV News* (5 April 2017), online: <http://www.ctvnews.ca/canada/innisfil-ont-chooses-uber-over-buses-in-canadian-first-1.3355348>.

CHAPTER VII

The Sharing Economy and Trade Agreements: The Challenge to Domestic Regulation

Michael Geist[1]

I. Introduction

The growth of the sharing economy has attracted increased attention as the disruption of longstanding, well-established market
sectors such as transportation and hotel accommodation creates new
opportunities and threatens powerful economic interests. In recent
years, the sharing economy debate has focused on two companies—
Uber and Airbnb—which have both dramatically reshaped their
respective business sectors.

The emergence of Uber and Airbnb as significant marketplace
competitors is notable not only because they are big businesses, but
also because of their impact on local businesses. The development
of those companies on a city-by-city, community-by-community
basis has ensured that policies and regulation often involve local or
regional authorities.

Much like the arrival of Walmart in small towns a generation
ago, the arrival of Uber or Airbnb has proven to be controversial and
contentious in most communities. Indeed, the perceived threats to
small businesses—whether the local stores in the days of Walmart
or local taxi drivers today—remain much the same. The existing
marketplace—licensed taxi drivers or accredited hotels—typically
respond with demands that the services cease operations, noting that
they conduct business without the necessary licensing or regulatory

approvals and that despite the consumer benefits, they threaten the viability of longstanding businesses.[2]

In many respects, the response to online competitors is as old as the commercial Internet. For the past two decades, it has been the Internet's never-ending story. Established, successful businesses face Internet upstarts who leverage the advantages of a global network and new communications technology to offer better prices, more choice, or innovative services.

In the 1990s, it was online retailers such as Amazon who presented more selection at lower prices than most bookstores could offer. In the 2000s, Wikipedia brought the decades-old encyclopedia business to an end, online music services provided greater convenience than conventional record stores, Internet telephony technologies used by companies like Skype changed the rules of international voice and video calls. Today, Netflix has challenged conventional broadcast models, Craigslist and Huffington Post have challenged conventional media, and services such as Uber and Airbnb have upended the taxi and hotel worlds.

In these David-versus-Goliath-type battles, the established businesses rarely fade away without a fight. Using their remaining influence, they often look to laws and regulations that increase costs, prohibit activities, restrict consumers, or regulate pricing to create barriers for the new entrants.[3] There is a danger that the public interest is cast aside in favour of rules that hamstring new competitors and cost consumers. From copyright reforms that blocked online video retransmitter iCraveTV from operating in Canada nearly fifteen years ago[4] to continued calls for local content requirements and fees on online video services such as Netflix,[5] the goal is too often to use law to stop or stall new Internet-enabled competition.

For example, Amazon was initially prohibited from operating in Canada as opponents cited restrictions on the foreign ownership of booksellers. The company proceeded to launch in 2002 without a physical presence (using Canada Post for order fulfillment)[6] and only formally entered the country, over the objection of the Canadian Bookseller Association, in 2010.[7] Similarly, the Canadian Radio-television and Telecommunications Commission, Canada's broadcast and telecom regulator, tried to regulate the pricing of Internet telephone services in Canada in 2005 before the Canadian government overruled it on the issue.[8]

Given that history, the current fights against companies such as Uber and Airbnb should come as little surprise. The battles are being waged in city halls around the world as the established businesses lobby for regulations that would either block the services or require price controls to increase costs. While Uber has faced mounting legal challenges involving labour and fair business practice issues which led to dramatic changes among corporate leadership in June 2017, the applicability of sector-specific rules and regulations have remained murky, with Uber and similar sharing economy companies frequently falling through the cracks and avoiding conventional legal requirements.

The question of new regulations is a complex one, but the aim of this paper is not to assess the merits of specific regulations or even address the perceived need to regulate. Beyond debates about the appropriate form of regulation is the question of the right to regulate. Regardless of one's position on the benefits or harms of the sharing economy, it seems reasonable to conclude that local, regional, and national governments should have the authority to determine for themselves and their citizens whether to implement regulatory frameworks.

Yet that right to regulate has been gradually overtaken by the expansion of trade agreements that have extended their ambit beyond conventional tariff reduction into economic regulation. In fact, the initial shift into issues such as intellectual property protection and trade in services has largely given way to agreements that cover virtually every aspect of a modern economy, including environmental protections, labour rights, and educational standards. This expansion will soon include the sharing economy, with rules that will govern key aspects of sharing economy services as the agreements make inroads into the digital economy, often before a sector is fully developed. In doing so, the regulatory powers currently vested in national, regional, and local governments to establish regulations governing this emerging economic powerhouse will give way to regulation through trade agreements, with legal, policy, and regulatory standards made within the context of global trade flows.

This paper examines the intersection between the sharing economy and international trade agreements. The result of such intersections is likely to restrict the right to regulate, and disputing the wisdom of using closed-door negotiations that typify the negotiating framework for massive trade deals to address an increasingly challenging policy matter.

Trade agreements and global trade rules have become a critical aspect of the digital economy. Often characterized as "harmonization" of rules for aspects of the economy that operate on a global platform, the resulting rules run the risk of "Americanization," with the export of standards from the United States (the dominant digital economy) to other markets.

The paper assesses the intersection between the sharing economy and international trade agreements in three parts. Section II focuses on recent efforts to regulate Uber and Airbnb, two of the leading sharing economy companies. While there are many other examples of disruptive sharing economy businesses, the pressure to address Uber and Airbnb upon entry into a local market has been mirrored around the globe. Drawing on examples from North America, Europe, and Asia, the paper highlights how politicians and regulators have sought to block, harness, or embolden sharing economy businesses by relying on an evolving regulatory toolbox.

Section III highlights how global trade rules and treaties have been used to establish legal frameworks for the digital economy, often before the full development of those sectors. The paper focuses on two treaty initiatives—the World Intellectual Property Organization's Internet treaties in the 1990s and the Anti-Counterfeiting Trade Agreement in the 2000s—to demonstrate how incumbent businesses frequently use their political and market power to establish rules that govern how emerging technologies can be used in the marketplace. The development of rules before new businesses and new business models can fully develop invariably means that the resulting regulations favour the established players, creating significant barriers to entry.

Section IV considers what happens when sharing economy regulation intersects with emerging global trade agreements. The analysis centres on two agreements: the Trans Pacific Partnership (TPP), which was concluded in 2015, and the Trade in Services Agreement (TiSA), which is still the subject of ongoing negotiation. Moreover, it notes that the North American Free Trade Agreement (NAFTA), which was embroiled in a contentious renegotiation process that began in the fall of 2017, has identified the digital economy as a key area for discussion. These agreements feature (or are likely to feature) provisions with direct implications for the regulation of sharing economy services, including restrictions on local regulations, privacy and data transfer rules, and provisions on localization requirements.

II. Growth of the Sharing Economy and Emergence of Regulatory Demands

Companies such as Uber and Airbnb are less than ten years old, yet both (alongside many other sharing economy businesses) have had a remarkable disruptive effect on the economy and longstanding regulatory approaches. Uber, based in San Francisco, currently operates in 662 cities and eighty-two countries around the world.[9] It offers several tiers of service, ranging from upscale town cars with professional drivers (Uber), to low-cost privately owned "regular cars" driven by amateur or part-time drivers (UberX, or UberPOP in Europe). Uber XL (oversized vehicles, used for hauling cargo) is another subdivision of Uber. While the company is losing money, it now generates more than $5 billion in revenue annually.[10]

Uber is not regulated in the vast majority of cities in which it operates, but that is slowly changing. Most regulation occurs at the municipal level, although as detailed below, some states and provinces have regulated it (often in conjunction with supporting municipal legislation). Moreover, the Philippines recently became the first country to legislate Uber at the national level.

The growth of Airbnb is similar to Uber. The company is also based in San Francisco, offering a digital platform for short-term rentals of private accommodation. Airbnb currently features over 2 million listings in 34,000 cities and 191 countries. It is a privately held company, but estimates suggest that its bookings are valued at over $10 billion annually.

Given their popularity and significant revenues, the two companies have been the prime targets for regulation.[11] This part of the paper examines the regulatory challenges faced by governments at all levels in seeking to adapt conventional regulation to the sharing economy environment, highlighting the myriad of legal strategies that have been adopted around the world.

i. Uber
Uber considers itself a digital service connecting drivers and passengers rather than a transport service. The distinction is critical, since

transport services are typically subject to extensive rules on driver qualifications, road rules, and insurance requirements.[12] Uber and similar platforms argue that they are technology companies or platforms that do not themselves provide a transport service but rather facilitate the provision of transport services by individual drivers.[13]

The European Union's highest court is set to rule on the issue next year.[14] The complexity of the issue is illustrated by the court's description of the case, which arises from proposed regulations in Spain:

> If the service provided by UBER SYSTEMS SPAIN, S.L. were not to be considered to be a transport service and were therefore considered to fall within the cases covered by Directive 2006/123, the question arising is whether Article 15 of the Law on Unfair competition—concerning the infringement of rules governing competitive activity—is contrary to Directive 2006/123, specifically Article 9 on freedom of establishment and authorisation schemes, when the reference to national laws or legal provisions is made without taking into account the fact that the scheme for obtaining licences, authorisations and permits may not be in any way restrictive or disproportionate, that is, it may not unreasonably impede the principle of freedom of establishment.
>
> If it is confirmed that Directive 2000/31/EC is applicable to the service provided by UBER SYSTEMS SPAIN, S.L., the question arising is whether restrictions in one Member State [regarding] the freedom to provide the electronic intermediary service from another Member State, in the form of making the service subject to an authorisation or a licence, or in the form of an injunction prohibiting provision of the electronic intermediary service based on the application of the national legislation on unfair competition, are valid measures that constitute derogations from paragraph 2 in accordance with Article 3(4) of Directive 2000/31/EC.[15]

At the heart of the regulatory debate is whether Uber is, as it claims, operating as a pure technology company, providing a matchmaking service to willing participants, or whether it is operating in effect as an unlicensed taxi service.[16] While the distinction is critical in many jurisdictions, being treated as a technology company does not guarantee the ability to operate. For example, Uber is registered in Taiwan as a software company and not a taxi service, however the government has still not permitted it to operate within the country.[17]

Early indications suggest that the court is likely to rule that Uber should be viewed as a transportation service. In May 2017, the European Court of Justice's advocate general, Maciej Szpunar, ruled that Uber may be innovative, but it falls within the field of transportation.[18] If upheld, the ruling would mean that Uber would fall under national regulations and would be required to obtain the necessary licences and authorizations. The opinion noted the central role of Uber in virtually all aspects of the service, including price setting and establishing conditions on drivers. In light of its active control, the advocate general ruled that it could not be viewed as a mere intermediary.

As Uber has grown, so too have efforts to impose regulation with numerous jurisdictions employing a wide range of measures.[19] In the United States, twenty-two states passed comprehensive ride-hailing legislation in 2015 alone.[20] Some cities have endeavoured to establish equivalent regulations for traditional taxis and Uber drivers. For example, regulators in Austin, Texas, insisted that Uber drivers (and competitors such as Lyft) be fingerprinted in the same manner as taxi drivers. The issue became particularly urgent after the police investigated at least seven alleged sexual assaults by ride-share drivers in 2015. The companies challenged the city measure, but lost in a public vote, leading both to halt operations in the city.[21]

Safety measures are a common regulatory requirement for Uber and similar services.[22] The company ceased operations in Kansas after the *Kansas Transportation Network Company Services Act* imposed stricter insurance and driver screening requirements. The bill requires companies to certify that drivers have comprehensive and collision insurance, and requires new drivers to undergo a background check performed by the Kansas Bureau of Investigation.[23] The city of Eugene, Oregon, sued Uber in March 2015, and went to court to stop the company from operating until it met what the city described as "minimum safety requirements."[24]

Rather than focusing on operational safety rules, some cities have passed regulations that challenge Uber's business model. For example, Uber stopped operating in Anchorage, Alaska, after the city demanded its drivers accept cash payments, contrary to its credit-card only approach.[25] In 2016, the Indian city of Delhi banned the use of surge pricing, a controversial practice that increases Uber rider costs during busy periods.[26]

Another regulatory approach has been to focus on regulating the technology used by Uber, namely smartphone apps. For example, in Texas, the Houston City Council took steps to regulate smartphone apps that connect drivers with passengers, such as Uber and Lyft.[27]

Canadian cities have frequently focused their regulatory efforts on revenue generation. Uber is active and regulated in five Canadian cities: Toronto, Waterloo, Ottawa, Niagara, and Edmonton.[28] In Niagara and Ottawa, Uber pays a $7,253 annual licensing fee, plus 11 cents per trip; in Toronto, the company paid a $20,000 upfront one-time fee, a $15 per driver annual fee, and 30 cents per trip; in Edmonton, it pays $50,000 a year and 6 cents a trip; in Waterloo it also pays $50,000 a year, plus 11 cents a trip.

At the provincial level, the Legislative Assembly of Alberta passed Bill 16, the *Traffic Safety Amendment Act, 2016*, which came into force on May 27, 2016.[29] One of the major effects is the creation of an administrative penalty of a maximum of $50,000 to a transportation network company for each day of non-compliance with the legislation. The province has left the burden of inspection to the companies themselves, and the mechanical inspections to the cities.

In the United States, statewide regulations tend to be more general, while municipal regulations are more focused and specific.[30] As concerns regarding Uber and antitrust have begun to mount, there has been some consideration to the applicability of federal antitrust rules.[31] The Federal Trade Commission is an independent agency tasked with promoting consumer protection and eliminating and preventing anticompetitive business practices. By law, the FTC's power to regulate interstate commerce is just as broad as that of Congress. Since the 1980s, the FTC has been critical of taxi and limousine commissions for being anti-competitive, and has brought suits against cities. In 1984, the FTC brought cases against Minneapolis and New Orleans regarding their taxi regulation practices, merely because interstate travellers take taxis to and from the airport when they fly across state lines. The FTC has yet to become active against companies such as Uber, which may be California-based, but operates in multiple states.

American antitrust laws, however, allow states some exceptions to adopt anticompetitive business regulations, but these rights do not extend to cities. Cities are subject to federal antitrust laws unless states pass legislation absolving them. For example, Minneapolis ended up avoiding the 1984 taxi lawsuit by acceding to the FTC and permitting more competition. New Orleans, on the other hand, succeeded in lobbying the state of Louisiana to authorize its anti-competitive actions, to the detriment of consumers.[32] This raises questions of whether city-based regulations could override national anti-trust rules.

The city of Philadelphia serves as an interesting case study for jurisdictional issues. Since state law overrides local policies, Philadelphia faced a blurred line between city and state politics. The Philadelphia Parking Authority (PPA) has worked aggressively to halt transportation network company (TNC) operations by ticketing drivers and impounding cars. The mayor of Philadelphia has no juris-diction over the PPA because it is a state-chartered agency, and has not openly challenged PPA activity around ride-sharing. However, the Philadelphia City Council passed a resolution supporting ride-sharing and urging statewide action to permit TNCs in Philadelphia. Elsewhere in Pennsylvania, TNCs may now operate legally thanks to a two-year experimental licence recently issued by the state's Public Utilities Commission.[33]

Washington State law allows municipalities to regulate licens-ing for taxis and other vehicles, while the state oversees limousines. TNC lobbyists are making a push to change Washington law and give the state jurisdiction over all vehicle licensing, which would provide uniformity across markets.[34]

While regulation in the United States and Canada has generally focused on operational and taxation issues, other countries have tar-geted the freedom to operate. In the European Union, regulators in the Netherlands, Portugal, France, Spain and Germany have taken action based on existing legal frameworks that resulted in administrative or criminal charges against Uber drivers and management. In response, Uber submitted complaints to the European Commission against Spanish, German, and French court bans for violation of Article 49 (right of establishment) and Article 56 (freedom to provide services) of the *Treaty on the Functioning of the European Union*. In other countries, such as Denmark, legal decisions are still pending.[35]

Legal actions challenging Uber's right to operate are not uncom-mon in Europe with judges targeting both the company and its execu-tives. For example, in France a judge slapped Uber with an €800,000 fine for running the "illegal" UberPOP service, using unlicensed drivers. It also fined two of the company's senior executives €50,000.[36]

Similarly, a Dutch court banned UberPOP on the grounds that it ran afoul of licensing laws for commercial drivers. Uber is challenging that ruling.[37]

The Philippines was the first country to regulate Uber on a national basis.[38] Uber has urged other countries to use the Philippines' legislation as a model to create similar nationwide legislation.[39] The Philippines law provides nationwide regulations for app-based transport services. It introduced a new type of classification called transportation network vehicle service that allows TNCs such as Uber to operate within the existing regulatory framework.[40] The Philippines' Uber requirements feature several technical requirements including limits on the age of vehicles, inclusion of a GPS system, use of sedans, and clearance requirements for drivers. The rules also establish citizenship and national ownership requirements. All drivers must provide evidence of Filipino citizenship and companies offering the services must demonstrate at least 70 per cent domestic ownership.[41]

ii. Airbnb

Airbnb offers a digital platform for short-term rentals of private accommodation. Airbnb is not regulated in the vast majority of cities in which it operates. Where it is regulated, most regulation occurs at the municipal level, although some states or provinces have begun to take notice of potential regulatory authority. At the country level, both Iceland and Aruba have pursued national regulation.

The chief anti-Airbnb concern typically focuses on affordable housing, as critics argue that Airbnb rentals make it difficult for full-time residents to find affordable housing in cities such as Berlin, Paris, and Vancouver. Airbnb has faced persistent criticism from city officials in Barcelona and Paris over its impact on local housing markets.[42]

The European Commission released a report in 2016 urging governments to *not* ban Airbnb unless it is the last resort.[43] The commission concluded that banning short-term lets of apartments "appears difficult to justify" when limits on the maximum number of days that apartments can be rented out would be a more appropriate measure.[44]

In 2014, Airbnb and the city of Amsterdam entered into a partnership that was the first of its kind in Europe. The municipality only allows residents to rent out their homes for up to sixty days per year,

and customers are supposed to pay a tourist tax via Airbnb (enforcement is questionable as Airbnb would have to share data with the
city). Without this regulation, Airbnb would create an incentive for
illegal renting with negative consequences for the local residents
(higher rents, nuisance, and speculation).[45]

Most Canadian cities have not regulated Airbnb. The only
jurisdictions that have passed regulations are the Province of Quebec
and two British Columbia towns, Tofino and Penticton. Quebec's
regulations took effect in April 2016. They require the collection of
lodging taxes (up to 3.5 per cent), and business registration for those
who rent out accommodations on a full-time basis.[46] Violations carry
fines that range from $500 to $50,000.

Vancouver has pledged to target properties dedicated to being
Airbnb rentals with an "empty-homes tax," which carries a maximum
fine of $10,000 for anyone who evades the applicable charge.[47] It has
also proposed

> a new business-licence system for short-term rentals through
> websites like Airbnb to deal with "dangerously" low vacancy
> rates. [...] [T]he new regulations would allow short-term rent-
> als in principal residences that are either owned or rented[,] [b]
> ut the proposed changes would make daily or weekly rentals
> illegal in homes that aren't principal residences or are structures
> like boats or trailers.[48]

Current regulations that require a minimum thirty-day rental period
will be amended to permit short-term rentals.[49]

Taxation is another concern associated with Airbnb. In 2016,
the Province of Ontario convinced the company to email hosts in
the province to urge them to declare their Airbnb-generated income
for income tax purposes. The company also reminded hosts about
consumer protection laws and their responsibilities regarding cancellations and refunds.[50]

Some jurisdictions have established legal restrictions on who
may rent properties using Airbnb. For example, the city of San Luis
Obispo, California, passed a comprehensive ordinance that requires
that the dwelling be owner-occupied; owner presence is encouraged
but not mandated in the ordinance due to difficulties in enforcing
such a requirement. However, to alleviate neighbourhood concerns,
the city requires homestay hosts or a "designated responsible party"

to be within a fifteen-minute drive of the property and available via telephone 24-hours a day, seven days a week, while rentals are occurring.[51]

Some cities have established limits on rentals, including how often people can rent space, how many rentals must occur before the city collects taxes, and how often hosts must rent their space before inspections are required. After a certain number of rentals, the city requires inspections to ensure adherence to applicable building codes.[52]

The most restrictive approach is a full ban on the service. The State of New York passed an anti-home-sharing law in 2016 that threatens to fine New Yorkers up to $7,500, for advertising their home on sites like Airbnb. While the law effectively makes Airbnb illegal, many properties remain advertised for rent on the platform.

Other cities simply restrict the ability to rent out specific properties. In May 2016, Berlin officials implemented one of the world's toughest clampdowns on Airbnb. City officials have promised to reject 95 per cent of requests by landlords to rent places on a short-term basis. City officials have received more than 500 legal complaints over the murky provisions of the new law, which were challenged by Wimdu, a German Airbnb competitor.[53]

While most regulation arises at the municipal level, there are at least two examples of national legislation. Iceland established national rules that limit the right to rent homes for more than ninety consecutive days or to generate revenue that exceeds 1 million Icelandic krona ($12,000).[54] Moreover, permits, including approvals from health and fire departments, are required to operate an Airbnb rental.[55] Airbnb recently signed an agreement with the Aruba government that is said to help "create a framework to allow the Aruba Tourism Authority and Airbnb to address the issue of taxes, host accommodation standards and regulations and ensure that it is in line with Aruba's tourism policy."[56]

Sharing economy regulation at the national, provincial/state, and local levels has emerged as a global issue with a myriad of rules and regulations becoming increasingly common. Those rules typically reflect local policy choices as communities grapple with both the benefits and drawbacks of new services that disrupt longstanding business models. Yet just as the markets for services such as taxis and accommodation have been disrupted by Uber and Airbnb, so too are trade agreements disrupting conventional regulatory models by overtaking policy choices that have traditionally been developed and implemented by local or regional governments. The power of trade agreements to shape digital policy is the subject of section III of this paper.

III. How Trade Agreements Can Shape Digital Policy

Trade agreements and international economic treaties are typically associated with measures designed to enhance trade through tariff reduction. Indeed, for decades trade negotiations were largely premised on increasing the flow of goods across borders by lowering tariffs applied to imports. While tariff reduction remains an important component of many trade deals, newer agreements frequently focus on economic regulation such as intellectual property enforcement, health regulation, and environmental standards. Trade agreements are often a poor place to negotiate these issues, which have traditionally fallen within the purview of international organizations that develop consensus-based treaties with broad stakeholder participation. A fuller examination of emerging treaties such as the TPP and TiSA is contained at section IV of this chapter.

This part examines how trade agreements and global treaties can shape digital policy by considering two treaties: the World Intellectual Property Organization's (WIPO) Internet treaties and their inclusion of anti-circumvention rules, as well as the Anti-Counterfeiting Trade Agreement (ACTA), which contained various measures designed to regulate Internet-based providers and activities. In the case of the WIPO Internet treaties, the anti-circumvention rules became firmly entrenched within domestic laws worldwide and had a significant impact on many Internet-based businesses. In the case of ACTA, the treaty has yet to take effect, but the Internet-related provisions have resurfaced in other trade deals.

Given the early-stage development of the sharing economy and the regulations associated with companies such as Uber and Airbnb, the experience with the two treaties provides an early warning on how established organizations can often shape laws well before new entrants have fully developed and therefore hamper domestic regulations, as well as potential competitors and their disruptive business models.

i. WIPO and Anti-Circumvention Rules

Since their conclusion in 1996, the World Intellectual Property Organization's Internet treaties—the WIPO Copyright Treaty (WCT) and WIPO Performances and the Phonograms Treaty (WPPT)—have had a transformative impact on the scope of copyright law, creating what some experts have referred to as "super-copyright"[57] or "para-copyright."[58] Both treaties feature a broad range of provisions targeting digital copyright issues; however, the most controversial provisions mandate the establishment within ratifying states' national law of anti-circumvention provisions that provide "adequate legal protection and effective legal measures" against the circumvention of effective technological protection measures.[59]

The promise of technological protection measures (TPMs) was long touted by movie, music, and software industry associations as providing important protections for their products, by using technology to prevent unauthorized access or use. Despite the support for TPMs, many advocates have acknowledged that all TPMs can be defeated. For example, in 2000, the Secure Digital Music Initiative (SDMI) launched a public challenge to encourage the public to test whether it could crack the digital lock system, viewed at the time as unbreakable technological protections.[60] A team of security researchers cracked SDMI with relative ease, confirming the technology community's view that no system is foolproof.[61]

Given the flawed protection provided by TPMs, supporters of technological protections lobbied for additional legal protections to support them. Although characterized as copyright protection, this layer of legal protection does not address the copying or use of copyrighted work. Instead, it focuses on the protection of the TPM itself, which in turn attempts to ensure that the content distributor, not necessarily the creator or copyright owner, controls how the underlying content is accessed and used.

Both the WCT and WPPT contain anti-circumvention provision requirements. Article 11 of the WCT provides that

> Contracting Parties shall provide adequate legal protection and effective legal remedies against the circumvention of effective technological measures that are used by authors in connection with the exercise of their rights under this Treaty or the Berne Convention and that restrict acts, in respect of their works, which are not authorized by the authors concerned or permitted by law.[62]

Similarly, Article 18 of the WPPT provides that

> Contracting Parties shall provide adequate legal protection
> and effective legal remedies against the circumvention of
> effective technological measures that are used by performers
> or producers of phonograms in connection with the exercise of
> their rights under this Treaty and that restrict acts, in respect of
> their performances or phonograms, which are not authorized
> by the performers or the producers of phonograms concerned
> or permitted by law.[63]

The initial work behind the WIPO Internet treaties began in 1989, with work on model provisions for legislation in the field of copyright.[64] The interplay between law and technology—which later would come in the form of anti-circumvention legislation—did not start in earnest until December 1994.[65] The issue did take hold, however, and over the next two years, several committee sessions followed by a WIPO Diplomatic Conference, in December 1996, led to the agreement on the treaties.[66]

The diplomatic conference in December 1996, which ultimately resulted in the conclusion of the WIPO Internet treaties, featured debate in both the main committee and within the plenary on the anti-circumvention provisions. The starting point for the diplomatic conference was the United States–backed "Basic Proposal" that provided that

> (1) Contracting Parties shall make unlawful the importation,
> manufacture or distribution of protection-defeating devices, or
> the offer or performance of any service having the same effect,
> by any person knowing or having reasonable grounds to know
> that the device or service will be used for, or in the course of,
> the exercise of rights provided under this Treaty that is not
> authorized by the rightholder or the law.
> (2) Contracting Parties shall provide for appropriate and effec-
> tive remedies against the unlawful acts referred to in paragraph
> (1).[67]

Several countries called for narrowing the scope of the provisions. For example, Jamaica noted that "in the view of her Delegation, the formulation 'any of the rights covered by the rights under the Treaty' was too broad and imprecise and its proposed amendment would not contravene the basic intention of the Article."[68] The Australian delegation sought to modify the provision to "confine its operations to clear cases of intended use for copyright breaches."[69] The Norwegian delegation "agreed with those who had proposed narrowing the scope of those provisions, for the main reason that such provisions should not prevent legitimate use of works, for example, private and educational uses, and use of works which had fallen into the public domain."[70] The German delegation also "joined those Delegations which had considered that the scope of the provisions in question should be narrowed."[71] Only three delegations—the United States, Columbia, and Hungary—were substantially satisfied with the scope of the proposal.

United States law professor Pam Samuelson chronicles what followed given the rising opposition to the basic proposal in her 1997 law review article, "The U.S. Digital Agenda at WIPO":

> Facing the prospect of little support for the Chairman's watered-down version of the U.S. White Paper proposal, the U.S. delegation was in the uncomfortable position of trying to find a national delegation willing to introduce a compromise provision brokered by U.S. industry groups that would simply require states to have adequate and effective legal protection against circumvention technologies and services. In the end, such a delegation was found, and the final treaty embodied this provision in article 11.[72]

The compromise position was to adopt the far more ambiguous standard: "to provide adequate legal protection and effective legal remedies." Not only does this language not explicitly require a ban on the distribution or manufacture of circumvention devices, it does not specifically target both access and copy controls. In fact, the record makes it readily apparent that the intent of the negotiating parties was to provide flexibility to avoid such an outcome. Countries were free to implement stricter anti-circumvention provisions consistent with the basic proposal (as the United States ultimately did), but consensus was reached on the basis of leaving the specific implementation to individual countries with far more flexible mandatory requirements.

While that may have been the intent of the treaty provision, its aftermath has been far different. As one of the primary supporters of the WIPO Internet treaties, the United States was one of the first to attempt to implement the obligations into national law. Several implementing bills were tabled before the United States Congress. Then Senator (later Attorney General) John Ashcroft introduced the *Digital Copyright Clarification and Technology Education Act of 1997*.[73] Rick Boucher (D-VA9) and Tom Campbell (R-CA15) introduced parallel legislation in the House of Representatives as the *Digital Era Copyright Enhancement Act of 1997*.[74] Neither bill included provisions on anti-circumvention devices.

The Ashcroft and Boucher bills were abandoned, however, after legislation that ultimately led to the *Digital Millennium Copyright Act* (DMCA) gained congressional momentum. Representative Howard Coble introduced what would later become the DMCA with the *WIPO Treaties Implementation Act*.[75] During hearings on the bills, United States government officials acknowledged that the implementing legislation went beyond WIPO Internet treaty requirements. The United States' chief policy spokesperson and proponent of the DMCA, Assistant Secretary of Commerce and Commissioner of Patents and Trademarks, Bruce A. Lehman, admitted during his congressional testimony that the provisions went beyond the requirements of the treaties.[76] Lehman stated that the administration's aim was not confined to changing United States law. Rather, it hoped that the United States model would be used to convince others to implement the WIPO Internet treaties.

That approach remains in place today, with the United States the lead proponent of the Anti-Counterfeiting Trade Agreement and the TPP (both discussed below) which include anti-circumvention provisions designed to narrow the flexibility found in the WIPO Internet treaties and provide a model for other countries to follow.[77]

The history of the anti-circumvention legislation is notable because it demonstrates the enormous influence that international agreements can have over domestic legislation. Indeed, there is a great likelihood of unintended consequences when crafting rules before technology and the market have fully developed. In the case of anti-circumvention rules, it meant applying regulations to consumer products and digital services that simply did not exist at the time of treaty negotiations. For sharing economy services that are at an early stage of development, the anti-circumvention rule experience highlights how global rules may ultimately have a significant impact over the future regulatory environment.

ii. ACTA and the Internet

On October 23, 2007, the United States, the European Union, Canada, Japan, and a handful of other countries announced plans to negotiate the ACTA.[78] The behind-the-scenes discussions had apparently been ongoing for several years, leading some countries to believe that a full agreement could be concluded within a year, to coincide with the end of the Bush administration. Few paid much attention, as the agreement itself was shrouded in secrecy. ACTA details slowly began to emerge, however, including revelations that lobby groups had been granted preferential access, the location of various meetings, and troubling details about the agreement itself.

As the public pressure mounted, the talks dragged along with participating countries increasingly defensive about the secrecy and the substance. The agreement was ultimately concluded in 2010—years after the initial target—and some of the most troubling provisions were abandoned. Yet the final agreement still raised serious concerns, both for the way the agreement was concluded as well as for the substance.

When ACTA was formally signed by most participants, in October 2011 in Tokyo, Japan, few would have anticipated that less than a year later, the treaty would face massive public protests and abandonment by leading countries. But with tens of thousands taking to the streets in Europe in the spring of 2012, ACTA became the poster child for secretive, one-sided intellectual property agreements that do not reflect the views and hopes of the broader public. By July 2012, the European Parliament voted overwhelmingly against the agreement, effectively killing ACTA within the EU.[79]

ACTA's lack of transparency was a consistent source of concern throughout the negotiation process. In December 2007, before formal negotiations began, the United States government asked other participating countries to agree to a confidentiality agreement. The agreement classified all correspondence between ACTA parties as "national security" information on the grounds that it is confidential "foreign government information."[80]

The lack of transparency throughout the ACTA process eroded public confidence in the entire agreement. While ACTA supporters pointed to secret releases to European Parliament committees, the exclusion of the public from the consultation process bred enormous distrust in the entire agreement.[81] The lack of transparency highlights one of the major problems with negotiating in secret trade agreements that have broad-based implications. The failure to include experts throughout the negotiation process caused significant damage to the substance of the agreement, with numerous legal concerns as a result. The prospect of replicating similar oversights due to the lack of public and expert consultation and participation with emerging agreements such as TiSA could lead to unintended consequences for sharing economy regulations caught within the ambit of the agreement.

From a substantive perspective, ACTA raised several concerns with respect to the expansion of international intellectual property laws as it applies to the Internet. For example, the emphasis on secondary liability, which potentially holds third parties liable for the infringing actions of others, represented a significant shift in international intellectual property law.

While many countries have codified secondary liability principles within their domestic laws, there are relatively few provisions aimed at secondary liability in international law. Within ACTA, Article 8 on Injunctions applied to both infringers and third parties as did Article 12 on Provisional Measures, which can be applied to third parties. Both Article 8 and Article 12 apply in a civil enforcement context.

The Internet provisions within ACTA also target third parties. Article 27(2) provided that "each Party's enforcement procedures shall apply to infringement of copyright or related rights over digital networks, which may include the unlawful use of means of widespread distribution for infringing purposes."[82] In other words, the potential liability extends beyond those infringing to those who are seen to facilitate infringing activity. In fact, the provision could be applied to peer-to-peer networks, blogging platforms, and other technologies that facilitate the dissemination of content.

The ACTA also sought to establish universal rules for the response of Internet service providers to allegations of infringement on their networks. Article 27(4) on Enforcement in the Digital Environment, stated that parties "may provide, in accordance with its laws and regulations, its competent authorities with the authority to order an online service provider to disclose expeditiously to a right holder information sufficient to identify a subscriber whose account was allegedly used for infringement." The article on the disclosure of subscriber information is broader than the equivalent provision in Article 47 of the *Agreement on Trade Related Aspects of Intellectual Property Rights* (TRIPS).[83]

ACTA sparked a global discussion on intellectual property issues and the optimal balance between privacy and intellectual property rights in the digital environment. Its defeat—only Japan has ratified the agreement—highlights the risk associated with using international trade and treaty negotiations to address complex public policy issues in relative secret without public consultation and transparency. This is particularly true for issues that touch directly on individuals in tangible ways. The risk for sharing economy regulation with services that are both provided and used by millions is heightened where rules are established behind closed doors without adequate public participation. That approach has been typified by agreements such as the TPP, which is further discussed in section IV, on future trade agreements and the sharing economy.

IV. Future Trade Agreements and the Sharing Economy

As the sharing economy continues to grow, it is likely to attract increased attention from local, regional, and national regulators. While individual communities and countries are free to regulate as they see fit, the steady expansion of trade agreements may have a significant impact on domestic regulation. The intersection between local regulations and trade agreements is best illustrated by two trade agreements, each with membership that represents a sizable portion of the global economy: the TPP and the TSA. This part also briefly discusses NAFTA, which is likely to turn to these issues during a forthcoming renegotiation.

i. Trans-Pacific Partnership

The Trans-Pacific Partnership (TPP), a massive trade agreement that covers nearly 40 per cent of world GDP, wrapped up years of negotiation in 2015. The agreement involves twelve countries, the United States, Canada, Australia, Mexico, Malaysia, Singapore, New Zealand, Vietnam, Brunei, Japan, Peru, and Chile.[84]

Donald Trump's surprise victory in the United States presidential election resulted in an overhaul of its trade policy, including the immediate end of support for the TPP and a renewed focus on NAFTA. While President Barack Obama held out hope that the TPP could be salvaged during the lame-duck session of Congress that occurs immediately after the election, his administration was quickly forced to concede that the deal had become politically toxic and stood no chance of passage. Since United States ratification was required for it to take effect, the original TPP is effectively dead. In its place, Japan has led an effort to create TPP11, a slightly modified version of the agreement featuring new implementation rules, minus the United States. As of November 2017, a final agreement on TPP11 had eluded the remaining countries, with Canada leveraging its position as the second-largest economy left in the TPP to extract significant concessions on intellectual property, culture, and the auto sector. The original digital economy provisions remain largely unchanged in the TPP11.

Notwithstanding its political difficulties, the agreement's provisions provide a roadmap for future efforts to merge trade policy with the digital economy, including sharing economy businesses. The TPP's impact would be felt in two ways: regulatory pre-emption, which would restrict the ability for regulators to implement their own laws or regulations; and regulatory mandates, which would prescribe specific requirements within domestic rules.

The potential for regulatory pre-emption is best illustrated by the complex array of regulations for service industries in the TPP. Many trade agreements feature obligations to specific service sectors based on commitments from negotiating parties. These are relatively clear and make it easy for businesses to understand the new rules and for governments to identify their regulatory requirements.

The TPP adopts a much different approach, featuring a series of generally applicable restrictions or requirements for services. These include national treatment, most favoured nation status, market access requirements, and restrictions on local presence requirements. These generally applicable conditions apply to all services, unless specifically excluded in the agreement or within annexes applicable to individual countries.[85]

Article 10.3 of the TPP on national treatment provides:[86] "Each Party shall accord to services and service suppliers of another Party treatment no less favourable than that it accords, in like circumstances, to its own services and service suppliers." As noted above, the services chapter also includes a most favoured nation requirement in Article 10.4:[87] "Each Party shall accord to services and service suppliers of another Party treatment no less favourable than that it accords, in like circumstances, to services and service suppliers of any other Party or a non-Party."

The effect of these provisions is that countries are required to treat service providers—regardless of which country they come from—in an equal manner. When combined with a restriction on local presence requirements, regulatory measures for services such as Uber already found in some jurisdictions that target foreign operators would run afoul of the TPP.

These rules are particularly noteworthy within the context of local regulations. The TPP excludes existing local government regulation from the scope of the service requirements in Article 10.7 (1)(a) (iii).[88] This also applies to renewals of existing rules and amendments "to the extent that the amendment does not decrease the conformity of the measure."[89]

While that may grandfather existing rules, local municipalities would face restrictions on future sharing economy regulations should they further decrease conformity with the obligations. For example, if a municipality does not currently feature a local presence requirement in taxi regulations, instituting a new presence requirement for TNCs could violate the TPP. Similarly, establishing new expensive licensing requirements that restrict the likelihood of Uber drivers entering the market might violate Article 10.8(5) which stipulates that "[e]ach Party shall ensure that any authorisation fee charged by any of its competent authorities is reasonable, transparent and does not, in itself, restrict the supply of the relevant service."[90]

The issue may be even more pronounced where ride-sharing services are also regulated at the provincial, state, or national level. For example, the Province of British Columbia has the power to regulate Uber[91] and similar services through the *Passenger Transportation Act*.[92] The province has thus far resisted mounting calls for it to act.[93] The provincial regulations establish requirements related to licensing, safety, inspections, and insurance, and establish the rates that may be charged by anyone operating a vehicle who charges or collects compensation for transporting passengers.[94] Without a broad provincial government exclusion, these rules would presumably be caught by the TPP. The province has identified why it believes it needs to regulate the sector and announced plans for updating the regulatory environment, but should the TPP apply, it could pre-empt the provincial regulatory power given the absence of an exclusion and the difficulty in relying on public policy grounds for non-compliant regulations.[95]

Pre-emption of local regulations is only part of the TPP's potential impact on sharing services. Services such as Uber and Airbnb rely upon a business model that depends upon open data transfers, with personal data frequently stored or processed offshore. As noted above, some jurisdictions have begun to consider regulations that would require local storage of data or local presence requirements for sharing economy companies. The TPP seeks to address the issue by mandating open data transfers and restricting the potential use of data localization requirements. These rules benefit cloud-based sharing services but run the risk of restricting the ability of countries (or local and regional governments) from establishing regulations to address consumer concerns regarding their personal information.

For example, data transfer restrictions are a key element of the European approach to privacy, which restricts data transfers to those countries with laws that meet the "adequacy" standard for protection. That approach is becoming increasingly popular, particularly in light of the Snowden revelations about governmental surveillance practices. Several TPP countries, including Malaysia, Singapore, and Chile,[96] are moving toward data transfer restrictions, as are countries such as Brazil and Hong Kong.[97]

Yet the TPP included a restriction on data transfer limitations. Article 14.11 (2) states:[98] "Each Party shall allow the cross-border transfer of information by electronic means, including personal information, when this activity is for the conduct of the business of a covered person." There are similar restrictions with respect to data localization. Data localization has emerged as an increasingly popular legal method for providing some additional assurances about the privacy protection for personal information. Although heavily criticized by those who fear that it harms the free flow of information, requirements that personal information be stored within the local jurisdiction is an unsurprising reaction to concerns about the lost privacy protections if the data is stored elsewhere. Data localization requirements[99] are popping up around the world[100] with European requirements in countries such as Germany,[101] Russia, and Greece; Asian requirements in Taiwan, Vietnam, and Malaysia;[102] Australian requirements for health records, and Latin America requirements in Brazil.[103] Canada has not been immune to the rules either, with both British Columbia and Nova Scotia creating localization requirements for government data.[104]

Despite the momentum toward data localization as a privacy protection measure, Article 14.13 of the TPP establishes a restriction on legal requirements to do so:[105] "No Party shall require a covered person to use or locate computing facilities in that Party's

territory as a condition for conducting business in that territory."
This general provision is subject to at least three exceptions. First,
government services are excluded. Second, there is an exception for
financial services, which has sparked protest from some members
of the United States Congress.[106] The exclusion is reportedly due to
demands from the United States Treasury, which wanted to retain
the right to establish restrictions on financial data flows.[107]

The third exception is cited by supporters of the TPP as evidence that privacy protections are still a possibility. The exception
states:[108]

> Nothing in this Article shall prevent a Party from adopting or
> maintaining measures inconsistent with paragraph 2 to achieve
> a legitimate public policy objective, provided that the measure:
> (a) is not applied in a manner which would constitute a means of
> arbitrary or unjustifiable discrimination or a disguised restric-
> tion on trade; and
> (b) does not impose restrictions on the use or location of comput-
> ing facilities greater than are required to achieve the objective.

When combined with a 1999 World Trade Organization reference to
privacy,[109] the argument is that privacy could be viewed as a legitimate public policy objective and therefore qualify for an exception.

The problem is that the historical record overwhelmingly
suggests that reliance on this exception is unlikely to succeed. As
the advocacy group Public Citizen noted in a study on the general
exception language:[110]

> the exceptions language being negotiated for the TPP is based
> on the same construct used in Article XX of the World Trade
> Organization's (WTO) General Agreement on Tariffs and Trade
> (GATT) and Article XIV of the General Agreement on Trade
> in Services (GATS). This is alarming, as the GATT and GATS
> exceptions have only ever been successfully employed to actu-
> ally defend a challenged measure in one of 44 attempts. That is,
> the exceptions being negotiated in the TPP would, in fact, not
> provide effective safeguards for domestic policies.

In other words, the exception is illusory since the requirements are
so complex (each aspect must be met) that countries relying on the

exception have failed in forty-three out of forty-four cases. For countries concerned about the weakened privacy protections, the TPP restricts the use of data localization requirements as a remedy just as more and more countries are exploring such rules.

The data transfer and data localization regulations function much like the WIPO Internet treaty approach to anti-circumvention with the establishment of rules that are likely to have long-term consequences for businesses and business models that are at the early stage of development. By subscribing to a specific set of legal requirements, governments may be eliminating the ability to implement new regulations that respond to public concerns. Indeed, some early regulatory responses to sharing services such as Uber and Airbnb have sought to implement data localization or residency requirements.

A similar concern arises with respect to the TPP's restriction on the ability to require companies to supply access to source code. Article 14.17 (1) states:[111] "No Party shall require the transfer of, or access to, source code of software owned by a person of another Party, as a condition for the import, distribution, sale or use of such software, or of products containing such software, in its territory." While much of the concern associated with the source code regulation has focused on its security implications, it is conceivable that countries could introduce source code disclosure requirements on sharing economy companies as a mechanism to introduce algorithmic transparency. For example, concerns about discriminatory practices for ride-sharing or accommodation rental services that avoid servicing some neighbourhoods might be addressed through mandated disclosures of the underlying code used to operate the service. The TPP would prohibit such provisions.

There is considerable merit to anti-discrimination provisions that ensure that all businesses are treated equally with respect to regulatory requirements. These provisions could prove enormously important for the purposes of sharing economy regulation given the likelihood that many service providers will be foreign owned and therefore face the prospect of heightened regulation simply by virtue of their ownership or residency status. However, the TPP provisions extend far beyond ensuring equal treatment. The rules within the trade agreement may pre-empt regulation altogether or establish restrictions on regulations that are otherwise preferred by local, regional, or national governments. This points to a likely future clash between trade agreements and sharing economy regulations.

ii. Trade in Services Agreement (TiSA)

The Trade in Services Agreement (TiSA) is a trade agreement currently being negotiated by many of the world's largest economies, accounting for approximately 70 per cent of the global trade in services. Launched in March 2013, participants include the United States, European Union, Japan, Canada, and many other developed economies. The future of TiSA shares some of the same uncertainties as the TPP in light of the change in the United States administration. As of November 2017, there had been twenty-one rounds of negotiations, with further negotiations on hold. Unlike the TPP, which is now public, the draft text of TiSA remains secret. The only sources of the TiSA text come from several leaks posted on Wikileaks.

Given the lack of official text, it is difficult to fully assess the impact of TiSA provisions. However, the leaked documents published to date point to the prospect of a similar impact as found in the TPP. For example, the International Trade Union Confederation (ITUC) published a detailed analysis of leaked negotiating texts of TiSA on October 20, 2016. According to these documents, "TiSA would legally fortify and economically facilitate the operation of the 'platform economy'—a term (also known as the 'gig economy' or 'sharing economy') describing the online, on-demand business model of international companies like Uber."[112]

The leaked version of TiSA also includes data localization and data transfer provisions that are similar to those found in the TPP. The draft article on data transfer provides:

> [CA/TW/CO/JP/MX/US propose: No Party may prevent a service supplier of another Party [CO/JP propose: or consumers of those suppliers,] [CA/CO/JP/TW/US propose: from transferring, [accessing, processing or storing] information, including personal information, within or outside the Party's territory, where such activity is carried out in connection with the conduct of the service supplier's business.[113]

The U.S. has also proposed restrictions on data localization requirements. Article 9 states:

No Party may require a service supplier, as a condition for supplying a service or investing in its territory, to:

a) use computing facilities located in the Party's territory;

b) use computer processing or storage services supplied from within the Party's territory; or

c) otherwise store or process data in its territory.[114]

The data localization provision would severely restrict regulatory efforts on sharing economy companies to retain data within the local jurisdiction.

Concern regarding the TiSA provisions prompted the European Parliament to adopt a resolution in February 2016 containing its recommendations to the European Commission on the TiSA negotiations. The recommendations included

- ensuring that European citizens personal data flow globally in full compliance with the data protection and security rules in force in Europe;
- immediately and formally opposing the US proposals on movement of information;
- ensuring that national security clauses are grounded in appropriate necessity;
- comprehensively prohibiting forced data localisation requirements in order to prevent geoblocking practices and to uphold the principle of open governance of the internet.[115]

The Parliament's emphasis on data flows in compliance with European data protection rules points to a likely source of conflict with TiSA rules aimed at eliminating restrictions on data transfers and national data protection rules that depend upon some limitations in order to safeguard user privacy.

As an agreement dedicated to increasing trade in services, TiSA unsurprisingly features provisions aimed at fostering market access, reducing regulatory requirements, and eliminating discriminatory domestic provisions. These are laudable goals, yet the implications of a broad-based trade services agreement on Internet-based companies would be particularly pronounced given the ability to service a global market from a single jurisdiction. For sharing economy businesses, TiSA could usher in an era of limited regulations and requirements for uniform regulatory models across member countries. Such an outcome might enhance the commercial potential of those businesses, but would also necessarily restrict the ability of local jurisdictions to implement their own regulatory solutions.

iii. NAFTA

The election of Donald Trump has placed renewed focus on NAFTA, with the United States having filed a notice of renegotiation, paving the way for talks that commenced in the summer of 2017. The renegotiation involves much more than just a few tweaks, as the Trump administration has emphasized that new NAFTA chapters should be crafted to reflect the digital economy. The emphasis on digital policies foreshadows a new battleground that will have enormous implications for the sharing economy, as NAFTA rules are likely to have a direct impact on how those entities are regulated.

Some of the digital economy policies, including online contract enforcement and consumer protection, should be relatively uncontroversial. More contentious, however, will be rules similar to those found in the TPP regarding data localization and data transfers, the lifeblood of digital sharing economy companies. Data localization has become an increasingly popular policy measure as countries respond to concerns about United States–based surveillance and the subordination of privacy protections for non–United States citizens and residents.

In response to the mounting public concerns, leading technology companies such as Microsoft, Amazon, and Google have established or committed to establish Canadian-based computer server facilities that can offer localization of information. These moves follow on the federal government's 2016 cloud computing strategy that prioritizes privacy and security concerns by mandating that certain data be stored in Canada. The TPP included restrictions on data localization requirements at the insistence of United States negotiators. Those provisions are likely to resurface during the NAFTA talks and could have an impact on how companies such as Uber and Airbnb conduct their business. For Canadian regulators of sharing economy companies, attempts to establish a domestic presence for regulatory purposes could face restrictions from NAFTA provisions prohibiting data localization requirements.

So too will potential limitations on data transfer restrictions, which mandate the free flow of information on networks across borders. United States Internet companies have been particularly vocal about the need to restrict such rules. Those rules are important to preserve online freedoms in countries that have a history of cracking down on Internet speech but, in the Canadian context, could restrict the ability to establish privacy safeguards. In fact, should the

European Union mandate data transfer restrictions, as many experts expect, Canada could find itself between a proverbial privacy rock and a hard place, with the European Union requiring restrictions and NAFTA prohibiting them. These rules could have a significant impact on domestic regulations on the sharing economy that may restrict data transfers for reasons of privacy or workplace conditions.

V. Conclusion

As the sharing economy continues to grow, the prospect of local, regional, and national regulation is likely to grow. Companies such as Uber and Airbnb have quickly become multi-billion dollar global entities that simultaneously offer new commercial opportunities, consumer choice, and market competition. Sharing economy services are not without their negative impacts, however, leading to controversy and calls for regulation.

Those regulations include fundamental questions of how best to characterize sharing economy businesses such as Uber, the introduction of safety and licensing requirements designed to create a level playing field with incumbent providers, and newly crafted regulations specifically targeting services such as Airbnb.

Individual communities and countries are typically free to regulate as they see fit, yet the steady expansion of trade agreements may have a significant impact on domestic regulation. There is considerable merit to agreements that open markets. Moreover, anti-discrimination provisions that ensure that all businesses are treated equally with respect to regulatory requirements facilitate global commerce on a level playing field. These provisions could prove enormously important for the purposes of sharing economy regulation given the likelihood that many service providers will be foreign owned and therefore face the prospect of heightened regulation simply by virtue of their ownership or residency status. However, trade agreement rules now extend far beyond ensuring equal treatment, potentially pre-empting regulation altogether or establishing restrictions on regulations that are otherwise preferred by local, regional, or national governments. This points to a likely future clash between trade agreements and sharing economy regulations.

This chapter does not advocate for specific regulations for the sharing economy. Rather, it maintains that regulators should be free to act in the public interest, consistent with local values and policies. There is a need to consider the long-term implications of trade agreements that undermine the regulatory role of local officials by establishing restrictions on future regulatory measures. Public debate and comprehensive analysis is particularly challenging given the secrecy and lack of transparency associated with many current trade negotiations. Looking ahead—whether to TPP11, TiSA, NAFTA, or the myriad of regional trade agreements currently under consideration—greater transparency and inclusion of officials from all levels of government could help avoid the unintended consequences that may come from treaty provisions that lack insight into future directions of the digital economy.

Notes

1. Canada Research Chair in Internet and E-commerce Law, University of Ottawa. My thanks to Teresa Scassa, Derek McKee, and Finn Makela for their invitation to participate in their exceptional workshop on the sharing economy; to workshop participants at the University of Sherbrooke, the University of Haifa, and Tel Aviv University for their helpful comments on earlier drafts of this chapter; to Melissa Arseniuk, Hubie Yu, and Emma Germain for their exceptional research assistance, to the peer reviewers for their helpful comments; and to the Canada Research Chair program and Social Sciences and Humanities Research Council of Canada for their financial assistance. Any errors or omissions are the sole responsibility of the author.

2. See e.g. Mike Smyth, "Threat of Uber Looms Large for Vancouver Taxi Drivers," *The Province* (16 October 2016), online: <http://theprovince.com/opinion/columnists/mike-smyth-threat-of-uber-looms-large-for-vancouver-taxi-drivers>.

3. For example, new taxes on ride-sharing apps: Laura Payton, "Budget 2017: More Taxes Coming on Alcohol, Uber," *CTV News* (22 March 2017), online: <http://www.ctvnews.ca/politics/budget-2017-more-taxes-coming-on-alcohol-uber-1.3336253>.

4. Stikeman Elliott, "Internet TV Copyright Issues to Be Clarified" (December 2001), *Intellectual Property Update* (blog), online <https://web.archive.org/web/20061118033111/http://www.stikeman.com/newslett/IPDEC01.PDF>.

5. "CRTC Eases Canadian-Content Quotas for TV" *CBC News* (12 March 2015), online: <http://www.cbc.ca/news/business/crtc-eases-canadian-content-quotas-for-tv-1.2992132>.

6. Omar El Akkad & Marina Strauss, "Amazon Given Green Light to Set Up Shop in Canada" *The Globe and Mail* (12 April 2010), online:

<https://www.theglobeandmail.com/technology/amazon-given-green-light-to-set-up-shop-in-canada/article1314313/>.

7. *Ibid.*

8. *Telecom Decision*, 2005 CRTC 28, online: <http://www.crtc.gc.ca/eng/archive/2005/dt2005-28.htm>.

9. *Uber Cities*, online: Uber Estimator <http://uberestimator.com/cities>.

10. Eric Newcomer, "Uber, Lifting Financial Veil, Says Sales Growth Outpaces Losses," *Bloomberg Technology* (14 April 2017), online: <https://www.bloomberg.com/news/articles/2017-04-14/embattled-uber-reports-strong-sales-growth-as-losses-continue>.

11. Raymond H Brescia, "Regulating the Sharing Economy: New and Old Insights into an Oversight Regime for the Peer-to-Peer Economy" (2016) 95:1 Neb L Rev 87.

12. Julia Fioretti & Eric Auchard, "EU Cautions Governments Against Banning Uber, Airbnb," *Reuters* (31 May 2016), online: <http://www.reuters.com/article/us-eu-services-idUSKCN0YM2H0>.

13. Federal Trade Commission, "The 'Sharing' Economy: Issues Facing Platforms, Participants & Regulators" (November 2016), online: <https://www.ftc.gov/system/files/documents/reports/sharing-economy-issues-facing-platforms-participants-regulators-federal-trade-commission-staff/p151200_ftc_staff_report_on_the_sharing_economy.pdf> at 74; *Uber Guidelines for Law Enforcement Authorities – United States*, online: Uber <https://www.uber.com/legal/data-requests/guidelines-for-law-enforcement -united-states/en-US/>.

14. Fioretti & Auchard, *supra* note 12.

15. *Request for a preliminary ruling from the Juzgado Mercantil No 3 de Barcelona (Spain) lodged on 7 August 2015 — Asociación Profesional Élite Taxi v Uber Systems Spain, S.L. (Case C-434/15)*, online: InfoCuria <http://curia.europa.eu/juris/document/document.jsf?text=&docid=170871&pageIndex=0&doclang=EN&mode=req&dir=&occ=first&part=1&cid=413922>.

16. City of Calgary "Report to the Taxi and Limousine Advisory Committee – Review of Smartphone Application Options" (15 August 2014), online: <http://www.calgary.ca/CSPS/ABS/Documents/Livery-Transport-Services/TLAC-2014/08-15-2014-Agenda-ATT/TLAC2014-30 Review of Smartphone App options.pdf>.

17. "Uber Faces Ban in Taiwan," *BBC News* (3 August 2016), online: <http://www.bbc.com/news/technology-36966334>.

18. *Advocate General's Opinion in Case C-434/15 Asociación Profesional Elite Taxi v Uber Systems Spain, SL* (11 May 2017), online: InfoCuria https://curia.europa.eu/jcms/upload/docs/application/pdf/2017-05/cp170050en.pdf.

19. See e.g. Vanessa Katz, "Regulating the Sharing Economy" (2015) 30:4 BTLJ 1067.

20. Alison Griswold, "Uber Pulled Off a Spectacular Political Coup and Hardly Anyone Noticed," *Quartz* (21 January 2016), online: <http://qz.com/589041/uber-pulled-off-a-spectacular-political-coup-and-hardly-anyone-noticed/>.

21. Richard Parker, "How Austin Beat Uber," *New York Times* (12 May 2016), online: <http://www.nytimes.com/2016/05/12/opinion/how-austin-beat-uber.html?_r=0>.

22. Sofia Ranchordás, "Does Sharing Mean Caring? Recognizing Innovation in the Sharing Economy" (2015) 16:1 Minn J L Sci & Tech 413.

23. Ramkumar Iyler, "Uber Ceases Kansas Operations in Face of Stricter Oversight," *Reuters* (5 May 2015), online: <http://www.reuters.com/article/us-uber-kansas-idUSKBN0NR01720150506>.

24. *Ibid.*

25. *Ibid.*

26. Itika Sharma Punit, "Another Region of India Is Killing Surge Pricing," *Quartz* (18 April 2016), online: <http://qz.com/664131/another-region-of-india-is-killing-surge-pricing/>.

27. Dug Begley, "Houston Approves New Regulations, Allowing Uber and Lyft," *Houston Chronicle* (6 August 2014), online: <http://blog.chron.com/thehighwayman/2014/08/houston-approves-new-regulations-allowing-uber-and-lyft/>.

28. Nick Malawskey, "In Pa., Uber Is Here to Stay; Receives License from PUC," *Penn Live* (26 January 2017), online: <http://www.pennlive.com/news/2017/01/ubers_finally_legit_in_pa.html>.

29. Bill 16, *Traffic Safety Amendment Act, 2016*, 2nd Sess, 29th Leg, Alberta, 2016, online: <http://www.assembly.ab.ca/ISYS/LADDAR_files/docs/bills/bill/legislature_29/session_2/20160308_bill-016.pdf>.

30. Johanna Interian, "Up in the Air: Harmonizing the Sharing Economy through Airbnb Regulations" (2016) 39:1 Boston College Intl & Comp L Rev 129, noting at p 129 "the pervasiveness of Airbnb, and the sharing economy as a whole, exposes deficiencies in the federal laws that govern online behavior, revealing the necessity for such laws to be revisited."

31. For more on the challenge of competing federal and state jurisdiction to regulate, see S Paul Posner, "The Proper Relationship between State Regulation and the Federal Antitrust Laws" (1974) 49 NYUL Rev 693; Robert F Copple, "Cable Television and the Allocation of Regulatory Power: A Study of Governmental Demarcation and Roles" (1991–2) 44 Fed Comm LJ 1.

32. Marvin Ammori, "Can the FTC Save Uber?," *Slate* (12 March 2013), online: <http://www.slate.com/articles/technology/future_tense/2013/03/uber_lyft_sidecar_can_the_ftc_fight_local_taxi_commissions.html>.

33. Lauren Hirshon et al, "Cities, the Sharing Economy, and What's Next," online: National League of Cities Center for City Solutions and Applied

Research <http://www.nlc.org/sites/default/files/2017-01/Report%20 -%20%20Cities%20the%20Sharing%20Economy%20and%20Whats%20 Next%20final.pdf> at 21, 31–2.

34. *Ibid* at 32.

35. Filipa Azevedo & Mariusz Maciejewski, "Social, Economic and Legal Consequences of Uber and Similar Transportation Network Companies (TNCs)" (October 2015), online: European Parliament <http://www.europarl.europa.eu/RegData/etudes/BRIE/2015/563398/ IPOL_BRI(2015)563398_EN.pdf> at 5.

36. Rob Davies, "Uber Suffers Legal Setbacks in France and Germany," *The Guardian* (9 June 2016), online: <https://www.theguard-ian.com/technology/2016/jun/09/uber-suffers-legal-setbacks-in-france-and-germany>.

37. *Ibid.*

38. Davey Alba, "The Philippines Just Made Uber Legal Everywhere," *Wired* (11 May 2015), online: <https://www.wired.com/2015/05/ uber-philippines/>.

39. "LTFRB to Uber: No One is Above the Law" *Rappler* (14 August 2015), online: <http://www.rappler.com/move-ph/102571-ltfrb-uber-no-one-above-law>.

40. Disini Law Office, "Regulating Uber in the Philippines" (4 April 2016), online: eLegal.ph <http://www.elegal.ph/regulating-uber-in-the-philippines/>.

41. *Ibid.*

42. Fioretti & Auchard, *supra* note 12.

43. *Ibid*: "Total bans of an activity constitute a measure of last resort that should be applied only if and where no less restrictive requirements to attain a public interest can be used."

44. *Ibid.*

45. Koen Frenken et al, "Smarter Regulation for the Sharing Economy," *The Guardian* (May 20, 2015), online: <https://www.theguardian.com/ science/political-science/2015/may/20/smarter-regulation-for-the-sharing-economy>.

46. *Ibid.*

47. Laura Kane, "Vancouver Empty Homes Tax to Include Units Used for Airbnb," *CBC News* (20 September 2016), online: <http://www. cbc.ca/news/canada/british-columbia/vancouver-airbnb-empty-homes-tax-1.3771725>.

48. The Canadian Press, "Vancouver Proposes Licensed Short-Term Airbnb Rentals to Increase Supply," *Business News Network* (28 September 2016), online: <https://www.bnn.ca/vancouver-proposes-licensed-short-term-airbnb-rentals-to-increase-supply-1.575560>.

49. *Ibid.*

50. Keith Leslie, "Airbnb Agrees to Ontario Request to Send Email Telling Hosts to Pay Their Taxes," *Canadian Business* (19 February 2016), online: <http://www.canadianbusiness.com/business-news/airbnb-agrees-to-ontario-request-to-send-email-telling-hosts-to-pay-their-taxes/>.

51. Hirshon et al, *supra* note 33 at 22.

52. *Ibid* at 23.

53. Fioretti & Auchard, *supra* note 12.

54. *Ibid*.

55. "Police Raid Illegal Airbnb's in Reykjavik," *Iceland Monitor* (21 July 2016), online: <http://icelandmonitor.mbl.is/news/nature_and_travel/2016/07/21/police_raid_illegal_airbnb_s_in_reykjavik/>.

56. "Airbnb and Aruba Tourism Authority Sign Historic, Tourism Agreement" (7 November 2016), online: Aruba Tourism Authority <http://www.aruba.com/our-island/airbnb-and-aruba-tourism-authority-sign-historic-tourism-agreement>: "Aruba embraces the shared economy and is eager to formalize the first partnership in our region with Airbnb. Together as industry leaders, we will add value to authentic travel experiences while ensuring this on-island development is managed successfully," saidRonella Tjin Asjoe-Croes, CEO of the Aruba Tourism Authority.

57. Canada, Industry Canada, *Technological Measures Circumvention Provisions* (Ottawa: Davies, Ward & Beck, 2000), online: <https://web.archive.org/web/20060510125337/http://strategis.ic.gc.ca/epic/internet/inippd-dppi.nsf/vwapj/davieseng.pdf/$FILE/davieseng.pdf> at 5.

58. Dan L Burk, "Anticircumvention Misuse" (2003) 50 UCLA L Rev 1095 at 1096.

59. *WIPO Copyright Treaty*, 20 December 1996, 36 ILM 65 (entered into force 6 March 2002) [WCT]; *WIPO Performances and Phonograms Treaty*, 20 December 1996, 36 ILM 76 (entered into force 20 May 2002) [WPPT].

60. Janelle Brown, "Crack SDMI? No Thanks!," *Salon* (14 September 2000), online: <https://www.salon.com/2000/09/14/hack_sdmi/>.

61. Scott A Craver et al, "Reading Between the Lines: Lessons from the SDMI Challenge" (2001), online: USENIX <http://www.usenix.org/events/sec01/craver.pdf>. The "cracking" of the SDMI protection led soon thereafter to litigation with the Recording Industry Association of America (RIAA), after the RIAA threatened the researchers with liability if they publicly disclosed their analysis. The case was ultimately dismissed due to lack of standing, after the RIAA denied they had threatened any legal action. See Electronic Frontier Foundation, "Security Researchers Drop Scientific Censorship Case" (6 February 2002), online: <http://w2.eff.org/IP/DMCA/Felten_v_RIAA/20020206_eff_felten_pr.html>.

62. WCT, *supra* note 59, art 11.

63. WPPT, *supra* note 59, art 18.

64. WIPO, *Report of the First Session of the Committee of Experts on Model Provisions for Legislation in the Field of Copyright*, WIPO Doc CE/MPC/1/3, online: WIPO <http://www.wipo.int/mdocsarchives/CE_MPC_I_1989/CE_MPC_I_3_E.pdf>.

65. WIPO, *Report of the Fourth Session of the Committee of Experts on a Possible Protocol to the Berne Convention*, WIPO Doc BCP/CE/IV/3, online: WIPO <http://www.wipo.int/mdocsarchives/BCP_CE_IV_1994/BCP_CE_IV_1_E.pdf>.

66. WIPO, *Final Act of the Diplomatic Conference on Certain Copyright and Neighboring Rights Questions*, WIPO Doc CRNR/DC/98, online: WIPO <www.wipo.int/edocs/mdocs/diplconf/en/crnr_dc/crnr_dc_98.pdf>.

67. WIPO, *Basic Proposal for the Substantive Provisions of the Treaty on Certain Questions Concerning the Protection of Literary and Artistic Works to Be Considered by the Diplomatic Conference*, WIPO Doc CRNR/DC/4, online: WIPO <http://www.wipo.int/edocs/mdocs/diplconf/en/crnr_dc/crnr_dc_4.pdf> at 58.

68. WIPO, *Diplomatic Conference on Certain Copyright and Neighboring Rights Questions—Summary Minutes*, WIPO Doc CRNR/DC/102, online: WIPO <http://www.wipo.int/edocs/mdocs/diplconf/en/crnr_dc/crnr_dc_102.pdf> at para 531.

69. *Ibid* at para 536.

70. *Ibid* at para 537.

71. *Ibid* at para 539.

72. Pamela Samuelson, "The U.S. Digital Agenda at WIPO" (1996) 37 Va J Intl L 369 at 414.

73. US, Bill S 1146, *Digital Copyright Clarification and Technology Education Act of 1997*, 105th Cong, 1997.

74. US, Bill HR 3048, *Digital Era Copyright Enhancement Act*, 105th Cong, 1997.

75. US, Bill HR 2281, *WIPO Copyright Treaties Implementation Act*, 105th Cong., 1997.

76. In response to the question "Could we meet those requirements by adopting a conduct oriented approach as opposed to a device oriented approach?" from Rep. Rick Boucher, Mr. Lehman's response was "In my personal view... the answer is yes. But in my personal view also that [sic] the value of the treaties would be reduced enormously, and we would be opening ourselves up to universal piracy of American products all over this planet." See US, *WIPO Copyright Treaties Implementation Act and Online Copyright Liability Limitation Act: Hearing on H.R. 2281 and H.R. 2280 Before the Subcommittee on Courts and Intellectual Property Committee on the Judiciary U.S. House of Representatives*, 105th Cong, 1997 at 62 (Bruce Lehman), cited in Bill D Herman & Oscar H Gandy, Jr, "Catch 1201: A Legislative History and Content Analysis of the DMCA Exemption Proceedings" (2006) 24 Cardozo Arts & Ent LJ 121 at 134.

Years later, Lehman admitted that the DMCA approach had been a policy failure. See Bruce Lehman, "Digital Dystopia at McGill" (2007), online: Internet Archive <http://www.archive.org/details/bongboing. mcgill> at 00h:20m:30s.

77. Michael Geist, "U.S. Caves on Anti-Circumvention Rules in ACTA" (19 July 2010), online: Michael Geist <http://www.michaelgeist.ca/content/view/5210/125/>.

78. Electronic Frontier Foundation, "Anti-Counterfeiting Trade Agreement," online: <https://www.eff.org/issues/acta>.

79. Matt Warman, "European Parliament Rejects ACTA Piracy Treaty," *The Telegraph* (4 July 2012), online: <http://www.telegraph.co.uk/technology/news/9375822/European-Parliament-rejects-ACTA-piracy-treaty.html>.

80. Eddan Katz & Gwen Hinze, "The Impact of the Anti-counterfeiting Trade Agreement on the Knowledge Economy: The Accountability of the Office of the U.S. Trade Representative for the Creation of IP Enforcement Norms Through Executive Trade Agreements" (2009) 35:21 Yale J Intl L 24.

81. Michael Geist, "Treaty Consultation Process Snubs Public," *The Star* (3 November 2008), online: <https://www.thestar.com/business/2008/11/03/treaty_consultation_process_snubs_public.html>.

82. *Anti-counterfeiting Trade Agreement*, 1 May 2011, art 27(2) (not yet in force).

83. *Agreement on Trade-Related Aspects of Intellectual Property Rights*, 15 April 1994, 1869 UNTS 299.

84. Janyce McGregor, "TPP Deal 'in Best Interests' of Canadian Economy, Stephen Harper Says," *CBC News* (5 October 2015), online: <http://www.cbc.ca/news/politics/canada-election-2015-tpp-agreement-atlanta-1.3254569>.

85. *Trans-Pacific Partnership Agreement—Chapter 10—Cross-Border Trade in Services*, online: United States Trade Representative <https://ustr.gov/sites/default/files/TPP-Final-Text-Cross-Border-Trade-in-Services.pdf>.

86. *Ibid.*

87. *Ibid.*

88. *Ibid.*

89. *Ibid*, art 10.7 (1)(c).

90. *Ibid.*

91. *FACTSHEET: Uber* (28 October 2014), online: BC Gov News <https://news.gov.bc.ca/factsheets/factsheet-uber>.

92. *Passenger Transportation Act*, SBC 2004, c 39, online: Bclaws.ca <http://www.bclaws.ca/civix/document/id/complete/statreg/04039_01>.

93. "Time for Governments to Act on Ride-Sharing: Uber GM," *Global News* (21 February 2016), online: <http://globalnews.ca/news/2530884/time-for-governments-to-act-on-ride-sharing-uber-gm/>.

94. *FACTSHEET: Uber, supra* note 91.

95. "8 Whys for Regulating Commercial Ridesharing and Other Passenger Transportation" (7 March 2017), *TranBC* (blog), online: <https://www.tranbc.ca/2014/11/05/8-whys-for-regulating-commercial-ridesharing-and-other-passenger-transportation/>.

96. "Chilean Government Moving Toward Stronger Privacy Provisions" (17 February 2015), *Truste Blog* (blog), online: <www.truste.com/blog/2015/02/17/chilean-government-stronger-privacy-provisions/#sthash.RL8BiKOS.dpuf>.

97. Dana Post & Victoria White, "Hong Kong Puts Restrictions on Cross-Border Transfers: Are You Compliant?" (27 January 2015), *International Association of Privacy Professionals* (blog), online: <https://iapp.org/news/a/hong-kong-puts-restrictions-on-cross-border-transfers-are-you-compliant/>.

98. *Trans-Pacific Partnership Agreement—Chapter 14—Electronic Commerce*, online: United States Trade Representative <https://ustr.gov/sites/default/files/TPP-Final-Text-Electronic-Commerce.pdf> [*TPP Chapter 14*].

99. "Data Localization: A Challenge to Global Commerce and the Free Flow of Information" (September 2015), online: Albright Stonebridge Group <www.albrightstonebridge.com/files/ASG%20Data%20Localization%20Report%20-%20September%202015.pdf>.

100. Hogan Lovells, "It's 2014. Do You Know Where Your Data Is, or Came From?" (22 July 2014), *International Association of Privacy Professionals* (blog), online: <https://iapp.org/news/a/its-2014-do-you-know-where-your-data-is-or-came-from/>.

101. "German Parliament Adopts Data Retention Law with Localization Requirement" (16 October 2015), *Privacy & Information Security Law Blog* (blog), online: <www.huntonprivacyblog.com/2015/10/16/german-parliament-adopts-data-retention-law-with-localization-requirement/>.

102. Shaun Waterman, "Trans-Pacific Partnership Will Ban Data Localization Laws" (5 October 2015), *FedScoop* (blog), online: <http://fedscoop.com/tpp-will-ban-data-localization-laws>.

103. Nigel Cory, *Cross-Border Data Flows: Where Are the Barriers, and What Do They Cost* (May 2017), online: Information Technology and Innovation Foundation <http://www2.itif.org/2017-cross-border-data-flows.pdf?_ga=2.248428289.743653034.1513627633-526308577.1513627633>.

104. *Ibid.*

105. *TPP Chapter 14, supra* note 98.

106. *Letter from Mike Kelly et al., Members of Congress, to the Honorable Secretary Jacob J Lew et al.* (11 January 2016), online: <http://kelly.house.gov/sites/kelly.house.gov/files/documents/Kelly%20Paulsen%20Moulton%20Kuster%20Data%20Localization%20Letter%20to%20USTR%20Treasury%20NEC%20SIGNED%201-11-2016.pdf>.

107. William C, "Treasury Opposed Relaxing Data Localization Requirements for Financial Services Sector in TPP #tpp #trade #congress #politics" (2 December 2015 at 9:12am), online: Twitter <https://twitter.com/wcrozer/status/672100982424236032>. Treasury opposed relaxing data localization requirements for financial services sector in TPP Treasury opposed relaxing data localization requirements for financial services sector in TPP #tpp #trade #congress #politics Treasury opposed relaxing data localization requirements for financial services sector in TPP #tpp #trade #congress #politics Treasury opposed relaxing data localization requirements for financial services sector in TPP #tpp #trade #congress #politics Treasury opposed relaxing data localization requirements for financial services sector in TPP #tpp #trade #congress #politics

108. *TPP Chapter 14, supra* note 98, art 14.13(3).

109. WTO, *Work Programme on Electronic Commerce (Progress Report to the General Council)*, WTO Doc S/L/74 (1999), online: WTO <http://trade.ec.europa.eu/doclib/docs/2004/may/tradoc_117019.pdf>.

110. "Only One of 44 Attempts to Use the GATT Article XX/GATS Article XIV 'General Exception' Has Ever Succeeded: Replicating the WTO Exception Construct Will Not Provide for an Effective TPP General Exception," *Public Citizen* (August 2015), online: <www.citizen.org/documents/general-exception.pdf>.

111. *TPP Chapter 14, supra* note 98.

112. Yorgos Altintzís, "A Global Trade in Services Agreement Would Put Workers and Consumers at Risk" (10 November 2016), online: Equal Times <https://www.equaltimes.org/a-global-trade-in-services?lang=fr#.WigmvouDPR1>.

113. Wikileaks, *Trade in Services Agreement (TiSA)—Annex on Electronic Commerce* (3 June 2015), online: <https://wikileaks.org/tisa/ecommerce/TiSA%20Annex%20on%20Electronic%20Commerce.pdf> at 2.

114. *Ibid* at 7.

115. *2015/2233(INI)–03/02/2016 Text Adopted by Parliament, Single Reading*, online: European Parliament / Legislative Observatory <http://www.europarl.europa.eu/oeil/popups/summary.do?id=1422570&t=e&l=en>.

PART IV

REGULATING MARKETS

CHAPTER VIII

Should Licence Plate Owners Be Compensated when Uber Comes to Town?

Eran Kaplinsky[1]

I. Introduction

> [T]he abstractions of law are basically conservative; they tend to
> preserve the status quo, to protect property and those who hold
> it, and to resist innovations of organization or method whether
> these originate from the private or governmental sector.[2]
> As often happens during an evolutionary period, the older,
> vested interests turned to the state for protection against the
> innovative elements within the industry and sought regulation
> that would preserve their traditional monopoly.[3]

The sharing economy represents a profound change in the way
goods and services are exchanged. New technological platforms
help connect consumers with goods and services providers and promote better utilization of assets and fuller realization of economic
rights over resources.[4] It is no surprise that the new way of doing
things threatens vested interests, in the same way that, as famously
described by Harry Miskimin, organizational innovations in the tex-
tile industry in sixteenth-century England threatened the traditional
guild structures.[5] But history suggests that change is inevitable, even
if its timing and direction cannot be anticipated fully; and when
change comes, there are winners and losers. It is the latter who are
the subject of this chapter. Specifically, do taxi licence owners have
a right to compensation when their municipally issued licences are

devalued as a result of local sanctioning of ride-sharing services such as Uber? This chapter argues that no such legal right exists, and while there may be compelling arguments to compensate plate owners, municipalities may lack the statutory authority to provide compensation under existing law. The chapter proceeds as follows: section II provides a broad description of taxi regulations in Canadian cities and the recent and ongoing legalization of ride-sharing. The main point of the section is to demonstrate that the transition to the new system based in the sharing economy is socially desirable overall, but comes largely at the expense of taxi plate owners. Section III examines the case for compensation. While there are powerful arguments in favour of compensation based in equity and efficiency, there is very likely no right to compensation as a matter of Canadian law. Section IV considers how a scheme of compensation might be implemented. As a preliminary matter, there is some question as to the power of municipalities to offer compensation to licence holders, which may require clarification in their enabling legislation. The bulk of the section is dedicated to an assessment of compensation schemes recently implemented by several Australian states, which may provide useful lessons to policymakers in Canada. Section V concludes.

II. From Municipal Regulation to the Sharing Economy

i. Municipal Regulation of Taxis

Local control of taxis began in American cities in the 1920s. As the story goes, regulation came as a direct response to the results of free-for-all, "cut-throat" competition in flooded transportation markets, which resulted in long hours and low wages for drivers, unsafe cars, and dearth of third-party liability insurance.[6] Local ordinances were promulgated to address these problems by implementing licensing requirements, limits on the number of local taxis, and regulated fares, as campaigned for by professional cab associations, as well as safety, service, and insurance standards demanded by consumers.[7] Taxi regulations in Canadian cities were historically driven by the same concerns,[8] and at least until recent reforms, have exhibited the same essential features. Municipal bylaws enabled by provincial legislation set licensing requirements for taxicabs and taxi drivers, and prescribe the terms under which taxi services may be offered. While the details vary across Canadian cities, the bylaws typically require taxicabs to meet municipal safety, insurance, and appearance standards; taxi drivers to be trained and accredited;[9] and taxi fares to be regulated and metered.[10]

Controlling the number of local taxis is a central feature of municipal regulations.[11] Calgary's system, challenged before and described by the Alberta Court of Queen's Bench in 1998 in *United Taxi Drivers' Fellowship of Southern Alberta v. Calgary (City of)*[12] is representative. Only a licensed taxi driver operating a licensed taxicab could legally provide a taxi ride in Calgary, but whereas any individual who met the prescribed qualifications could obtain a driver's licence, the number of taxi licences issued by the city was capped at a number previously set in 1986 by the city's taxi commission.[13]

Municipal supply management of taxis (or pharmacies or single-family homes for that matter) is premised on the local government's ability to anticipate demand and set the optimal quotas and fares. The evidence of such ability is, however, to the contrary. David Seymour observed, in 2009, that in more than one prairie city, taxi quotas had remained frozen for significant periods. Saskatoon's numbers had not changed in twenty-two years, and in Winnipeg they were largely unchanged since 1947. Calgary adhered to a cap imposed twenty-three years earlier, even though the city's workforce had almost doubled since.[14]

The strict municipal quota system has also the effect of turning taxi licences (referred to sometimes as taxi "plates" or "medallions"; the terms are interchangeable) into very desirable government-created property.[15] Because taxi licences confer an exclusive privilege (strictly speaking, an oligopoly) to engage in remunerative point-to-point transport, which is transferable with very few restrictions, they are openly traded at prices disproportionally higher than nominal licence fees.[16] The best available data on the transfer prices of taxi licences in Canadian cities prior to the emergence of ride-sharing services is based on a 2007 report commissioned by the City of Edmonton.[17] Reported transfer prices were as high as $55,000 in Edmonton, $185,000 in Ottawa, $280,000 in Winnipeg, and $500,000 in Vancouver. More recent newspaper articles cite even higher figures.[18] Further, due to the historical advantages of dispatch booking, taxicabs tend to be affiliated with one of a handful of large local operators, and in most cities taxi plates are concentrated in the hands of powerful operators who own the licences outright, or manage them on behalf of non-driver owners.[19] As a result, most individuals who wish to earn an income as taxi drivers cannot obtain their own taxi licence and are often forced to rent licences at high premiums and on unfavourable terms. A 2008 report on working conditions of taxi drivers in Toronto noted a great financial strain on drivers, long working hours, low morale, and a feeling of resentment against the industry and city council. Meanwhile, plate owners and agents have been collecting an estimated $30 million annually in rental fees.[20]

Studies reveal that the quota or plate/medallion system produces a net social loss.[21] A 1984 staff report by the United States Federal Trade Commission concluded that "[r]estrictions on the total number of firms and vehicles and on minimum fares waste resources and impose a disproportionate burden on low income people. Similarly, there is no economic justification for regulations that restrict shared-ride, dial-a-ride, and jitney service."[22] In a study of Metropolitan Toronto, the cartelization of the taxi industry was estimated to reduce consumer surplus by $39.2 million in 1987 alone. Whatever economic advantages the system yielded were concentrated in the hands of a few, while higher social costs were widely dispersed among consumers.[23] More recently, in 2014, the Economic Regulation Authority of the State of Western Australia modelled the costs and benefits of taxi regulations in Perth and concluded that while there were benefits to maintaining taxi and driver standards, licence number restrictions resulted in a net loss to the public. The study estimated the benefit to taxi plate owners at AUD$27.7 million ($26 million) and to taxi drivers at AUD$4.4 million annually, whereas the cost to the public was between AUD$45.7 to AUD$70.7 million in higher prices and longer waiting times.[24] The net effect of restricting the supply of taxis was an annual loss of up to AUD$38.6 million.[25]

The artificial shortages resulting from taxi quotas become evident whenever barriers to entry are removed. In Ireland, the deregulation of taxis in 2000 resulted in a trebling of their numbers in Dublin.[26] Similarly, Uber's entry into urban centres has increased the volume of rides for hire and lowered fares, suggesting that previously there was unmet demand for point-to-point transportation and, further, that the regulated price was too high and the existing service inadequate. There may have been periods during which taxis stood idle for lack of business, but that could only indicate that committing a fixed number of vehicles to round-the-clock taxi use is highly inefficient. So is committing private vehicles to full-time personal or domestic use. Ride-sharing services attempt to address both problems.

ii. Ride-Sharing and Its Advantages

Uber is the best known, and at the time of writing, the most successful ride-sharing service. Since its founding in 2009, it has grown to be the world's largest transportation provider, currently in some 600 cities in eighty countries. The popularity of transportation network companies such as Uber is attributable to the rapid growth of the sharing economy, their efficient business models, and their competitive advantage over regulated operators, but above all, the superiority of their booking technology. By allowing passengers and drivers to match based on an online directory of user experience and global positioning service (GPS) technology, ride-sharing companies reduce search costs and fares, and create a point-to-point transportation market much more reflective of supply and demand.[27]

In lieu of municipal taxi regulations, transportation network companies offer standard contractual terms governing the relationship between the company, its partner drivers, and its consumers, which serve as private regulations. Under Uber's standard terms, for example, the company grants its partner drivers a private operating licence, which is in effect the right to be listed in Uber's location-based directory of point-to-point transportation providers.[28] Each partner driver must meet the company's standards, including liability insurance, vehicle standards, driver's licensing requirements, and more. The company reserves to itself a fixed percentage from each fare and the right to set each fare, which it collects directly from passengers using its application.[29] As opposed to the fixed regulated rates charged by taxi drivers, Uber's fares vary in response to demand and supply in real time (allowing, for example, to attract more service providers in peak demand times), and its platform matches drivers and consumers depending on mutual interest.

Uber is the largest, but not the only ride-sharing service.[30] It still enjoys a first-mover advantage due to the recognition of its brand, the popularity of its phone application, and its database of driver and passenger ratings; but it faces competition from existing services such as Lyft and from emerging platforms, such as a new Australian company, Mum's Taxi, which promises to serve female and child passengers by matching them with female-only driver partners to "provide safer transport for women and children, and help women who are looking for safe and flexible work."[31] The infrastructure requirements for ride-sharing services are minimal, the barriers to entry relatively low, and the business easy to emulate. Drivers can, and often do, work for more than one service, where available. In such an environment, ride-sharing services can be expected to compete on multiple fronts, including not only lower fares and commissions but also flexible terms of service to respond to the preferences of drivers and passengers. This is an important point given that Uber's business models and practices are very much a work in progress and given the allegations made against it from time to time for exploiting consumers and drivers. Some of these concerns can be addressed by labour and employment laws and consumer protection legislation, but competition among ride-sharing providers is more likely to produce terms of service more favourable to drivers and passengers than top-down municipal regulations that dictate every aspect of the service, from the number of vehicles to the cost of the ride.

According to one estimate, "[f]or each dollar spent by consumers, about [USD]$1.60 of consumer surplus is generated. Back-of-the-envelope calculations suggest that the overall consumer surplus generated by the UberX service in the United States in 2015 was [USD]$6.8 billion."[32] Ride-sharing may also produce important indirect public benefits. Location- and fare-based matching tends to decrease driving distances and times between rides, make better use of existing fleets, and reduce the number of cars committed to private travel, as well as the amount of urban land devoted to parking. Because the use of vehicles is associated with the externalities of carbon and air pollution, ride-sharing may also improve environmental outcomes. These additional effects have not been fully investigated.[33]

iii. Ride-Sharing in Canadian Cities

Thirteen Canadian cities in Alberta, Ontario, and Quebec (the list continues to grow) currently allow Uber or other transportation network companies to operate within their boundaries,[34] while progress has been slower elsewhere.[35] The Federal Competition Bureau has called on provincial and municipal regulators "to allow the forces of competition to shape how the industry will move forward [... and to] re-think existing regulations to provide an even playing field upon which ride providers can compete."[36] The bureau recommended that taxi regulations be relaxed, and more stringent regulations be imposed on new providers to secure public safety and other legitimate policy objectives.[37] Local policymakers have responded by relaxing licensing requirements and reducing licence fees for taxis on the one hand, and on the other hand, regulating ride-sharing services by requiring safety inspections for cars, background checks for drivers, and mandatory insurance.[38] In the most recent federal budget, a sales tax on ride-sharing had been announced.[39]

The traditional taxi industry has been disrupted by the introduction of ride-sharing, but has not collapsed entirely. Neither have those Canadian jurisdictions that opened their doors to Uber abolished altogether their old licensing systems. Taxi plates continue to confer a right to engage in a remunerative trade, but this right is no longer exclusive. Most municipalities still limit ride-sharing to pre-arranged rides and allow only taxis to respond to street hails, but to the extent that an Uber ride can substitute for a taxi, quotas have been rendered irrelevant. As a result, taxi plates retain some portion of their value for now, at least until the future of ride-sharing in Canada is settled.

iv. Ride-Sharing's Losers

Uber's introduction into Canadian cities was preceded by massive lobbying efforts. These campaigns could be explained as attempts to secure favourable terms of operation and perhaps to enhance the company's reputation, but are also indicative of the stakes held by the incumbent taxi industry, which engaged openly in heavy protesting[40] and lobbying[41] against ride-sharing. The transition to the sharing economy and the introduction of competition for point-to-point transportation services can create not only winners, but losers also.

Some taxi drivers may be made worse off by the opening up of local markets to ride-sharing services, but others who choose to work for Uber, or one of its competitors, may benefit from greater independence and flexibility, higher hourly wages, and more favourable terms:

> one veteran Toronto cabbie driver called Uber his saviour, allowing him to escape the grind of 12-hour shifts in a rented taxi that paid dividends to an absentee plate-holder: "I am no longer charged an astronomical price to drive a taxi [...] I can take a day off – take my kid to his hockey practice and my daughter to her after-school activities without the fear of being charged. I have a choice."[42]

Data from the United States for the years 2009 to 2015 does show that in cities where Uber operates the average hourly earnings of taxi drivers fell up to 10 per cent relative to cities where it does not, consistent with a decline in the volume of taxi passengers due to competition.[43] But the data also showed an overall growth in point-to-point transportation services, including self-employed and salaried taxi drivers, and increased hourly earnings for self-employed drivers due to their higher capacity utilization.[44] Despite a concern about a displacement by the sharing economy of traditional service jobs, in sum there was "little evidence of adverse impacts on labour market outcomes in point-to-point transportation services."[45]

There is very limited data on the effect of ride-sharing on the Canadian local government. A decline in the number of taxis and taxi drivers could deprive the municipality of substantial licensing fees, but these would be offset by revenue generated from licensing ride-sharing companies and their partner drivers. Municipal licensing departments will be expected to adapt to new regulatory responsibilities, and powerful municipal taxi commissions will eventually lose their power to set quotas. For example, following its decision to allow ride-sharing services, the City of Toronto created a new vehicle-for-hire group within its business licensing and permitting group, using staff previously employed in taxicab driver training (which is no longer mandated under the city's changed regulations). The restructuring has not resulted to date in significant changes in the bureaucracy's resource requirements.[46] The same appears to hold for Edmonton's vehicle-for-hire licensing department.[47]

The stakeholders who are most likely to be adversely affected by deregulation and competition from ride-sharing are the owners of taxi licences. The prospect of the introduction of ride-sharing in Canadian cities precipitated a sharp decline in taxi licence values. According to source data from the City of Toronto, while rental prices generally held, taxi plate prices began to plummet in 2012—from a peak of $360,000 in September 2012 to an average of $118,235 in 2014.[48] Media reports suggest prices in Edmonton fell from around $200,000 in 2013 to $70,000 in 2016.[49] Taxi plate transfer prices also fell in Ottawa[50] and Calgary.[51] The reported decline in taxi licence prices in Canadian cities where ride-sharing is authorized or expected is consistent with the experience in other countries. In Dublin, for example, licence values fell within two years after the deregulation of the taxi industry in Ireland and the removal of barriers to entry by qualified drivers from £90,000 in 2000 to £13,224.[52] Similarly, recent analysis of data from three American cities (New York City, Chicago, and Philadelphia) concluded that "the number of Uber drivers in the market is negatively correlated with the price of a taxi medallion, as expected. It is statistically and economically significant; each additional Uber driver reduces the price of a taxi medallion by [USD]$22 to [USD]$45."[53]

III. The Case for Compensating Taxi Plate Holders

i. Is There a Normative Case for Compensation?

The financial losses incurred by taxi plate owners due to competition from ride-sharing companies pose a policy choice dilemma: Should those losses be compensated or ignored? This question engages a broader concern about the social impact of the sharing economy. A *prima facie* case for compensation can be made on normative grounds of economic efficiency and fairness.[54]

Louis Kaplow has argued that government assurance of compensation or other relief to private actors negatively affected by welfare-enhancing policy changes will encourage those actors to invest excessively in reliance on existing regulations. In his view, private actors should not presume that regulatory regimes are immutable and should anticipate and prepare for regulatory uncertainty as they do for uncertainty in the market.[55] In contrast, other scholars argue that a requirement of compensation is conducive to welfare-enhancing policymaking.[56] A change in policy is socially desirable, other things being equal, if it produces overall gain. However, in the absence of an *ex-ante* commitment to compensation (as a matter of law or general policy), there is a risk that policymakers might disregard the costs of proposed regulations and consider only the benefits to the public, the same way a private manufacturer making a production decision might disregard the social cost of pollution.[57] A general rule requiring compensation to those adversely affected by regulation forces regulators to internalize the costs of their decisions and encourages efficient policy. Suppose, for example, that in one city there are 1,000 plate owners and that the new policies under consideration would cause each of those licences to be devalued by $30,000. The new policies should only be adopted if the sum of their benefits is greater than $30 million. (To put this number in context, according to Statistics Canada, in the twelve months before October 2016, ride-sharing services collected $241 million in Canada.[58]) One of the purposes of compensation would be to deter policymakers from proceeding with the changes unless they are prepared to pay that amount. However, Quinn and Trebilcock have pointed out that because the benefits of regulatory transition are rarely captured in full by policymakers (in the case of taxicab and ride-sharing reforms, the benefits are largely captured by consumers and ride-sharing companies), a compensation requirement is not certain to promote cost-benefit analysis and efficient outcomes.[59]

Another allocative function of compensation is to facilitate socially desirable public initiatives. Stakeholders who stand to lose from proposed policies, but who are nevertheless assured of compensation, have a smaller incentive to engage in political lobbying efforts to stop them. On the other hand, the promise of compensation may encourage rent-seeking over eligibility for compensation as well as its amount, but the cost of these may be comparatively small given the lower stakes.

It might be argued that in cities where the transition from traditional taxi regulations to a new system offering the advantages of the sharing economy has been found already to be in the public interest, adopting a policy of compensation will not improve efficiency. Compensation cannot incentivize local officials after they have made their policy decisions (councils who previously voted to legalize ride-sharing may reverse course, but may then be required to compensate ride-sharing interests instead), or reverse the wasteful expenditures and delays already incurred in the course of the political battle over ride-sharing. But a commitment to compensation can improve decision-making by municipalities still contemplating a transition, and more importantly, by every municipality that may consider other policy changes involving the sharing economy in the future. It is less clear whether or not compensation can facilitate regulatory transition in the future: an offer of compensation on the heels of massive political pressure may encourage more of the same.

One final economic consideration is what Frank Michelman called "settlement costs,"[60] which includes the cost of identifying the victims of regulation, putting a dollar value on the harms they sustain, and providing them with compensation. Because taxi licences are registered with the municipality and must be renewed annually, the class of eligible claimants is readily ascertainable. Assessing the harm and providing compensation according to some formula should be straightforward.

A different set of arguments in support of compensation relates to the distribution of regulatory benefits and burdens. Government action that focuses disproportionate regulatory burdens on particular individuals or groups is inconsistent with societal notions of justice and fairness. A policy of compensation provides some assurance against such hardships being endured, without unduly restraining government from carrying out its objectives. The ride-sharing reforms generate sizable benefits to consumers, but also to the transportation network companies and their drivers—largely at the expense of taxi plate owners. This redistribution of benefits is ancillary to the purpose of improving point-to-point transportation markets, rather than the impetus for the reforms, so compensating the losers would not frustrate a public purpose.

Whether compensation is required as a matter of fairness in any particular instance may turn on the extent of the harm, the degree to which the political interests of the claimants are adequately represented, the extent and legitimacy of reliance on existing policies, and how the entitlement which is to be protected by compensation was acquired.[61] Two general observations can be made about taxi licence plate holders as a group. The first is that they are in no way an under-represented constituency deserving of special protection, but rather constitute a well-organized and traditionally effective municipal lobby.[62] The second is that whatever one might think of the existing licence system, current plate owners cannot be said to have acquired them unjustly. But other generalizations about plate owners should be made with caution, and the cogency of the claims will vary depending on the circumstances. The most sympathetic case would be the holder of a taxi licence acquired not too long before the advent of ride-sharing, to whom the licence is both a primary source of income and an investment for retirement, very likely an immigrant to Canada.[63] To an individual in such circumstances, the devaluation of the licence may constitute significant, even catastrophic, economic hardship.[64] This sentiment was expressed before the Legislative Assembly of Western Australia in a debate over the compensation previously offered to taxi plate owners by the government:

> This motion is all about treating small business people and small investors fairly. Taxi plate owners are often drivers, but, in any event, taxi plate owners are generally small business people. They have often invested their life savings and are

often people from migrant communities who have arrived in
Australia and used all their savings—often all their families'
and extended families' savings—to invest in a business that, up
until now, has been regulated and competitors have been unlawful. That approach to taxis that has now been in place for time
immemorial has meant that the value of a taxi plate has been
significant and that people invested on the basis of the existing
law as it stood. These taxi plate investors have relied upon the
law in their investment decisions [...]. It is a matter of fairness
how these investors—these people—are treated based upon the
situation that now exists.[65]

In contrast, a less sympathetic case would be that of a taxi-plate
baron who has made a fortune by accumulating licences and renting them out to drivers. Two arguments for limiting compensation
can be made in this case. The first is that claimants in this category
are better able to protect themselves against catastrophic economic
injury by diversifying their investments. The second is that the
regulatory risk inherent in the quota system tends to be reflected
in the premiums that licences command in the market. Simply put,
allowing plate owners to enjoy excessive rents over a long period
of time, coupled with full compensation when the monopoly is
removed, would amount to double-dipping. One way of addressing these differences without sacrificing the interest of those most
likely to be affected the hardest (albeit at the expense of economic
efficiency) is to set a cap on the number of licences for which compensation is provided.

Once a policy of compensating plate owners is adopted, there is
the matter of who should fund it. The compensation could be funded
from general revenues, or from charges levied on the beneficiaries of
the regulation. The latter policy is more equitable in aligning more
closely the costs of transition with the benefits, and reduces the
incentives of special interest groups to lobby for policies that benefit
them at the expense of other groups or of the public. One obvious
way to shift the cost of ride-sharing reforms to the beneficiaries is to
compensate plate owners out of a fund collected from ride-sharing
passengers and transportation network companies. Whoever bears
the economic incidence of compensation would depend on relative
market power. In localities where a single operator such as Uber
faces no competition, the cost of compensation will be shifted to

passengers, whereas in localities with healthy competition, the operators can be expected to shoulder them.

ii. Do Taxi Plate Owners Have a Legal Right to Compensation?
Are taxi licence holders entitled, as a matter of law, to compensation
for municipal regulations accommodating ride-sharing? As the following analysis suggests, the answer is not entirely straightforward, but
more than likely negative.[66] The question has not yet come before the
Canadian courts, but has recently been dealt with in the United States.

In 2016, the Federal Court of Appeals (Seventh Circuit) held in
Joe Sanfelippo Cabs, Inc v Milwaukee (City of)[67] that the repeal of a local
restriction on the number of taxi permits issued by the defendant did
not constitute a "taking" within the meaning of the Fifth Amendment
to the United States constitution.[68] Judge Richard Posner accepted
that the taxi permits issued to the plaintiffs were "property," but reasoned that property can take many forms and, in this case, consisted
of nothing more than the (transferable) right to operate a taxicab in
the city. Importantly, the taxi permits did not confer on the plaintiffs
a property right "to be an oligopolist [and] to exclude others from
operating taxis."[69] Moreover, the former ordinance which provided
that no further taxi permits be issued by the city gave the plaintiffs
no guarantee that it would remain in effect indefinitely. In consequence, no property of the plaintiffs was "taken."[70] Judge Posner, an
avowed proponent of free enterprise, added:

> [u]ndoubtedly by freeing up entry into the taxi business the
> new ordinance will reduce the revenues of individual taxicab
> companies; that is simply the normal consequence of replacing
> a cartelized with a competitive market. But the plaintiffs exag-
> gerate when they predict ruination for themselves. Buses and
> subways and livery services and other taxi substitutes have not
> destroyed the taxi business; nor has Uber or Lyft or the private
> automobile or for that matter the bicycle. Taxicabs will not go
> the way of the horse and buggy—at least for some time.[71]

Comparisons to American takings jurisprudence must be tempered
with caution.[72] As Cromwell J.A. (as he then was) emphasized in
Mariner Real Estate Ltd v Nova Scotia (AG),[73] an American court is
tasked with deciding the constitutional validity of an uncompensated regulatory action, whereas the mandate of a Canadian court

is limited to determining whether compensation is required as a matter of statutory interpretation. The questions are "fundamentally different."[74] Indeed, in the absence of constitutional protection of private property, the Canadian jurisprudence has recognized a right to compensation only in two categories of cases. First, compensation is payable where it is expressly provided in, or can be implied from, the statute authorizing the exercise of regulatory powers. Second, compensation is payable, in the absence of contrary intention, where the exercise of regulatory powers amounts to a *de facto* expropriation of property.[75] Neither ground for compensation is likely to be made out by taxi plate owners.

The proprietary status of taxi licences in Canada may not be completely settled,[76] but the courts have recognized that taxi licences may be regarded as property in specific contexts: for example, for the purpose of division of marital property pursuant to provincial family law,[77] or for the purpose of personal property security registration and bankruptcy proceedings.[78] A plain reading of the taxi bylaws in several major Canadian cities may suggest that the licences are not property. Edmonton's *Vehicles for Hire Bylaw,* for example, states that, "[e]very licence issued pursuant to this bylaw [...] does not confer any property rights and remains at all times the sole property of the City,"[79] and similar provisions appear in the bylaws of Toronto, Ottawa, Vancouver, and Calgary. However, the rights conferred by a taxi licence are both valuable and transferable,[80] qualities often described as hallmarks of property.[81] In *Re Foster,*[82] the court summarized the relevant authorities as follows:

> [w]hat this case law reveals is a tension between the commercial reality that licences, like any commodity in restricted supply, have a value and may be traded, and the legal impact of the legislator's desire to maintain, in varying degrees, control over the industry in question. Where the control is absolute and unfettered, no property interest exists even though there is a market [...] where there is a market and a practical, historical assurance of renewal, the licensee has a right akin to a chose in action, and hence property [...]. It is obvious from all the cases that the regulatory framework is a decisive factor.[83]

In *Surdell-Kennedy Taxi Ltd v Surrey (City of),*[84] local taxi companies challenged the city's decision to issue additional taxi licences and allocate them by way of a public auction. The city relied on its corporate powers pursuant to the provisions in section 176 of the B.C. *Local Government Act*, "to acquire [...] and dispose of [...] personal property or other property, and any interest or right in or with respect to that property [on] any terms and conditions it considers appropriate."[85] The court followed *Re Foster* in holding that a taxi licence becomes intangible personal property in the hands of the licensee, and becomes then capable of being transferred or encumbered (but not before it is issued, so section 176 did not apply).

Assuming that municipally issued taxi plates can be regarded as private property, the traditional position in Canada is that any right to compensation for expropriation or regulation of private property must invariably be founded in statute. The rule was first stated by the Privy Council in a case involving injurious affection to land,[86] but remains the starting point in any discussion concerning compensation for regulation.[87] The courts, while reluctant to recognize a common law right to compensation,[88] are prepared, in principle, to infer a statutory right to compensation in appropriate circumstances, even where it is not provided expressly. For example, it is a recognized rule of construction that "unless the words of the statute clearly so demand, a statute is not to be construed so as to take away the property of a subject without compensation."[89] This principle was applied by the Supreme Court of Canada in *Manitoba Fisheries v R*.[90] There, pursuant to federal legislation, a government monopoly to export freshwater fish was given to a Crown corporation, effectively putting the long-established plaintiff out of business. The court held that the effect of the legislative scheme was to acquire the plaintiff's business goodwill, and insofar as nothing in the legislation authorized such a taking without compensation, the plaintiff was entitled to compensation.[91]

Nevertheless, the Canadian courts have resisted extending the principles upon which compensation may be founded beyond the ruling in *Manitoba Fisheries*.[92] On the contrary, subsequent case law interpreted the right to compensation quite narrowly. The rule of construction requiring compensation barring clear demonstration of opposite intention has been held inapplicable in circumstances where the owner's rights were extinguished, but the government did not acquire title to the property in question,[93] although it is a plausible and arguably the better rule.[94] In addition, the judicial standard for constructive expropriation is notoriously difficult to meet.[95] Under that test, a *de facto* expropriation entitling the owner to compensation (unless expropriation without compensation is expressly authorized) requires both an acquisition of a beneficial interest in the property or flowing from it, and a removal of all reasonable uses of the property.[96] Some of the most stringent regulations and restrictions would not ordinarily pass this test: as long as some reasonable private use is left to the owner, or as long as no interest is acquired by the public authority, then no compensation is payable, even if the property is rendered worthless.[97]

In light of this discussion, it is doubtful that municipal bylaws sanctioning ride-sharing would give rise to a right to compensation to incumbent taxi plate owners for the devaluation of their property. Such bylaws, like the repeal of the permit freeze in *Joe Sanfelippo Cabs Inc*,[98] and unlike the legislation in *Manitoba Fisheries*,[99] do not deprive the licence holders of any of their rights or affect their usage, and do not therefore constitute an actual or constructive taking of property. Moreover, although provincial legislation could easily specifically authorize compensation, none of the enabling statutes under which taxi and livery regulations are adopted currently authorize compensation expressly, or imply that compensation is intended, for licence quota changes or for any acts short of revoking licence holder's rights.

Doctrinal restrictions on the power of municipalities further militate against an implied right to compensation. Municipal councils are prohibited from ceding, bargaining away, or otherwise fettering their legislative powers unless authorized to do so by the legislature. Thus, a direct promise to enact, or maintain, or refrain from enacting a bylaw is illegal on its face.[100] In *Pacific National Investments Ltd v Victoria (City of)*, the Supreme Court of Canada held that the enabling legislation did not give the municipality an implied power to enter into a bargain with a private developer that would implicitly guarantee the developer compensation in case of a future rezoning of the developer's lands in exchange for the developer's contribution of public amenities. The majority of the court reasoned that such an obligation on the part of the city would constitute an indirect fetter of council's legislative powers.[101] Justice LeBel, for the majority, expressed skepticism at the notion of "an implication of an implication [which] begins to tax the imagination."[102] The dissenting opinion was prepared to recognize an implied right to compensation on the grounds that the arrangement would otherwise be "contrary to business sense and to all obligations of fairness."[103] The majority's reasoning would hinder a claim by taxi licence holders for an implied right to compensation, and in the absence of corresponding contributions by plate owners, the claim would fail even under the dissent's business sense test.[104]

IV. Compensating Taxi Licence Holders

As the preceding section shows, an argument for compensation for private losses occasioned by regulatory changes to facilitate the sharing economy can be made on policy grounds of efficiency and equity. A commitment to compensation can curtail lobbying and promote welfare enhancing reforms and in spreading the costs of transition, compensation is consistent with notions of fairness where there is no particular reason to let the losses lie. Compensation to taxi plate owners, whose economic interests are seriously jeopardized by municipal sanctioning of ride-sharing, represents an important test case and should be considered in light of the above arguments. As it is unlikely that taxi licence holders can establish a legal right to compensation before the courts, it is up to policymakers to enable and design a compensation scheme that can appropriately account for the local effects of regulatory transition on the industry and the factors which may affect the merits of any given claim, as well as a source of funding for any compensation.

i. Do Municipalities Have the Power to Compensate?

On May 3, 2016, the Toronto City Council directed the executive director of the Municipal Licensing and Standards Committee to report on the feasibility of establishing a transition fund for taxicab plate owners whose "investments have been negatively impacted by new market entrants."[105] In the absence of specific authority in their enabling legislation, the power of Canadian municipalities to extend assistance to taxi licence owners is not clear. In several provinces, the legislation expressly prohibits councils from extending direct financial assistance to any person or business beyond what is ordinarily offered to other ratepayers or inhabitants.[106] The *Municipal Act* of Ontario still contains such a prohibition,[107] as does the *Community Charter* of British Columbia[108] and the *Municipal Government Act* of Nova Scotia.[109] Section 82 of the *City of Toronto Act* provides that "the City shall not assist directly or indirectly any manufacturing business or other industrial or commercial enterprise through the granting of bonuses for that purpose."[110] The historic purpose of "anti-bonusing" provisions was to restrain municipalities from jeopardizing their financial positions by competing for business. None of the cases involving allegations of bonusing dealt with an attempt by a council to mitigate the adverse impact of its own policies. In addition, although the rule against bonusing is still in the books, many of the rules restricting municipalities have been abandoned, and a broad and purposive approach to the interpretation of enabling legislation has been embraced.[111] In recent decisions, anti-bonusing provisions have been construed in light of this approach. For example, in *Friends of Lansdowne Inc v Ottawa (City of)*,[112] the Court of Appeal held that the Ontario provision only prohibits the granting of an "obvious advantage or undue benefit [which] on the spectrum of benefits, [...] falls closer to providing a party with an unmerited windfall."[113] Arguably this definition would preclude a municipality from extending transition relief to affected plate owners. Judicial guidance or legislative changes may be required to clarify such a power.

ii. Compensation Schemes in Australia

Local policymakers might draw useful lessons from the Australian experience with compensation schemes. As in Canada, Australia's taxi industry has been shaken up by competition from transportation network companies offering ride-sharing services. Most Australian states have moved to regulate sharing and to reform the commercial point-to-point transportation sector. Regulatory and licensing requirements for traditional taxis have been relaxed to even the playing field, and only taxis are still permitted to provide hail services. Taxi licence values have plummeted, and the governments of several of the states have announced or implemented transition assistance, including partial compensation for plate owners. Unlike in Canada, the taxi industry is not regulated at the local or metropolitan level, but by state law.

Taxi licence prices in Sydney, New South Wales, had slumped by the end of 2015 to AUD$220,000 from an average of AUD$425,000 four years earlier,[114] in part due to the issuance of additional licences by the authorities, and in part due to ride-sharing. In June 2016, the New South Wales government passed the *Point to Point Transport (Taxis and Hire Vehicles) Act*, which provides a single regulatory framework for taxi services and ride-sharing. The Act explicitly provides that no compensation is payable by the state as a consequence of the enactment, its operation, or any statement or conduct related to it.[115] At the same time, the Act provided for regulations to establish transitional assistance funds for eligible taxi licence holders. Under these regulations, AUD$20,000 was payable to each holder of one taxi licence and AUD$40,000 was payable to each holder of two or more licences.[116] Provisions have been made for additional transition assistance, but these have not yet been implemented. Additionally, a small fund has been established for business advisory services, to help the taxi and hire car industries adapt to the point-to-point transport industry reforms. The government plans to introduce a AUD$1 surcharge on all trips booked by a taxi or ride-sharing company.

The government of Victoria announced comprehensive reforms to the taxi and ride-sharing industry in August 2016. Metropolitan Melbourne licence prices had dropped from about AUD$376,000 in 2012–13 to AUD$159,000 in 2015–16, and no transfers have been recorded after October 2016.[117] The government announced a support package for taxi and hire-car licence holders. An AUD$50 million "fairness fund" was established to assist eligible taxi licence holders who were experiencing significant financial hardship as a result of the proposed reforms, including a loss of income, significant difficulty in meeting ongoing debt obligations related to the licence, or a lack of available funds to meet financial commitments.[118] In addition, the government said that it will provide transition assistance payments to taxi licence holders in the amount of AUD$100,000 for the first licence, and up to AUD$50,000 for each additional licence up to a total of four licenses for each licence holder.[119] Finally, the government plans to introduce a universal AUD$2 levy per ride on all taxi and ride-sharing trips. The levy will replace annual licence fees and will support existing licence holders.

Queensland had legalized ride-sharing in September 2016, although Uber had been operating in Brisbane since 2014. Taxi licence prices were worth over AUD$500,000 in 2014 according to industry data, but fell sharply in the following year.[120] The Queensland government approved an industry assistance package that offered transitional assistance to eligible licence holders in the amount of AUD$20,000 for one taxi licence and AUD$40,000 for two or more licences. The assistance was recently enlarged by a further AUD$9,000 for a licence holder/operator, and AUD$4,500 for each licence held but not operated, up to ten payments in total. The government has similarly announced a "Hardship Fund" and funding for business advice to assist taxi and limousine businesses to adapt to the new regulatory framework.[121]

The government of Western Australia established a "Transition Adjustment Assistance Grant" to eligible taxi plate owners in metropolitan Perth in the amount of AUD$20,000 for each multi-purpose taxi plate and AUD$6,000 for each restricted plate, with no maximum.[122] The transition assistance program under development includes a "Hardship Fund" for owners suffering severe financial hardship as a direct consequence of industry reforms, and innovation funding administered through the Small Business Development Corporation to assist taxi plate owners and lessees to adjust and transition their business models was previously announced.[123]

The government of South Australia, where ride-sharing was legalized in July 2016, has also announced an assistance program that will offer AUD$30,000 per taxi licence, with no maximum, and AUD$50 per week for a maximum of eleven months for lessees of taxi licences.[124] In contrast, no compensation or other assistance has been announced by the governments of Tasmania, which legalized ride-sharing in late 2016, or the Australian Capital Territory, where ride-sharing was legalized in late 2015. The latter intends to reassess its policies in two years, when the effect of industry reforms on taxi licence values would be known.

Several features of the above schemes stand out. First, the implementation of compensation (and the regulation of point-to-point transportation) is carried out by state government pursuant to primary legislation, which removes any question of *vires*. Second, efficiency concerns provide a weak explanation for the schemes: the decision to offer compensation (or not) in each state was taken after the reforms had been decided, and no basis for the sum provided has been offered; at any rate, the amounts do not correspond to the actual losses. Third, the cap on the number of licences for which compensation is available in some states provides more protection to owner-operators and small investors than to holders of multiple licences. This is consistent with the fairness concerns outlined earlier.[125]

V. Conclusion

The technological developments of the sharing economy have thrown into question existing business models and regulatory arrangements. In Canada, the introduction of ride-sharing exposed a taxi industry whose time has passed, resistant to innovation and propped up by local regulations that serve taxi plate owners at the expense of the public. For the most part, the regulation of ride-sharing shifts the focus of government supervision away from market supply and demand, and to the enforcement of safety and quality standards. It is clearly not the deal the taxicab drivers asked for a century ago. But the responsibility of local government is to the public at large. Nevertheless, the government, which is responsible for putting in place a dysfunctional system, should consider compensating the adversely affected by the transition to the new regulatory framework. A policy of compensating the losers is fairer and makes for better public decisions by encouraging governments to consider the welfare implications of regulations.

There are sound arguments against compensating taxi plate owners for a devaluation of their licences. For years, many have reaped windfall profits at the expense of their passengers and some of their drivers. Moreover, licence values already reflect the regulatory risk of reliance on existing entitlement. Finally, it is difficult to disentangle the effects of regulation from those of technological changes and market changes in general. Yet, letting the losses lie will inflict ruinous harm on individual plate owners who are at fault for nothing more than investing poorly.

Canadian law does not establish a legal right to compensation for the effects of regulatory changes generally or for the devaluation of taxi licences specifically, but policymakers can follow the Australian example in recognizing the case for compensation and other forms of assistance. Compensation schemes should be devised to reflect the losses as closely as possible and the differences in circumstances between different plate owners. This will a require careful study of local markets.

Notes

1. Associate Professor, Faculty of Law, University of Alberta. I am grateful to Shaun Campbell and Victoria Rudolf for their excellent research assistance, and to Malcolm Lavoie, to Derek McKee, and to an anonymous

reviewer for providing helpful comments on earlier drafts. Any errors and inaccuracies are mine.

2. Harry A Miskimin, *The Economy of Later Renaissance Europe: 1460–1600* (Cambridge, UK: Cambridge University Press, 1977) at 4.

3. *Ibid* at 92.

4. See Yoram Barzel, *Economic Analysis of Property Rights*, 2nd ed (Cambridge, UK: Cambridge University Press, 1997).

5. Miskimin, *supra* note 2.

6. See Paul Stephen Dempsey, "Taxi Industry Regulation, Deregulation & Reregulation: The Paradox of Market Failure" (1996) 24:1 Transportation LJ 73; Roger F Teal & Mary Berglund, "The Impact of Taxicab Deregulation in the USA" (1987) 21:1 J Transport Economics & Policy 37 at 37.

7. See Brishen Rogers, "The Social Costs of Uber" (2015) 82 U Chicago L Rev Dialogue 85 at 87.

8. See Benoit-Mario Papillon, "The Taxi Industry and Its Regulation in Canada" (1982) Economic Council of Canada Working Paper No 30; Donald F Davis, "The Canadian Taxi Wars, 1925–1950" (1998) 27:1 Urban History Rev 7. See also the chapter by Eric Tucker in this volume, "Uber and the Unmaking and Remaking of Taxi Capitalisms: Technology, Law, and Resistance in Historical Perspective" [ed.].

9. For examples of taxi regulations currently in force in Canadian cities, see City of Vancouver, by-law No 6066, *Vehicles for Hire* (19 October 2016), online: <http://former.vancouver.ca/bylaws/6066c.PDF>; City of Edmonton, by-law No 17400, *Vehicle for Hire Bylaw* (27 June 2017), online: <https://www.edmonton.ca/documents/Bylaws/C17400.pdf>; City of Toronto, by-law No 546, *Licensing of Vehicles-for-Hire* (7 October 2016), online: <http://www.toronto.ca/legdocs/municode/toronto-code-546.pdf>; City of Montreal, by-law No 10-009, *By-Law Concerning Taxi Transportation* (15 October 2015), online: <http://ville.montreal.qc.ca/pls/portal/docs/page/bur_taxi_fr/media/documents/RCG10-009_en.pdf>. In Manitoba, the province has proposed only recently to delegate the regulation of taxis to municipalities: see Bill 30, *The Local Vehicles for Hire Act*, 2nd Sess, 41st Leg, Manitoba, 2016, online: <http://web2.gov.mb.ca/bills/41-2/b030e.php>.

10. See e.g. *Municipal Government Act*, RSA 2000, c M-26, ss 7, 8. In particular, section 8(c.1) provides local councils with the express power to pass a bylaw to "establish and specify the fees, rates, fares, tariffs or charges that may be charged for the hire of taxis or limousines."

11. See e.g. *City of Toronto Act, 2006*, SO 2006, c 11, Schedule A, s 94(1)(c).

12. *United Taxi Drivers' Fellowship of Southern Alberta v Calgary (City of)*, 1998 ABQB 184, ultimately aff'g 2004 SCC 19 [United Taxi Drivers].

13. *Ibid* at para 12. For an example of the methods by which a municipality might set its taxi quotas, see Hara Associates Inc, "Scoping Study:

Determining a Better Structure for the Calgary Taxi Industry" (31 August 2011), online: Livery Transport Services, City of Calgary <http://www.calgary.ca/CSPS/ABS/Documents/Livery-Transport-Services/LPT2011-90-EvaluationofTaxiLimousineAdvis-Att4.pdf>.

14. David Seymour, "The Case for Taxi Deregulation" (2009) 55 FCPP 1 [Seymour, "The Case for Taxi Deregulation"].

15. As famously characterized in Charles A Reich, "The New Property" (1964) 73 Yale LJ 733 at 735.

16. See Barry Prentice, Charles Mossman & Adam van Schijnde, "Taxi Fares and the Capitalization of Taxi Licenses" (Paper delivered at the Canadian Transportation Research Forum, May 2010), (2010), Canadian Transportation Research Forum, Proceedings Issue, 45th Annual Meeting 769; David Seymour, "Who Owns Taxi Licenses?" (2009) 67 FCPP 1 at 9 [Seymour, "Who Owns Taxi Licenses?"].

17. Hara Associates Inc, "Assessment of Changes in Edmonton Taxi Demand and Supply" (7 April 2008), online: City of Edmonton <webdocs.edmonton.ca/OcctopusDocs/Public/Complete/Reports/.../2008PDD003.doc>. The highest reported transfer prices for taxi licenses in each of the following cities: Toronto, Montreal, Calgary, Ottawa, Edmonton, Mississauga, Winnipeg, Vancouver, Windsor, Saskatoon, and Regina, are cited by Seymour, "Who Owns Taxi Licenses?," *supra* note 16 at 15.

18. As high as $200,000 for an Edmonton taxi license in early 2015. See e.g. "More Cabs, Cheaper Plates Will Cripple Taxi Industry, Say Some Drivers," *CBC News* (23 January 2015), online: <http://www.cbc.ca/news/canada/edmonton/ more-cabs-cheaper-plates-will-cripple-taxi-industry-say-some-drivers-1.2929295>.

19. See e.g. Seymour, "The Case for Taxi Deregulation," *supra* note 14 at 17.

20. See Sara Abraham, Aparna Sundar & Dale Whitmore, *Toronto Taxi Drivers: Ambassadors of the City* (Toronto: Ryerson University and University of Toronto-Mississauga, 2008). See also Peter Cheney, "'We Get Something and They Steal It Away,'" *The Globe and Mail* (6 September 2003), online: <http://www.theglobeandmail.com/news/national/we-get-something-then-they-steal-it-away/article25578026>; Peter Cheney, "How Uber Is Ending the Dirty Dealings Behind Toronto's Cab Business," *The Globe and Mail* (16 July 2015), online: <https://www.theglobeandmail.com/globe-drive/adventure/red-line/how-uber-is-ending-the-dirty-dealings-behind-torontos-cab-business/article25515301>.

21. See e.g. Adrian T Moore & Ted Balaker, "Do Economists Reach a Conclusion on Taxi Deregulation?" (2006) 3:1 Econ J Watch 109; Prentice, Mossman & Schijnde, *supra* note 16.

22. United States, The Bureau of Economics of the Federal Trade Commission, *An Economic Analysis of Taxicab Regulation*, by Mark W

Frankena & Paul A Pautler (Washington, DC: US Government Printing Office, 1984) at 155.

23. D Wayne Taylor, "The Economic Effects of the Direct Regulation of the Taxicab Industry in Metropolitan Toronto" (1989) 25:2 Logistics & Transportation Rev 169.

24. The opportunity costs to qualified individuals who are denied a licence were not included in the calculation. See Austl, WA, Economic Regulation Authority, *Inquiry into Microeconomic Reform in Western Australia: Final Report* (Perth, WA: Economic Regulation Authority, 2014) ch 7.2.

25. *Ibid.*

26. Sean D Barrett, "Regulatory Capture, Property Rights and Taxi Deregulation: A Case Study" (2003) 23:4 Econ Affairs 34.

27. For a famously "tweeted" schematic explaining Uber's success, see David Sacks, "Uber's Virtuous Cycle. Geographic Density Is the New Network Effect" (6 June 2014 at 5:34 p.m.), online: Twitter <https://twitter.com/DavidSacks/status/475073311383105536>.

28. Uber's terms of service for passengers can be accessed on its website. See "Terms of Service," online: Uber Terms <https://www.uber.com/legal/terms/ca>. A copy of Uber's "Technology Services Agreement" with partner drivers (December 11, 2015) is on file with the author.

29. *Ibid.*

30. See Igor Dosen & Helen Rosolen, "Uber and Ridesharing" (2016) Parliament of Victoria Research Paper No 2 ("[i]n Australia, Uber remains the major rideshare provider, although other service providers are beginning to increase their market share" at 3).

31. "Mums Taxi" (4 May 2016), online: GoFundMe <https://www.gofundme.com/mumstaxi>.

32. Peter Cohen et al, "Using Big Data to Estimate Consumer Surplus: The Case of Uber" (2016) National Bureau of Economic Research Working Paper No 22627.

33. See Amanda Eaken, "NRDC Urban Solutions to Lead First Climate Analysis of Uber and Lyft" (13 November 2015), *Expert Blog* (blog), online: <https://www.nrdc.org/experts/amanda-eaken/nrdc-urban-solutions-lead-first-climate-analysis-uber-and-lyft>.

34. According to Uber's website, it currently operates in Calgary, Edmonton, Gatineau, Hamilton, Kingston, Kitchener-Waterloo, Lethbridge, London, Montreal, Ottawa, Quebec City, Toronto, and Windsor, in addition to the "Niagara Region." See "Uber Cities," online: Uber Ride <https://www.uber.com/en-CA/cities>.

35. See e.g. Rhianna Schmunk, "Uber Is Coming to B.C., Province Announces," *CBC News* (7 March 2017), online: <http://www.cbc.ca/news/canada/british-columbia/bc-taxi-1.4013315>; "Halifax to Stay an

Uber-Free Zone," *The Chronicle Herald* (1 April 2016), online: <http://thechronicleherald.ca/metro/1353524-halifax-to-stay-an-uber-free-zone>.

36. Canada, Competition Bureau, *Modernizing Regulation in the Canadian Taxi Industry*, (Gatineau, QC: Competition Bureau, 2015), online: <http://www.competitionbureau.gc.ca/eic/site/cb-bc.nsf/eng/04007.html>.

37. *Ibid.*

38. See e.g. City of Ottawa, by-law No 2016-272, *Vehicle for Hire* (30 September 2016), online: <http://ottawa.ca/en/vehicle-hire-law-no-2016-272>.

39. Dean Beeby, "Budget 2017: Hello Uber Tax, Goodbye Transit Credit," *CBC News* (22 March 2017), online: <http://www.cbc.ca/news/politics/federal-budget-2017-uber-bonds-transit-tax-1.4036893>.

40. See e.g. "Ontario Taxi Drivers Protest Uber on Parliament Hill," *CBC News* (2 February 2016), online: <http://www.cbc.ca/news/canada/ottawa/taxi-driver-protest-against-uber-parliament-hill-1.3430284>; Elise Stolte, "Edmonton Taxi Drivers Protest Uber, Shouting and Tearing Off Their Shirts at City Council Meeting," *National Post* (23 September 2015), online: <http://news.nationalpost.com/news/canada/edmonton-taxi-drivers-protest-uber-shouting-and-tearing-off-their-shirts-at-city-council-meeting>.

41. See e.g. David Reevely, "One of Ottawa's Taxi Barons Leads National Anti-Uber Effort," *Ottawa Citizen* (10 July 2015), online: <http://ottawacitizen.com/news/national/reevely-one-of-ottawas-taxi-barons-leads-national-anti-uber-effort>. For reported data comparing lobbying by Uber and the taxi industry in Toronto, see Peter Kim, "Uber and Taxi Industry Lobbying Data for the City of Toronto," *Global News* (3 May 2016), online: <http://globalnews.ca/news/2675643/uber-and-taxi-industry-lobbying-data-for-the-city-of-toronto>.

42. Peter Cheney, "Why Uber is the Best Thing to Happen to Toronto's Taxi Industry," *The Globe and Mail* (2 May 2016), online: <http://www.theglobeandmail.com/news/toronto/why-uber-is-the-best-thing-to-happen-to-torontos-taxi-industry/article29825194>.

43. See Thor Berger, Chinchih Chen & Carl Benedikt Frey, "Drivers of Disruption? Estimating the Uber Effect" (2017) Oxford Martin School Working Paper, online: <http://www.oxfordmartin.ox.ac.uk/downloads/academic/ Uber_Drivers_of_Disruption.pdf>.

44. This is consistent with the findings of earlier studies. See Jonathan V Hall & Alan B Krueger, "An Analysis of the Labor Market for Uber's Driver-Partners in the United States" (2016) National Bureau of Economic Research Working Paper No 22843.

45. Berger, Chen & Frey, *supra* note 43 at 10.

46. Correspondence with Vanessa Fletcher, Acting Manager of Policy and Planning for Toronto Municipal Licensing and Standards, on file with the author.

47. Correspondence with Kayla Matteoti, licensing and policy advisor, City of Edmonton, on file with the author.

48. Patrick Cain, "Toronto Taxi Licence Prices Are Plummeting. Is Uber to Blame?," *Global News* (22 January 2015), online: <http://globalnews.ca/news/1780260/toronto-taxi-licence-prices-are-plummeting-is-uber-to-blame>. Some taxi licenses are transferred within the same family for $1, and are not included in the analysis.

49. Tim Querengesser, "Edmonton's Taxi Plate Market Begins Collapsing," *Metro News* (8 February 2016), online: <http://www.metronews.ca/news/edmonton/2016/02/08/edmonton-taxi-plate-market-collapsing.html>.

50. David Reevely, "City Hall Blog: What a Taxi Plate Goes For," *Ottawa Citizen* (12 April 2016), online: <http://ottawacitizen.com/news/local-news/city-hall-blog-what-a-taxi-plate-goes-for>.

51. Helen Pike, "Calgary's Taxi Plate Market Tanking After Uber, New Plate Approval," *Metro News* (2 December 2016), online: <http://www.metronews.ca/news/calgary/2016/12/01/calgary-taxi-plate-market-tanking-uber-new-plate-approval.html>.

52. Barrett, *supra* note 26.

53. Richard William Kelly, "The Uber Effect" (2016) Western University Undergraduate Awards Paper No 8, online: <http://ir.lib.uwo.ca/cgi/viewcontent.cgi?article=1007&context=ungradawards_2016>.

54. See generally Frank I Michelman, "Property, Utility and Fairness: Comments on the Ethical Foundations of 'Just Compensation' Law" (1967) 80 Harv L Rev 1165; John Quinn & Michael J Trebilcock, "Compensation, Transition Costs, and Regulatory Change" (1982) 32:2 UTLJ 117 at 135. The normative argument for compensating taxi licence owners affected by local ride-sharing sanctioning ordinances is considered in David K Suska, "Regulatory Takings and Ridesharing: 'Just Compensation' For Taxi Medallion Owners?" (2016) 19 NYUJ Legis & Pub Pol'y 183.

55. Louis Kaplow, "An Economic Analysis of Legal Transitions" (1986) 99:3 Harv L Rev 509.

56. See Michelman, *supra* note 54; Lawrence Blume & Daniel L Rubinfeld, "Compensation for Takings: An Economic Analysis" (1984) 72 Cal L Rev 569; William A Fischel, *Regulatory Takings: Law, Economics, and Politics* (Cambridge, MA: Harvard University Press, 1995) at 141–82.

57. Failure to account for private losses in public decision-making is sometimes referred to in the literature as the "fiscal illusion" problem. See Blume & Rubinfeld, *supra* note 56. For criticism, see Bethany R Berger, "The Illusion of Fiscal Illusion in Regulatory Takings" (2017) 66 Am U L Rev 1.

58. Canada, Statistics Canada, *The Sharing Economy in Canada*, (Ottawa: Statistics Canada, 28 February 2017), online: <http://www.statcan.gc.ca/daily-quotidien/170228/dq170228b-eng.pdf>.

59. See Quinn & Trebilcock, *supra* note 54 at 135.

60. Michelman, *supra* note 54 ("'[s]ettlement costs' are measured by the dollar value of the time, effort, and resources which would be required in order to reach compensation settlements adequate to avoid demoralization costs. Included are the costs of settling not only the particular compensation claims presented, but also those of all persons so affected by the measure in question or similar measures as to have claims not obviously distinguishable by the available settlement apparatus" at 1214).

61. Some of these concerns are reflected in the American "regulatory takings" jurisprudence, and in particular, the "ad hoc, factual inquiry" standard sketched in *Penn Central Transp Co v New York (City of)*, 98 S Ct 2646 (US 26 June 1978). See section III.ii, *below*, for the differing law in Canada. The same concerns are mimicked in the foreign investor protection provisions of the North American Free Trade Agreement.

62. See David Seymour, "The End of Taxi Regulation: Why GPS-Enabled Smartphones Will Send Traditional Taxi Regulation the Way of the Dodo" (2011) 105 FCPP 1.

63. According to the 2006 census, one in two taxi drivers in Canada was an immigrant—double the ratio of immigrants in Canada in the same age group. See Canada, Citizenship and Immigration Canada, *Who Drives a Taxi in Canada?*, by Li Xu (Ottawa: Citizenship and Immigration Canada, 2012).

64. Accordingly, compensation in such circumstances is also arguably more strongly warranted on efficiency grounds, because of the higher marginal utility of the lost income/wealth (i.e., "risk aversion"). See Robert D Cooter & Thomas Ulen, *Law & Economics*, 5th ed (Boston, MA: Pearson/Addison Wesley, 2008) at 49–52.

65. Austl, WA, Legislative Assembly, *Hansard* (21 June 2016) at 1 (Mr. McGowan, Rockingham—Leader of the Opposition).

66. The discussion of the right to compensation is limited to the law in Canada's common law provinces.

67. *Joe Sanfelippo Cabs, Inc v Milwaukee (City of)*, 839 F (3d) 613 (7th Cir 2016) [*Joe Sanfelippo*].

68. See US Const amend V, which famously provides: "nor shall private property be taken for public use, without just compensation."

69. *Joe Sanfelippo*, *supra* note 67 at para 1.

70. *Ibid* at para 1.

71. *Ibid* at para 3.

72. In addition, Michael Trebilock recently argued that a focus on the American taking clause has led the academic debate on compensation to losers "astray." In his view, discourse should focus on political institutions, which are more suited to tailoring transitional solutions to regulatory transitions than courts tasked with "all-or-nothing" arbitration of constitutional rights. See Michael Trebilcock, *Dealing with Losers: The Political Economy of Policy Transitions* (New York: Oxford University Press, 2014) at 29.

73. *Mariner Real Estate Ltd v Nova Scotia (AG)*, 1999 NSCA 98 [*Mariner Real Estate*].

74. *Ibid* at para 40.

75. See Eran Kaplinsky, "Property Rights, Politics, and Community in Canada, and the Alberta Land Stewardship Act" (2012) 45:1 Hosei Riron JL & Pol 78.

76. For discussion of government licences as property rights, see Christopher Essert, "Property in Licenses and the Law of Things" (2014) 59 McGill LJ 559 (arguing that licences ought to be treated as property rights).

77. See *Wehbe v Wehbe*, 2016 ONSC 1445.

78. See *Re Foster*, [1992] O.J. No 352, 1992 CanLII 7428 (ON SC); *Re Rogers*, 2001 ABQB 551.

79. *City of Edmonton, supra* note 9, s 22.

80. See e.g. *ibid*, ss 24–25.

81. Thomas GW Telfer, "Statutory Licences and the Search for Property: The End of the Imbroglio?" (2007) 45 Can Bus LJ 224. For discussion of this approach and the question of the status of government licenses for registration of securities and bankruptcy, see *Saulnier (Receiver of) v Royal Bank of Canada*, 2008 SCC 58.

82. *Re Foster, supra* note 78.

83. *Ibid* para 18 [citations omitted].

84. *Surdell-Kennedy Taxi Ltd v Surrey (City of)*, 2001 BCSC 1265.

85. *Ibid*.

86. *Sisters of Charity of Rockingham v R*, [1922] 2 A.C. 315, 1922 CanLII 489 (UK JCPC).

87. For examples of Canadian cases recognizing the statutory compensation rule, see *R v Tener*, [1985] 1 SCR 533, 1985 CanLII 76 [*Tener*]; *Johnson v Nova Scotia*, 2005 NSCA 99 at para 49; *Rock Resources Inc v British Columbia*, 2003 BCCA 324 at para 168, leave to appeal to the SCC refused, [2003] SCCA No 375; *Semiahmoo Indian Band v Canada*, [1997] FCJ No 842 at para 112, 1997 CarswellNat 1316 (FCA); *Steer Holdings Ltd v Manitoba*, [1993] 2 WWR 146 at para 4, 1992 CarswellMan 150 (Man CA); *Woods Manufacturing Co v R*, [1949] Ex. C.R. 9, 1948 CarswellNat 55, rev'g on other grounds [1951] SCR 504, 1951 CarswellNat 272. The statutory

nature of the right to compensation remains a part of English law. See *Waters v Welsh Development Agency*, [2004] UKHL 19 ("[c]ompulsory expropriation of land is a creature of statute. There is no common law right or extant crown prerogative that allows such a thing. So it might reasonably be thought that the basis on which compensation would be paid for land compulsorily acquired would be provided for by statute. And so it is" at para 84). See further Eran Kaplinsky & David R Percy, "The Impairment of Subsurface Resource Rights by Government as a 'Taking' of Property: A Canadian Perspective" in Bjorn Hoops et al, eds, *Rethinking Expropriation Law II: Context, Criteria, and Consequences of Expropriation* (The Hague, Netherlands: Eleven International Publishing, 2015) 223.

88. *Contra* Paul A Warchuk, "Rethinking Compensation for Expropriation" (2015) 48 UBC L Rev 655 (arguing for a right to compensation for a taking at Canadian common law). See also Russell Brown, "'Takings': Government Liability to Compensate for Forcibly Acquired Property" in Karen Horsman & J Gareth Morley, eds, *Government Liability: Law and Practice* (Aurora: Canada Law Book, 2007) 4-1 at 4–33.

89. *De Keyser's Royal Hotel Ltd, Re*, [1920] AC 508 (HL (Eng)), citing *London & North Western Railway Co v Evans*, [1893] 1 Ch 16, 28 [*De Keyser's Royal Hotel*].

90. *Manitoba Fisheries Ltd v R*, [1979] 1 SCR 101, 1978 CanLII 22 [*Manitoba Fisheries*].

91. *Ibid* at para 36.

92. For a rare exception, see *Lynch v St. John's (City)*, 2016 NLCA 35, leave to appeal to SCC refused, [2016] SCCA No 390.

93. See e.g. *Tener, supra* note 87 ("[w]here land has been taken the statute will be construed in light of a presumption in favour of compensation but no such presumption exists in the case of injurious affection where no land has been taken" at para 56) [citations omitted].

94. In *De Keyser's Royal Hotel, supra* note 89, the question was whether an owner whose hotel property was requisitioned during World War I was entitled to compensation as a question of the proper interpretation of the legislative scheme, which was ambiguous at best. The House of Lords imputed to Parliament an intention to compensate the owner, because the legislature cannot fairly be supposed to intend that one individual suffer an uncompensated deprivation in the name of the public interest. Lord Atkinson stated accordingly that it would be almost inconceivable for the Crown to claim for national security purposes the right to knock down fences, or cause any buildings to be destroyed without being legally bound to compensate the owners. The presumption of compensation is not therefore dependent on any acquisition by the state.

95. For criticism, see Russell Brown, "The Constructive Taking at the Supreme Court of Canada: Once More, Without Feeling" (2007) 40 UBC L Rev 315.

96. See *Canadian Pacific Railway v Vancouver (City of)*, 2006 SCC 5 at para 30.

97. *Ibid; Mariner Real Estate, supra* note 73.

98. *Joe Sanfelippo, supra* note 67.

99. *Manitoba Fisheries, supra* note 90.

100. See *Vancouver (City of) v British Columbia (Registrar of Land Registration District)*, [1955] 2 DLR 709, 1955 CanLII 275 (BC CA).

101. *Pacific National Investments Ltd v Victoria (City of)*, 2000 SCC 64 [*Pacific National*]. In follow-up proceedings between the same parties, based on unjust enrichment, the SCC held that the City was required to disgorge the benefits it received from the developer under the contract. See *Pacific National Investments Ltd v Victoria (City of)*, 2004 SCC 75.

102. *Pacific National, supra* note 101 at para 42.

103. *Ibid* at para 84.

104. But see *Adefarakan v Toronto (City of)*, [2000] OJ No 3555, 2000 CanLII 22819 (ON SC). The case involved claims by certain taxicab drivers in Toronto, that in exchange for agreeing to adhere to a code of conduct they were promised that they would be included on a waiting list to acquire new transferable taxi licenses from the city. The city subsequently passed new regulations providing that all new licences issued by the city would be non-transferable. The plaintiffs sued for breach of contract, negligent misrepresentation, expropriation, and breach of fiduciary duty, and demanded compensation. The court refused the city's motion to strike the plaintiffs' pleadings, and allowed the case to go trial. See also J Gareth Morley, "Sovereign Promises: Does Canada Have a Law of Administrative Contracts?" (2010) 23:1 Can J Admin L & Prac 17.

105. Toronto City Council, "A New Vehicle-for-Hire Bylaw to Regulate Toronto's Ground Transportation Industry, Item 2016.LS10.3" (3 May 2016) at para 92, online: Toronto.ca <http://app.toronto.ca/tmmis/viewAgendaItemHistory.do?item=2016.LS10.3>.

106. See Stanley M Makuch, Neil Craik & Signe B Leisk, *Canadian Municipal and Planning Law*, 2nd ed (Toronto: Carswell, 2004) at 41.

107. *Municipal Act*, SO 2001, c 25, s 106.

108. *Community Charter*, SBC 2003, c 26, s 25.

109. *Municipal Government Act*, SNS 1998, c 18, s 57(2).

110. *City of Toronto Act, supra* note 11, s 82(1).

111. See *Shell Canada Products Ltd v Vancouver (City of)*, [1994] 1 SCR 231, 1994 CanLII 115; *Nanaimo (City of) v Rascal Trucking Ltd*, 2000 SCC 13; *United Taxi Drivers, supra* note 12.

112. *Friends of Lansdowne Inc v Ottawa (City of)*, 2012 ONCA 273.

113. *Ibid* at para 49.

114. Austl, NSW, Roads and Maritime, *Sydney Metropolitan Transport District Taxi Licence Transfers* (Sidney: Roads and Maritime Service, 2017), online: <http://www.rms.nsw.gov.au/about/corporate-publications/statistics/public-passenger-vehicles/licence-transfers/sydney.html>.

115. *Point to Point Transport (Taxis and Hire Vehicles) Act 2016* (NSW), s 157.

116. *Point to Point Transport (Taxis and Hire Vehicles) Regulation 2016* (NSW), Schedule 1.

117. For annual reports of the Victoria Taxi Services Commission, see "Taxi Services Commission," online: TSC <http://taxi.vic.gov.au>.

118. Austl, Vic, Economic Development, Jobs, Transport and Resources, *Support Package for Taxi and Hire Car Licence Holders* (Victoria: Victoria State Government, 2017), online: <http://economicdevelopment.vic.gov.au/transport/rail-and-roads/taxis/support-package-taxi-and-hire-car-reform>.

119. *Ibid.*

120. Alexandria Utting, "Queensland Taxi Licence Owners Fear Price Drop as Uber Gains Traction," *The Courier Mail* (10 April 2015), online: <http://www.couriermail.com.au/business/queensland-taxi-licence-owners-fear-price-drop-as-uber-gains-traction/news-story/58fd901a0d913054cf3c553f176e0a54>. Public data on transfer prices has not been released since 2015.

121. Austl, Qld, Queensland Rural and Industry Development Authority, *Taxi and Limousine Industry Assistance Scheme Regulation 2016* (Brisbane: Queensland Government, 2017), online: <http://www.qraa.qld.gov.au/current-programs/taxi-and-limousine-industry-assistance-scheme-regulation-2016-industry-hardship-assistance-scheme>.

122. *Taxi Act 1994* (WA), ss 30J-30M.

123. Austl, WA, Department of Transport, *Hardship Fund*, online: <http://www.transport.wa.gov.au/On-demandTransport/hardship-fund.asp>; Austl, WA, Department of Transport, *On Demand Transport Reform, Questions & Answers*, online: <http://www.transport.wa.gov.au/mediaFiles/taxis/ODT_F_AppHardshipFundFAQ.pdf>.

124. Austl, SA, Government of South Australia, *State Government to Reform the Taxi and Chauffeur Vehicle Industry*, News Release (12 April 2016), online: <https://www.premier.sa.gov.au/index.php/jay-weatherill-news-releases/381-state-government-to-reform-the-taxi-and-chauffeur-vehicle-industry>.

125. Further discussion of a specific fairness consideration (the extent of the harm) is found at 15–17, *above*.

CHAPTER IX

Competition Law and Policy Issues in the Sharing Economy

Francesco Ducci[1]

I. Introduction

W hat are the main challenges that the sharing economy phenomenon poses for competition law and policy? Despite its positive role in providing market access for a number of small providers and enabling innovative ways of offering goods and services, the emergence of sharing economy platforms has raised competition law concerns, largely related to the fear that this phenomenon may enable new forms of anti-competitive conduct and create conditions for possible abuses of market power. Emerging case law and evidence pertaining to the increasing levels of concentration and market shares possessed by dominant sharing economy platforms seem to corroborate these fears, and would appear to suggest a potential need for stronger competition law enforcement, or potentially an *ad hoc* approach given the specificities of sharing economy markets.

This chapter offers a contribution to the many legal puzzles raised by the sharing economy phenomenon, by providing a perspective on the scope of competition law and policy. Various policy reports have been published on the regulatory issues raised by the sharing economy. The German Competition Authority report,[2] for instance, in discussing specific controversies related to the phenomenon, examines the need to create a level playing field between traditional and new service providers, problems of asymmetric information and negative externalities, distinctions between commercial and private suppliers, taxation, employment policy aspects, and market concentration. Similarly, the United States Federal Trade Commission (FTC) report concerning the sharing economy[3] discusses various regulatory issues, including market power, the role of trust mechanisms, privacy, and collection of applicable taxes.

In this chapter, I conduct my analysis within the narrower framework of market power, in order to evaluate possible needs for regulatory interventions through competition law and economic regulation. The goal of my study, rather than providing a comprehensive analysis of possible competition law issues, is to single out and identify whether there is anything specific to the sharing economy with regard to addressing possible issues of market power, in order to evaluate possible novel competition policy implications that emerge from this phenomenon, and in order to provide a guiding light for emerging competition law issues.

In my view, although the emergence of the sharing economy raises a plethora of competition law questions, there is nothing specific to the sharing economy as a phenomenon in and of itself. On the one hand, the central competition policy questions that are likely to emerge in this context, in particular those related to abuse of dominance and monopolization, find their source in the emergence of the platform model of intermediation in markets characterized by two-sided network externalities. However, as I show in this chapter, these questions are not unique to the sharing economy. The lessons emerging from the growing literature on two-sided markets, together with the role of big data in competition policy[4] and the possible anti-competitive issues raised by algorithms,[5] offer important insights about the role of technology in shaping contemporary competition policy. However, these strands of scholarship reflect much broader economic and technological transformations in the nature of today's markets, which apply within and beyond the sharing economy framework. On the other hand, other competition law questions have also emerged as a result of the controversial legal and policy issues regarding the nature of work. Although some of these issues have been framed in terms of competition law, they should in fact be considered from the perspective of other areas of law, in particular labour law. To illustrate this point, I use the case of Uber and the ongoing price-fixing investigation against the ride-sharing platform to demonstrate that no unique competition law issues emerge in the sharing economy context. I further suggest that some of the issues that have been framed in terms of competition law should instead be framed from the perspective of more appropriate areas of law.

The roadmap for the chapter is as follows. It starts by defining the sharing economy and delineating in greater detail the characteristics of sharing economy markets. The chapter then analyzes the specific form of market intermediation that prevails in this context, in order to highlight some of the challenges faced by competition law and the potential role of alternative regulatory instruments to tackle issues of market power in two-sided markets. The chapter then shows the complex interconnections between employment issues and competition law concerns raised by the emergence of these new business models, by analyzing some recent investigations in the taxi and ride-sharing industry. The chapter concludes that, although the interplay of the predominant platform business model and the unsolved nature of work in the sharing economy appear to validate the idea that there are sharing-economy-specific concerns about market power, there is nothing substantially novel from a competition law and policy perspective.

II. Key Characteristics of Sharing Economy Markets

The success of the sharing economy is based on technologies that enable unused or underutilized assets to be turned into productive resources, and significantly reduce the transaction costs of matching those underused assets to those willing to pay or employ such assets. By creating new ways of providing goods and services and spurring innovation into existing ones, the sharing economy radically changes the conditions of consumption, with goods and services increasingly offered to consumers "on demand" and ownership being replaced by access to or rental of shared assets.[6] Economic activity also drastically changes the conditions of supply, with firms organized as platforms rather than as centralized hierarchies and the emergence of hybrid forms of employment characterized by flexible labour, with contract work and micro-entrepreneurship replacing full-time employment.[7]

Although the scope, nature, and normative implications of the sharing economy and its implications for regulators are not fully clear,[8] the economic impact of the sharing economy is significant and growing at a rapid pace. According to a 2015 report by PricewaterhouseCoopers, "five key sharing sectors—travel, car sharing, finance, staffing, and music and video streaming—have the potential to increase global revenues from roughly $15 billion today to around $335 billion by 2025."[9] Airbnb for instance, has now more than 50,000 guests per night, has served over 50 million guests since it was founded in 2008, and has a market capitalization of well over $20 billion.[10] Uber "operates in more than 250 cities and as of February 2015 was valued $41.2 billion."[11]

The growth rate of the sharing economy and its impact on transportation, hospitality, media, and many other sectors has profound legal and policy implications, ranging from employment law, tax law, privacy, anti-discrimination, consumer safety, and sectoral regulation. For instance, the application of labour standards becomes problematic when trying to classify platform users as either employees or individual contractors, or in attempting to identify the role of the platform as simply an enabler of exchange or as a more centralized unit controlling the behaviour of its users—hence, carrying liability for the activities they help coordinate. Similarly, the data-intensive nature of platforms raises complex issues of privacy and data portability. Anti-discrimination and accessibility concerns also emerge when platforms operate in regulated sectors, such as transportation or hospitality, and can escape specific regulatory requirements for providing services that incumbents have to comply with. Such legal questions and, more generally, the scope, form, and timeliness of regulation for the sharing economy are at the heart of the struggles that many legal systems face in dealing with technological change in market dynamics.

The literature on the sharing economy emerging from disparate fields, including sociology, economics, or more policy-oriented reports, does not provide a clear-cut definition on the sharing economy, which sometimes include terms such as "collaborative consumption," "peer-to-peer exchange," or "access-based consumption."[12] For the purposes of this chapter, I use the following definition of the sharing economy, composed of two necessary but distinct elements: (1) specific developments in market design allow for the creation of thick, liquid, and safe markets[13] for direct exchange between independent providers and consumers, where the intermediary serves the role of a matchmaking platform among independent providers and consumers; and (2) there are specific assets owned by private individuals that are not utilized at full capacity, and the owners are willing to put these personal assets to professional use, making them available to third parties through a platform. This definition excludes non-commercial or non-profit forms of sharing or pure business-to-consumer models—where the intermediary is more a reseller than a platform—and concentrates on consumer-to-consumer, or peer-to-peer type of exchanges intermediated by a platform.[14] As I discuss in greater detail below, most of the central competition law and policy questions in the sharing economy are related to the emergence of platforms as the prevalent form of intermediation in markets that have been labelled as "two-sided" in industrial organization literature, in particular the winner-take-all dynamic that characterizes these markets.

Original concerns about market power that led to the enactment of the *Anti-Combines Act* in Canada in 1889 and the *Sherman Act* in the United States in 1890 were the results of significant technological and economic transformations.[15] The call for public intervention to correct market imperfections, which resulted in the proliferation of competition law regimes around the world, was driven by fears of abuses of economic power by big corporations that emerged due to advances in telecommunication and transportation technologies and the development of capital markets in the nineteenth century.[16] In a similar way, today's technological transformations that have given rise to the sharing economy, and online platforms more generally, raise the issue of how to design competition law rules to tackle possible anti-competitive conduct enabled by these novel technological changes, whether such conduct takes the form of collusion among competitors, anti-competitive mergers, or abuse of dominance. There are a plethora of these challenges relevant to the sharing economy: When can a sharing economy platform facilitate collusion among its members, perhaps through its pricing algorithms? What are the strategies that dominant platforms can adopt to exclude competitors? How should the emerging possibility of perfect or behavioural price discrimination be treated? To what extent are network effects a barrier to entry for competitors? What is the impact of big data on competition law, particularly regarding merger policy for platforms?

At a general level, the relationship between competition policy and the sharing economy is inherently ambiguous. On the one hand, sharing economy platforms increase competitive conditions in the provision of various services, by allowing small service providers with low fixed costs to access a previously unavailable market. On the other hand, the problem of market power appears ubiquitous in the sharing economy, because many of these markets are dominated by one or a few platforms. It is important to note that, under competition law, a high level of concentration or market power is not a problem in itself. However, the current level of concentration in many platform markets, including sharing economy platforms, has raised legitimate concerns that some form of regulatory intervention may soon be needed to deal with dominance in these winner-take-all markets. This problem has recently been noted even among the more conservative schools of antitrust.[17]

The following section will examine in greater detail how the evaluation of the central competition law questions—the existence of market power in a given relevant market, the emergence of possible forms of anti-competitive conduct, and the best policy tools to deal with these concerns—ultimately revolve around the centrality of the predominant platform business model of intermediation. In doing so, it will highlight how the emergence of platform markets represents, at the same time, a much broader phenomenon for which the policy implications exceed the sharing economy and apply in many other two-sided markets, including, among others emphasized in the literature, advertising-based media, online search, and payment card networks.[18] After analyzing some of the legal and economic issues that emerge in two-sided markets and the possible anti-competitive concerns that may be relevant in the sharing economy context, the subsequent section will consider the ways in which the distinguishing feature of the sharing economy related to the marketization of private underutilized assets and the resulting unclear nature of work have created the arguably mistaken perception that novel competition law issues (at the intersection with employment law) have emerged in the sharing economy sphere. Using the ongoing price-fixing investigations against Uber in the United States as an example, this chapter seeks to demonstrate how these questions reflect controversies that are ultimately more pertinent to the problematic classification of work in the sharing economy, rather than substantial or standalone antitrust issues, and should therefore be framed as issues of labour law rather than competition law.

III. Competition Law Issues in the Sharing Economy

Most of the sharing economy is based on a business model whereby firms act as matchmakers operating through platforms that connect different types of users willing to interact with each other.[19] Uber, for instance, connects passengers and drivers in a similar way that Airbnb connects homeowners and guests. This business model thrives in the sharing economy but is also predominant in other sectors of the economy and has entailed a critical transformation of the nature of the firm.

Markets operated by platforms have been labelled "two-sided markets" in industrial economics literature and have increasingly drawn the attention of economists, legal scholars and policy makers.[20] Roughly speaking, in economic terms, the key feature of these markets is that different user groups with interrelated demand match through a platform that exploits indirect network externalities.[21] Usually, network externalities are thought of as the extra value that one user of a good or service creates for the other people using it. The value of owning a telephone, for example, depends on the number of other people also owning one. These are defined as direct network effects because they entail within-group effects. In the case of platforms, the network effects are also indirect, whereby the value for one group of users depends on the presence of another distinct group of users that join the platform. For instance, a taxi and ride-sharing platform connects drivers and passengers. Unlike the telephone network example, the value of joining the platform for drivers mostly depends on the number of passengers that also join the platform, and vice versa. Users on one side of the market care about the number and type of users on the other side, and the platform acts as a catalyst enabling a match among different user groups that would not otherwise be able to interact.

Although the presence of a specific user group affects the utility of the other group, individual users do not take this cross-market effect into account when making a decision to join or use a specific platform. The role of the platform is to internalize these indirect network externalities in order to enhance the chances of matches across users on different sides of the platform. Such intermediaries achieve this result by setting a skewed price structure that takes into account not only the elasticity of demand and the cost of serving each side, but also the externalities that each side creates for the other. As a result, pricing in two-sided markets often entail subsidizing one side and charging more to the other side.

The literature on two-sided markets is also connected with older literature on the theory of the firm and vertical integration. In 1937, Ronald H. Coase argued that the boundaries of the firm are determined by the relative transaction costs of organizing economic activity, either through markets and the pricing system or within the hierarchy of the firm.[22] The economic theory of two-sided markets is related to the question of firm structures because platforms blur the traditional boundaries between markets and hierarchies and enable a new form of intermediation, where the typical make-or-buy decision of vertical integration becomes "enable or employ" in the context of two-sided intermediaries.[23] The latter dichotomy involves a preference for contractual relationships between buyers and sellers, to which the two-sided intermediary is not a party, but merely an enabler of such contractual relationships.[24]

To be sure, two-sided markets are not a new economic phenomenon. The village market maker, in some sense, is itself an older example of a two-sided matchmaker between buyers and sellers. What is new about today's phenomenon is that modern information and communication technologies have exponentially scaled up the viability and efficiency of the multi-sided platform business model, which thrives especially in the online world. As a result, firms can have incentives to transform themselves from hierarchical organizations (directly controlling transactions with customers) into simple enablers of exchanges and transactions among users.

Not only is the two-sidedness of markets not new, but it is also not an intrinsic technological feature of specific markets. More specifically, it is possible to identify a spectrum of intermediation forms, ranging from pure platforms to input suppliers, resellers, and vertically integrated organizations. Through the design of their contracts, firms can choose to adopt one model or another, with a view to specific trade-offs.[25]

Nor is the choice of a business model fixed. A firm may start as a single-sided intermediary, preferring to be a reseller in order to avoid the initial chicken-and-egg problem of balancing demand from different sides, and once successfully established, switch to a platform model in order to attract third parties to trade directly with buyers via the firm's marketplace. Amazon, for instance, started as a reseller of books and then introduced a platform marketplace for certain products, enabling third-party sellers to trade directly with consumers on its website, thereby maintaining two coexisting business models.[26] How and why intermediaries make decisions to adopt specific business models, or why intermediaries decide to integrate with one of their sides, are important policy questions that have implications both for competition law and the future of the sharing economy phenomenon.

These market dynamics and trade-offs among different firm structures, which at a high level connect back to Coase's theory of the firm, apply to the sharing economy as well. First, there are often significant direct and indirect network externalities at play in sharing economy platforms, such as in the case of ride-sharing services where the number of drivers increases the value of the platform for passengers, and vice versa. Second, a platform usually faces the "enable or employ" question when deciding whether to employ providers directly or allow them to be independent contractors based on specific trade-offs.[27] Third, platforms can locate themselves along a spectrum of centralization and decentralization, with the possibility of heterogeneous platform design. For instance, although Uber argues that drivers are independent service providers, it nevertheless exerts significant control over them, imposing specific requirements, rating standards, and pricing. A platform like Airbnb, however, delegates much more control to its users on either side. One of the reasons for this difference is that Uber offers a relatively homogenous service and creates a market for quick on-demand rides, which requires some degree of centralization and coordination to ensure rapid availability of rides and transactions. That is why, among other things, platforms like Uber set prices centrally instead of delegating pricing decisions to individual drivers. In contrast, Airbnb offers a service that has a much higher level of product heterogeneity and that allows for greater delays between requests and offers of supply. Both of these elements suggest the desirability of a higher level of delegation to users over price and other aspects of the transaction. The choice of centralization within a platform is ultimately a trade-off between keeping transaction costs low and using information efficiently to ensure individual product choice.[28] Lastly, the choice of a business model is not fixed. This point is important because in the future one might witness a fundamental shift away from the sharing economy paradigm towards a more centralized and ownership-oriented model.

i. Legal and Economic Issues in Two-Sided Markets

The economic literature on two-sided markets has identified some central fallacies that can arise when two-sided platforms are examined under the lens of traditional one-sided markets.[29] These fallacies are for the most part associated with the different pricing strategies adopted in two-sided markets, and with the complexities of defining the relevant market when multiple user groups are affiliated with a platform. With regard to pricing, Julian Wright, for instance, notes that an efficient price structure in two-sided markets does not have to reflect the relative cost of serving each side in isolation.[30] As a result, a high price-cost margin does not necessarily indicate market power, and a price below marginal cost cannot in itself indicate predation.[31] Similarly, an increase in competition will not necessarily result in more efficient or balanced price structures.[32] As a result of these characteristics, legal treatment of various practices in two-sided markets has shifted from illegality per se, to full-blown rule of reason in various countries.[33] This literature on two-sided markets has been central, for instance, to the regulatory and antitrust investigations into payment card networks, and the role of the interchange fees charged to merchants for credit card transactions.[34]

Regarding market definition, there are technical issues associated with the two-sided nature of a market.[35] Questions have been raised in the literature as to how many markets should be defined in competition law cases—a broad platform market or individual markets for each side—in order to take into account the interlinks and feedback effects between each group of users. Although market definition is just a tool, it is a central step of the analysis that can affect the finding of market power. A broad market definition would make it harder to establish the presence of market power, compared to an analysis that defines a separate market for each side of a two-sided market and then looks at the feedback effects between each of these markets. Similarly, the choice of how to define the market affects the scope of possible countervailing efficiencies. Efficiencies are usually taken into account only when they arise within the boundaries of the relevant market as defined in each individual case. However, because of the "waterbed effect" at play between the sides of two-sided markets, it may be the case that a narrow market definition that focuses only on one side of the market could overlook the countervailing efficiencies that occur on the other side of a two-sided market.

Beyond these important technical issues in applying competition law tools in two-sided markets, this literature is also related to other strands of research that examine the increasing importance of algorithms and big data for competition policy. For instance, recent scholarship has identified possible risks of collusion and price-fixing through the use of algorithms, which can create new opportunities for anti-competitive conduct.[36] A pricing algorithm can either become an instrument for collusion, both among platforms and among members of the same platform, or a mechanism that, by enhancing market transparency, can enable new forms of tacit collusion without the presence of any anti-competitive agreements.

The importance of big data also has important implications for competition policy in platform markets.[37] As noted recently by *The Economist*, "a century ago, the resource in question was oil. Now similar concerns are being raised by the giants that deal in data, the oil of the digital era."[38] Data creates additional network effects that make a dominant platform's position hard to challenge. One of Uber's advantages, for instance, can be partially attributed to its ownership of the biggest pool of data about driver and passenger supply and demand for on-demand ride services.[39] These interconnected strands of legal and economic literature, although still at early stages of research, may have significant implications for the sharing economy and raise possible issues of market power and anti-competitive conduct.

ii. Possible Anti-Competitive Concerns in the Sharing Economy

From a more structural perspective, the central issue that emerges from the two-sided nature of these sharing economy markets is likely to be the question of dominance. Due to network effects and the aggregation of data, most markets tend to be oligopolistic or characterized by a single dominant platform, raising concerns about the possible presence of significant barriers to entry and fears of potential abuse of market power by dominant incumbents to exclude competitors.

The dilemma of dominance in platform markets, including in the sharing economy context, is that there seems to often be a natural tendency towards market concentration. This occurs as a result of various forms of network externalities, which can be direct (among users of the same kind) or indirect (between different users on each side of the market), and as a result of the accumulation of data. Concentration may also be fostered by increasing returns to scale, when platforms have high fixed costs and low variable costs. At the same time, there are countervailing forces that can reduce the tendency toward market concentration, including congestion externalities, differentiation among platforms, and the possibility of users using multiple platforms.[40] The extent of concentration will vary depending on the specific characteristics of each individual market, and different policy tools can be adopted to deal with possible abuses of market power and concerns over excessive concentration.

One way to approach dominance is to intervene *ex-post* to punish specific behaviours that are deemed to be anti-competitive. Major concerns of abuse of dominance that can be expected to appear in the sharing economy include attempts by dominant platforms to artificially increase user barriers and costs of switching to other competing platforms; attempts to reduce multi-homing, for example, through exclusive contracts; or attempts to leverage monopoly power from one market to another through tying and bundling.

A different and more prophylactic approach is to prevent the creation of dominance *ex-ante* with tighter merger policies. In analyzing the effects of such mergers, the two-sided nature of the market and the importance of data aggregation play important roles that can be overlooked when viewed through a traditional competition law lens. Usually, competition authorities scrutinize the possible effects of a proposed merger on price and look for possible efficiencies and synergies that are created by the merger.[41] When platforms are merging, this assessment is further complicated by multiple factors. For example, higher prices on one side may lead to lower prices on the other side of the market, requiring an assessment of the welfare effects on each side of the market. Moreover, additional utility due to the aggregation of network externalities in a single platform could outweigh the negative effects of a price increase post-merger, even in the absence of efficiency gains. This additional utility may play an important role in assessing a proposed merger even if price increases are possible. Furthermore, aggregation of data may encourage mergers between firms that are competing in different markets, potentially escaping competition law scrutiny. Taking fears of excessive market concentration seriously requires careful consideration of these kind of issues when scrutinizing mergers among platforms.

A third and more structural policy approach to the issue of market power and dominance is economic regulation. In markets characterized by network externalities, such as markets characterized by economies of scale, trying to induce more competition through the application of competition law may be neither feasible nor desirable. This conclusion suggests a different perspective on the possibility of dealing with market power *ex-ante* through economic regulation, treating a dominant platform as an essential facility or a natural monopoly. This policy option, rather than trying to induce more competition among platforms, would accept a single platform provider as the most efficient market outcome, while also requiring a form of public utility regulation of prices and non-discriminatory access to the platform to deal with possible abuses of market power. As David S. Evans notes, a two-sided market can be considered a natural monopoly under certain conditions.[42] In particular, this can be the case when there are no significant dis-economies of scale on the cost side, no congestion effects on the demand side, and homogenous consumers on both sides, so that it would not be optimal to have differentiated platforms. In such a case, as long as possible dis-economies of scale in cost do not outweigh the benefits of consolidating demand, it would be optimal to have a single platform serving the entire market. Glen Weyl and Alexander White, for instance, argue that the main problem in platform markets can often be one of over-fragmentation, and argue that regulation rather than competition law may be the best policy tool to address market power in these winner-take-all markets.[43]

In sum, the competition law issues that are likely to be central in the sharing economy are those that emerge from the growing importance of two-sided markets, coupled with possible new anti-competitive concerns created by algorithms and the increasing importance of big data for competition law and policy, in particular with regard to issues of abuse of dominance. As will be discussed in the next section, the sharing economy adds an additional layer of complexity to these issues, as a result of the marketization of private underutilized assets, but this additional element does not create specific competition law concerns. Rather, it reflects policy questions that are only tangential to competition law, which should instead be seen through the lenses of more appropriate areas of law.

IV. Regulatory Concerns and the Nature of Work in the Sharing Economy

The regulatory issues that have emerged in the sharing economy are rooted in the fact that private individuals provide access to their own underutilized assets. For example, the problem of asymmetric information is exacerbated at one level by the fact that providers of services in the sharing economy are not professionals, but more often part-time providers without the necessary training, licensing, or legal requirements that are usually imposed on the professional provision of services. The use of reviews and online ratings is a mechanism of self-regulation implemented by platforms to solve such pervasive information asymmetries. In this regard, there are various debates as to whether these tools are sufficient to solve consumer protection and safety concerns.[44]

I believe that there is a need for a balanced approach that recognizes the important role of public regulatory intervention to complement these self-regulatory mechanisms. On the one hand, the success of many sharing economy platforms proves that these self-regulatory systems have worked relatively well. On the other hand, ratings and reviews have shortcomings and must be complemented by public regulation. Similarly, problems of negative externalities can emerge, such as accidents resulting from unsafe driving or unsafe vehicles. Such negative externalities are exacerbated by the fact that providers may not have certifications or commercial forms of insurance. Non-customers lack contractual relationships with the platforms and cannot rely on contracts to shape a platform's behaviour.[45] Again, a balanced approach, combining platform mechanisms with publicly imposed requirements, appears to be the best policy approach, as suggested by the United States FTC report.[46] Such an approach should include imposing insurance requirements to close possible gaps that can result in serious negative externalities.

In addition to these market failures, the marketization of private assets also raises the important question of the characterization of work in the sharing economy. This question highlights the critical tension between purported forms of micro-entrepreneurship and forms of direct and full-time employment. In the taxi industry, for instance, the novelty created by the sharing economy phenomenon is that any individual with a car can become, in an easy way, a part-time taxi driver. On the one hand, the fact that individuals are the owners of the key assets and have control of when and how to provide the services gives rise to a dynamic where each individual provider may appear to be an independent service provider. On the other hand, ride-sharing platforms often exert substantial control over these independent providers, to the point where they may appear more like platform employees than independent contractors. The classification of workers in the sharing economy has been challenged in various courts around the world. For instance, in the United Kingdom[47] and in California[48] court decisions have concluded that drivers should be considered as employees, while in other American states drivers

have been classified as independent contractors.[49] In other countries, including Canada, the resolution of this question still remains
uncertain. Recently, the advocate general of the Court of Justice of
the European Union held, in a recent reference for a preliminary
ruling, that Uber drivers do not pursue an autonomous activity that
is independent of the platform. The advocate general concluded that
Uber could not be regarded as a mere intermediary between drivers and passengers, because it controlled economically important
aspects of the transport service, which amounts to the organization
and management of a comprehensive system for on-demand urban
transport.[50]

These doubts about the nature of work in the sharing economy
have raised puzzling questions at the intersection of competition
and employment law, where different legal characterizations of
work have appeared to substantially affect the scope of competition
law in the sharing economy and possibly raise novel competition
law issues. This is clearly reflected in *Meyer v Kalanick*,[51] an ongoing
American price-fixing investigation against Uber's pricing policies.
In this case, it appears that classifying drivers in one way may create
the conditions for certain competition law claims to emerge, while if
drivers are characterized in another way, this automatically appears
to negate the possibility for the same claim to arise, even when the
competitive conditions are the same under each legal classification.

In particular, *Meyer v Kalanick* revolves around the claim that
Uber is illegally colluding with drivers in violation of section 1 of
the *Sherman Act*, by controlling the prices of car rides through Uber's
pricing algorithm and for fixing price surcharges. If it is accepted that
Uber does not employ drivers, the allegation goes, independent drivers should compete, among other things, on prices to obtain passengers. However, under this perspective, the central pricing algorithm
reduces price competition and enables a form of collusion and price-
fixing orchestrated by the platform and the drivers. Uber faces both
a claim for horizontal price-fixing conspiracy between Uber drivers
themselves and vertical conspiracy between the platform and drivers.

The challenging questions raised by this price-fixing case lie at
the heart of the sharing economy business model, because in a hypo-
thetical counterfactual situation, where Uber directly employed drivers, a price-fixing claim would simply be not possible. Competition
law doctrines have recognized that coordination within a firm is
necessary, while coordination among firms, except in specific cases,

is treated as per se illegal. Whereas the coordination of employees is required for the efficient operation of a firm, coordination among firms reduces price competition to the detriment of consumers and social welfare. In the case of Uber, a different classification of drivers can shift the boundaries of the firm, raising the possibility of a competition law claim in the case of independent drivers. In such a case, the allegation is that centrally set prices create the possibility of price-fixing, since independent drivers would be expected to compete on price. But are there valid grounds to advance a competition law claim against such a price mechanism, solely based on the classification of drivers under different labour law standards? I argue that such concerns are the result of unsolved legal questions about the nature of work in the sharing economy, and are in fact only tangentially relevant to substantial competition law issues.

In my view, given the characteristics of this market, a centralized price mechanism is necessary to properly organize supply and demand of rides in real time. A narrower concern may be raised on the basis of the fact that Uber has a stake in how much drivers earn (increasing fares also increases Uber's profits, as a result of the percentage taken from drivers). In response to such concerns, however, rather than eliminating centralized pricing or requiring drivers to set their own prices, an alternative would be to impose on Uber a different mechanism for obtaining revenue from drivers. This would be a much narrower and well-defined claim. Regardless of whether drivers are considered employees or independent contractors, a form of centralized pricing is not only necessary, but efficient, and the answer regarding possible price-fixing cannot depend on a formal classification of work, when the competitive conditions remain unchanged in each scenario.

Regarding the possible legal characterization of the issues underlying *Meyer v Kalanick*, competition law doctrines have the necessary tools to analyze such price-fixing allegations. As for horizontal conspiracy, the court could characterize the contractual relationships as a "hub-and-spoke" agreement.[52] A hub-and-spoke arrangement refers to a scenario where an entity at one level of the market structure (the hub) coordinates an agreement among competitors at a different level upstream or downstream (the spokes). *United States v Apple Inc*[53] is an important recent precedent dealing with hub-and-spoke agreements. In that case, Apple orchestrated a conspiracy among six publishers to enter the e-book market, where Amazon had been the leader since 2009. The business strategy adopted by Amazon was to sell at a discount price of $9.99 certain new releases and bestsellers (the "loss-leader pricing strategy") and to distribute e-books under a wholesale model. Publishers were reluctant to see the e-book market expand, because that would negatively affect both the sale of hardcover books and the viability of brick-and-mortar stores, and because they were concerned that consumers would become accustomed to such low prices. Since publishers perceived that each of them, individually, would not be able to force Amazon to change its pricing strategy, they saw an opportunity in Apple's desire to enter the e-book market. Apple, aware of these concerns, proposed a strategy to the publishers in the form of contractual conditions which included the establishment of an agency model and "Most-Favoured-Nation" (MFN) clauses. Such conditions effectively allowed publishers to impose the agency model on Amazon and other retailers as well. If Amazon continued selling e-books for $9.99, publishers were, in practice, forced to set the same price for books sold on the iBookstore. However, the entry of Apple into the e-book market increased the bargaining power of publishers vis-à-vis Amazon and allowed them to impose an agency model on Amazon, ultimately resulting in higher e-book prices. The court found that these vertical agreements with Apple were used to facilitate horizontal collusion among publishers, and that this arrangement entailed a per se violation of section 1 of the *Sherman Act*.

As noted by other commentators, in the case of Uber, there is a parallel dynamic in that the platform is accused of orchestrating price-fixing among drivers by making use of its pricing algorithm that drivers must accept when joining the platform, which results in an increase in the price of fares.[54] There are many difficulties in characterizing Uber's pricing as a per se illegal horizontal price-fixing conspiracy. First, as it was explained before, cooperation within a single economic entity is generally allowed under competition law, which does not consider wholly unilateral conduct to be illegal.[55] However, the claim goes to the heart of Uber's business model, because Uber's claim that drivers are not employees makes this argument unavailable. Second, there must be evidence of an agreement or tacit coordination facilitated by the platform, which may be inferred from the fact that drivers accept the terms and conditions imposed by the platform, although it is unclear whether this would suffice to classify the price mechanism as a per se illegal price-fixing agreement. Third, the price mechanism may escape per se liability for efficiency reasons under the logic of *Broadcast Music Inc v Columbia Broadcasting System Inc*,[56] or be characterized as an ancillary restraint.[57] In this decision, copyright holders agreed to offer a blanket licence by pooling together their copyrights. The agreement was not considered price-fixing because the defendants had created something new that created pro-competitive efficiencies, despite its *prima facie* resemblance to per se illegal horizontal collusion. Similarly, the ancillary doctrine can exempt certain agreements that are ancillary to a lawful agreement.

Under the alternative rule of reason analysis of vertical conspiracy, the negative effects of reduced price competition among drivers are balanced against the benefits resulting from centralized pricing. The plaintiff must first establish anti-competitive effects. If the plaintiff establishes the likelihood of such effects, the burden shifts to the defendant to offer pro-competitive justifications. Then, the burden shifts back to the plaintiff to show that the anti-competitive effects outweigh the pro-competitive effects. There are various pro-competitive explanations that can play in favour of Uber's algorithm,[58] including price predictability, reduced transaction costs for users, and increased exploitation of network externalities, based on the fact that unrestricted price competition among drivers may drive down the price of fares in the short run to the extent that it would be less attractive for drivers to join the platform. This, in turn, would also reduce the value for consumers using the platform.

In sum, although the Uber case raises intriguing questions, from a legal perspective, the dynamics at play in this case are within the reach of well-established competition law doctrines. The claim of price-fixing appears to be an attack on the specific model and classification of work adopted by Uber, rather than a concern about collusion per se. In my view, a claim regarding the way prices are centrally set by the platform is misguided, to the extent that it focuses too broadly on the polar options between centrally set prices versus decentralized price competition among drivers. The issue would be more precise if it focused on how Uber extracts revenue from drivers within a centralized pricing system. Ultimately, the case appears to be concerned more with the controversial classification of workers adopted by Uber than with competition law, and it would be preferable to approach these issues from the perspective of more appropriate areas of law.

V. Conclusion

In evaluating the possible broad competition policy concerns at play in the sharing economy, I have identified the following central elements. First, there are important issues raised by the likely two-sided nature of sharing economy markets. The literature on two-sided markets has important implications for how to apply competition law tools in possible scenarios of collusion, abuse of dominance, and mergers when a market is two-sided or multi-sided. Moreover, the importance of big data and the role of algorithms in these markets, issues that have been recognized in the scholarship as increasingly relevant, raise additional questions and challenges for the future enforcement of competition policy. These, arguably, are the central competition law concerns raised by the sharing economy, in particular those related to the tendencies of such markets toward concentration and dominance. However, the policy implications emerging from this body of literature are not specific to the sharing economy, but apply more broadly to markets with two-sided characteristics.

Second, in the sharing economy there are additional issues arising from the fact that private individuals use their underutilized assets for professional purposes, which raises the question of whether service providers should be considered independent contractors or employees of the platform. This characterization of work is the source of the many central regulatory problems related to possible market failures in the sharing economy, such as asymmetric information and negative externalities. However, as far as competition law is concerned, I have attempted to show that the controversial nature of work does not raise in itself new paradigmatic problems for the application of competition law.

There is arguably a third, more speculative, concern, which is related to the possibility of vertical integration and a more radical shift away from the sharing economy model itself.[59] In fact, it is often assumed that sharing economy platforms own the means of connection across decentralized users without providing, themselves, goods or services. However, it is not clear at all that this has to be the case in the future, and it is not unlikely that platforms may soon have incentives to fully or partially integrate with one of their sides. Imagine, for instance, that Uber or another dominant taxi and ride-sharing platform, after establishing itself as the dominant player in the market, introduces self-driving cars. By directly providing the driving service, the platform will cease to be a platform and will become more like a traditional taxi company, owning significant physical assets used to sell a specific service to end customers. Certainly, the competitive dynamics would then look very different from what they are today. As recognized by the United States FTC report concerning the sharing economy,[60] by changing the nature of competitive dynamics, possible forms of vertical integration may add additional layers of complexity regarding market power and the scope of competition law and policy in the sharing economy. However, it is hard to speculate about the future of this phenomenon—which, in many regards, is still at its early stages.

In conclusion, the sharing economy raises many challenging legal and policy questions. This chapter attempts to provide a competition law perspective on some of these issues by offering a glimpse into the complexities behind the evaluation of market power and the anti-competitive concerns that are likely to emerge in a context characterized by disruptive innovation, new business models, and unique market dynamics. As argued in the chapter, these complexities are, however, not unique to the sharing economy. On the contrary, they represent broader phenomena that have implications for competition policy both within the sharing economy context and beyond. These issues can become subtler in this context, given the complex interplay between competition law issues and other legal concerns, but questions raised by complex puzzles, such as the controversial nature of work in the sharing economy, should be addressed from the standpoint of more appropriate areas of law, rather than competition law and policy.

Notes

1. S.J.D. Candidate, University of Toronto, Faculty of Law. Email: francesco. ducci@mail.utoronto.ca. The author is grateful to Derek McKee and anonymous reviewers for comments on earlier drafts. He also thanks the participants to the Sharing Economy Workshop for insightful discussions on these issues.

2. Germany, Monopolkommission, *Twenty-First Biennial Report by the Monopolies Commission* (Chapter V), online: <http://www. monopolkommission.de/images/HG21/HGXXI_Chapter_V.pdf> [Monopolkommission].

3. US, Federal Trade Commission, *The "Sharing" Economy: Issues Facing Platforms, Participants & Regulators* (A Federal Trade Commission Staff

Report, 2016), online: <https://www.ftc.gov/system/files/documents/reports/sharing-economy-issues-facing-platforms-participants-regulators-federal-trade-commission-staff/p151200_ftc_staff_report_on_the_sharing_economy.pdf> [Federal Trade Commission].

4. See e.g. Maurice E Stucke & Allen P Grunes, *Big Data and Competition Policy* (Oxford: Oxford University Press, 2016).

5. See Ariel Ezrachi & Maurice E Stucke, *Virtual Competition: The Promise and Perils of the Algorithm-Driven Economy* (Cambridge, MA: Harvard University Press, 2016).

6. See Aaron Perzanowski & Jason Schultz, *The End of Ownership: Personal Property in the Digital Economy* (Cambridge, MA: MIT Press, 2016).

7. See Geoffrey G Parker, Marshall W Van Alstyne & Sangeet Paul Choudary, *Platform Revolution: How Networked Markets Are Transforming the Economy—And How to Make Them Work for You* (New York: W. W. Norton & Company, 2016).

8. See Arun Sundararajan, *The Sharing Economy: The End of Employment and the Rise of Crowd-Based Capitalism* (Cambridge, MA: The MIT Press, 2016); Yochai Benkler, "Sharing Nicely: On Shareable Goods and the Emergence of Sharing as a Modality of Economic Production" (2004) 114 Yale LJ 273; Tom Slee, *What's Yours Is Mine: Against the Sharing Economy* (New York: OR Books LLC, 2015).

9. "The Sharing Economy: Consumer Intelligence Series" (2015), online: PricewaterhouseCoopers <http://www.pwc.com/en_US/us/technology/publications/assets/pwc-consumer-intelligence-series-the-sharing-economy.pdf> ["The Sharing Economy"].

10. "Airbnb Summer Travel Report 2015," *At Airbnb* (blog), online: <http://blog.airbnb.com/wp-content/uploads/2015/09/Airbnb-Summer-Travel-Report-1.pdf>.

11. "The Sharing Economy," *supra* note 9.

12. See Cristiano Codagnone & Bertin Martens, "Scoping the Sharing Economy: Origins, Definitions, Impact and Regulatory Issues" (2016) European Commission Institute for Prospective Technological Studies Digital Economy Working Paper No 2016/01.

13. See Alvin E Roth, *Who Gets What – and Why: The New Economics of Matchmaking and Market Design* (New York: Houghton Mifflin Harcourt, 2016).

14. See Monopolkommission, *supra* note 2.

15. See Alfred D Chandler, Jr, *The Visible Hand: The Managerial Revolution in American Business* (Cambridge, MA: Harvard University Press, 1977); Michael Trebilcock et al, *The Law and Economics of Canadian Competition Policy* (Toronto: University of Toronto Press, 2003).

16. See Massimo Motta, *Competition Policy: Theory and Practice* (Cambridge, UK: Cambridge University Press, 2004).

17. See "The University of Chicago Worries About a Lack of Competition," *The Economist* (12 April 2017), online: <http://www.economist.com/news/business/21720657-its-economists-used-champion-big-firms-mood-has-shifted-university-chicago>.

18. See David S Evans & Richard Schmalensee, "The Antitrust Analysis of Multi-Sided Platform Businesses" (2012) Coase-Sandor Institute for Law & Economics Working Paper No 623 [Evans & Schmalensee, "The Antitrust Analysis"].

19. See David S Evans & Richard Schmalensee, *Matchmakers: The New Economics of Multisided Platforms* (Boston, MA: Harvard Business Review Press, 2016).

20. See Mark Armstrong, "Competition in Two-Sided Markets" (2006) 37:3 Rand J Econ 668.

21. See B Caillaud & BM Jullien, "Chicken and Egg: Competition Among Intermediation Service Providers" (2003) 34:2 Rand J Econ 309; Jean-Charles Rochet & Jean Tirole, "Two-Sided Markets: A Progress Report" (2006) 35 Rand J Econ 645.

22. Ronald H Coase, "The Nature of the Firm" (1937) 4:16 Economica 386.

23. See Andrei Hagiu & Julian Wright, "Multi-Sided Platforms" (2015) Harvard Business School Working Paper No 15-037.

24. *Ibid* at 4.

25. *Ibid* at 6.

26. See Andrei Hagiu & Julian Wright, "Marketplace or Reseller?" (2015) 61:1 Management Science 184.

27. *Ibid*.

28. See Liran Einav, Chiara Farronato & Jonathan Levin, "Peer-to-Peer Markets" (2016) 8 Annu Rev Econ 615.

29. See Jean-Charles Rochet & Jean Tirole, "Platform Competition in Two-Sided Markets" (2003) 1:4 J Eur Econ Assoc 990; Evans & Schmalensee, "The Antitrust Analysis," *supra* note 18; Julian Wright, "One-Sided Logic in Two-Sided Markets" (2004) 3:1 Rev Network Econ 44.

30. Wright, *supra* note 29 at 47.

31. See e.g. Trib com Paris, 31 January 2012, *Bottin Cartographes c Google Inc. & Google France*, (2012 15ᵉ sem).

32. Wright, *supra* note 29 at 49.

33. See *National Bankcard Corp (NaBANCO) v VISA U.S.A. Inc*, 779 F (2d) 592 (11th Cir 1986); EC, *Groupement des Cartes Bancaires (CB) v European Commission*, [2014] OJ, C 67/13.

34. See *United States v Visa U.S.A. Inc*, 163 F Supp (2d) 322 (SDNY 2001); EC, *MasterCard and Others v European Commission*, [2014] OJ, C 382/12. For some literature on competition law and regulatory issues in payment card network markets, see especially Robert Hunt, "An Introduction to the Economics of Payment Card Networks" (2003) Federal Reserve

Bank of Philadelphia Working Paper No 03-10; Jean-Charles Rochet & Jean Tirole, "An Economic Analysis of the Determination of Interchange Fees in Payment Card Systems" (2003) 2:2 Rev Network Econ 69; Julian Wright, "The Determinants of Optimal Interchange Fees in Payment Systems" (2004) 52:1 J Ind Econ 1; Richard Schmalensee, "Payment Systems and Interchange Fees" (2002) 50:2 J Ind Econ 103; Richard Schmalensee & David S Evans, "The Economics of Interchange Fees and Their Regulation: An Overview" (2005) MIT Sloan Working Paper No 4548-05; Alan O Sykes, "Antitrust Issues in Two-Sided Network Markets: Lessons from in Re Payment Card Interchange Fee and Merchant Discount Antitrust Litigation" (2015) NYU Law and Economics Research Paper No 14-45.

35. See Lapo Filistrucchi et al, "Market Definition in Two-Sided Markets: Theory and Practice" (2014) 10:2 J Comp L & Econ 293.

36. See Ezrachi & Stucke, *supra* note 5; see also "Price-Bots Can Collude Against Consumers," *The Economist* (6 May 2017), online: <https://www.economist.com/news/finance-and-economics/21721648-trustbusters-might-have-fight-algorithms-algorithms-price-bots-can-collude>.

37. See Stucke & Grunes, *supra* note 4.

38. "The World's Most Valuable Resource Is No Longer Oil, but Data," *The Economist* (6 May 2017), online: <http://www.economist.com/news/leaders/21721656-data-economy-demands-new-approach-antitrust-rules-worlds-most-valuable-resource>.

39 See "Data Is Giving Rise to a New Economy," *The Economist* (6 May 2017), online: <https://www.economist.com/news/briefing/21721634-how-it-shaping-up-data-giving-rise-new-economy>.

40. See Monopolkommission, *supra* note 2.

41. See e.g. section 96 of Canada's *Competition Act* (RSC 1985, c C-34), which contains an efficiency defence, allowing mergers where the efficiencies are greater than, and offset, the anti-competitive effects of the merger. The scope of the efficiency defence was discussed in *Canada (Commissioner of Competition) v Superior Propane Inc*, 2003 FCA 53.

42. David S Evans, "Economics of Vertical Restraints for Multi-Sided Platforms" (2013) Coase-Sandor Institute for Law and Economics Working Paper No 626 at 9.

43. Glen Weyl & Alexander White, "Let the Best 'One' Win: Policy Lessons from the New Economics of Platforms" (2014) Coase-Sandor Institute for Law and Economics Research Paper No 709.

44. See Sundararajan, *supra* note 8; Benjamin G Edelman & Damien Geradin, "Efficiencies and Regulatory Shortcuts: How Should We Regulate Companies like Airbnb and Uber?" (2016) 19 Stan Tech L Rev 293.

45. Edelman & Geradin, *supra* note 44.

46. Federal Trade Commission, *supra* note 3.

47. See Hilary Osborne, "Uber Loses Right to Classify UK Drivers as Self-Employed," *The Guardian* (28 October 2016), online: <https://www.theguardian.com/technology/2016/oct/28/uber-uk-tribunal-self-employed-status>.

48. See Mike Isaac & Natasha Singer, "California Says Uber Driver Is Employee, Not a Contractor," *The New York Times* (17 June 2015), online: <https://www.nytimes.com/2015/06/18/business/uber-contests-california-labor-ruling-that-says-drivers-should-be-employees.html?_r=0>.

49. See *McGillis v Florida (Department of Economic Opportunity)* (1 February 2017), Florida 3D15-2758 (Fla 3d Ct App), online: Third District Court of Appeal <http://www.3dca.flcourts.org/Opinions/3D15-2758.pdf>.

50. Court of Justice of the European Union, Press Release, 50/17, "According to Advocate General Szpunar, the Uber Electronic Platform, Whilst Innovative, Falls Within the Field of Transport: Uber Can Thus be Required to Obtain the Necessary Licences and Authorisations Under National Law" (11 May 2017), online: CVRIA <https://curia.europa.eu/jcms/upload/docs/application/pdf/2017-05/cp170050en.pdf>.

51. *Meyer v Kalanick* (3 October 2016), New York 1:15-cv-09796 (NY Dist Ct), online: Justia US Law: <http://law.justia.com/cases/federal/district-courts/new-york/nysdce/1:2015cv09796/451250/37>.

52. See e.g. Nicholas Passaro, "How *Meyer v. Kalanick* Could Determine How Uber and the Sharing Economy Fit into Antitrust Doctrine," Case Comment, (2016) Social Science Research Network, online: <https://ssrn.com/abstract=2880204>.

53. *United States v Apple Inc*, 952 F Supp (2d) 638 (SDNY 2013); *United States et al v Apple Inc et al* (30 June 2015), 13-3741-cv at 28-29 (2d Cir 2015), online: Justia US Law <http://law.justia.com/cases/federal/appellate-courts/ca2/13-3741/13-3741-2015-06-30.html>.

54. See Passaro, *supra* note 52.

55. See *Copperweld Corp v Independence Tube Corp*, 467 US 752 at 768–69 (Sup Ct 1984).

56. *Broadcast Music Inc v Columbia Broadcasting System Inc*, 441 US 1 at 5 (Sup Ct 1979).

57. See *United States v Addyston Pipe & Steel Co*, 85 F 271 (6th Cir 1898).

58. See Passaro, *supra* note 52.

59. See Federal Trade Commission, *supra* note 3.

60. *Ibid* at 28.

PART V

REGULATING LABOUR

CHAPTER X

The Legal Framework for Digital Platform Work: The French Experience

Marie-Cécile Escande-Varniol[1]

I. Introduction

1.0 , 2.0, 3.0, 4.0 … the digitization of the economy is like a stopwatch, ticking off the seconds in the race to innovation. By the time a few experts become familiar with one issue, a brand new system is in place. And woe to those with no smartphone or apps, no plans to ride-share or have dinner at a stranger's home, and no way to find a plumber at 8:00 p.m., at the lowest possible rates. As young people eagerly rush to meet this new, wide-open universe head on, their parents feel like they've missed the bus, while their grandparents have simply stayed home.

And where does the law fit in? Its role is to govern society with general, permanent, acceptable rules, known to all. Should it leap ahead and strain to answer all the questions these new tools raise, at the risk of contradicting itself? Or should it take its time and seek a broader perspective? It might make intuitive sense for legislators to sit back and reflect and let judges resolve the specific cases that come before them. But French law has been swept up in the frenzy of digital communication, and only a few years in, we already find ourselves with a sufficiently consistent "digital law" to justify publishing legal encyclopaedia[2] and specialized law journals.[3] Although this area of the law is diffuse, and its enactment has in many cases been disorderly, it has nevertheless inserted itself into numerous branches of French and European law, particularly in commercial law, tax law, consumer law, and—since August 2016—labour law.

The Université de Sherbrooke has created an opportunity for joint reflection on the "sharing economy," a small planet in this new digital universe. The remarks presented here are supplemental, limited as they are to a consideration of the legal status of digital workers. Many economists and sociologists in particular have predicted that the collaborative economy sounds a death knell for salaried employment,[4] but French scholarly commentary on labour law has so far paid little attention to the issue.[5]

This universe has its own language—circular economy, sharing economy, social and solidarity economy, collaborative economy, service economy—that needs to be decoded if we are to properly understand the new realities.[6] All these terms express the need for societal change felt by their users. To varying degrees, they refer to human labour, and the practices they describe all came into being before the large-scale development of the digital platforms that are now their primary means of deployment. The original model based on the sharing of goods and services had altruistic and not-for-profit ambitions.[7] Wikipedia is a prime example. That model, however, failed to take into account the capitalist propensity to seize on opportunities for financial gain. The societal impact of these new forms of consumption has been magnified as a result of digitization, first through peer-to-peer networks, then through digital platforms acting as intermediaries between those who offer and those who seek goods or services. The "platform economy" is the newest term in the lexicon of economic forms,[8] and Uber has emerged as its emblematic company.

Of course, the altruistic, interdependent, and volunteer spirit that was there at the beginning is still present in the way many of these platforms operate. The ones that interest us here, however, are those that promise a way to obtain work performed for remuneration. The rapid success of platforms of this type is due in large part to their flexibility and low-cost positioning.[9] In these days of high unemployment in France, many workers see them as opportunities for new sources of income.

The Uber platform, established in more than 600 cities in eighty countries, has revealed to everyone a new way of working, which has caught on worldwide.[10] But this tree conceals a forest. In addition to taxi drivers, even less visible service providers with even fewer protections can be hired through crowdsourcing, opening up a new global labour market[11] and sparking large-scale competition among workers.[12] This ultra-flexible job market is the world created by TaskRabbit, Mechanical Turk, OpenWork, and other gig providers for so-called self-employed workers.

Should this work be regulated? If so, how? The answer depends on the country. In countries where informal work dominates, digital platforms might present an opportunity to regulate.[13] But in countries like France, where tax and social welfare regimes are supported in large part by salaried work, informal work is unacceptable because it undercuts the social system as a whole and leaves some of the often very vulnerable working population without protection.[14]

Under French law, digital platforms are defined as "Businesses, whatever their place of establishment, that connect persons remotely by electronic means for the purpose of the sale of a good, the provision of a service, or the exchange or sharing of a good or service."[15] The definition is sufficiently broad to include all situations, paid or not, involving these platforms. But the fact that the provision appears in the *Code général des impôts* (General Income Tax Code) in a section concerning the income generated by intermediary activities reveals the economic significance of the phenomenon and the source of income it represents.

This definition is repeated in the French *Code du travail* (Labour Code), in provisions dealing with "self-employed workers who, to perform their professional activities, use one or more platforms connecting persons by electronic means as defined in article 242 *bis* of the *Code général des impôts.*"

These are the workers that interest us here: those who perform remunerated work obtained via platforms that operate for profit. The three main participants here are the worker, his or her "customer," and the platform that connected them. In most cases, there is nothing new about the work being performed, and the same operation could probably take place without the platform. However, only digital platforms have the scope to make this work truly profitable. Their greatest innovation is their capacity to disseminate information broadly and connect people easily through smartphones. That is their main difference from traditional classified ads.[16]

From the perspective of labour law, which we take here, these new forms of work prompt us to consider the characterization of the relationship and status of the participants. Is the worker a salaried employee? That would presuppose an employment contract between the worker, who is easy to identify, and the employer, who is much less so. Indeed, most large platforms describe themselves as intermediaries and reject the label of employer, even as they define the terms under which the work is to be performed. And the workers, for their part, are often self-employed and therefore benefit from little protection, despite their heavy economic dependence on the platforms that give them work.

This paper seeks to understand the highly disruptive nature of this new labour relations model and consider potential solutions to this disruption by undertaking a review of labour law from three main perspectives: the performance of the work, the workers, and the employer/platform. The roots of the *Code du travail* are in industrial legislation, and the protections it offers were forged in that historical context, although it has of course evolved significantly since then, through both legislation and court rulings. We hope that, by examining the notion of work as understood by the law and considering the notions of worker and employer as defined by labour law, we may achieve a better understanding of the protections these new digital workers need.

II. Work as Understood by the Law

As Professor Cyril Wolmark states, it is pointless to seek a definition of work in books on the subject of labour law.[17] The law understands work only through its result or through the activity it denotes and the contracts that regulate it. It is not the activity itself that is the important thing; the way it is performed is what matters.[18]

Labour law, with its much-vaunted protective virtues, applies only to subordinate workers, and classifying gig economy workers as self-employed therefore deprives them of its protection. Finding new protections to ensure that these workers are treated decently requires a broader definition of false self-employment.

Indeed, work itself must be defined,[19] given that our interest here is work as a human activity, or the performance of labour. But any human activity can be characterized as work. The same person can be a computer engineer toiling for a company during the week and a volunteer lifeguard for the Red Cross on Sundays. Some people are professional soccer players, while others are amateurs. The only way to distinguish work from a hobby is remuneration.

Collaborative platforms further muddle the already vague borders. Some rely on unpaid contributions for specialized tasks that were once remunerated. Wikipedia, for example, has established itself as a recognized encyclopedia worldwide thanks to volunteer contributors, pushing out *Encyclopædia Universalis*, whose authors were paid for their expertise. Other platforms are moving the other way, transforming unpaid services—such as driving, having people over for dinner, babysitting the neighbour's children, or sorting photographs—into paid services. These activities, traditionally seen as unpaid friendly behaviour or mutual assistance, now take place on a larger scale thanks to the power of the algorithm and platform marketing. The long-distance car sharing service BlaBlaCar costs more than hitchhiking, and since it involves cost-sharing, drivers benefit by saving the money they would spend if they drove solo. Similarly, Airbnb, VizEat, and VoulezVousDiner are transforming friendly, unpaid hosting into new jobs. And the list goes on.

Often, these approaches have many initial charms, their limitations and deficiencies becoming apparent only later. The platforms, for example, provide none of the protections available under labour law. For indeed, although labour law may not define its own subject matter, it still protects workers, takes care of their health, limits the number of hours they have to work, imposes mandatory breaks, requires a minimum wage, and organizes to defend the collective interests of workers, in exchange for the employer's managerial prerogatives. This is the *quid pro quo* born of industrial legislation, a model first strongly challenged by the service industries and today threatened with extinction by the digital industries. Platforms, which present themselves as nothing more than intermediaries, seem to allow parties to set the conditions of the performance themselves in an apparent return to individual autonomy of the will. Some of them, however, impose very high requirements on the service provider.

Since the late twentieth century, numerous books and reports have delved into this "new labour question,"[20] seeking a broader understanding of this type of work that would accommodate systems to protect workers. Protections should cover every type of work, since all individuals will potentially have different jobs over the course of their lives. In addition to salaried employment, the protections should cover domestic work, professional training, different employment statuses, and periods of lower employment, among other things. French law currently shows signs of such a reckoning: so-called portable rights allow salaried employees to preserve their right to continued vocational training throughout their lives, among other things.[21] However, while there might be progress, it affects salaried employees only and does not resolve the major problems facing precarious workers, who are the ones taking on the often poorly paid piecework available through collaborative commercial platforms.

Labour law has become the law governing employment, "understood as the totality of the guarantees surrounding salaried activity,"[22] and it is precisely these guarantees that unsalaried digital workers lack. Thus, the question remains: How can all activities be taken into account in the creation of a status that guarantees the same rights to decent work for all?

The answer probably lies in recognizing the fundamental rights of all workers, without distinction according to status. In the summer of 2015, two French authors published a small book listing fifty fundamental principles and rights of workers.[23] The labour minister would have liked to include these principles in the preamble to the labour code, but the French Parliament demurred.[24] Labour law scholars have also been harsh, criticizing the book for addressing the subject of salaried workers only marginally.[25] Nevertheless, the principles might still serve as a starting point for defining minimum rights for all workers, whatever their status, including those who are "false self-employed."

But in a context where human activity is dematerialized, thus permitting competition among Mechanical Turks worldwide, another gap has appeared between non-relocatable proximity services and intellectual services that cannot be dematerialized. States govern the labour market only as far as their territory extends. The International Labour Organization (ILO), for its part, has been promoting the fundamental rights of workers globally for decades and is currently reconsidering non-standard work;[26] however, it lacks the jurisdiction to limit the large-scale social dumping created by these digital platforms on a worldwide scale. Uber has simply revealed an upheaval in the world of work arising from a simultaneous decrease in industrial labour, an increase in service industry jobs, digitization, and digital intermediation. The verb "to uberize" has entered the lexicon of more than one language,[27] and its definition illustrates the difficulty of pinning down the activity it describes.

Platform work presents a radical challenge to labour relations as they developed in law throughout the twentieth century.

Designed to respond to the needs of industry, labour law relies on a very concrete reality of that era: the unity of location, time, and action. The masses of workers, moving away from rural labour, had to be disciplined to follow regular schedules, no matter the weather, and to work together towards the same goal (assembly lines, mining, or other types of extraction).[28] Orders were given by the boss, supervised by the foreman, and performed by the worker within a specific time frame. But this harmonious unity has been fractured by digitization. Now, nothing is material: orders can be given from the other side of the planet; the foreman has ceded way to the consumer who supervises and evaluates the worker; and the algorithm generates an alert, determining payment, reward, or sanction. This new model revives piecework, unpredictable salaries, and *non-standard* or informal employment.[29]

Since long before the current tripartite employment relationship existed, the law has been responding to labour developments. Over the course of a century, the salaried worker class expanded to encompass service professionals and intellectual workers, leading to court decisions in France and elsewhere in Europe adapting the application of the law to take these new situations into account.[30]

However different things might appear today, at the heart of labour relations still remain human beings—workers—who are treated differently by the law depending on the legal form of their work.

III. Digital Platform Workers: Dependently Self-Employed

Now that our area of inquiry has been limited to platform work performed with a view to earning financial income, we must consider the legal characterization of the employment relationship in these circumstances. Under the law, each legal category has a legal effect. We must determine whether platform workers truly constitute a new category of worker that requires its own new regime or whether aspects of the traditional categories still underlie the new working methods.

The answers will of course be nuanced and often depend on the actual conditions in which the activity is performed. A few people have already staked out a specific employment status somewhere between salaried employees and self-employed workers,[31] to be known as "collaborative workers."[32] But challenges to the salaried status began before digital platforms appeared, and reflection on "the new faces of subordination" concerns much broader changes in labour that have taken place in the post-industrial era.[33]

Our task is therefore to consider the various employment statuses that might be used to characterize these new forms of labour.

i. Subordinate Workers?

Today, in a time of slashers[34] and the multiple jobs encouraged by so many platforms, it can be useful to recall that the industrial labour force grew out of the pluriactivity of rural people looking to supplement their income at the factory, and out of the flexibility of labour at home. It took some time before subordination, a characteristic of employment contracts today, became the norm. The French Revolution was informed more by the belief in freedom of enterprise and the freedom to work than in the work of servitude.

The 1804 *Code civil* devoted only two articles to what was then referred to as *"louage de services"* (lease of personal service) and the contrasting *"louage d'ouvrage"* (contract for services).[35] In the first case, the object of the contract is the person's *performance* of the work, while in the second it is the *product* of such work. In a rural France, with few industrial workers, this notion found its origin in the *ancien droit*—in the pre-Revolutionary French law inspired by Roman law.[36]

There is nothing enviable in the position of someone leasing the performance of their work. The differences between a labourer and a slave are remuneration and a limit on the number of hours worked, yet in each case the work is done on another's orders and thus requires the alienation of a part of the worker's freedom.[37] Those contrasting definitions of work is still where the line is drawn today between employees (*travailleurs dependants*), who perform work under an employment contract, and self-employed workers (*travailleurs indépendants*), who are described as independent and undertake to deliver a product under a contract for services.

In the early twentieth century, the legal characterization of an employment contract was the subject of important scholarly debate against the backdrop of cautious court decisions. Was the employment contract defined by economic dependence, or by the relationship of subordination it described?

In a landmark judgment rendered on July 6, 1931, the Cour de Cassation found that

> the legal condition of workers in relation to the persons for
> whom they work cannot be determined by the economic weak-
> ness or dependence of the said workers and cannot arise solely
> from the contract between the parties; the status of employee
> necessarily implies the existence of a legal relationship of sub-
> ordination of worker to employer.[38]

Since then, this legal relationship of subordination has been the
test of an employment contract. Discussion on this point has never
ceased, however, and every once in a while the issue of economic
dependence reappears as an undercurrent in certain judgments.

The appeal of the employment contract certainly cannot be
explained by a desire on the part of a majority of French citizens to
obey and submit to others. But in the late nineteenth century, the
laws protecting first labourers and then employees started attracting a large number of workers that continued to grow along with the
number of laws providing protections, such as access to social insurance, a guaranteed minimum wage, dignified working conditions,
stronger systems of representation, protections against dismissal, and
unemployment benefits. This legislation made it possible for wage
earners to evolve toward a type of salaried employee status. The subordination imposed in exchange has been circumscribed by labour
law, which has developed alongside this work performed under a
special contract, which, in its standard form, has an indefinite term
and stipulates that the employment is full-time.[39]

In addition to rights directly related to working conditions, we
must also take into account the structure of society that has taken
shape around this activity and become so entrenched that we now
speak of a society of salaried workers.[40] In France, it is estimated
that over 85 per cent of the working population is "salaried."[41] Social
and tax contributions are collected primarily from wages. Thus, the
welfare state is based on salaried workers, and any innovation that
calls this system into question is perceived as a threat. This is, of
course, the case with platform-generated work.

In all industrialized and developing countries, as well as in
the European Union (EU), the relationship of subordination is an
identifying feature of employment contracts. Although EU law
refers the definition of labour relations back to the member States,
the European Court of Justice (ECJ) has ruled on the contours of
this relationship, resulting in contrasting judgments. The European

definition of an employment contract also has a legal subordination requirement,[42] but when faced both with the transformation in employment and a need to establish a broader spectrum of protective employment standards, Europe has broadened the characterization, sometimes taking a pragmatic position to ensure that the protective standards achieve their purpose.[43]

Although the French labour code still does not define the employment contract, the case law has developed a definition, in two leading cases in particular.[44] In 1996, it was decided that

> the relationship of subordination is characterized by the performance of work under the authority of an employer who has the power to give orders and directives, to control its performance, and to sanction breaches by the subordinate; and that work for an organized service may be an indication of a relationship of subordination when the employer unilaterally determines the conditions of performance of the work.

Then, in 2000, it was determined that

> the existence of an employment relationship does not depend on either the will expressed by the parties or the name they give to their agreement, but on the actual conditions in which the workers' activities are performed.

The remark from the judgment rendered on December 19, 2000, is of particular interest to us here. The case concerned a taxi driver (this was before Uber, but things were already moving in that direction) who leased his vehicle from a specialized business with which he had entered a contract to "lease a car for use as a taxi." The contract was breached, and the driver brought an action before the labour division of the Conseil des Prud'hommes demanding that it be recharacterized as a contract of employment. The courts hearing the merits declined jurisdiction, but the Cour de Cassation quashed the appeal judgment on the basis of the interpretation quoted above.

That judgment is far removed from the former article 1134 of the *Code civil*.[45] It is pragmatic, leaving little room for the will of the parties. The name or characterization of the contract (lease, contract of enterprise, contract for professional services) initially agreed upon is of no importance in light of the reality of the facts related before

the judge. This point should be emphasized here, as this is the jurisprudential analysis that will probably make it possible for French
judges to redefine the contracts of some digital platform workers as
employment contracts, as certain American and English judges, as
well as the Chinese authorities, have done.[46] This pragmatism reflects
the attention that judges pay to the economic weakness of one of the
parties to a contract of successive performance.[47] Although the Cour
de Cassation did not ignore the requirement of a legal relationship
of subordination, it analyzed the situation of dependence of the
driver vis-à-vis his lessee, who not only took care of the car, but
also handled the administrative responsibilities and social security
declarations in the place of the driver. The financial consideration
requested by the lessor was such that the driver had to work long
hours, ultimately for low pay. This situation is identical to Uber drivers and pizza delivery drivers.

It should not be assumed, however, that all currently self-
employed taxi drivers operating via digital platforms can easily
have their contract of self-employment redefined as an employment
contract. After the judgment in 2000, many have tried, but outcomes
are uncertain.[48] The analysis of the relationship of subordination
has been narrowed again, and drivers have to prove the authority
of direction of the work provider (in this case the lessor) directly
over the work, not just over the vehicle, if they want the contract
recharacterized.

As for Uber drivers, the relationship of subordination should
not be difficult to prove, given the numerous requirements the
company imposes, which go beyond what a mere intermediary can
demand, including car choice, dress code, logo display, and, especially, a compulsory system of remuneration.[49] The subordination
is evident merely in the details from Uber UK contracts remarked
upon by the English judge in the case referred to above.[50] Uber exerts
constant control through digital devices, smartphones, including
geotracking, and, above all, the systematic customer ratings on the
platform. Its authority to discipline is evident in the right it reserves
to terminate the contract by simply disconnecting the driver in the
event of poor ratings or a breach of obligations.

It is clear, however, that the full-time employment contract of
indeterminate duration established by industrial legislation is not
suitable to the type of work at issue here. The small number of actions
brought before the courts in France seeking a recharacterization of

such contracts seems to indicate that the workers themselves do not want to enter into a contract that is essentially defined by legal subordination. Requalifying contracts by reshaping the facts is not a tenable solution in the long term.

But does that mean that platform workers are self-employed?

ii. Self-Employed Workers?

Since the end of the twentieth century, self-employment (*travail indépendant*) seems to have caught the wind in its sails, thanks to both certain legislative trends and the younger generations—even though studies have shown no increased numbers in this type of work.[51] Indeed, self-employed is the status chosen by most digital platform workers, and this is the reason the statute enacted on August 8, 2016, included special provisions.

The notion of self-employment refers to a legal status of independence in opposition to a worker bound by contract to an employer to whom obedience is owed. This independence, however, does not resolve the inherent problem of the economic dependence of the worker. A person who derives income through work by selling either the performance of a service or the product of that performance is in a state of economic dependence vis-à-vis the person who orders the work. While labour law has created a protected status, it is limited to its field of application, which comprises essentially private-sector wage-earning employees. The legislature vacillates between strengthening these protections and encouraging an exodus from the ranks of salaried employees. For the last thirty years, the economic dependence of self-employed workers and the autonomy of salaried employees have inspired numerous proposals for reform that have done more to complicate labour law than to simplify it. For the time being, then, workers who are not in a legal relationship of subordination are independent and therefore self-employed. This binary vision of the legal categories explains the contortions on the part of the legislator and then judges, as we have seen, to categorize workers whose independence is established as salaried employees.[52]

Unlike other European countries, France has not created an intermediate status. Germany, Italy, and Spain have established a special status for "dependent self-employment"[53] that more or less recognizes the status of employee for self-employed workers with one main client (that is, representing more than 50 per cent of their activity). This status lets these workers benefit from certain rights and protections, although not all labour law protections apply to them. However, while these categories might appear attractive, they are apparently rarely used, and Italy has even eliminated this "quasi-employee" status.

In France, as early as 1994, a presumption of unsalaried status for workers entered in the business, trade, or commercial agent registries or registered with social agencies was added to the first articles of the *Code du travail*. The presumption could be rebutted if the worker had proof of a "permanent legal relationship of subordination" vis-à-vis a client.[54] Reflecting political changes, the provision was amended on numerous occasions. Today, its equivalent can be found in article L. 8221-6 of the *Code du travail*, in a section on illegal work.

All these provisions, whether they recognize a special status or require workers to prove their dependence on an exclusive client, are ill-suited to digital platform workers, who are often registered on several platforms to be sure they get enough work. It bears noting that exclusivity clauses, such as those originally in Uber's contracts, have tended to disappear as the number of court sanctions have increased.[55]

Self-employed workers therefore must be registered and declared as merchants, artisans, or commercial agents in accordance with the rules for each status, failing which they commit the offence of *"travail dissimulé par dissimulation d'activité"* (concealed work by the concealment of paid employment).[56] This offence, punishable by three years imprisonment and a €45,000 ($68,500) fine, is committed when a worker has not met the formal requirements referred to above or has failed to make the mandatory declarations to social agencies before starting to work.

The provisions directly concern collaborative economy workers. Any income they earn through an activity obtained via a platform will be characterized as "concealed work" unless they can prove that the income is merely a reimbursement of costs (for example, BlaBlaCar ride-sharing) or that the platform conducts itself as the main client.[57]

Since August 2016,[58] the groundwork has been laid in the French labour code for "the social responsibility of platforms" through the recognition of workers' collective rights, the right to unionize, and the right to collective action. The recognition of the freedom of association and the rights to collective action might be essential, but it is in fact nothing more than declarative. As fundamental rights, they are recognized for all workers under the French constitution and numerous international agreements; France, for example, has ratified the fundamental ILO Conventions, the *European Convention on Human Rights* and the *European Social Charter*. Nevertheless, it is interesting, at least symbolically, that the labour code has now recognized a new legal category of worker. Platform workers have also formed unions and sparked far-reaching social movements. Led by Uber drivers, among others, they have demonstrated their capacity to regain their collective strength by defending workers.[59]

Collective bargaining can also sometimes place salaried employees and self-employed workers on an equal footing when their situations are the same. The European Court of Justice applied competition law when ruling on the validity of a collective agreement that favoured setting identical minimum fees for replacement workers (in this case orchestra musicians), whether hired as self-employed workers or employees (ECJ 4 December 2014, C-413/13, FNV Kunsten). The court, continuing to see self-employed workers as "enterprises," did not move away from the European definition of worker, which essentially presupposes a relationship of subordination. Nonetheless, it saved the provision in the agreement by proposing the label "false self-employed" for these workers when they are under the legal subordination of the client. Thus, the ECJ's judgment was attenuated: although the collective agreement provision submitted to the judges was saved, the social dialogue regarding the fate of self-employed workers was not acknowledged, even though their status is often more precarious than that of salaried employees. Such a recognition would have protected employees from social dumping, which represents a danger to everyone, since the growing number of self-employed workers can incite competition potentially leading to lower salaries and decreased employee benefits.

The trend pushing workers towards new forms of self-employment preceded the development of digital platforms. Specific regulations have appeared gradually, supported by a political will to encourage the development of "auto-enterprises," an individual incorporated status available to self-employed workers. More recent protective measures also tend to take "career paths" into account, establishing a certain portability of rights.

iii. *Auto-Entrepreneurs?*

Unlike subordinate work, self-employment can be exercised under many statuses, including: artisan, merchant, and professional. These statuses are defined by other fields of law, primarily commercial law and business law. Beyond labour law considerations, considerable differences between these statuses can be identified in their respective social protection regimes. Self-employed workers cannot claim the same rights as employees, and this situation is prejudicial to those self-employed workers who are economically dependent, who have several clients, and whose situation is often very precarious.

Freedom of enterprise, enshrined in the French constitution, allows anyone to start his or her own business. For years, the French legislature has encouraged this type of activity, seeing it as a remedy to de-industrialization and mass unemployment. In this spirit, the "modernization of the economy" statute[60] enacted on August 4, 2009, established a simplified social and taxation regime for self-employed workers with low sales revenue, known as the "auto-entrepreneur" regime. Since January 1, 2009, it has been available to natural persons who create or already own an individual business to perform a principal or supplementary commercial activity, either artisanal or professional (with some exceptions), if this individual business meets the conditions of the micro-enterprise tax regime and chooses to operate under a VAT exemption.[61] On January 1, 2016, auto-enterprises became known as micro-enterprises, but the regime remained the same. It is not a special legal status, contrary to what is often believed because of the rapid development of the mechanism, but a regime that simplifies the processes, declarations, and burdens related to social security and income tax. It is intended for self-employed workers with sales revenue below €82,200 or whose income as service providers is below €32,900.

Workers who wish to benefit from this regime must register with the chamber of commerce and industry, the directory of trade workers and artisans, or, if they are professionals, the URSSAF (the organization that collects social contributions). As early as 2010 there were more than 660,000 workers registered, and by the end of 2015 there were over one million, three-quarters of whom say they would not have launched their own business without this regime.[62] The auto-entrepreneur regime is chosen by 54 per cent of all those starting out as self-employed workers. However, while "traditional" self-employed workers earned an average of €3,110 a month in 2012, auto-entrepreneurs earned only €450 on average.

The ease of registering for the auto-entrepreneur regime, which can be done online, helps explain its early popularity as well as the fact that nearly half of those registered are economically inactive. Auto-entrepreneurs often operate multiple businesses (38 per cent) or are unemployed and in retraining (28 per cent).

The regime would thus appear to be suitable for digital platform workers, who have similar profiles. And in fact it is the regime recommended (if not required) by a certain number of platforms (Deliveroo,[63] Uber, and the like). In this way, the platforms take advantage of the presumption of unsalaried status set out in article L 8221-6 of the *Code du travail*, which *a priori* protects them from the possibility of the contract being characterized as an employment contract since the workers are registered as merchants or artisans. These workers, however, are in extremely precarious situations because they lack a protected status. Their working conditions, working hours, workplace health and safety, time off, holidays, and the provision and loss of work are neither guaranteed nor protected. They fall outside both administrative controls and the jurisdiction of the labour tribunals (Conseils de Prud'hommes).

But then again, the courts have oversight, and they sanction those who defraud the auto-entrepreneur regime.[64] For example, in 2009, a training company breached a contract with its teachers and then immediately proposed rehiring them as auto-entrepreneurs. The Cour de Cassation upheld the decisions on the merits, which had recharacterized the situation as an employment contract. The action had been brought by URSSAF, since the rate of contribution for self-employed workers who pay on their own is lower than that of salaried employees, whose contributions are shared by the employers and employees.[65]

Digital workers' rights can be protected by the reinterpretation of labour law based on a new labour relations model, as certain official reports have recognized:

> Beyond the traditional definition of salaried work, which remains relevant to the vast majority of them, the new forms of work taking place outside the salaried realm suggest it would be appropriate to consider broadening the notion based on new indicators emerging from an economic rather than a legal

economic assessment. Thus, much like the Department of Labour under the Obama Administration, France must reflect on how court rulings on the characterization of salaried employees can be modernized. Such an evolution, which could be based on broader criteria (the degree of autonomy at work, who decides matters of remuneration, the exclusivity of the worker's services, etc.), will make it possible to characterize the worker's status as either salaried or, on the contrary, self-employed (in its generic sense).[66]

Many parties, including the European Commission (EC), also urge the recognition of a legal relationship under labour law and protections for digital workers. However, in the view of the EC, the collaborative economy is first and foremost an economic opportunity, and hampering the development of the platforms, which it sees as potential sources of employment, should not be risked by enacting overly restrictive legislation. Thus, for the EC, while worker protections are necessary, they must be flexible and safe enough to ensure the development of these new activities.[67]

While the new labour relations model being created through digital platforms requires us to reconsider the two pillars of the employment relationship—work and the status of the person performing it—its true innovation resides in the establishment of a tripartite relationship. The legal characterization of the platform in that relationship, however, remains to be determined.

IV. Platform/Intermediary/Employer

We have now come to the truly innovative aspect of the "sharing economy." What makes digitization possible is the nearly unlimited range at which information—in this case, job offers and applications—can be disseminated. The broader the dissemination, the greater the likelihood of a balance between "sharing" and "economy." Dissemination is ensured via digital platforms, which have taken the place of traditional advertisers.

The term "platform" entered the lexicon with the arrival of Web 3.0. Until then, people were more likely to refer to communities, networks, hosts, or operators.[68] Once beyond the sales and information stage, the term was established in response to the rise of intermediation between various actors. It has since been set down in various legal provisions, to the point where the term "digital platform law" has become accepted.[69] The EC states, "'Online platform' refers to an undertaking operating in two- (or multi)-sided markets, which uses the Internet to enable interactions between two or more distinct but interdependent groups of users so as to generate value for at least one of the groups."[70] In France, these platforms are defined not only in the general income tax code referred to above but also the consumer code.[71] But not all platforms operate according to the same model: "The 'platform' galaxy is populated by various participants. We are now in the realm of 'platform capitalism' but the contrast between participants is so pronounced that its maps have yet to be drawn."[72]

The primary characteristic of platforms is their mission of intermediation, which leads to two consequences of direct interest to us here: their self-proclaimed lack of accountability, and their violation of existing regulations and organizational forms. Uber and Airbnb are prime examples. Since they do not define themselves as a taxi company[73] and a hotel company, they do not, in their view, have to comply with the obligations incumbent on operators in those industries in place all over the world.[74] The activities they took on were antiquated or outmoded,[75] and they have created a new global model for consumption, the success of which is based on ease of access, new lifestyles, and very competitive prices made possible by their refusal to take on industry obligations.[76] As a result, entire industries (taxi, hotel) have been destabilized. Long subjected to demanding regulations, these industries have found themselves battling "lawless pirates" who feel entitled to set up business in the same industry without following the rules. In response, a new type of regulation has begun to emerge, particularly in the service sector we are interested in here, seeking to both protect consumers and maintain public order.[77]

Digital platforms always present themselves as mere inter-mediaries, but their legal status remains to be clarified.[78] Indeed, the very term "intermediary" evokes numerous and varied legal characterizations. As this discussion is limited to the entities that connect workers and customers with one another, it will touch on the characterizations of platforms under commercial law and labour law. Are they brokers or mandataries? A medium for posting job offers, or a way to obtain illegal temporary work?

i. The Contractual Relationship Between Workers and Online Service Platforms

As we have seen, if a platform worker is not a salaried employee (which they rarely are), there is a presumption that he or she is a self-employed merchant or artisan. In such a case, the platform must be considered a provider, mandatary (agent) or broker.[79] A cluster of contracts is created between the various providers. One is a general contract between the platform and the worker for the performance of a service, entered into when the worker registers on the platform as a driver, host, cook, housecleaner, and the like, depending on the platform's specialization. The worker undertakes to perform the service promised by the platform, which in turn undertakes to register the provider in its pool and to forward any requests to the worker that correspond to the offer given.

At the same time, another general contract is formed with the customer, who requests a service, when he or she signs up on the smartphone app. This second contract is a kind of subscription allowing access to the service available only to subscribers. It falls under the purview of consumer law and the new "duty of loyalty" incumbent on platforms under the statute enacted on October 7, 2016.[80] This principle of loyalty applies only to the relationship between the business operators and consumers, however, and not that between the workers who provide the services. This is regrettable for those workers in a position of weakness vis-à-vis the platform.[81]

Entering into these contracts requires nothing more than a single click on the "I agree" or "I accept the general user conditions" button. Rarely does anyone, whether provider or customer, read the entire contract. Besides, more often than not these contracts are illegible, contain contradictions, and incorporate by reference other documents that can be accessed only through a hyperlink.

The work itself is performed the same way, whether the platform connects the worker and the customer through the smartphone app or the website. This operation can take various legal forms, giving rise to equally diverse legal characterizations. Some platforms do no more than connect the parties, allowing them free rein to negotiate financial terms and performance. In such cases, the platform is indeed a "mere intermediary," comparable to traditional advertisers but with the possibility of endless classified ads. In other cases, the platform is involved in the formation of the contract for services, and the characterization of the contract becomes much more elusive. When payment for the service is made via the platform—which then forwards the fee after having taken its commission off the top—the operation takes place through a network of mandates conferred by the parties via their initial contracts. When the platform sets the conditions of performance, the chances that the contract will be recharacterized as a contract of employment become more likely.

The ability of the customer to choose the worker who performs the service can also vary. In the Uber, Deliveroo, and other taxi or delivery service models, the client has no choice at all, and the platform decides on the basis of proximity. Human intervention in that decision is virtually non-existent; the app's algorithm ensures the service is rendered as quickly as possible. The *intuitu personae* character of the relationship between the worker and customer is weak, and the customer pays a flat rate set by the platform. In contrast, in other models, the platform connects the offer of service and the request, giving customers broad leeway in their choice of who will perform it. This latter type of contract is the model for professional or amateur hotels (Booking and Airbnb), as well as OpenWork and other crowdsourcing platforms based on competitive systems.

Platforms become more involved in the relationships between the performer of services and the customer by acting as dispute arbitrator for the parties. In the event of a user complaint, platforms reserve the right to hold back some or all of the service fee.[82] These contracts, which their creators define as *sui generis*, contain clauses that are similar from one country to the next and handily ignore specific local legal requirements.[83] Of course, these requirements are only made known after the platform sets up business, when the consumers' needs or desires make them necessary and entail the reform of national laws to accommodate this type of UCO (unidentified contractual object). Only then are the contracts subjected to judicial review, with varying outcomes for the platforms.[84]

ii. Legal Risks for the Platforms

Legal risks are numerous and vary according to the subject of the dispute. The major international platforms know this and do not hesitate to legally optimize their operations. Uber, for example, set up its headquarters in the Netherlands[85] and its customer service relations in Morocco.[86] Legal optimization is pursued essentially for tax reasons,[87] but also to save on labour costs.

From the perspective of labour law, a distinction can be drawn on the basis of the activity offered. Platforms like Airbnb, which offer essentially the enjoyment of a good (lodging), though the lodger does provide some personal services (hotel services), are not at much risk as they traditionally fall under the framework of business law. In contrast, services providing human activities (taxi service, delivery, cooking, housecleaning, babysitting, and so on), whether or not the type of work is generally regulated, are profoundly affected by the systems of platform intermediation operating outside of any legal framework.[88] Often these activities are performed by workers who, like nineteenth-century labourers, have only their hands to live by—or to be more precise, have only their smartphones and cars or bikes to make a living.

The taxi industry appears to have been the most affected by digital platform intermediation. Accordingly, the French legislator intervened on December 29, 2016,[89] enacting a single statute to cover all providers of this service, including digital intermediaries.

Heetch and UberPOP are the platforms that managed to operate with the greatest degree of deregulation. Both connect non-professional drivers using their own cars with customers seeking cheap transportation. This low-cost system is of course possible because the business assumed no tax or social contribution burdens whatsoever. Admittedly, as these platforms emphasized in France, they gave unemployed people a means of gainful employment, and Heetch, which operated only between 8:00 p.m. and 6:00 a.m., argued that it did not engage in unfair competition, focusing as it did on trips to the suburbs that were served very little by taxis and not at all by public transit. Nevertheless, the fact remains that their services were not provided as volunteer activities and could therefore be characterized as illegal work. The liability of the platforms remained to be established.

Following a court ruling against UberPOP,[90] Heetch and its directors were found guilty by the Tribunal Correctionnel de Paris on March 2, 2017.[91] After nearly 1,500 taxi drivers had filed complaints, the company was prosecuted for organizing an illegal system connecting customers with persons transporting others for remuneration, complicity in the illegal exercise of the taxi profession, and misleading business practices. The court upheld all the charges, finding that the platform was responsible because the system could only work through the platform and that the price it suggested was generally the one customers paid, due to the strong incentives to do so provided by the platform itself. The company was ordered to pay a €200,000 fine, its directors were fined €10,000 each, and €500,000 was ordered in compensation for the plaintiffs.

In addition to criminal convictions applicable in respect of any type of informally exercised work that tends to evade various laws and regulations, platforms must also take into account the specific rules of labour law.[92] Articles L. 8221-5 and following of the *Code du travail* define concealed work by the concealment of paid employment, an offence punishable by three years' imprisonment and a €45,000 fine. It takes place when an employer fails to file the proper declarations to social agencies, make required social contributions, or issue pay slips to its employees. The sanctions are imposed solely as a consequence of the relationships under an employment contract, once again indicating the importance of the characterization of the contract and the consequences of judicial recharacterization. If the judge finds that the platform conducted itself as an actual employer (direction, control, and discipline of employees), he or she will recharacterize the relationship and impose both civil and criminal sanctions.[93]

Having created a new social relationship model without concerning themselves with national laws in any way, digital platforms now find themselves in a position of great legal insecurity. And yet, though they are responsible for the situation they are now in, they have also revealed the public appetite for these new types of relationships. It has therefore become necessary to enact new, suitable, and balanced legislation, applicable to everyone.[94]

iii. What Status for Digital Intermediary Service Platforms?

In any work undertaken on this subject, two words constantly reappear: transition and disruption. In legal terms, transition is ensured by adapting existing solutions to new ways of operating. As for disruption, the term is as new as the model to which it applies.

The labour law solution so far adopted—that is, the recharacterization of the relationship as an employment contract giving rise to compensation—is neither satisfactory nor suitable.[95] Aside from the fact it can only be imposed after the fact and even then only rarely, it also inadequately protects workers, who are often precarious and whose numbers continue to grow. Platforms must be held accountable and bear obligations similar to those the legislator imposed first on industrial employers and then eventually on all employers, creating what we know today as labour law.

French labour law is already well acquainted with a number of forms of labour intermediation. One avenue that has already been attempted[96] is business and employment cooperatives that define workers as salaried entrepreneurs.[97] Another possibility is the temporary work option. Once again, however, the French legislator has intervened, as this new labour relations model represents a threat due to its similarity with slavery or at least servitude (lease of a person to perform work at the pleasure of the lessor). Very strict legislation circumscribes this type of work in France, and breaches are punished criminally as illegal subcontracting. These provisions might be adapted, and the legislator might be inspired to circumscribe the activities of the many platforms, but for the moment, in a situation of high unemployment, it is easier to encourage the development of the platforms than to protect workers. Indeed, this attitude is evident all over Europe. The EC is urging its member states to deregulate more and more professions and to open themselves up to these innovations, in the hopes of encouraging economic recovery.[98] But this approach seems to ignore the fate of workers, who often have to work twice as many hours as salaried employees do and earn no more than minimum wage.

With the statute enacted on August 8, 2016,[99] France opted to legislatively compel the "social accountability of platforms." Like any corporate social responsibility, this is a minimum obligation that depends greatly on the goodwill of the platforms. Although the legislature has not abandoned the salaried work/self-employed work dichotomy, it has included a title in the *Code du travail* explicitly dealing with self-employed workers using electronic remote connection platforms.[100] These provisions apply to self-employed workers who, for the purpose of exercising their professional activity, use one or more electronic remote connection platforms as defined in article 242 *bis* of the *Code général des impôts* (General Income Tax Code).[101] That provision contemplates enterprises, regardless of their place of business, who use electronic means to remotely connect persons with a view to the sale of a good, the provision of a service, or the exchange or sharing of a good or service, and states that they are required to provide, upon each transaction, candid, clear, and transparent information regarding the tax and social obligations incumbent on persons who use them as intermediaries to carry out commercial transactions.

Platforms have few obligations.[102] The *Code du travail* does provide that, "when a platform determines the characteristics of the performance of service or of the good sold and sets its price, that platform bears a social responsibility towards the workers concerned."[103] This responsibility consists in contributing to workplace accident insurance and ensuring workers' rights to occupational training as soon as the service provider achieves a certain level of sales revenue via the platform.[104]

This recent reform gives rise to two observations. On the one hand, the workers concerned are excluded from the application of the *Code du travail*, which can only be seen as regrettable. On the other, platforms that until very recently operated entirely outside the realm of labour law are now starting to bear some obligations. As the Projet pour un autre Code du travail suggests, however, a solution that would offer more protection might have included these digital workers within an expanded definition of the employment contract.[105]

Labour law was conceived and built for an industrial society exploiting a large and stationary labour force that it wanted to supervise and discipline.[106] It is now time to rewrite the labour code for the twenty-first century, so that it may govern all forms of subordinate or autonomous work performed for others and safeguard the social rights of workers, whether their work is defined by the performance of a service or by the result of such a performance.[107]

The task before us now remains: the creation and establishment of social law that protects digital platforms workers.[108]

Notes

1. Senior lecturer, Institut d'Etudes du Travail de Lyon, Université Lumière Lyon2 France, CERCRID UMR 5137. Text translated by Vera J. Roy. Unless otherwise indicated, all translations of legislation and of judgements are unofficial.

2. Michel Vivant et al, *Le Lamy—Droit du Numérique* (Paris: Wolters Kluwer, 2016).

3. *Communication—Commerce Electronique*, online: Lexis Nexis <http://boutique.lexisnexis.fr/4529-communication-commerce-electronique/>.

4. Jeremy Rifkin, *The End of Work: The Decline of the Global Labor Force and the Dawn of the Post-Market Era*, 2nd ed. (New York: Penguin, 2004); Philippe Escande & Sandrine Cassini, Bienvenue dans le capitalisme 3.0 (Paris: Albin Michel, 2015), ch 3, 49; Stephen Bouquin, "Fin du travail ou crise du salariat ?" (1997) Revue Banlieu-Ville et Lien Social 1, online: <http://

www.espaces-marx.net/IMG/pdf/FinWcriseSal.pdf>. The expression is frequently used in the mainstream press: Elsa Dicharry, "L'Urssaf déclenche l'arme atomique contre Uber" Les Échos.fr (17 May 2016), online: <http://www.lesechos.fr/idees-debats/dossiers/travail-emploi-uberisation-salariat-chomage-protectionsociale/index.php>; Chloé Dussapt, "La fin du salariat est-elle inéluctable?" Challenges (15 March 2016), online: <http://www.challenges.fr/challenges-soir/la-fin-du-salariat-est-elle-ineluctable_34412>; *La fin du salariat: comment l'ubérisation change le travail*, online: L'Express <http://lexpansion.lexpress.fr/actualite-economique/la-fin-du-salariat-comment-l-uberisation-change-le-travail_1733397.html>.

5. Very few articles have been published in French specialized legal journals on the subject, even if the question of the transformation of work and the impact of the digital age on salaried work has been debated since the beginning of the century.

6. See the definitions suggested in "Économie collaborative, une révolution?" (2016) 3128 Problèmes économiques 1 at 12; Loïc Jourdain, Michel Leclerc & Arthur Millerand, Économie collaborative et Droit (Limoges: Fyp, 2016) at 23. As for the European Commission, "the term 'collaborative economy' refers to business models where activities are facilitated by collaborative platforms that create an open marketplace for the temporary usage of goods or services often provided by private individuals. The collaborative economy involves three categories of actors: (i) service providers who share assets, resources, time and/or skills—these can be private individuals offering services on an occasional basis ('peers') or service providers acting in their professional capacity ('professional services providers'); (ii) users of these; and (iii) intermediaries that connect—via an online platform—providers with users and that facilitate transactions between them ('collaborative platforms'). Collaborative economy transactions generally do not involve a change of ownership and can be carried out for profit or not-for-profit." *Communication on a European agenda for the collaborative economy* (2 June 2016) at 3, online: European Commission <http://ec.europa.eu/DocsRoom/documents/16881>.

7. Valérie Peugeot et al, "Partager pour Mieux Consommer" (2015) 7 Esprit 19; Jean-François Dortier, "L'économie du partage, une alternative au capitalisme?" 266 Sciences Humaines 34; "Économie collaborative, une révolution?," *supra* note 6 at 5, 17; Damien Demailly & Anne-Sophie Novel, "Économie du partage : Enjeux et opportunités pour la transition écologique" (2014) 3 IDDRI 1, online: <http://www.iddri.org/Publications/Economie-du-partage-enjeux-et-opportunites-pour-la-transition-ecologique?fr>.

8. Orly Lobel, "The Gig Economy and the Future of Employment and Labor Law" (2017) 51:1 USF L Rev 51; *People First: The Primacy of People*

in a Digital Age, online: Accenture <https://www.accenture.com/ca-en/ insight-trends-insurance-technology-vision-2016-infographic>.

9. Patrick Thiébart, "Pour une réglementation a minima de l'économie collaborative" (2016) 1706 Sem Soc Lamy.

10. Evgeny Morozov, "Résister à l'ubérisation du monde" *Le Monde diplomatique* (September 2015), online: <https://www.monde-diplomatique. fr/2015/09/MOROZOV/53676>.

11. Christophe Degryse, *Les impacts sociaux de la digitalisation de l'économie* (Brussels: ETUI, 2016), online: <https://www.etui.org/ fr/Publications2/Working-Papers/Les-impacts-sociaux-de-la-digitalisation-de-l-economie>.

12. Henceforth, a distinction can be made between the workers operating within proximity services (drivers, delivery persons, babysitters), for whom a national regulation is foreseeable, and those operating in a dematerialized context (accountants, secretaries, translators, encoding workers) that can be made to compete on a global level, with the income distortions one might imagine. After the relocation of factories, we are witnessing the relocation of office jobs.

13. The platforms offer the opportunity to organize collectively. Workers in the informal economy aren't isolated anymore, as they can independently create their own platform to defend their rights. Namely, Uber drivers, far from being isolated, very quickly collectively organized or unionized.

14. In France, the prohibition of UberPOP, the European version of UberX, by judicial action was very quick, condemned as a concealed work infraction.

15. *Code Général des Impôts,* s 242bis. Another definition can also be found at section L. 111-7 of the *Code de la consommation,* which is essentially the same, but targets more specifically the obligations of the platforms towards consumers.

16. According to the official website of the French Ministry for the Economy and Finance: "Today more than 90,000 start-ups constitute the global sharing consumption market. In 2013, the total revenue of the sector is estimated at 20 billion Euros, to reach 302 billion Euros before 2025, which represents an average annual growth rate of + 36.4% and a market multiplication of more than 20 in 10 years. Moreover, 89% of the French population states having taken part at least once in a sharing consumption practice." (*"Aujourd'hui plus de 90 000 startups composent le marché mondial de la consommation collaborative. En 2013, on estime à 20 milliards d'euros le chiffre d'affaires du secteur et à 302 milliards d'euros d'ici 2025, ce qui représente un taux de croissance annuel moyen de + 36,4 % et une multiplication du marché par plus de 20 en 10 ans. Par ailleurs, 89% de la population française déclare avoir déjà réalisé au moins une fois une pratique*

de consommation collaborative."). *Les chiffres clés de l'économie collaborative* (20 July 2016), online: French Ministry for the Economy and Finance <http://www.economie.gouv.fr/vous-orienter/entreprise/numerique/chiffres-cles-leconomie-collaborative>.

17. Cyril Wolmark, "Quelle place pour le travail dans le droit du travail?" (2016) 5 Dr soc 439.

18. Participation in a game show can be re-qualified as a work contract once participants can demonstrate their subordinate position towards the production company: Cass soc, 3 juin 2009, (2009) Bull civ, 141, No 08-40.981 et al ["Île de la Tentation"]; *Communiqué relatif à l'arrêt n° 1159 du 3 juin 2009 de la Chambre sociale*, online: Cour de Cassation <https://www.courdecassation.fr/jurisprudence_2/chambre_sociale_576/arret_n_12906.html>. Among the many comments on the topic, see Jean-Marc Béraud & Christophe Radé, "Protéger qui exactement? Le tentateur? Le sportif amateur? Le travailleur?" (2013) 3 Dr Soc 197.

19. Alain Supiot, *Critique du Droit du travail*, 3rd ed (Paris: Presses Universitaires de France, 2015); Dominique Méda, *Le travail*, 5th ed (Paris: Presses Universitaires de France, 2015).

20. Namely, Robert Castel, *Les métamorphoses de la question sociale: une chronique du salariat* (Paris: Fayard. 1995); Jean Boissonnat, *Le travail dans vingt ans* (Paris: Odile Jacob, 1995); Alain Supiot, *Au-delà de l'emploi* (Paris: Flammarion, 1999).

21. The "Compte Personnel d'Activité" (CPA), provided for in a 2013 Act, implemented by the *Loi n° 2016-1088 du 8 août 2016 relative au travail, à la modernisation du dialogue social et à la sécurisation des parcours professionnels*, JO, 25 September 2017, text 3 [*Loi n° 2016-1088*], and the *Ordonnance n° 2017-53 du 19 janvier 2017 portant diverses dispositions relatives au compte personnel d'activité, à la formation et à la santé et la sécurité au travail dans la fonction publique*, JO, 20 janvier 2017, text 43, grants rights related to training to the active population from sixteen years old. See: Selma Mahfouz, "Le compte personnel d'activité, de l'utopie au concret" (2016) 10 Dr soc 789; and the other articles in this special issue of the journal.

22. Wolmark, *supra* note 17.

23. Robert Badinter & Antoine Lyon-Caen, *Le travail et la loi* (Paris: Fayard, 2015).

24. Comité chargé de définir les principes essentiels du droit du travail, *Rapport au Premier Ministre* (January 2016), online: <http://www.gouvernement.fr/sites/default/files/document/document/2016/01/25.01.2016_remise_du_rapport_badinter.pdf>.

25. Pascal Lokiec, "Les idéologues de la simplification" (2015) 1677 Sem soc Lamy, online: <http://www.wk-rh.fr/actualites/detail/85108/les-ideologues-de-la-simplification.html>; Emmanuel Dockès, "Préservons un système qui protège les salariés," *Le Monde* (27 June 2015), 5; Emmanuel

Dockès, "La commission Badinter vaporise le droit du travail" (2016)
812 Le Droit ouvrier 114; Gérard Filoche, "Analyse détaillée des 61
mesures du rapport Badinter" (29 January 2016), *Le blog de gerardfiloche*
(blog), online: <https://blogs.mediapart.fr/gerardfiloche/blog/290116/
analyse-detaillee-des-61-mesures-du-rapport-badinter>.

26. *Non-Standard Employment Around the World: Understanding Challenges,
Shaping prospects* (14 November 2016), online: International Labour
Organization <http://www.ilo.org/global/publications/books/
WCMS_534326/lang--en/index.htm> [*Non-Standard Employment Around
the World*]; *Recommendation No. 204 concerning the Transition from the
Informal to the Formal Economy* (23 June 2015), online: International
Labour Organization <http://www.ilo.org/ilc/ReportsavailableinArabic/
WCMS_377774/lang--en/index.htm>.

27. *Le Robert*, 2016, *sub verbo* "Ubériser": "destabilize, transform a business
sector with an innovative economic model by drawing on new technologies." ("déstabiliser, transformer un secteur d'activité avec un modèle
économique innovant en tirant parti des nouvelles technologies").

28. To learn more about this part of labour law history: Jacques Le Goff, *Du
silence à la parole*, 3rd ed (Rennes: Presses universitaires de Rennes, 2004);
Jens Thoemmes, "Du temps de travail au temps des marches" (2009) 10
Temporalités, online: <http://temporalites.revues.org/1149>; Edward P
Thompson, *Temps, discipline du travail et capitalisme industriel* (Paris: La
Fabrique, 2004).

29. *Non-Standard Employment Around the World*, *supra* note 26.

30. Thomas Pasquier, "Sens et limites de la qualification de contrat de
travail" (2017) 2 RDT 95.

31. Bruno Mettling, Transformation numérique et vie au travail (September
2015), online: La documentation française <http://www.ladocumenta-
tionfrancaise.fr/var/storage/rapports-publics/154000646.pdf>; *Rapport
au Premier Ministre*, *supra* note 24; Nathalie Andireux et al, "Travail,
emploi, numérique: les nouvelles trajectoires" (January 2016), online:
Conseil national du numérique <http://www.ladocumentationfrancaise.
fr/rapports-publics/164000018/index.shtml>.

32. Nicolas Amar & Louis-Charles Viossat, *Les plateformes collaboratives,
l'emploi et la protection sociale* (2015), online: Inspection Générale des
Affaires Sociales <http://www.igas.gouv.fr/spip.php?article551>.

33. Alain Supiot, "Les nouveaux visages de la subordination" (2000) 2 Dr
soc 131.

34. Recent expression used to refer to persons exercising numerous professional activities at once, usually of short duration. The development
of smartphone apps and of Internet fosters new parallel activities.
Donald Hébert, "Ils ont plusieurs métiers: slasher, mode d'emploi,"
L'Obs (6 December 2015), online: <http://tempsreel.nouvelobs.com/

bien-bien/20151102.OBS8720/ils-ont-plusieurs-metiers-slasher-mode-d-emploi.html>. The number of "slashers" is estimated at 4.5 millions of persons, representing 16 per cent of the active population: *Slashers ou pluri-actifs... Qui sont ces nouveaux (et futurs) entrepreneurs?* (15 September 2015), online: Le Salon des micro-entreprises <http://www.salonsme.com/espace-telechargements/CP_Slasheurs_15092015.pdf>.

35. Claude Didry, *L'institution du travail. Droit et salariat dans l'histoire* (Paris: La Dispute, 2016).

36. Gérard Aubin & Jacques Bouveresse, *Introduction historique au droit du travail* (Paris: Presses Universitaires de France, 1995); Le Goff, *supra* note 28.

37. Robert-Joseph Pothier, whose writings inspired the drafters of the French Civil Code, wrote: "only services that are pedestrian and subject to a price, such as those of servants, labourers and artisans, may be the object of a contract of service." ("*il n'y a que les services ignobles et appréciables à prix d'argent qui soient susceptibles du contrat de louage, tels que ceux des serviteurs et servantes, des manœuvres, des artisans, etc.*"). Robert-Joseph Pothier, *Oeuvres de Pothier*, 2nd ed (Paris: Cosse et Marchal & Henri Plon, 1861) at 7.

38. Cass civ, 6 July 1931, DP 1 131, note P Pic.

39. *Code du travail*, s L. 1221-2: "The indefinite duration contract of employment is the normal and general form of an employment relationship." ("*Le contrat de travail à durée indéterminée est la forme normale et générale de la relation de travail.*").

40. Castel, *supra* note 20.

41. This designation is meant to be understood broadly, encompassing all jobs in the private and public sectors; "Emploi, chômage, population active: bilan de l'année 2014" (2015) 050 Dares analyses 1, online: <http://travail-emploi.gouv.fr/IMG/pdf/2015-050_.pdf>.

42. *Lawrie-Blum v Land Baden-Württemberg*, C-66/85 [1987] ECR 02625.

43. *Dita Danosa v LKB Līzings SIA*, C-232/09, [2010] ECR I-11405: pregnant workers must benefit from the protection stipulated by the directive.

44. Emmanuel Dockès et al, *Les grands arrêts du droit du travail*, 4th ed (Paris: Dalloz, 2008) at 5 ff; Cass Ass plén, 4 March 1983, (1983) D 381; Cass soc, 13 November 1996, (1996) Bull civ V 275, No 386; Cass soc, 19 December 2000, (2000) Bull civ V 337, No 437.

45. (1815-) [C civ], s 1103: "Contracts that have been legally concluded constitute law for those who have concluded them." ("*Les contrats légalement formés tiennent lieu de lois à ceux qui les ont faits.*").

46. Even if it is impossible to generalize on the level of entire countries, some interesting decisions should still be mentioned: *Aslam v Uber BV* (2016), [2017] IRLR 4 [*Aslam*]; Aiqing Zheng, "What protection for workers acting via digital platforms in a market economy?" (Panel

intervention delivered at the LLRN3 Conference, 25 June 2017); Marie-Cécile Escande-Varniol, "L'Ubérisation un phénomène global: Regard de droit comparé" (2017) 3 RDT 171.

47. Antoine Jeammaud, "L'avenir sauvegardé de la qualification de contrat de travail: à propos de l'arrêt Labbane" (2001) 3 Dr soc 227.

48. The Cour de Cassation referred the review of the facts and evidence allowing for contract characterization back to the trial judges. If the driver "remained in control of his work schedule as well as of vacation periods, and he was not held accountable for the origin of the funds earmarked for the payment of the fee" ("demeurait maître de ses horaires ainsi que de ses périodes de vacances et qu'il ne lui était pas demandé de comptes sur l'origine des fonds destinés à payer la redevance"), for example, the court approves the refusal to re-characterize the contract. The worker is excluded from the benefits and advantages provided by the application of the work contract. Cass soc, 17 September 2008, No 07-43.265; Cass soc, 5 May 2010, No 08-45323; Cass soc, 22 September 2015, No 14-15381; Cass soc, 18 March 2016, No 14-28987; Cass soc, 6 October 2016, No 15-19776.

49. This compensation system was responsible for numerous conflicts between Uber France drivers and the platform. In December 2017, the platform, after decreasing the imposed rates for rides, increased its management fees collected on the rides, from 20 to 25 per cent. The drivers retaliated by blocking access to Paris train stations and airports, forcing the Ministry of Transport to intervene as a mediator.

50. *Aslam, supra* note 46.

51. Jacques Barthélémy & Gilbert Cette, *Travailler au XXIème siècle: L'Ubérisation de l'économie* (Paris: Odile Jacob, 2017).

52. The French labour code includes many such provisions, pertaining to very diverse professions such as journalists, models, artists and others, as well as to "independent" workers.

53. Olivier Leclerc, "La dépendance économique en droit du travail: éclairages en droit français et en droit comparé" (2010) 3 RDT 149.

54. *Loi n° 94-126 du 11 février 1994 relative à l'initiative et à l'entreprise individuelle*, 25 July 2010, s 49.

55. In reality, such platforms try to ensure the exclusivity of their best providers through other means than an exclusivity clause. Since they are sufficiently warned by their counsels, they use legal subtleties to their advantage.

56. *Code du travail, supra* note 39, s L. 8221-3.

57. The UberPOP platform stopped operating in France due to this infraction: Laurent Gamet, "Uber Pop (†)" (2015) 11 Dr soc 929.

58. *Loi n° 2016-1088 supra* note 21, s 60.

59. See e.g. about Foodora Francine Aizicovici, "En colère les livreurs de repas se mobilisent de nouveau pour leurs conditions de travail"

Le Monde (26 August 2017), online: <http://www.lemonde.fr/econo-mie/article/2017/08/26/en-colere-les-livreurs-de-repas-se-mobi-lisent-de-nouveau-pour-leurs-conditions-de-travail_5176952_3234.html>; see also Mark Graham & Alex Wood, "Why the digital gig economy needs co-ops and unions" (15 September 2016), online: openDemocracy <https://www.opendemocracy.net/alexwood/why-digital-gig-economy-needs-collectif-ops-and-unions>.

60. *Loi n° 2008-776 du 4 août 2008 de modernisation de l'économie*, 1 January 2017.

61. *Définition—Auto-entrepreneur* (13 October 2016), online: Institut national de la statistique et des études économiques <https://www.insee.fr/fr/metadonnees/definition/c2066>.

62. Claire Hagège & Clotilde Masson, *La création d'entreprise en 2009 dopée par les auto-entrepreneurs* (21 January 2010), online: Institut national de la statistique et des études économiques <https://www.insee.fr/fr/sta-tistiques/1281078>; Jocelyn Beziau, Sylvie Rousseau & Henri Mariotte, *Auto-entrepreneurs immatriculés en 2014 54 % de ceux qui démarrent en font leur activité principale* (8 September 2016), online: <https://www.insee.fr/fr/statistiques/2121605>.

63. For example, Deliveroo asks its bike couriers to sign a contract in which it characterizes itself as a "client" towards the courier, charac-terized as a "provider," the latter "being registered in the Registre du Commerce et des Sociétés or in the Registre des Métiers, and carrying out an independent courier activity." It is impossible in the context of this general analysis to further detail the provisions of this contract, but the power imbalance between parties is obvious, and the risk of re-characterization appears significant.

64. Cass civ 2ᵉ, 7 July 2016, (2016) Bull civ No 15-16110; Jean Mouly, "Quand l'auto-entreprise sert de masque au salariat" (2016) 10 Dr soc 859.

65. Similar proceedings brought against Uber are currently underway before the Parisian jurisdiction.

66. Mettling, *supra* note 31 at 51.

67. EC, Commission, A European agenda for the collaborative economy (Brussels: EC, 2016), online: <http://eur-lex.europa.eu/legal-content/EN/TXT/PDF/?uri=CELEX:52016DC0356&from=FR>.

68. Mélanie Clément-Fontaine, "La genèse de l'Economie Collaborative: le Concept de Communauté" (2017) 3 Dalloz IP/IT 140.

69. Grégoire Loiseau, "Vers un droit des plateformes numériques" (2016) 6 Comm Com Elec 28.

70. *Have Your Say on Geo-blocking and the Role of Platforms in the Online Economy* (24 September 2015), online: European Commission <http://europa.eu/rapid/press-release_IP-15-5704_en.htm>.

71. *Code de la Consommation, supra* note 15, s L111-7: "I. – Platform operator shall mean any natural or legal person offering, in a professional capacity, in a paid manner or not, an online, publicly available communication service based on: [...] 2° connecting several parties in order to sell goods, to offer services or to exchange or share content, goods, or services." ("*I.- Est qualifiée d'opérateur de plateforme en ligne toute personne physique ou morale proposant, à titre professionnel, de manière rémunérée ou non, un service de communication au public en ligne reposant sur : [...] 2° la mise en relation de plusieurs parties en vue de la vente d'un bien, de la fourniture d'un service ou de l'échange ou du partage d'un contenu, d'un bien ou d'un service.*").

72. Judith Rochfeld & Célia Zolynski, "La « loyauté » des « plateformes ». Quelles plateformes ? Quelle loyauté ?" (2016) 11 Dalloz IP/IT 520.

73. This self-proclamation could be contradicted by the Court of Justice of the European Union if it follows the conclusions of its advocate general: *According to Advocate General Szpunar, the Uber electronic platform, whilst innovative, falls within the field of transport: Uber can thus be required to obtain the necessary licences and authorisations under national law* (11 May 2017), online: Court of Justice of the European Union <https://curia.europa.eu/jcms/upload/docs/application/pdf/2017-05/cp170050en.pdf>. According to him, Uber is indeed a taxi company.

74. Célia Zolynski & Charly Berthet, "Quelle loyauté pour les plateformes numériques?" (2016) 36 JAC 14: "This handful of inescapable actors is the source of information oligopolies. They are centralizing amongst them a considerable power, which frequently allows them to exert influence on individuals, traditional institutions (states, companies) and regulatory inclinations." ("*Cette poignée d'acteurs incontournables est à l'origine de véritables oligopoles informationnels. Ils centralisent entre leurs mains un pouvoir considérable qui leur permet souvent de prendre un ascendant sur les individus, les institutions traditionnelles (Etats, entreprises) et les velléités de régulation.*").

75. Suffice it to recall that the idea for the Uber platform was born out of the shortage of taxis in both San Francisco and Paris identified by the inventors of the platform.

76. Nathalie Martial-Braz, "De quoi l'« ubérisation » est-elle le nom?" (2017) 3 Dalloz IP/IT 133.

77. Manuella Péri, "La régulation de l'« ubérisation »" (2017) 3 Dalloz IP/IT 144.

78. Xavier Delpech, "De la responsabilité des plateformes en ligne" (2017) 194 Juris Tourisme 3.

79. Grégoire Loiseau, "Le mystère contractuel des relations triangulaires impliquant une plateforme de mise en relation en ligne" (2016) 7-8 CCE 30.

80. *Loi n° 2016-1321 du 7 octobre 2016 pour une République numérique*, JO, 7 October 2016, s 49-53, imposes to platforms selling goods and services the delivery of loyal, clear, and transparent information to consumers.

81. Lucie Cluzel-Métayer, "La loi pour une République numérique: l'écosystème de la donnée saisi par le droit" (2017) 6 AJDA 340.

82. See the chapter by Nofar Sheffi in this volume, "The Fast to the Furious."

83. Alexandre Fabre, "Plateformes numériques : gare au tropisme « travailliste »!" (2017) 3 RDT 166.

84. On September 27th, 2017, the Paris Conseil des Prud'hommes rejected the request of Take Eat Easy workers asking for the re-characterization of their contracts into work contracts: "Des anciens coursiers de Take Eat Easy déboutés aux prud'hommes" *Le Monde* (27 September 2017), online: <http://www.lemonde.fr/economie-francaise/article/2017/09/27/des-anciens-coursiers-de-take-eat-easy-deboutes-aux-prud-hommes_5192496_1656968.html>. See also Antoine Jeammaud, "Uber, Deliveroo: requalification des contrats ou dénonciation d'une fraude à la loi?" (2017) 1780 Sem Soc Lamy [Jeammaud, "Uber, Deliveroo"].

85. One of the elements debated in *Aslam*, *supra* note 46, was precisely related to which law is applicable to the case, the defendant requesting the application of Dutch law due to the location of its headquarters.

86. "Uber a progressivement délocalisé son service relation client de 25 pays vers le Maroc" *Medias 24*, online: <https://www.medias24.com/print17321910052017Uber-a-progressivement-delocalise-son-service-relation-client-de-25-pays-vers-le-Maroc.html?layout=default&>.

87. "Le montage financier d'Uber pour payer moins d'impôts" *Le Parisien* (21 February 2014), online: <http://www.leparisien.fr/economie/le-montage-financier-d-uber-pour-payer-moins-d-impots-21-02-2014-3612633.php>.

88. Barbara Gomes, "Le *crowdworking*: essai sur la qualification du travail par intermédiation numérique" (2016) 7-8 RDT 464.

89. *Loi n° 2016-1920 du 29 décembre 2016 relative à la régulation, à la responsabilisation et à la simplification dans le secteur du transport public particulier de personnes*, JO, 29 December 2016, text 4.

90. CA Paris, 31 March 2015, No 15/00371; Cons const, 22 September 2015, (2015) Rec 17083, 2015-484 DC; CA Paris, 7 December 2015, (2016) JCP Jur 1074, No 05; Gamet, *supra* note 57.

91. As the decision hasn't been published, for a thorough report see: "Jugement du procès #Heetch: une condamnation sévère" (3 March 2017), *Droit du partage* (blog), online: <https://droitdupartage.com/2017/03/03/jugement-du-proces-heetch-une-condamnation-severe/>.

92. This type of work is all the more unacceptable in a country in which the social protection system is extensive, and inasmuch as it jeopardizes the individual protection of the informal worker, but also of the system as a whole, weakened at the source in its funding system.

93. Jeammaud, "Uber, Deliveroo," *supra* note 84.
94. Martial-Braz, *supra* note 76.
95. Fabre, *supra* note 83.
96. Elsa Lederlin, "Le travail numérique à l'épreuve du droit social: l'appréciation du lien de subordination selon le principe de réalité" (2015) 47 Sem Jur 1415; Gescop Alpha Taxis (*Alpha Taxis: une coopérative qui roule!* (30 January 2013), online: economie.gouv.fr <https://www.economie.gouv.fr/ess/alpha-taxis-cooperative-qui-roule?language=fr>), Alliance Taxis and others.
97. *Décret n° 2015-1363 du 27 octobre 2015 relatif aux coopératives d'activité et d'emploi et aux entrepreneurs salariés*, JO, 27 October 2015, 20116.
98. A European agenda for the collaborative economy, *supra* note 67.
99. *Loi n° 2016-1088*, *supra* note 21.
100. *Code du travail, supra* note 39, ss L. 7341-1 - L. 7342-6.
101. The fact that the definition of collaborative platforms can be found in the *Code général des impôts* demonstrates the extent to which this economy has capitalized itself in order to become a financially important source of income and commercial exchanges.
102. As an author states: "the new title given to "workers using an electronic linking platform" by the labour code leads to *a minima* social progress for the workers using this platform. Such measures therefore appear insufficient to halt the "Uberization" movement within certain sectors of our economy." ("*le nouveau titre consacré aux « travailleurs utilisant une plateforme de mise en relation par voie électronique » par le code du travail concède des avancées sociales a minima pour les travailleurs utilisant ces plateformes. De telles mesures semblent ainsi insuffisantes à enrayer le mouvement « d'ubérisation » de certains pans de notre économie.*"). Arnaud Casado, "Droit des travailleurs indépendants utilisant des plateformes de mise en relation" (2017) 194 Juris Tourisme 30.
103. *Code du travail, supra* note 39, s L. 7342-1.
104. *Décret n° 2017-774 du 4 mai 2017 relatif à la responsabilité sociale des plateformes de mise en relation par voie électronique*, JO, 4 May 2017, text 45, s D. 7342-1 - D. 7342-5. The amount of revenues set by the law is low; for 2017, it is set at € 5,099.64.
105. A "Project for a Different Labour Code" ("*Projet pour un autre Code du travail*") developed by a group of academics proposes an inclusive definition of the work contract: "11-3. The worker is a natural person who is engaged in work under the power of, or dependant upon, another person. 11-4. Power is defined as the practical capacity of a person to command another and to be obeyed. 11-5. Economic dependency is the weak position that can be identified: – when the major part of a person's income derives from the work relation the person has with another person, – when the activity of a person depends on the means or the will

of another person." ("*11-3. Le salarié est une personne physique qui exécute un travail sous le pouvoir ou sous la dépendance d'autrui. 11-4. Le pouvoir de fait est la capacité pratique dont dispose une personne d'en commander une autre et de s'en faire obéir. 11-5. La dépendance économique est la situation de faiblesse qui peut être constatée : – lorsqu'une personne tire la part essentielle de ses revenus du rapport de travail qu'elle a avec une autre personne, – lorsque l'activité d'une personne dépend des moyens ou de la volonté d'autrui.*"). Groupe de recherches pour un autre Code du travail, *Proposition de Code du travail* (Paris: Dalloz, 2017).

106. Jean Vercherand, "« Les chauffeurs Uber découvrent la même problématique que le monde ouvrier au xixᵉ siècle »" *Le Monde* (17 January 2017), online: <http://www.lemonde.fr/idees/article/2017/01/17/uber-entreprise-du-xixe-siecle_5063748_3232.html>.

107. Nicolas Lagrange, "Economie collaborative: un modèle fiscal et social à inventer" *Alternatives économiques* (17 December 2015), online: <https://www.alternatives-economiques.fr/uberisation/economie-collabora-tive-un-modele-fiscal-et-social-a-inventer-201512171900-00002783.html>.

108. Bernard Guilhon, "Uber: analyse de l'effet de domination" *The Conversation* (30 May 2017), online: <https://theconversation.com/uber-analyse-de-leffet-de-domination-78440>.

CHAPTER XI

Uber and the Unmaking and Remaking of Taxi Capitalisms: Technology, Law, and Resistance in Historical Perspective

Eric Tucker[1]

I. Introduction

From a neoliberal economic perspective, the emergence of new digital technologies portends the possibility of an economic revolution, in which there will be greater human freedom and a democratization of economic opportunity. Digitally enabled workers will transform themselves into micro-entrepreneurs, able to work for themselves "whenever they want from any location and at whatever level of intensity needed to achieve their desired standard of living."[2] Of course, there is also recognition that this bright future will not be decided by technology alone. Even for the most technological utopian, human liberation is not merely an app away, and there is recognition that other institutional and policy changes are required for the emancipatory potential of the platform economy to be unlocked.[3] But it is seen as possible within what Arun Sundararajan, a leading sharing economy optimist, calls "crowd-based capitalism."[4]

For others, the impact of the platform economy is much darker. The title of Steven Hill's book succinctly encapsulates this perspective: *Raw Deal: How the "Uber Economy" and Runaway Capitalism are Screwing American Workers.*[5] Here the emphasis is on the ways in which these platforms are shifting uncertainty and risks onto workers who lack employment security and face a shredded safety net in hyper-competitive, globalized labour markets.

Woodcut by Philippe Maurais, c. 1995. Reproduced with permission of the artist.

On the surface there seems to be a common agreement that capitalism is central to understanding the operation of the platform economy and its implications for the workforce, yet neither Sundararajan nor Hill actually make capitalism and the social relations of production central to their analytic framework. Thus, one goal of this chapter is to put capitalism at the centre of the analysis, drawing on Nick Srnicek's recent book, *Platform Capitalism*.[6] In doing so, there is a need to recognize that capitalism is not a static system operating uniformly over time and space, but rather takes very different forms. The debate about the varieties of capitalism draws on this insight, but focuses on the political framework within which capitalism functions and the extent to which it is embedded in particular institutional arrangements.[7] The concern here is more focused on the inner workings of capitalist regimes of accumulation. In particular, this chapter inquires into and seeks to account for the distinct ways that workers are subsumed into platform capitalism.

A second goal is to use this refined political economy framework to place Uber and the taxi industry in historical perspective. As we shall see, taxi capitalisms have been made, unmade, and remade several times over the past hundred years in response to changing technology law, and resistance to these changes by workers and segments of capital which shape both law and technology. Using Toronto as a case study, this chapter examines the rise of Uber and its platform technology in the context of the broader history of taxi capitalisms.

II. Theoretical Starting Points

Although Sundararajan titled his book *The Sharing Economy,* he recognizes this is a misnomer, since there is actually very little sharing that takes place in the world of the platform economy.[8] Rather, the so-called sharing economy is dominated by technologically facilitated commercial exchanges, and in recognition of this reality Sundararajan's preferred term is "crowd-based capitalism." As I draw on Nick Srnicek's work, I prefer the term "platform capitalism," but regardless of the adjective used to describe the kind of capitalism that exists, it is important in the first instance not to lose sight of the analytical significance of its *capitalist* character. In particular, venture capitalists fuel the platform economy, seeking to increase their private fortunes by finding new ways of extracting value from socially produced wealth. Platforms are digital infrastructures that enable individuals and groups to interact and are thus intermediaries. What makes them capitalist is that these infrastructures are privately owned and operated to extract profits by becoming the ground on which transactions take place. Users must pay quasi-monopoly rents to access the platform while the platform itself is uniquely positioned to collect data provided by its users, which is then commodified and sold to other profit-seeking businesses.[9]

The identification of the platform as a vehicle for capitalist accumulation, however, only begins the analysis, and here is where the adjectives come in. What kind of capitalism does the platform produce? A good place to begin this discussion is with Sundararajan's subtitle, *The End of Employment and the Rise of Crowd-Based Capitalism*. This juxtaposition might seem paradoxical at first glance, since capitalism has long been associated with the primacy of waged work as the mechanism through which capitalists extract surplus value from labour. But Sundararajan is not a Marxist, and neither sees his claim as paradoxical nor as requiring an explanation of what makes crowd-based capitalism capitalist. However, he does describe the elements of crowd-based capitalism as being market-based, providing greater opportunities to more fully deploy assets, and to source labour and capital from decentralized crowds. He also describes it as blurring the lines between the personal and professional by commercializing activities that used to be considered personal, and as blurring the lines between fully employed and casual labour, between independent and dependent employment, and between work and leisure.[10]

This combination of characteristics seems to describe a decentralized market economy in which the lifeworld is pervasively commodified and in which labour is seemingly provided on a spot market finely tuned to meet ever-shifting demand. What is missing, however, are several structural features of capitalism that differentiate it from a simple trading economy. First, there is no recognition that underlying capitalism is a particular structure of property and class relations in which the means of production are substantially owned by a small minority of the population while the majority are dependent on their labour in order to survive.[11] Second, there is no recognition that capitalism is driven by the relentless pursuit of profits and expansion. Economic value in capitalism is not generated by simple exchange but in the ability of capital to extract profits from socially produced wealth through relations of domination and exploitation. If crowd-based capitalism was a world in which the predominant social relation of production was between relatively equal, truly independent, property-owning commodity and service producers, it would not be capitalist because it would not have a capitalist property and class structure.[12]

We will return to a discussion of Uber later, but the evidence seems pretty clear that the predominant structure of the platform economy does not resemble a world of truly independent commodity/ service producers selling directly to consumers through platform-mediated transactions, but rather one in which workers are subordinated to platform enterprises bent on maximizing profits and expanding to become dominant players, if not monopolists, in their markets. For example, leaving open the question of whether Uber drivers are legally employees or not, what is clear is that they are not economically independent in any meaningful way, but rather exist in a subordinate relation with Uber, a privately held company with a valuation estimated to be over $60 billion. This is the underlying reality that motivates Uber drivers to act collectively to redress what they perceive to be their domination and exploitation in that relation.[13]

So even if Sundararajan does not satisfactorily explain how capitalism works in the platform economy, the question is centrally important, not just theoretically, but also practically. Platform capitalism fits within a larger political economic transformation that has seen the decline of the standard employment relationship central to the post–World War II era of welfare-state capitalism and the growth of precarious work, including own-account self-employment and temporary work, associated with the rise of neoliberal capitalist formations.[14]

This is not to deny that technological change plays a significant role in the evolution of capitalism. Marx was acutely attentive to the "constant revolutionizing of the instruments of production" that was endemic to capitalism, but he did not consider technology in isolation. Rather, he was concerned with the way that technology revolutionized "relations of production and with them the whole relations of society."[15] It was the first industrial revolution that was Marx's primary focus, and in *Capital* he famously described the process by which capitalist relations of production supplanted simple commodity production by freeing workers from ownership of the means of production, making them "free" to sell their labour as rights-bearing individuals to the equally rights-bearing owners of capital. He then followed these personae into the factory—the hidden abode of production—where the capitalist, having purchased the workers' capacity to work, extracted surplus value by his control over the labour process. Thus the wage relation came to be seen as the paradigmatic mode of labour exploitation in Marxist theory.

However, as Wallace Clement reminds us, pockets of commodity production continued in areas such as fishing and farming, so the process of proletarianization was never complete.[16] But even where simple commodity production continued, it was not hived off from the capitalist economy, but rather became linked to it in various ways that also produced economic domination and exploitation. For example, commodity producers retained possession and formal ownership of the means of production, but once market exchange ceased to be predominantly within integrated local economies, they increasingly became tied to and dependent upon capitalist firms to acquire necessary inputs (including financing) and to transport, store, and sell the outputs of commodity production. As a result, capital gained real economic control over commodity producers and with that the ability to extract surplus from their efforts. Indeed, as Jairus Banaji has demonstrated, historically, capitalism is compatible with a wide variety of modes of labour exploitation that may co-exist at any particular conjuncture.[17] Moreover, as we shall see in the case of Uber, the lines between proletarianization and other modes of labour exploitation, such as petty commodity production, are not always clear in social reality, which opens up space to argue about their legal characterization as well.

Clement also examined the question of the determinants of the mode of labour exploitation. When does capital proletarianize workers from whom it extracts surplus value directly or leave them as dependent commodity producers from whom it extracts surplus value indirectly through commercial transactions? Focusing on farming and fishing, he pointed to the ways capital benefited by retaining dependent commodity production, including a reduction in its exposure to risks of nature, elimination of the cost of investment in the first stages of production, and lower labour supervision costs.[18]

Clement's Marxist analysis can be connected with and supplemented by Coase's theory of the firm, which asks when firms will make (that is, manufacture with its own employees) rather than buy.[19] In a world of zero transaction costs there would be no firms and no employment, because there would be no benefit from managing (which always has a cost) compared to costless contracting. However, in the real world, where transaction costs are endemic at some level, firms will form and employees will be hired where the costs of making and managing are less than the cost of negotiating contracts. These decisions will be significantly affected by technology. For example, where technological developments allowed productivity to be enhanced through capital-intensive investments in machinery and a refined division of labour, individualized dependent commodity production was replaced by proletarianized social labour coordinated by capital in factory settings. For Marx, writing in the third quarter of the nineteenth century, the factory was the paradigmatic site of the hidden abode of production where the capitalist extracted surplus labour from the proletarianized worker. Dependent commodity production seemed to be destined for the dustbin of history. As a result, theorizing about the social relations of production in dependent commodity production was relatively uncommon.

However, the shift from buying to making was never complete and, as Rubery and Wilkinson demonstrate, there is no economic law dictating that the movement from dependent commodity production to factorization will always be in one direction. Looking specifically at outwork, they identified a number of factors that interact to shape the decision whether to produce in-house or outsource. These include the type of technology available, the potential for fragmenting the production process, the role of capital-intensive investment, the cost of labour supervision, and the avoidance of collective action and legal regulation, among others.[20]

David Weil has also approached this issue through his exploration of the phenomenon of fissuring, which involves once integrated lead businesses choosing not to make things themselves but to shift the production of goods and services outside the firm to smaller businesses through outsourcing, franchising, and supply chains. As a result, employment is also shifted outside lead firms and into smaller business, which in turn may seek to shift work out to so-called independent contractors or "micro-entrepreneurs." Technological change is a significant factor that makes fissuring both feasible and attractive. "Over the past three decades, it has become far less expensive to contract with other organizations—or create new organizational forms—to undertake activities that [...] alte[r] the calculus of what should be done inside or outside enterprise boundaries."[21] Again it is important to remember that it is not just technology that drives fissuring, but rather it is the drive for profit maximization that leads firms to adopt and adapt technology for that purpose.

To the extent that Marxist theory is centred on the paradigm of extracting surplus value through employment in the hidden abode of the factory, it now faces the challenge of analyzing the new relations of production and modes of labour exploitation that are becoming prominent features of twenty-first-century capitalist economies. Various theorists are beginning to take up this task. A collection of essays edited by van der Linden and Roth challenges the theoretical centrality of proletarianized wage work and calls for an examination of the "extraordinary multiplicity and multifacetedness of the constellations of exploitation" that coexist, including self-employment.[22] Steffen Böhm and Chris Land argue that there is a need to prize open, new, hidden abodes of production outside of employment to incorporate new sites of value production.[23] Finally, Ursula Huws, a pioneer in theorizing the implications of cybernetics for capitalist development, has explored the question of how enterprises generate profit in the digital age. She makes the useful distinction between labour that is performed directly for a capitalist employer by a worker who is dependent on her or his labour for subsistence (workers whom she dubs "inside the knot"—the classic proletariat) and groups that she characterizes as being less directly involved in capitalist social relations, including people engaged in petty commodity production, trade or small-scale rent, groups that she says have been given a new lease on life by the Internet. Being less directly involved, however, does not translate into being outside capitalist relations of production, and so Huws points to the need to specify and analyze these relations, including the process of generating profits by rent or trade rather than commodity production. For example, she suggests that online employment agencies and car-sharing services may be thought of as profiting from rent rather than commodity production, but such a claim requires close scrutiny of the actual relations between these platforms and the workers who use them. Her larger point, however, remains valid; we need to think about the ways capitalism operates "outside the knot."[24]

The identification of different modes of labour exploitation is the first step, but does not end the discussion, because one mode is not necessarily preferable to another. We must also take the next step and explore and assess the extent of domination and exploitation that exists within these relations. A number of factors are likely to be influential, including the extent to which laws effectively limit workers' market vulnerabilities or facilitate (or obstruct) their ability to act collectively to protect their interests. Then, within the spaces available for collective action, there is the question of the forms collective action takes (for example, unions or cooperatives) and their success. More generally, the broader political economic context sets the conditions within which laws are enacted and enforced, collective action occurs, and capital exercises power.

With this in mind, we turn to a historical exploration of taxicab capitalisms and the social relations of production that characterized them through a case study of Toronto. However, one final theoretical clarification is necessary. It may seem odd, perhaps, to speak of taxi capitalisms as if they were distinct forms of capitalism on the same order as, say, liberal market capitalism or welfare-state capitalism. That is not the intention. Rather, the discussion of taxi capitalisms recognizes that the taxi industry operates within a larger capitalist social formation, but also understands that different sectors of capitalist industry are organized according to the distinctive technologies, market structures, regulatory arrangements, and worker resistance they experience. The historical account that follows aims to elaborate on these distinctive features without losing sight of the larger capitalist environment in which they operate.

III. Taxi Capitalisms Before Uber

i. Taxi Capitalism 1.0: Standard Capitalism and the Standard Employment Relation

The history of the taxicab industry and the impact of technological change logically should begin with the horse-drawn trade of the nineteenth century and the impact of the automobile, but there is too little Canadian research for this to be feasible, so the chapter begins with the motorized taxi trade dating from the second decade of the twentieth century.[25] Initially, the cost of entry was high. Motor cars were a luxury item affordable by few, and municipal regulations required cabs to have special features which made them more expensive than standard cars. Since cruising the streets looking for fares was not an efficient way of doing business, taxis depended on cabstands and telephone dispatch systems. Cabstands in prime locations often operated as private concessions, for which hefty fees were charged, and telephone dispatch required the installation of call boxes around the city, where drivers could wait for assignments, also requiring a significant investment. Another cost was taximeters, favoured by some segments of the public and by some owners as a means to protect themselves against petty fraud by drivers.

As a result of the high cost of entry, the trade was initially dominated by larger fleet owners who hired drivers as employees in the classic, or what I will call "standard capitalist," mode of production.[26] Yet despite the hopes of early investors that high entry costs would produce an oligopolistic industry structure in which quasi-monopoly profits could be extracted, independent operators soon found ways into the industry, increasing competition and reducing profits. For example, even by 1910, thirty-six automobile dealerships and other companies in Winnipeg leased taxis to drivers who competed for business with the taxi fleets.[27] The involvement of these companies also marked an early attempt by rentiers to profit from the taxi industry by selling services to those directly involved in producing taxi services.

The nature of the work also did not favour direct management of a large labour force, as there was little scope for extracting more surplus value by a refined division of mass labour. As well, because cab drivers worked alone and were geographically dispersed across the city, employers had difficulty exercising a high level of managerial control and intensifying the labour process. Beyond phone systems, significant economies of scale were simply not available.

Finally, the existing regulatory regime also did not create barriers to entry. Older municipal regulations, dating back to the horse-drawn trade, required licences, but there was no limit on their number, and fees were not particularly high. Rules governed other matters such as fare structures and driver behaviour, but none of this strongly favoured large taxi fleets over small ones or independent operators.[28]

For all these reasons, taxi capitalism 1.0 failed to thrive, even without significant collective resistance by employee drivers.[29]

ii. Taxi Capitalism 2.0: Unregulated Petty Commodity/Service Production

Conditions for fleet owners worsened in the 1920s and 1930s as the cost of entering the business dropped. The growth of the mass-production auto industry and the increase in real wages during the 1920s made car ownership more affordable, and municipalities failed to enforce vehicle regulations, allowing less specialized cars to operate as taxis. Public taxi stands in some cities replaced or provided an alternative to private concessions, and taxi driver and cab owner licences remained readily available at low cost. In Toronto, for example, the number of taxi driver licences issued annually increased from 1,043 in 1921 to 2,009 in 1929, while the number of owner licences issued grew from 541 to 1,313 over the same period. By 1931, there was only one fleet with more than fifty licensed cabs, and fleets with ten or more cars accounted for only about a third of the trade. Small fleets with fewer than ten cars comprised about a quarter of the trade, while individual owner-operators made up the other 40 per cent.[30] Finally, in some cities taxi brokers entered the field, providing a bundle of services to taxi owners, including advertising, a garage, and telephone dispatching, further reducing the economies of scale that favoured larger fleets.[31] As a result, petty commodity/service production came to dominate the industry.[32]

iii. Taxi Capitalism 3.0: Regulated Petty Commodity Production

The triumph of petty production, however, did not bring prosperity to its participants. As one observer of the highly competitive cab business in London, England, commented at the turn of the century, "It is a poor man's industry."[33] This was the case in Canada too, particularly after the onset of the Great Depression in 1929, which not only reduced demand for taxi services but also triggered an increase in the number of operators as unemployed workers tried their hand at earning an income by driving a cab.[34] Cab fares dropped and operators and drivers struggled to make a living. In Toronto, an Advisory Committee on Taxicabs was struck in 1931 and in its 1932 report found that "the business is badly overcrowded" and the earnings of most drivers "meagre." Although there was some variation between different industry sectors, the report found that drivers typically worked about twelve hours a day, six days a week and earned about $17 a week, less than the wage of a general labourer. In Montreal in 1934, it was estimated that both drivers and owner-operators of a single cab took home about $13.50 a week.[35]

The advisory committee was also highly critical of the emerging role of rentier capital in the industry. As noted earlier, taxi brokerages were formed to sell taxi owners a bundle of services, including dispatch. They have not been the subject of much research, so there are still unanswered questions, but it seems that, initially, some brokerages were created as cooperatives by small fleet owners to take advantage of economies of scale. By the early 1930s, however, most brokerages were businesses in their own right, selling services to industry participants who did not have an ownership stake in the brokerage. The advisory committee was particularly critical of the role of these rentier brokerages, finding "that in a great many cases cab brokers have conducted their businesses in an irresponsible manner and largely at the expense of the cab owners whom they have induced to subscribe to their service." The committee recommended that brokers should be licensed and that licences should only be issued to persons who were licensed cab owners.[36]

Another avenue for rentier capitalists to profit from the taxi industry was through cab leasing, a phenomenon that first appeared a decade earlier but that expanded in the 1920s. The advisory committee explained how it operated. A private company would buy a number of inexpensive cars and would then lease a car to a driver for one year, with payments made daily. The driver purchased fuel from the leasing company and paid for repairs, which were done at the company's garage. The company might also provide telephone dispatch services. If the driver lived up to the terms of the contract, the driver would obtain title to the car at the end of the year. Taxi leasing became more attractive as the Depression deepened because it provided unemployed workers without capital an opportunity to get into the business, but the advisory committee found that they fared poorly. "As far as financial results are concerned, however, the real and only beneficiaries have been the companies disposing of automobiles." It proposed to eliminate the practice by requiring that owners or their employers operate all cabs. Rentier capitalism was not welcome in the industry or, at the very least, the limited opportunities to profit from selling services to operators were to be hoarded for industry insiders.[37]

Driver resistance to poor working conditions took a variety of forms. In a few instances, employed drivers tried to unionize, but Canadian labour law during this period did not compel employers to recognize and bargain with unions, so it was a tough slog.[38] As well, in a depressed industry where profits were hard to generate, there were severe limits on what drivers could gain through collective bargaining, although there were some successes. In 1936, 500 Montreal taxi drivers, joined by 873 licensed cab owners, struck to secure reduced brokerage fees. The city intervened and a committee was created to address the drivers' and owners' concerns.[39] In 1938, 720 members of the Toronto taxi drivers' local of the Teamsters struck against sixty-three taxi companies, demanding union recognition, a minimum weekly wage, overtime after ten hours, and other improvements. The strike was substantially successful, and its terms were extended to the entire industry under the *Industrial Standards Act*. The following year, the union struck again and made further gains.[40]

Drivers also worked with local labour councils to protect workers' interests when municipal taxi regulations were being considered.[41] However, it was not just taxi drivers who acted collectively; the chief players in municipal taxi regulation were associations of taxi owners, whose demands included restrictions on entry, rate regulation, mandatory meters, tougher vehicle standards, and a requirement that brokers be cab owners. The politics of regulation were complicated as different segments of the industry formed into different associations to represent their distinct interests.[42] There is no detailed account of how these politics unfolded in Toronto after the 1932 report but, like in most North American cities, taxi regulation restricted entry, regulated fares, and limited rentier capital's access to the industry.[43]

iv. Taxi Capitalism 4.0: Medallion Capitalism

The intent of the new taxi licensing bylaws was to create a regulated regime of owner-operator petty commodity/service production. The adoption of a quota on licences (commonly known as the medallion system) restricted entry, enabling licence holders to gain an economic rent that otherwise would have been dissipated by competition, and the restrictions on dispatchers aimed to keep these rents in the hands of those directly providing taxi services. Moreover, because taxi licences were widely dispersed among small firms and individual owner-operators, municipal regulators anticipated that the rents would be widely shared. Finally, price regulation protected customers against licence holders taking undue advantage of limits on competition. However, the regulations also permitted medallion owners to treat their licences as alienable private property that its owner could sell, lease, or devise,[44] and this paved the way for the creation of a different mode of taxicab capitalism, which I have dubbed "medallion capitalism."

We can begin the story of the development of medallion capitalism by examining the industry's evolving social relations of production. Under the medallion system, employment in the taxi industry initially increased as workers seeking to become taxi drivers could not easily obtain a licence and go into business for themselves. For many, the only option was to become an employee of a licence holder, who needed additional drivers to keep the car on the road as many hours as possible to maximize the revenue the licence produced. Since many drivers faced the prospect of remaining employees for several years until a medallion became available for purchase, they had a greater interest in engaging in collective action to improve their terms and conditions. More generally, there was a high level of labour militancy at the end of the war, as returning veterans and workers generally sought to share in the post-war prosperity and have a collective voice in workplace decision-making. The adoption of the Wagner Act model of collective bargaining in Canada at the end of the war facilitated this desire through an administrative regime of compulsory union recognition, coupled with a duty to bargain in good faith.

Although the labour legislation embraced a highly fragmented model of enterprise bargaining, taxi unions in Toronto not only managed to organize drivers but also to bargain on a broader basis. For example, in the late 1940s, Teamsters Local 488 bargained with the Federal Association of Taxi Cab Operators on behalf of 800 drivers employed by the association's forty members and with the Diamond Taxi Cab Association on behalf of 300 drivers employed by its members. As a result, taxi unions were successful in securing improved terms and conditions for drivers.

As the union pressed for contract improvements in the early 1950s, medallion owners took steps to end employment in the taxi industry. Instead of hiring drivers as employees, medallion owners adopted a leasing system in which drivers leased the car on either a long- or short-term basis, typically including dispatching services. Drivers who rented taxis either paid a percentage of the fares to the owner or, more commonly, paid a fixed fee and kept the fares, but were responsible for fuel. In part by push and perhaps in part by pull (the lure of being independent), the leasing system became so widespread that employment virtually disappeared and Local 488 collapsed.[45]

A second development that produced and shaped medallion capitalism was the departure of owner-operators, the intended beneficiaries of regulated petty commodity/service production, from the industry. Driving a cab is hard work, involving long hours, and so owner-operators often looked for exit strategies. As the value of licences went up, some owner-operators cashed out, sometimes selling their medallions to drivers who replaced them as owner-operators, but often selling medallions to small fleet owners looking to expand their operations. Each medallion that went to a fleet owner reduced the number of owner-operators, and the movement was largely in one direction. Another exit strategy for owner-operators was to retain ownership of the medallion as an income-generating asset. In this scenario, medallion operators stopped driving and became full-time rentiers by leasing it to other drivers or fleet owners. Often the owner hired an agent to manage the medallion on the owner's behalf. In fact, as we shall see, the use of agents became quite widespread. The overall result of this process was that not only did the great majority of medallion owners become rentiers but also a second layer of rentiers became interposed between the medallion owner and the driver.

A third change in the relations of production involved the growing role of taxi associations providing dispatch services. The development of radio displaced telephone dispatching and new economies of scale became available. Diamond Taxi was typical. It was formed after the war by ten small fleet owners who collectively operated 200 cars. By 1957, the number of medallions associated with the dispatch increased to 410. Diamond Taxi operated as a branded fleet with all of its associated taxis painted in the same colours and carrying rooftop signs, so that to the customer it would appear that Diamond Taxi was a single branded business. Diamond also developed corporate accounts, which provided a valuable and important source of fares at a time when credit card usage was not as widespread as it is today.[46]

If these associations (or brokerages, as they came to be known) remained cooperatives providing services to their members, they would have been a barrier against, rather than an entry for, rentier capitalism. However, they became incorporated for-profit businesses that provided dispatching and other services to medallion owners and lessees who did not have ownership shares in the brokerage. This created another layer of rentier capitalism, characterized by unequal power relations between the brokerages and the remaining owner-operators of single vehicles who contracted for their services.

The structure and operation of the industry in the early 1990s was described in detail in two Ontario Labour Relations Board (OLRB) decisions from that period.[47] There were about 3,500 cab licences in Toronto, half of which were held by an owner having one medallion. The other half were held by about 600 individuals or corporations that owned multiple licences. As well, there were 7,000 licensed drivers who were not medallion owners. However, as we noted, some medallion owners, including single owners, were not drivers but rather leased out their medallions to another individual who operated the vehicle or appointed an agent, typically a principal of a brokerage, to manage the medallion on their behalf.

The largest brokerage at the time was Diamond, which had 299 associates who collectively owned or leased 605 medallions. Of these, 248 associates owned or leased a single medallion, while the remaining fifty-one associates owned or leased 357 medallions. Only a small number of associates ran ten or more medallions with Diamond, the largest associate having thirty-nine.[48] Diamond was governed by a nine-member board of directors, almost all of whom were associates of the brokerage, and was managed by a president and vice-president. Although Diamond itself did not own any cabs, the president and vice-president acted as designated agents for owners of 173 medallions, giving them control of more than a quarter of the licensed vehicles operating under the Diamond banner. Other brokerages had different structures, but the OLRB noted there were often personal, commercial, or family connections between the larger associates who effectively controlled the brokerages. As a result, medallion capitalism created opportunities for both rentier capitalists and an increasing concentration of ownership and control of medallions.

Under these conditions, there were two principal groups from whom profits could be extracted: drivers who rented cars by the shift, and owner-operators who either owned or leased a single medallion—and both groups organized to resist what they perceived to be their exploitation. Initially, owner-operators and drivers were concerned with the disciplinary actions of the licensing authority, but by the 1960s they increasingly focused on their relationship with the brokerages and/or the multiple medallion owners. Access to protective employment law and collective bargaining, however, was impeded by their designation as self-employed, with little prospect of successfully challenging that status.[49]

Operating from an industrial pluralist perspective, in 1965 Professor Harry Arthurs recognized the unfairness of depriving economically vulnerable individuals access to industrial citizenship to redress unequal power relations, regardless of whether that vulnerability was created by the employment relationship or through commercial contracts. He proposed that the law should recognize a category of "dependent contractors" who would be given access to the collective bargaining regime and specifically identified "taxicab operators" as a group that fit this category.[50] Arthurs' article opened a conceptual crack in the door to employee status, but it took years of struggle by taxi drivers and owner-operators to get through it.[51]

Drivers unsuccessfully attempted to unionize on several occasions in the 1960s. In the early 1970s, the Canada Labour Congress chartered the Toronto Union of Taxi Employees as a direct local, and by 1972 it had 500 members. Efforts to claim coverage under the recently enacted *Employment Standards Act*[52] (ESA) failed when a court ruled that drivers were not employees, and talk of expanding the Act's coverage in the Ministry of Labour came to naught. However, in 1975 the Ontario government amended the *Labour Relations Act* (LRA) to include a dependent contractor provision, which gave employment status to a person who

> whether or not employed under a contract of employment, and whether or not furnishing his own tools, vehicles [...] performs work or services for another person for compensation [...] on such terms and conditions that he is in a position of economic dependence upon, and under an obligation to perform duties for, that person more closely resembling the relationship of an employee than that of an independent contractor.[53]

No similar provision was added to the ESA at the time or has been to this day.

The dependent contractor provision clearly did not make all people in unequal economic relations employees. For example, if taxi drivers entered into fuel supply contracts with companies in an oligopolistic supply industry, the law would not transform them into fuel supply company employees simply because of unequal power relations and economic dependency. Exploitive relations of production in purely rentier capitalism were outside the scope of the law. So if all brokerages did was sell taxi drivers dispatch and related services, they could successfully argue that this did not create a dependent contractor relationship for the purposes of the law, even if the taxi brokerages were able to extract value from the labour of the rental drivers and owner-operators.

However, the relationship between brokers and drivers went beyond merely selling dispatch and related services. Taxi brokerages were branded businesses selling a product to the public, and to build and maintain their goodwill they were driven to impose contractual obligations on members and drivers in order to provide a more-or-less standardized product and to ensure reasonably prompt service. As well, the brokerages needed to prevent drivers from gaming or cheating the dispatch. The first goal was achieved primarily by requiring that associates' vehicles have common colours and signs, and be kept clean. As well, drivers were subject to dress and behaviour codes, with disciplinary measures available if the rules were violated. The provision of prompt service and the prevention of gaming required the exercise of managerial controls related to the use of the dispatch service, such as prohibitions on booking into an area when not in it or while engaged in transporting a passenger or parcel, and prohibitions on rejecting or failing to respond promptly to a fare offered by the dispatch. These rules were enforced by a system of sanctions.[54]

These elements of control made it possible to argue that as a matter of law taxi drivers were dependent contractors of the dispatches, not merely the purchasers of dispatch services. This is not the place to delve into a detailed analysis of the complex legal test of who is an employee or dependent contractor,[55] but it will be helpful to look at the organizational and legal complexity that Toronto taxi unions faced when they attempted to organize the industry in the 1990s.

Although in the first case, the OLRB rejected a claim by owner-operators that they were dependent contractors employed by brokerages, organizing drives continued, reflecting workers' widespread dissatisfaction with how they were being incorporated into medallion capitalism. Eventually, one case was successful.[56] The fight to unionize in Toronto was an extended one. The Retail, Wholesale and Department Store Union (RWDSU) conducted an extensive organizing drive among drivers and individual owner-operators associated with nine different brokerages in the early 1990s, eventually filing simultaneous applications for certification, identifying the brokers as the employers. Votes were held and the ballot boxes were sealed pending a determination of whether the workers were dependent contractors under the LRA. After a careful examination of the operation of the brokerages, the OLRB found that drivers and owner-operators

> regularly and consistently derive a substantial portion of their income from a single entity which exercises detailed control over the performance of their work by means of an elaborate system of written or unwritten rules and disciplinary responses which effectively penalize anyone failing to meet its standards [...].

The board noted that although drivers could opt to work outside the dispatch system, "economic pressures substantially limit the exercise of those freedoms." It also recognized that while owner-operators were at liberty to change brokers, their freedom was no greater than the freedom of employees to change employers, a freedom that merely shifted their dependency from one broker to another, but did not alter the basic condition of dependency.[57]

Having been found to be dependent contractors and therefore employees under the LRA, the ballot boxes were opened, and in 1993 the union was certified as the bargaining agent for the drivers and owner-operators of three of Toronto's largest brokerages: Diamond, Co-op, and Metro. Negotiations took place in 1994 but were unsuccessful, and the workers went on strike in August. After three weeks of demonstrations and protest, leading to unfair labour practice claims and criminal charges, the parties agreed to have outstanding issues resolved by arbitration. Part of the problem in negotiations was that some of the issues that needed to be resolved related directly to the rental and shift fees that associates charged drivers, a matter not governed by the brokerages' rules. To address this problem, the union applied to have the members of the brokerage who owned or leased more than one medallion declared related employers to force them to the bargaining table.

The arbitration was held before the related employer application was heard, but to defend their interests, the association representing the small fleet owners associated with the brokerages sought to intervene. Although the arbitrator denied the fleet owners intervenor status, his award, issued in December 1994, identified them as parties to the agreement along with the union and the brokerages. However, the arbitrator refused to include a provision in the two-year agreement regarding the rental and licensing fees charged by the associates.

Hearings on the union's related employer application began in 1995. Ironically, although the associates previously sought to be represented in the arbitration proceedings, they now opposed the related employer application, presumably to avoid having their fees become subject to future collective negotiations. To determine whether the associates and the brokers were related employers, the OLRB had to consider whether they were carrying on associated activities under common control and direction. The board recognized that the fundamental goal of the related employer provision was to make collective bargaining viable in the face of organizational arrangements that fragmented the employer function, a situation that David Weil has since popularized as "fissuring."[58]

Based on an extensive analysis of the relationship between the brokerages and their associates, the board found a high degree of functional integration, such that the drivers were dependent contractors of both and that there was common control and direction. The brokerages exercised control over the associates through the associates' dependency on their services, as well as through the brokerages' control over the associates' drivers, while the associates were found to exercise a degree of influence over the brokers, particularly the larger fleet owners who were often involved in running the brokerage. In the result, board found the brokerages and their associates to be related employers, and arrangements were made for them to be represented in future bargaining.[59]

That future was short-lived. The parties managed to negotiate a second collective agreement but could not resolve the issue of rental and lease fees, a matter that was vital to the determination of compensation for drivers and owner-operators who leased but did not own a plate. As a result, by the end of the decade, the union collapsed, and collective bargaining and representation disappeared, a victim of the fragmented structure of the Toronto taxi industry and the unequal power relations it produced.

The failure of taxi drivers and owner-operators to achieve industrial citizenship meant these workers were unable to gain a reasonable share of the rents produced by medallion capitalism. Instead, these were being captured by the various rentiers.[60] A 1998 task force report found numerous problems in the taxi industry, including the fact that transferability allowed absentee ownership of medallions, which produced a layer of middlemen. Concerns were raised that the structure contributed to "deplorable working conditions," exacerbated by the redistribution of fare-box revenues to non-driving agents, lessees, and owners.[61]

In an effort to lessen the role of rentier capital in the Toronto taxi industry, two key changes were made to the bylaw in 1999 that aimed to get medallions back into the hand of drivers and recreate a regime of regulated petty commodity production. The first froze the number of medallions and placed limits on their transferability, while the second created a new "Ambassador" licence that could only be held by a full-time licensed driver who was prohibited from hiring another driver and/or transferring the licence in any way.[62]

A preliminary report prepared for an industry review in 2012 found that these changes were partially successful in achieving their goal. Ambassador licences did create a new group of owner-operators who had higher incomes than shift drivers, although many resented the restrictions on their ability to hire drivers or lease the vehicle.[63] Standard licences, however, were not getting back into the hands of drivers because owners found various ways to evade the transferability restrictions imposed in the bylaw. They had a strong incentive to do so as the market value of standard licences was skyrocketing from about $80,000 in 1998 to $210,000 in 2011. The final report, issued in 2014, found that two-thirds of the nearly 3,500 standard taxi licences were managed by agents and that the top twenty-seven agents managed 1,113 medallions.[64] Despite the reforms, rentier capital retained a large place in the industry.

To complete the transformation from medallion capitalism to regulated petty commodity production, Toronto would have to move more aggressively to decommodify standard taxi licences and get them into the hands of drivers, [65] and to retain restrictions on supply. Here is where Uber comes into the story.

v. Taxi Capitalism 5.0: Platform Capitalism Uber Style
Uber is commonly referred to as a ride-sharing company and as such part of the sharing economy, but Uber drivers no more share their cars with passengers than traditional taxi drivers do; they both sell a transportation service. Of course human interactions inevitably occur in these jointly occupied spaces and pleasant ones enhance the quality of the experience for the customer and add exchange value for the seller. In fact, many workers, including taxi and Uber drivers, may be required to perform affective labour as part of their jobs,

whether for their own protection or to satisfy employer demands, obtain high ratings from customers or earn tips, where tipping is permitted.[66] The transactional context of these "sharing" interactions makes it impossible to know whether one is experiencing authentic sociality or merely witnessing a good performance, and perhaps as consumers we don't really care.

A somewhat more accurate way to describe Uber is that it is a transportation network company that provides intellectual property (a computer platform) to connect passengers with drivers who are paid by the passenger to transport them from one location to another. However, from a consumer perspective, Uber is functionally no different than a taxi dispatch service. If I want a taxi, I telephone a dispatch (say, Diamond Taxi), which uses its technology to locate a driver in its network who is sent to pick me up and drive me to where I want to go, for which I pay a fare to the driver. If I want an Uber, I use my Uber app, which is a technology that locates a driver in Uber's network who is sent to pick me up and drive me to where I want to go, for which I pay a fare through my app. I may prefer Uber to taxi dispatch services because the app is cool and easier to use than making a phone call and paying the driver myself, or because Ubers arrive more promptly or are less expensive, but the service is nonetheless functionally equivalent to a taxi dispatch. They even use the same technology to transport the passenger—a car.

We will return briefly to the question of the legal characterization of Uber, but first we want to look underneath the hood, so to speak, at its social relations of production. At one level Uber might be characterized as a rentier capitalist selling a dispatch service to individual commodity producers, arguably much as like traditional taxi dispatch services claim. On that reading, drivers with cars are just micro-entrepreneurs using their own labour and means of production to sell transportation services to the public. The Uber app is merely a software platform that enables Uber drivers to reach that public, just as telephone and radio dispatch services enabled traditional taxi drivers to connect with customers. Like radio dispatchers, Uber owns no cars and has no drivers on its payroll. The technology is different, but the functional relation between Uber and its drivers and radio dispatchers and their drivers is nearly identical.

To stop there, however, would be to miss what happens beneath the surface. Uber does more than simply sell dispatch services to drivers. Just like taxi dispatches, it is also a brand and, therefore, is driven to impose additional obligations on its drivers to protect the brand by ensuring that certain service standards are met and that its network operates efficiently. Of course there are differences between brands. Taxi dispatches enhance their brands' visibility by requiring cars to be painted in its colours and to have rooftop signs, while Uber prefers to operate with a look more akin to a black car service, without identifying signs, but there is nothing fundamentally important about this difference.

To achieve its goals of maintaining standards and efficiency, Uber exercises considerable control over its drivers. Although Uber drivers are not required to book onto the service, once they do, they are governed by Uber's rules. For example, when a fare is offered to a driver, the driver has a very limited time to accept. If the driver does not respond in time, the fare is offered to another driver. Drivers who decline too many trips may be forcibly logged off the app for a period of time. The driver and the vehicle must meet quality standards set by Uber and are subject to customer reviews after each trip, with poor reviews potentially resulting in deactivation.[67] These controls sound remarkably similar to those imposed by traditional dispatches, which complicates Uber's claim that functionally it is merely a rentier capitalist selling digitialized dispatch services to drivers. Moreover, it is precisely these kinds of functional controls that make both traditional dispatches and Uber vulnerable to being legally classified the employer of the drivers in its network. Indeed, there is a rash of claims being brought by Uber drivers seeking employee status, whether for the purposes of collective representation or to gain the protection of minimum employment standards, as well as growing legal academic commentary on whether Uber employees are or should be considered employees.[68]

The argument that from a consumer and a driver point of view Uber is functionally a dispatch that operates much along the same lines as traditional taxi dispatches, however, does not lead to the conclusion that it is a medallion capitalist. To the contrary, Uber has disrupted medallion capitalism in a very important way: it operates without medallion capital and therefore threatens to destroy medallion capitalism.[69] Uber recruits drivers who may not be licensed as taxi drivers and, more importantly, who do not own or lease a taxi licence. As a result, it bypasses municipal taxi regulation and, if it is successful, taxi licences will cease to have either a use or an exchange value or, at the very least, that value will be substantially

diminished.[70] In short, Uber's major innovation is less a technological than a legal one.

The avoidance of taxi regulation has important consequences
for relations of production in the Uber model. In medallion capitalism, relations of production are complex and multilayered.
Dispatches sell services to medallion owners who in turn rent
licensed vehicles to drivers directly or through agents. Uber provides dispatch services directly to owner-operators, thus cutting
out medallion owners and their agents. There are no intermediary
rentiers between Uber and the driver.

Whether Uber's bold evasion of existing taxi regulations succeeds will depend on the regulators' response. In North America, this
will be a municipal decision. Toronto's new bylaw, which came into
effect on July 15, 2016, legalized and lightly regulated Uber's business model, while modifying standard taxi regulation by formally
terminating its attempt to (re)create an owner-operator model. Limits
on the number of taxi licences remain, but Ambassador licences were
rolled over into standard licences and limits on the accumulation of
licences by a single owner were ended.[71] It remains to be seen how
these changes will impact the future of medallion capitalism, but
even if Uber's success comes at its expense, it will not be the end
of taxi capitalism. Rather, we will have a new model of capitalism:
platform-facilitated petty commodity production by subordinated
workers. On one level, there will be thousands of so-called micro-
entrepreneurs selling taxi services through the Uber platform, but
on another Uber drivers will be engaged in a dependent relationship
characterized by unequal power relations that enable Uber to extract
profit from their labour and petty capital.

This dependency and inequality is not only a general characteristic of capitalist relations of production, but takes a specific form
in *platform* capitalism. Platforms are likely to be oligopolistic in their
structure. This is because, to be successful, Uber or other platforms
must develop both sides of the market in the sense that they need to
assemble large pools of sellers (drivers) and buyers (riders). Network
effects play an important role here. The more numerous the users, the
more valuable the platform becomes for both the users and the platform owner. According to Srnicek, "this generates a cycle whereby
more users beget more users, which leads to platforms having a
natural tendency towards monopolisation."[72] As a result, being there
first has a significant advantage, especially when the dominant player

is also heavily capitalized and can lock in its initial advantage by subsidizing rides when necessary to keep competitors at bay. Indeed, many observers argue that Uber's ambition, and the condition for its long-term success, is to establish itself as an unregulated monopoly provider.[73] A related feature of platform-facilitated petty commodity production is that unlike earlier versions, which pitted drivers against local petty capitalists, here drivers face a heavily capitalized global corporation that has the wherewithal to withstand short-term losses as well as unmatched resources to lobby government.

Uber's market power gives it the upper hand with its drivers, the petty service providers. As a price maker, Uber sets the fare structure and then takes a commission. It therefore exercises considerable control over what drivers can realistically earn. Since its launch, Uber has cut fares, increased its commission from 20 per cent to 25 per cent and tacked on a $1 safety fee. Uber drivers are using their own cars and bear the cost of gas, maintenance, insurance, and car depreciation. Although comparisons are not straightforward, one analyst estimates that Uber drivers make no more than taxi drivers. Not surprisingly, researchers find that Uber drivers consistently complain about low income.[74] Indeed, Uber drivers in numerous jurisdictions have alleged they are making less than the minimum wage. As well, Uber's claim that its drivers enjoy freedom and flexibility has been contradicted by the experience of its drivers.

> [T]he combination of blind passenger acceptance with low minimum fares and the algorithmic determination of surge pricing [...] reveal, respectively, how little control Uber drivers have over critical aspects of their work and how much control Uber has over the labor of its users (drivers).[75]

Finally, Uber's platform technology gives it a level of surveillance and managerial control that was impossibly costly for traditional taxi brokerages.

It is not surprising that Uber drivers have resisted what they perceive to be their exploitation in the same ways that other workers have historically. Indeed, because the relation between drivers and Uber is more direct and unmediated by other layers of rentier capital than is the case in medallion capitalism, the obstacles to securing labour and employment rights may be somewhat reduced. Uber drivers have sought to be declared employees entitled to the protection of employment standards and eligible for unemployment insurance, workers' compensation, and other benefits for which employers must make contributions. Many of these claims are still being litigated, but there have been some successes, including a decision in England, in 2016, by an employment tribunal that was scathing in its rejection of Uber's arguments.

> Any organization [...] resorting in its documentation to fictions, twisted language and even brand new terminology, merits, we think, a degree of scepticism.
>
> [I]t seems to us that the Respondents' general case and the written terms on which they rely do not correspond with the practical reality. The notion that Uber in London is a mosaic of 30,000 small businesses linked by a common 'platform' is to our minds faintly ridiculous.[76]

In New York, Uber drivers have been ruled eligible for unemployment payments and workers' compensation coverage.[77] There is also a major class-action lawsuit claiming that Uber has misclassified thousands of drivers in California and Massachusetts, depriving them of minimum wages and hours of work protections.[78]

Workers are also seeking to form unions in some locations. In New York, the Amalgamated Transit Union collected close to 14,000 signed union cards from Uber and Lyft drivers, but in order to avoid the issue of employee status under the *National Labor Relations Act*, union officials applied to the Taxi and Limousine Commission to hold an election.[79] The organizing drive occurred after Uber attempted to head off unionization by entering into an agreement with the Independent Drivers Guild, an organization affiliated with the International Association of Machinists, to represent its drivers in appeals of de-activations and in meetings with Uber, but without any authority to negotiate terms and conditions of employment or to strike.[80]

It is too early to tell whether Uber drivers in platform-enabled petty commodity production will gain the protection of labour and employment law and whether, if they do, Uber will find ways to re-transform taxi capitalism to enable it to operate without having the obligations of an employer. The important point for our purposes is that to talk sensibly about the future of platform capitalism in the taxi industry we must not only recognize that it is capitalist, but also understand the relations of production behind the app and the conflicts they generate.

IV. Conclusion

Platform capitalism Uber-style is not the end of taxi capitalism history. Changes in technology are part of the story, but so too is law and resistance. Indeed it is fair to say that the development of taxi capitalism is driven by their interactions. Medallion capitalism was made possible by law, but the law was a response to the actions of drivers and owner-operators unable to make a living in a regime of unregulated petty commodity production. The development and spread of a new technology, radio dispatching, provided an opportunity for rentier capitalism to gain a foothold in the industry, but medallion capitalism was also shaped by the conflict between drivers and dispatches and small fleet owners over how the value produced under medallion capitalism would be divided. In order to avoid collective bargaining and keep more of the value for themselves, dispatches and fleet owners ended employment and turned drivers into contractors. When labour law eventually changed to address this reality, drivers renewed their efforts to unionize as dependent contractors, but were ultimately defeated by the fissured relations in the industry.

Uber has introduced a new technology and created an unmediated relation between itself and its drivers, whom it too treats as self-employed micro-entrepreneurs. Yet here too law and resistance play an important role in shaping taxi capitalism Uber-style. Uber's boldest innovation is its legal claim that it is not subject to existing taxi regulation. Taxi regulation is being remade city by city, largely with the aim of creating a level playing field for both branches of the industry. At the same time, Uber is facing resistance from its drivers who seek to retain more of the value they produce through collective bargaining and employment law. It remains to be seen whether they will succeed and, if they do, how Uber will respond. It is already investing heavily in the development of driverless cars, which would lead to a new model of capitalism or, perhaps, post-capitalism.[81]

My argument is not that medallion capitalism is preferable to platform capitalism Uber-style. Under either form of taxi capitalism, the drivers who perform the work experience domination and exploitation. So, while technological change may open up possibilities for transformation, as long as the technology is deployed for the purposes of maximizing profits for the benefit of its owners, its emancipatory potential is unlikely to be realized. Capitalism is not a platform on which a sharing economy can be built.

Notes

1.   Professor, Osgoode Hall Law School, York University, and Distinguished Visiting Researcher, Cleveland-Marshall College of Law, Cleveland State University. Thanks to Alec Stromdahl and Tyler Fram for their research assistance and to Harry Ghadban and James Hayes for sharing their knowledge of the taxi industry and the challenges encountered in organizing. The chapter has benefited from the comments and questions of participants at presentations at Cleveland-Marshall College of Law, Cleveland, RMIT, Melbourne, the Australian Labour Law Association, Sydney, the Canadian Association of Work and Labour Studies, Toronto, and especially from Harry Glasbeek, Shelley Marshall, and Ron McCallum.

2.   Arun Sundararajan, *The Sharing Economy: The End of Employment and the Rise of Crowd-Based Capitalism* (Cambridge, MA: MIT Press, 2016) at 176. For a schematic overview of the conventional, neoliberal perspective, see Frank Pasquale, "Two Narratives of Platform Capitalism" (2016) 35:1 Yale L & Pol'y Rev 309.

3 .   Juliet Schor, "Debating the Sharing Economy" (October 2014) online: Great Transition Initiative <http://www.greattransition.org/images/ GTI_publications/Schor_Debating_the_Sharing_Economy.pdf> ("[b]ut technologies are only as good as the political and social context in which they are employed. Software, crowdsourcing, and the information commons give us powerful tools for building social solidarity, democracy, and sustainability. Now our task is to build a movement to harness that power" at 12).

4.   Sundararajan, *supra* note 2.

5.   Steven Hill, *Raw Deal: How the "Uber Economy" and Runaway Capitalism Are Screwing American Workers* (New York: St. Martin's Press, 2015). See also Tom Slee, *What's Yours Is Mine: Against the Sharing Economy* (New York: OR Books, 2015), especially ch 4, 5; Trebor Scholz, *Uberworked and Underpaid: How American Workers Are Disrupting the Digital Economy* (Cambridge, UK: Polity, 2017).

6.   Nick Srnicek, *Platform Capitalism* (Cambridge, UK: Polity, 2017).

7.   Peter A Hall & David Soskice, *Varieties of Capitalism: The Institutional Foundations of Comparative Advantage* (Oxford: Oxford University Press, 2001). For a critique, see Wolfgang Streeck, *Re-forming Capitalism:*

Institutional Change in the German Political Economy (Oxford: Oxford University Press, 2009), especially ch 12.

8.   Sundararajan, *supra* note 2 at 27. Indeed, the growth of the platform economy may be tilting the balance away from de-commodified altruistic or communal interactions. See Orly Lobel, "The Law of the Platform" (2016) 101:1 Minn L Rev 87 at 109.

9.   For a more detailed and nuanced account, see Srnicek, *supra* note 6 ch 2.

10. Sundararajan, *supra* note 2 at 27.

11. Erik Olin Wright, *Understanding Class* (London, UK: Verso, 2015).

12. Nick Dyer-Witheford, *Cyber-Proletariat: Global Labour in the Digital Vortex* (London, UK: Pluto, 2015) ("[s]ince the discovery of the microchip, promoters of the information revolution have argued that it dissolves class" at 9).

13. See e.g. Hill, *supra* note 5 ch 3; Slee, *supra* note 5 ch 4.

14. For a useful overview of and explanation for the rise and decline of the standard employment relation, see Judy Fudge, "The Future of the Standard Employment Relationship: Labour Law, New Institutional Economics and Old Power Resource Theory" (2017) 59:3 J Indus Rel 374. On precarious employment, see Gerry Rodgers & Janine Rodgers, eds, *Precarious Jobs in Labour Market Regulation: The Growth of Atypical Employment in Western Europe* (Geneva: International Institute for Labour Studies, 1989), online: <http://staging.ilo.org/public/libdoc/ilo/1989/89B09_333_engl.pdf>; Leah Vosko, ed, *Precarious Employment: Understanding Labour Market Insecurity in Canada* (Montreal: McGill-Queen's University Press, 2006); Katherine Stone & Harry Arthurs, *Rethinking Workplace Regulation: Beyond the Standard Contract of Employment* (New York: Russell Sage Foundation, 2013). On neoliberal capitalism, see David Harvey, *A Brief History of Neo-Liberalism* (New York: Oxford University Press, 2005).

15. Karl Marx & Friedrich Engels, *The Communist Manifesto* (Oxford: Oxford University Press, 2008).

16. Wallace Clement, *Class, Power and Property* (Toronto: Methuen, 1983), especially ch 9, 10. See also Wallace Clement, *The Struggle to Organize: Resistance in Canada's Fishery* (Toronto: McClelland and Stewart, 1986), especially ch 5.

17. Jairus Banaji, *Theory as History: Essays on Modes of Production and Exploitation* (Chicago: Haymarket Books, 2011). Also, see Genevieve LeBaron, "Unfree Labour Beyond Binaries: Insecurity, Social Hierarchy and Labour Market Restructuring" (2015) 17:1 Intl Fem J Pol 1.

18. Clement, *Class, Power and Property, supra* note 16 at 233.

19. Ronald Coase, "The Nature of the Firm" (1937) 4:16 *Economica* 386. See also: Alfred D Chandler, Jr., *The Visible Hand: The Managerial Revolution in American Business* (Cambridge, MA: Harvard University Press, 1977);

Bruce E Kaufman, "The Impossibility of a Perfectly Competitive Labour Market" (2007) 31:5 Cambridge J Econ 775.

20. Jill Rubery & Frank Wilkinson, "Outwork and Segmented Labour Markets" in Frank Wilkinson, ed, *The Dynamics of Labour Market Segmentation* (London, UK: Academic Press, 1981) 115 at 120—24. In a recent article, Matt Finkin usefully deployed this framework to explore the broad contours of the use of the "putting-out system" and its social relations of production. See Matthew W Finkin, "Beclouded Work, Beclouded Workers in Historical Perspective" (2016) 37:3 Comp Lab L & Pol'y J 603.

21. David Weil, *The Fissured Workplace: Why Work Became So Bad for So Many and What Can Be Done to Improve It* (Cambridge, MA: Harvard University Press, 2014) at 44.

22. Marcel van der Linden & Karl Heinz Roth, "Results and Prospects" in Marcel van der Linden & Karl Heinz Roth, eds, *Beyond Marx: Theorising the Global Labour Relations of the Twenty-First Century* (Chicago: Haymarket Books, 2014) 445 at 479. In that volume, see Sergio Bologna, "Workerism: An Inside View. From the Mass-Worker to Self-Employed Labour" 121 at 121.

23. Steffen Böhm & Chris Land, "The New 'Hidden Abode': Reflections on Value and Labour in the New Economy" (2012) 60:2 Sociol Rev 217.

24. Ursula Huws, *Labor in the Digital Economy: The Cybertariat Comes of Age* (New York: Monthly Review Press, 2014) at 162-63.

25. The only detailed Canadian study is Norman Beattie, "The Cab Trade in Winnipeg, 1871–1910" (1998) 27:1 Urban Hist Rev 36. For a brief discussion of the early cab trade in Toronto, see Kimberly M Berry, "The Independent Servant: A Socio-Cultural Examination of the Post-War Toronto Taxi Driver" (PhD Thesis, University of Ottawa Department of History, 2006) [unpublished] at 33–43. Drivers' unions seem to have been fairly common in major cities. See Eugene Forsey, *Trade Unions in Canada 1812–1902* (Toronto: University of Toronto Press, 1982).

26. Beattie, *supra* note 25 at 48; Donald F Davis, "The Canadian Taxi Wars, 1925–1950" (1998) 27:1 Urban Hist Rev 7 [Davis, "Taxi Wars"] at 7–8.

27. Beattie, *supra* note 25 at 48.

28. Beattie, *supra* note 25 at 39–42; Berry, *supra* note 25 at 37–41.

29. Canada Department of Labour, *The Labour Gazette* (Ottawa: Queen's Printer, 1900–1978) [LG] contains sporadic references to taxi driver unionization during this period, mostly from Montreal. For example, see *LG* (December 1922) at 1261 (application of Montreal taxi drivers for conciliation under the *Industrial Disputes Investigation Act* (IDIA)); (August 1923) at 870 (strike by seventy-seven taxi drivers over dismissal of an employee); and (June 1924) at 470 (another IDIA application from Montreal drivers).

30. *Report of the Advisory Committee on Taxi Cabs to the Board of Commissioners of Police of the City of Toronto* (12 April 1931), Toronto, City of Toronto Archives (Box No 225064, Item 2348) [*Advisory Committee on Taxi Cabs*] at 84–6.

31. In fact, many of the taxi brokerages, including the most powerful, the Diamond Taxicab Association, were initially created in Montreal by a decision of seven independents to share a switchboard. See Davis, "Taxi Wars," *supra* note 26 at 10.

32. *Ibid* at 8–11.

33. Vance Thompson, "The London Cabby" (1904) Outing 156, cited in Beattie, *supra* note 25 at 37.

34. Davis, "Taxi Wars," *supra* note 26, observes: "[d]riving a cab always has been a haven for the unemployed" at 11.

35. *Advisory Committee on Taxi Cabs, supra* note 30 at 55; Davis, "Taxi Wars," *supra* note 26 at 12–3; Berry, *supra* note 25 at 46–51.

36. *Advisory Committee on Taxi Cabs, supra* note 30 at 28–9; Berry, *supra* note 25 at 56–8; Donald F Davis, "Continuity and Discontinuity in Canadian Cab History" (1998) 27:1 Urban Hist Rev 3 at 4.

37. *Advisory Committee on Taxi Cabs, supra* note 30 at 31–2.

38. Judy Fudge & Eric Tucker, *Labour Before the Law: The Regulation of Workers' Collective Action in Canada, 1900–1948* (Toronto: Oxford University Press, 2001).

39. *LG* (September 1936) at 777–78.

40. *LG* (May 1938) at 486–88; (September 1938) at 1047; (August 1939) at 859–60. Berry, *supra* note 25 at 71–6.

41. There were also some efforts directed at obtaining protective provincial legislation. For example, in 1931 the Ontario Executive Committee of the Trades and Labour Congress lobbied for an eight-hour day for drivers of trucks, buses, and taxicabs. See *LG* (February 1931) at 188.

42. *Advisory Committee on Taxi Cabs, supra* note 30, contains all these demands and reproduces the submissions it received from seven different industry associations.

43. For a detailed discussion of the development of taxi regulation in Winnipeg during this period, see Davis, "Taxi Wars," *supra* note 26 at 14–7.

44. The scope of license transferability changed over time. A 2014 review of Toronto taxi regulation found that as of 1956, transfers were only permitted on the death of the license holder and then only to a family member. These restrictions were removed in 1963. See City of Toronto, *Toronto's Taxicab Industry Review, Final Report* (Toronto: January, 2014) [City of Toronto, *Final Report*] at 14–5. For an earlier discussion of the need to regulate transfers, see *Advisory Committee on Taxi Cabs, supra* note 30 at 30–2.

45. Berry, *supra* note 25 at 129–135.

46. *Ibid* at 84–7.

47. *RWDSU v Diamond Taxicab Assn. (Toronto) Ltd.*, [1992] OLRB Rep 1143 [*RWDSU v Diamond*]; *USWA, Local 1688 v Diamond Taxicab Assn. (Toronto) Ltd.*, [1995] OLRB Rep 753 [*USWA v Diamond*].

48. Some medallion owners were associates of more than one brokerage; they associated some of their medallions with one brokerage and some with another brokerage.

49. Berry, *supra* note 25 at 135–37. On the development of employment standards, see Mark Thomas, *Regulating Flexibility: The Political Economy of Employment Standards* (Montreal: McGill-Queen's University Press, 2009).

50. Harry Arthurs, "The Dependent Contractor: A Study of the Legal Problems of Countervailing Power" (1965) 16 UTLJ 89 at 89.

51. See Harry Arthurs, "The False Promise of the Sharing Economy," this volume, for Professor Arthurs' discussion of the "category problem" in the context of the sharing economy.

52. SO 1968, c 35.

53. SO 1975, c 76, s 1(1).

54. For a full description, see the two Diamond Taxi OLRB judgments at *supra* note 47.

55. See e.g. Judy Fudge, Eric Tucker & Leah Vosko, "Employee or Independent Contractor? Charting the Legal Significance of the Distinction in Canada" (2003) 10:2 CLELJ 193. More recent reviews of the issue in both domestic and international law include, Miriam A Cherry & Antonio Aloisi, "'Dependent Contractors' in the Gig Economy: A Comparative Approach" (2017) 66:3 Am U L Rev 635; Breen Creighton & Shae McCrystal, "Who is a 'Worker' in International Law?" (2016) 37:3 Comp Lab L & Pol'y J 691.

56. *Ontario Taxi Association v Seven-Eleven Taxi Ltd.*, [1976] OLRB Rep 134; Berry, *supra* note 25 at 138–56.

57. *RWDSU v Diamond*, *supra* note 47 at paras 56–7.

58. *Ibid* at paras 62–3; Weil, *supra* note 21.

59. *USWA v Diamond*, *supra* note 47 at paras 75–127.

60. There is a conventional economic analysis of the medallion system that focuses on its distorting effects and cost to consumers. See e.g. Benoit-Mario Papillon, "The Taxi Industry and Its Regulation in Canada" (1982) Economic Council of Canada Working Paper No 30; D Wayne Taylor, "The Economic Effects of the Direct Regulation of the Taxicab Industry in Metropolitan Toronto" (1989) 25:2 Logist Transp Rev 169.

61. City of Toronto, Toronto Task Force to Review the Taxi Industry, Report to Review the Toronto Taxi Industry (Toronto: October 1998), 15.

62. For a discussion and critique of the program, see Mariana Valverde, *Everyday Law on the Street: City Governance in an Age of Diversity* (Chicago: University of Chicago Press, 2012) at 168–174.

63. Indeed, because the newer drivers who held ambassador licences were predominantly from racialized groups, an unsuccessful human rights complaint was launched alleging that the program unlawfully discriminated: *Addai v Toronto (City)*, 2012 HRTO 2252.

64. City of Toronto, *Taxicab Industry Review, Preliminary Report* (Toronto: September 2012), at 37–42; City of Toronto, *Final Report, supra* note 44 at 12–5, 22–7, 38–9.

65. For unsuccessful efforts in this regard, see David Bush, "UberXploited: Behind the Toronto Taxi Wars," *RankandFile.ca* (11 December 2015), online: <http://rankandfile.ca/2015/12/11/uberxploited-behind-the-toronto-taxi-wars/>.

66. See Arlie Russell Hochschild, *The Managed Heart: Commercialization of Human Feeling* (Berkeley, CA: University of California Press, 1983); Marcia Facey, "'Maintaining Talk' Among Taxi Drivers: Accomplishing Health-Protective Behaviour in Precarious Workplaces" (2010) 16:6 Health and Place 1259.

67. For a detailed description of an Uber contract, see Joellen Riley, "Regulating Work in the 'Gig Economy'" (April 2017) Sydney Law School Working Paper No 17/30, online: <http://ssrn.com/abstract=2949631>.

68. The litigation is ongoing. In England, Uber drivers were recently found by an employment tribunal to be workers (not employees) employed by Uber for the purposes of the *Employment Rights Act* and the *Minimum Wage Act*. See *Aslam v Uber BV* (2016), [2017] IRLR 4 [*Aslam*]. The limits of this decision are discussed in Rabih Jamil, "Drivers Vs Uber—The Limits of Judicialization: Critical Review of London's Employment Tribunal Verdict in the Case of Aaslam Y. & Farrar J., Against Uber" (2017) 58 Papers in Political Economy, online: <https://interventionseconomiques. revues.org/3449>. For a recent review of claims, see Brishen Rogers, "Employment Rights in the Platform Economy: Getting Back to Basics" (2016) 10:2 Harv L & Pol'y Rev 479. See also Jeremias Prassl & Martin Risak, "Uber, Taskrabbit, & Co: Platforms as employers? Rethinking the Legal Analysis of Crowdwork" (2016) 37:3 Comp Lab & Pol'y J 619; Guy Davidov, "The Status of Uber Drivers: A Purposive Approach" (2017) 6:1–2 Spanish Lab L & Employment R J 6.

69. Conventional economic analysts celebrate this because of their critique of restrictions on entry. See David Seymour, *The End of Taxi Regulation: Why GPS-Enabled Smart Phones Will Send Traditional Regulation the Way of the Dodo* (May 2011), online: Frontier Centre for Public Policy <https:// fcpp.org/files/1/PS105_TaxiReg_MY02F3.pdf>.

70. The value of Toronto taxi licences has dropped from a high of $360,000 in 2012 to less than $100,000. See Patrick Cain, "Toronto Taxi Licenses are Plummeting. Is Uber to Blame?," *Global News* (22 January 2015), online: <http://globalnews.ca/news/1780260/toronto-taxi-licence-prices-are-plummeting-is-uber-to-blame/>.

71. City of Toronto, "Vehicle-for-Hire," online: Toronto.ca <http://www1.toronto.ca/wps/portal/contentonly?vgnextoid=b7d78b38956c5510VgnVCM10000071d60f89RCRD>.

72. Srnicek, *supra* note 6 at 45.

73. Simon Harding, Milind Kandlikar & Sumeet Gulati, "Taxi Apps, Regulation, and the Market for Taxi Journeys" (2016) 88:C Transp Res Part A 15; Justin Fox, "Uber is Still Trying to Figure Out if It's a Real Business," *Bloomberg View* (29 August 2016), online: <https://www.bloomberg.com/view/articles/2016-08-29/uber-is-still-trying-to-figure-out-if-it-s-a-real-business>; Yves Smith, "Can Uber Ever Deliver? Part Four: Understanding that Unregulated Monopoly Was Always Uber's Central Objective" (5 December 2016), *naked capitalism* (blog), online: <http://www.nakedcapitalism.com/2016/12/can-uber-ever-deliver-part-four-understanding-that-unregulated-monopoly-was-always-ubers-central-objective.html#_ednref10>.

74. Slee, *supra* note 5 at 63–7; Hill, *supra* note 5 at 84–90.

75. Alex Rosenblat & Luke Stark, "Algorithmic Labor and Information Asymmetries: A Case Study of Uber's Drivers" (2016) 10 Intl J Comm 3758 at 3762.

76. *Aslam, supra* note 68 at paras 87, 90. On the potential implications of the decision, see Gregor Gall, "Is Uber Ruling the Beginning of the End for Bogus Self-Employment?," *The Conversation* (4 November 2016), online: <https://theconversation.com/is-uber-ruling-the-beginning-of-the-end-for-bogus-self-employment-68010>.

77. Noam Scheiber, "Uber Drivers Ruled Eligible for Jobless Payments in New York State," *The New York Times* (12 October 2016), online: <https://www.nytimes.com/2016/10/13/business/state-rules-2-former-uber-drivers-eligible-for-jobless-payments.html>; Deborah Berkowitz & Rebecca Smith, *On-Demand Workers Should be Covered by Workers' Compensation* (21 June 2016), online: National Employment Law Project <http://nelp.org/content/uploads/Policy-Brief-On-Demand-Covered-Workers-Compensation.pdf>.

78. US Circuit Court of Appeals for the Ninth Circuit, *O'Connor v Uber Technologies Inc.*, online: <https://www.ca9.uscourts.gov/content/view.php?pk_id=0000000823>.

79. Matthew Flamm, "Union Seeks to Organize Rideshare Drivers in NYC," *Crain's [New York Business]* (26 September 2016), online: <http://www.crainsnewyork.com/article/20160926/TRANSPORTATION/160929902/>

amalgamated-transit-union-local-1181-seeks-to-organize-uber-drivers-in-nyc>.

80. Noam Scheiber & Mike Isaac, "Uber Recognizes New York Drivers' Group, Short of a Union," *The New York Times* (10 May 2016), online: <https://www.nytimes.com/2016/05/11/technology/uber-agrees-to-union-deal-in-new-york.html>; Josh Eidelson, "Uber Found an Unlikely Friend in Organized Labor," *Bloomberg Businessweek* (27 October 2016), online: <https://www.bloomberg.com/news/articles/2016-10-27/uber-found-an-unlikely-friend-in-organized-labor>. For a discussion of the Guild that locates it in an analysis of non-traditional forms of worker representation that enhance labour-management cooperation, see Jeffrey Hirsch & Joseph A. Seiner, "A Modern Union for the Modern Economy," Fordham L Rev [forthcoming in 2018], at 25–9.

81. Paul Mason, *Postcapitalism: A Guide to Our Future* (London: Allen Lane, 2015).

CHAPTER XII

Making Sense of the Public Discourse on Airbnb and Labour: What about Labour Rights?

Sabrina Tremblay-Huet[1]

I. Introduction

Popular sharing economy platforms, such as Airbnb, have been a frequent focus of public attention in recent years. Much of this attention has been driven by the numerous regulation challenges facing these platforms, either present ones through ongoing litigation, or prospective ones, through legislation drafting by governments. The media addresses evident legal issues, such as the fact that short-term rental laws are circumvented, as in the case of Quebec,[2] or the new regulations to curb illegal actions.[3] These issues speak the loudest, as they are immediate or imminent. What is lost, or what might be lost, in terms of the labour rights of workers, doesn't appear as urgent an issue. Opinion pieces, among others, have touched on this issue, alerting the reader to unsuspected problems appearing through the cracks of the bright portrait painted by the platforms. It doesn't appear, however, that labour rights are a central part of the public discourse on the sharing economy. What can be gained (for hosts, drivers, consumers, and others), rather than what can be lost, seems to receive much more attention. "Public discourse" is understood for the purposes of this chapter as being mainly constituted of media accounts on Airbnb, including news reports, opinion columns, and analytic journalism. It is understood as the information and analyses presented to the general population about Airbnb, rather than aimed at a specific audience such as academia.

The Airbnb platform will be used as a case study, along with its corollary, the traditional hotel industry, to explore the attention given to labour rights concerns in the context of a neoliberal era. This chapter is concerned with the question: Why aren't labour rights of hotel workers and of Airbnb host an important part of the Airbnb conversation? Furthermore, why aren't the labour rights of these two groups of workers addressed concomitantly, as a dependency relation can be traced between them? To contextualize the topic, the labour rights of workers in the tourist accommodation sector in Canada are presented. The acquired labour rights of hotel workers of Quebec are used as an example. The labour rights issues facing the hotel industry in Canada are also addressed, in order to consider a more holistic framing of their labour situation. The restricted labour rights and the extended duties of self-employed workers are then described, using once more the example of Quebec, considering that Airbnb hosts are usually acting under self-employment laws, in the context of this province's current worker statuses, and when declaring their hosting activities as an income source for income tax purposes. This characterization of self-employment is used as an example of the ways in which a worker loses labour rights protections afforded to workers under an employee status, acknowledging that not all Airbnb hosts can be, or are, characterized as such.

Next, this chapter is concerned with discerning how the discourse about Airbnb is framed regarding labour. This contribution draws on the public discourse, using only publicly available sources in Canada and the United States. I identify two groups of themes emerging from this discourse—freedom and monetization, and empowerment and accountability for oneself. I also argue that there is a missing connection: that of Airbnb and the labour rights (and eventually, right to labour) of workers in the hotel industry.

How do we make sense of this public discourse, from a perspective critical of the minimal presence of labour rights? I propose that this can be accomplished through a theoretical framing from Michel Foucault's *The Birth of Biopolitics: Lectures at the Collège de France, 1978–79*[4] and Wendy Brown's *Undoing the Demos—Neoliberalism's Stealth Revolution*[5] on neoliberal rationality. Their main arguments are presented, followed by a conceptualization of labour within a neoliberal governing rationality. The themes that emerged from the public discourse on Airbnb and labour are then revisited, using the theoretical framework offered by Foucault's and Brown's contributions. Deconstructing dominant themes to discern implicit assumptions allows for an uncovering of the preponderant logic at work. Organizing thoughts within the framework of a theoretical approach allows for a more concerted voicing of concerns and avenues for further reflection. Such concerns and avenues are offered as concluding thoughts.

II. The Context of Labour Rights in the Tourist Accommodation Sector in Canada

i. Hotel Industry in Canada: Acquired Rights and Current Labour Rights Issues

This section addresses the labour rights of workers in the hotel industry who are considered employees, using the context of Quebec law as an example. An employee, according to the *Act Respecting Labour Standards*,

> means a person who works for an employer and who is entitled to a wage; this word also includes a worker who is a party to a contract, under which he or she
> i. undertakes to perform specified work for a person within the scope and in accordance with the methods and means determined by that person;
> ii. undertakes to furnish, for the carrying out of the contract, the material, equipment, raw materials or merchandise chosen by that person and to use them in the manner indicated by him or her; and
> iii. keeps, as remuneration, the amount remaining to him or her from the sum he has received in conformity with the contract, after deducting the expenses entailed in the performance of that contract.[6]

The *Act Respecting Labour Standards* applies to employees.[7] The Act's Chapter IV, "Labour Standards," provides numerous labour rights. They concern wages,[8] hours of work,[9] statutory general holidays and non-working days with pay,[10] annual leave with pay,[11] rest periods,[12] absences owing to sickness, an organ or tissue donation for transplant, an accident or a criminal offence,[13] family or parental leave and absences,[14] psychological harassment,[15] termination of employment or layoff,[16] and collective dismissal,[17] retirement,[18] and other miscellaneous provisions. Numerous hotel employees are unionized, providing additional labour protections to the ones provided by the *Act Respecting Labour Standards*, such standards being of public order.[19] The Quebec hotel industry has even been termed a "model of solidarity" by a left-wing publication.[20]

Obviously, even within the context of being under the protection of the *Act Respecting Labour Standards* or another provincial labour act, there are many labour rights issues facing hotel industry workers. For example, the president of the board of directors of the Quebec Hotel Association (*Association hôtellerie Québec*) recently co-signed an opinion piece in *La Presse* opposing a minimum wage of $15 per hour.[21] Recently as well, unionized workers from the *Pur Hotel*, in Quebec City, were locked out by their employer, which according to a union leader "came out of nowhere," as negotiations were going well.[22] The employees responded with a vote overwhelmingly in favour of an unlimited general strike.[23] A few months before, eleven hotels in Montreal and Quebec City declared a one-day strike, mainly on grounds related to wages as well as vacation and severance pay.[24] Furthermore, as Chris Schenk demonstrates in the context of the hotel industry, "even unionized, full-time employees, successful in securing contractual gains in wages, benefits, and working conditions, are vulnerable to precarious employment, partly because of their occupational context and income level, and especially in the face of unpredictable events."[25]

The hotel industry in Canada also employs a significant number of temporary foreign workers. In March 2016, the Hotel Association of Canada (HAC) applauded "The Honourable MaryAnne Mihychuk, Minister of Employment, Workforce Development and Labour for recognizing the seasonal nature of the lodging industry and authorizing tourism businesses temporary foreign workers for up to a six month period."[26] The HAC has spoken about the industry's need for temporary foreign workers in the recent past, as it "is facing a nation-wide labour shortage crisis."[27] In the hotel industry, "back jobs," accomplished by workers who do not normally interact directly with guests, are largely held by immigrant women.[28] Temporary foreign workers, nonetheless, are protected under the relevant provincial labour and employment laws.[29]

The Canadian Temporary Foreign Worker Program (TFWP) has, of course, received its fair share of criticisms, a prominent critique being the fact that "precarious employment, unfree labour relations and precarious legal status are actively produced by employers and the state and negotiated by workers not as distinct 'categories,' but as interrelated conditions of labour market participation."[30] The spectrum of exploitation sometimes even leads to cases of human trafficking.[31] Under the program, workers are tied to a unique employer, and it does not automatically lead to permanent resident status or to citizenship.[32] In June 2016, Minister Mihychuk announced that she is "temporarily freezing at current levels the cap on the proportion of an employer's workforce that can consist of low-wage temporary foreign workers," citing the fact that the "program needs to change."[33]

ii. Airbnb in Canada: Self-Employed Status and the Example of Quebec

Airbnb hosts are not employees of Airbnb; hosts earn money directly from their clients (guests) and decide when they are to work and when their space is available. (These decisions, of course, are to be considered in the context of the pressures within the Airbnb market.) They determine the terms of this host-guest relation, as concerns house rules, for example. Under the Quebec *Act Respecting Labour Standards*, Airbnb hosts cannot be considered employees, as they do not work for a person. They are, in the context of this profit-making activity, self-employed workers, or "independent" workers. Therefore, the *Act Respecting Labour Standards* does not apply to them, and they thus do not benefit from its standards. Additionally, self-employed workers in Quebec must bear numerous costs for which employees are exempted, such as for statutory holidays they wish to take as a vacation,[34] for many public social welfare programs, including the Quebec Pension Plan[35] and the provincial occupational safety and health coverage,[36] as well as for other health-related insurances, such as dental care.[37] Already in 2006, before the rise of the "sharing economy," it was noted that "[t]he contemporary Canadian labour force is characterized by an expansion of self-employment."[38]

Perhaps this is not an evident problem at the moment when one thinks of Airbnb. If hosts do not operate an Airbnb business full-time, or if they own numerous properties and are thus financially secure, the issue doesn't appear relevant. However, Airbnb is profiting enormously from these hosts, as the mediating platform between them and their guests. Furthermore, Airbnb's continuous expansion could suggest that more hosts will be assuming this function full time. Also, interestingly, the *San Francisco Chronicle* published a study it undertook that shows that "Airbnb had 4,798 properties listed in the city. Almost two-thirds—2,984—were entire houses or apartments."[39] An article published in *Money* magazine pointed out that this finding "pok[es] holes in airbnb's [sic] 'folksy' argument that the vast majority of its hosts are simply small-time 'home sharers' who earn a few dollars here and there by occasionally renting out a spare room."[40] This is an even more serious cause for concern, in terms of the preservation of acquired labour rights, considering that Airbnb is expanding its services to "Trips," a service allowing tourists to book tours or similar activities with locals that would not be available otherwise.[41] Eventually, Airbnb will collect 20 per cent of the costs of such services,[42] while not offering hosts the labour protections offered by an employee status.

III. How Is the Public Discourse on Airbnb and Labour Framed in Canada and the United States?

This chapter is concerned with the potential loss of previously acquired labour rights for Airbnb hosts. As this labour force increases, are labour rights a serious part of the conversation on Airbnb? How is this labour characterized? Even if one of the premises of this chapter is that labour, indeed, isn't usually a central part of the public discourse on Airbnb, it sometimes is. And this type of labour deserves a more significant place within this conversation, considering the significance of such work occurring outside of the traditional employee/employer relation for which labour law affords important labour rights to workers. This is the case when labour issues themselves constitute a news event. For example, advanced negotiations between Airbnb and the United States–based Service Employees International Union have recently taken place, but have failed.[43] If this agreement had been adopted, Airbnb would have encouraged hosts to hire unionized workers and pay them $15 per hour or more.[44] Airbnb also reportedly approached another important union in the industry, Unite Here, which rejected the possibility of such an agreement.[45] This garnered media attention in popular outlets, such as *The Guardian*,[46] as well as in other, alternative ones.[47]

In any case, the arguments in this chapter imply that Airbnb hosts are indeed engaged in labour.[48] This is mentioned because it can elude us, when hosting is presented as a side occupation, or when it is presented using testimonials from hosts, stating: "Airbnb has brought the world to me. We sit around on my patio, and [guests] describe their lives,"[49] and when ads for the company state that it "strengthens our communities."[50] Arguably, for platforms such as Uber (for which work is accomplished in a public space), the recognition of labour as an eessential part of participating in the sharing economy hasn't been an issue. This use of public space is consistent with one ofthe most important contributions of feminist theory concerning the pubic/private divide and the devaluation of interest in the private sphere, ehere labour, paid and unpaid, is accomplished. [51] As Naomi Schoenbaum remarks,

> [t]he rise of the sharing economy then challenges the traditional sociological division between the "first place'" which is the home, the °second place," which is the workplace, and the "third place," which are communal spaces generally open to the public that may or may not be part of the market.[52]

Even though she acknowledges that this is not "entirely new or unique to the sharing economy,"[53] the magnitude of this emerging sector "presents challenges for legal regulation and the goals of sex equality."[54]

Hosting through Airbnb is not the same as hosting relatives or other people in your personal networks, nor is it like sharing your couch or a room in your home to strangers free of charge through platforms such as Couchsurfing.[55] Hosts are service providers and guests are clients. A portrayal of two Airbnb hosts in a *New York Times* article illustrates this point, when one is quoted as saying that "[h]osting on Airbnb wasn't a choice. It was decided for me," while the other woman portrayed is also "a host out of necessity," due to financial constraints related to the job market.[56]

How is the public discourse on Airbnb and labour framed, using the examples of Canada and the United States? I identify two pairs of themes that stand out in the public discourse on Airbnb and references made to labour within it. The positive themes of freedom and empowerment are often coupled with, for the former, monetization, and for the latter, accountability for oneself. Their associated themes can be portrayed as positive as well; but also negatively in the framework of a critique of neoliberalism. Each pair of themes will be revisited in the following section, through a deconstruction using the neoliberal governing rationality critique from Foucault and Brown. I end this section with thoughts on how there seems to be a missing connection between the labour of the hotel industry workers and Airbnb hosts, even though they constitute two major groups of workers in the accommodation industry.

i. Freedom and Monetization

Freedom is a value that is used by many to characterize Airbnb, presenting engagement with Airbnb as freedom from a desk job, financial freedom, freedom to dispose of one's property, freedom from state regulation, or even freedom of speech. "I like my freedom," says a woman whose income is provided solely by the labour she accomplishes in the framework of numerous sharing economy platforms, portrayed by a *New York Times* article.[57] A *Forbes* article quoted a study revealing that persons "who take advantage of 'free agent' contractual gigs, 'choose this workstyle for the freedom, flexibility, and entrepreneurial empowerment they experience with this independent approach to work and life.'"[58] Airbnb is presented as a way to live a dream life characterized by freedom, described in websites, guides, and books with titles such as *Portable Bed & Breakfast: Empower Your Freedom Lifestyle With Airbnb*.[59]

The promise of financial freedom is also the topic of numerous publications, such as *Overnight Success: Achieve Financial Freedom Through Airbnb*.[60] Freedom is furthermore associated with disposing freely of property. This was the case, for example, when the governor of Arizona signed a bill to prevent localities from banning platforms such as Airbnb, which was presented as being "about property owners regaining some small measure of freedom."[61] Freedom is understood as freedom from illegitimate state regulation, as this headline from *ABC News* in New Orleans makes clear: "City Begins to Consider More Freedom for Short-Term Rentals."[62] In Montreal, new regulations have been portrayed as "discouraging entrepreneurship" and "imposing obstacles on people's initiatives and who benefit from the new technologies"[63] [author's translation].

Even freedom of speech is becoming a significant element of the public discourse on Airbnb, as legal challenges on such grounds are emerging in places such as Anaheim (California),[64] New York City,[65] and San Francisco.[66] An article in the *Los Angeles Times* explains the logic behind such allegations, stating that

> [t]he lawsuit says the regulation violates constitutional rights to free speech and equal protection under the law as well as the 1996 Communications Decency Act, which prohibits states and local jurisdictions from holding Internet platforms liable for content created by users of the websites.
> The lawsuit also says that the ordinance "will have an impermissible chilling effect on speech" because Airbnb won't know which listings are lawful and which are not and therefore will have to stop publishing all listings from Anaheim.[67]

Freedom from having a boss, from imposed schedules, and the like also means, however, that a subsistence revenue must come from other sources than employment. This usually means being responsible for optimally monetizing one's own labour, in the form of production or services. "Monetization" is another term frequently used to describe the opportunity offered by Airbnb. Indeed, it is used on the Airbnb website itself as a sort of slogan: "[a]nd with world-class customer service and a growing community of users, Airbnb is the easiest way for people to monetize their extra space and showcase it to an audience of millions."[68]

Here as well, websites, guides, and books abound, with titles such as *Practical Guide on How to Turn Your House Into a Money Making Machine: Achieve Financial Security Today.*[69] Monetizing hobbies and homes is celebrated. "[T]he most successful businesspeople simply devise a means to monetize what they enjoy doing most," says an article about Airbnb co-founder Nate Blecharczyk.[70] "[Airbnb is] a great way for people to monetize their most valuable asset, which tends to be their home," the company's country manager for Canada is quoted as saying in a *Globe and Mail* article.[71] A *Bloomberg* article is ironically titled "The Sharing Economy: Monetize Your Life."[72] A *New York Times* opinion piece about Airbnb claims "dead capital" is a "problem," the term meaning "potentially productive assets owned by ordinary people who could use them if they could only find a way."[73]

What is freedom without monetization, after all, in a capitalist society?

ii. Empowerment and Accountability for Oneself
Another strong association made with Airbnb is entrepreneurship, and with that, empowerment. Here too, books abound, with titles

like *The Airbnb Entrepreneur: How to Earn Big Profits, Even if You Don't Own a Property*[74] and *The Airbnb Expert's Playbook: Secrets to Making Six-Figures as a Rentalpreneur.*[75]

Airbnb itself uses the term "empower" frequently. Headlines such as "Airbnb Unveils Expansive Suite of Personalized Tools to Empower Hosts"[76] or "New Airbnb Partnership Empowers Rural Indian Women"[77] grace the company's website. On last year's International Women's Day, Airbnb published a blog post titled "Celebrating and Empowering Women Around the World."[78] It stated that

> [w]omen are some of the most avid and adventurous travellers, and the warmest and most hospitable hosts and guides. Today, 55 percent of our hosts are women, and the income they earn helps with everything from sending their kids to school, to living independent lifestyles, to letting them pursue their passions.[79]

I will leave the gender analysis of essentialism to another time and place.[80]

"People generally know what's best for them, or at least they know better than government regulators. The peer-to-peer economy helps them get what they want, faster, cheaper and more efficiently," claims an opinion piece in the *Chicago Tribune*.[81] Independence is a key component of the promotion of the "sharing" economy consumers. We would (should) thus be seeking to empower ourselves independently in the face of undue state regulation.

Empowerment, especially when accomplished through entrepreneurial endeavours, can also have as a corollary accountability for oneself, which is not present to the same degree in the context of being employed. In the case of Airbnb, *Fortune Magazine* coined the following headline to express the company's business strategy: "Making a business out of not being responsible."[82]

The host is the one assuming the risks, not Airbnb. A contributing editor to *The Nation* magazine comments with irony about the public message on the sharing economy:

> [The sharing economy] sees us all as micro-entrepreneurs fending for ourselves in a hostile world. [...] Can't afford a place to live while attending grad school? Take a two-bedroom

apartment and rent one room out. You may lack health insurance, sick days and a pension plan, but you're in control.[83]

The Airbnb host is accountable for his or herself in the case of any changing life circumstances or fork in the road that he or she may encounter, such as pregnancy or disability.

Moreover, Airbnb is not necessarily about making money to afford additional luxuries. For example, in the case of Vancouver, Airbnb released a report stating that "more than half of the people who rent out their homes do so to afford their cost of living."[84] Airbnb's "Fast Facts" webpage informs us that "52% [of hosts] are moderate to low income" and that "48% of host income is used to pay for regular household expenses like rent and groceries."[85] While these statistics are presented as a promotion of the help Airbnb is offering society, this perspective implicitly accepts the fact that a vast number of people cannot afford to subsist while taking part in the traditional employed labour force. Indeed, many people are enticed into Airbnb hosting because of mortgage debt they cannot afford to pay.[86] A recent start-up, Loftium, even offers to pay for the down payment to buy a house, in exchange for one to three years of renting a room on Airbnb, save for eight days at the discretion of the new homeowners, and sharing the profits with the company.[87] Perhaps we are to question the structure creating such precariousness, rather than patching the holes with another form of precarious work. I argue that this structure is underpinned by the logic of neoliberalism, which will be deconstructed in section IV.

iii. The Missing Connection: Airbnb and Labour Rights (and Right to Labour) in the Hotel Industry

The precarious labour situation of many workers in both categories is prevalent. Indeed, this might not be so evident in the context of Airbnb hosts, whom we might think of as people who own property and are thus in a comfortable financial situation; however, the high percentage of persons who use this income for basic needs, as presented above, tells us otherwise. The labour rights issues of hotel industry workers presented above also paint a picture of, although not generalized, potentially prevalent labour precariousness. The situation can be even more complex when it is considered that Airbnb hosts might also be workers in the hotel industry at the same time, or that Airbnb hosts might contract with management companies to complete hosting-related tasks such as communication with guests or cleaning.[88] In the latter case, hotel-room attendants might then also provide cleaning services for an Airbnb host, for example.

It appears, though, that the connection is rarely made between the labour situations of hotel industry workers and Airbnb hosts. Of course, their situations are not comparable. But the rise of Airbnb could come to mean that the "low-skilled" hotel industry workers experience a right-to-labour situation, especially in the cases where they do not themselves have extra space to rent on Airbnb.

IV. Making Sense of the Discourse: Foucault's Neoliberalism and Brown's Economization of the Individual

Wendy Brown, a professor of political science at UC Berkeley,[89] delivered a sharp critique of neoliberalism and its threat to democracy in *Undoing the Demos—Neoliberalism's Stealth Revolution*. Its relevancy for making sense of the discourse on Airbnb and labour emanates both from the fact that Airbnb is coined as participating in the "democratization of services,"[90] and from the fact that the themes highlighted above, frequently used in the public discourse on the platform, can also be considered as pillars of neoliberalism. Her critique is based on Foucault's conceptualization of neoliberalism in *The Birth of Biopolitics: Lectures at the Collège de France, 1978–79*. Accordingly, Foucault's contribution will be briefly reviewed before Brown's work is presented in more detail, and applied to the themes of Airbnb and labour, identified above as a frame of reference for making sense of the public discourse on the topic.

i. The Main Arguments on Neoliberal Rationality from Michel Foucault's *The Birth of Biopolitics* and Wendy Brown's *Undoing the Demos*

Foucault delivered lectures at the Collège de France in Paris from 1971–84, and transcripts of his talks are collected in *The Birth of Biopolitics*. He speaks at length of neoliberalism, distinguishing between the German form and the American form,[91] a distinction that will not be maintained for the purposes of this chapter. For Foucault, neoliberalism is not a revitalization of forms of liberalism from the eighteenth and nineteenth centuries; rather, it is concerned with "whether a market economy can in fact serve as the principle, form, and model for a state which, because of its defects, is mistrusted by everyone on both the right and the left, for one reason or another."[92] In opposition with liberalism, "[t]he problem of neo-liberalism is rather how the overall exercise of political power can be modeled on the principles of a market economy."[93] Furthermore, Foucault identifies "a shift from exchange to competition in the principle of the market," from liberalism to neoliberalism.[94] Rather than constituting an equal relationship, free exchange is typically associated with inequality.[95] Competition is neither evident nor natural; it operates under a formal structure,[96] and as such, "[n]eoliberalism should not therefore be identified with laissez-faire, but rather with permanent vigilance, activity, and intervention."[97]

Foucault also addresses what he considers to be the neoliberal conception of unemployment:

> [w]hat is to be saved, first of all and above all, is the stability of prices [rather than full employment]. Price stability will in fact allow, subsequently no doubt, both the maintenance of purchasing power and the existence of a higher level of employment than in an unemployment crisis [...]. As, I think it was Röpke said, what is an unemployed person? [...] He is a worker in transit between an unprofitable activity and a more profitable activity.[98]

Foucault observes an "essential epistemological transformation" within neoliberal analyses, which he explains in the context of labour:

> [t]he problem of bringing labor back into the field of economic analysis is not one of asking about the price of labor, or what it produces technically, or what is the value added by labor. The fundamental, essential problem [...] is how the person who works uses the means available to him.[99]

What a neoliberal society wants of humans "is not the man of exchange or man the consumer; he is the man of enterprise and production."[100] This being the case, "there is a privileged connection between a society oriented towards the form of the enterprise [...] and a society in which the most important public service is the judicial institution," as more disputes necessitating legal arbitration are likely to emerge.[101]

Brown builds on Foucault's neoliberal governing rationality, in *Undoing the Demos*, to argue that neoliberalism not only dominates the economic sphere, but also all other social spheres. Therefore, neoliberalism is formulated somewhat differently and focuses on different deleterious effects. In contrast with an understanding of neoliberalism as a set of state policies, a phase of capitalism, or an ideology that set loose the market to restore profitability for a capitalist class, I join Michel Foucault and others in conceiving neoliberalism as an order of normative reason that, when it becomes ascendant, takes shape as a governing rationality extending a specific formulation of economic values, practices, and metrics to every dimension of human life.[102]

In this governing rationality, humans are *"homo oeconomicus."*[103] Brown brings this concept further than Foucault. Foucault conceived of it as meaning that humans are "driven by interest," while Brown argues that "this subject is so profoundly integrated into and hence subordinated to the supervening goal of macro-economic growth that its own well-being is easily sacrificed to these larger purposes."[104] As such, "market values are crowding out all others."[105]

An extended logic of neoliberal governing rationality comes to mean that "[r]eversing the liberal formulation in which a free market is defined and supervised by the state, [...] the state should be defined and supervised by the market."[106] Or, in the words of Foucault: "[o]ne must govern for the market, rather than because of the market."[107] Airbnb imposed on the state the regulation of its activities, as they were novel and disruptive. Heated public debates arose concerning the shape that such regulations should take, but at the end of the day, a significant proportion of them do not prohibit Airbnb from existing; they frame how it can exist, as it is considered an inevitable market force.

"Contemporary neoliberalism is unthinkable without governance,"[108] Brown states. Airbnb's constant negotiations with governments to secure regulations that allow it to maintain its activities in different cities resonate with Brown's description of governance, and with how we can conceive of Airbnb's societal power:

> [g]overnance replaces hierarchical, top-down mandates and enforcement with horizontal networks of invested stakeholders pursuing a common end. And governance replaces "command and control" with negotiation and persuasion. Effective governors create incentives for desired outcomes and negotiate over goals, even those that public action is to serve.[109]

The role of law in a neoliberal governing rationality is again taken further than Foucault by Brown, as "law becomes a medium for disseminating neoliberal rationality beyond the economy, including to constitutive elements of democratic life."[110]

Coming back to the fact that Airbnb is often presented as a form of democratization, it is interesting to take note of Brown's words in *Undoing the Demos'* epilogue: "[a]bove all, no doubt, neoliberal rationality has been extremely effective in identifying capitalism with democracy."[111]

ii. Labour in a Neoliberal Governing Rationality

Brown paints a dark picture for the future of labour within a neoliberal governing rationality:

> When everything is capital, labour disappears as a category, as does its collective form, class, taking with it the analytical basis for alienation, exploitation, and association among laborers.[112]

> [Therefore,] [a]s capitals, every subject is rendered as entrepreneurial, no matter how small, impoverished, or without resources, and every aspect of human existence is produced as an entrepreneurial one.[113]

This can be understood as the basis of a logic of turning hobbies into jobs; this is not to propose that one cannot and should not enjoy his or her work, but rather to state that there might be an underlying pressure to monetize time spent on hobbies as to not waste this time, or a constant lure to monetize them rather than be satisfied with enjoying them. The same can be true about Airbnb; guest rooms should not be considered as exclusively for welcoming a relative or friend, but rather as possible avenues for monetization of our private space. It almost appears as if one should ask themselves: why not turn this private space into a monetization avenue? If one's home is conceptualized as capital waiting to be monetized, then indeed a shift is operated between seeing labour as being accomplished outside of one's private resting space, to extracting value from capital at every turn in a normalized manner.

In this entrepreneurial, competition-driven environment, how do labour rights fit in? Harry Arthurs observes the following:

[b]y widening the gulf and shifting the numerical balance between workers still protected by labour law and those who are not, it [the rise of non-standard employment] may also have contributed to a new political dynamic in which have-not workers acquiesce in or support efforts to strip the haves of their advantages.[114]

As concerns Airbnb hosts, are we questioning who has access to extra space to monetize in the first place, or are we only concerned with sustaining a "healthy" competition between the Airbnb market and the traditional hotel market? Are we questioning the labour rights of Airbnb hosts, or are we only concerned with eschewing regulations that restrict their possibilities of accomplishing their hosting?

iii. Questioning the Themes Emerging from the Public Discourse on Airbnb and Labour

The four themes that I have identified as emerging from the public discourse on Airbnb and labour can all be presented as positive. On the other hand, freedom and empowerment are also sometimes deconstructed as illusions, and monetization and accountability for oneself are sometimes criticized for their negative societal effects. Here, I revisit the four themes using as a theoretical framework Brown's critic of neoliberalism, and necessarily in this context, that of Foucault as the underlying basis. The objective is to make sense of a public discourse that does not seem to take labour rights issues into serious consideration. In associating the themes with neoliberalism, and in positing neoliberalism as our current governing rationality, I seek to frame the underlying logic of the discourse and its coherency, to offer a more solid interpretation of why the public concentrates on certain issues and not others. The analyses emanating from the deconstruction of the four discourse themes seek to explore how we have cast, in a normalized manner, Airbnb labour as outside of the sphere of "traditional labour," the sphere within which labour rights have been acquired, under this neoliberal governing rationality.

1. Freedom and Monetization Revisited

In a neoliberal governing rationality, Brown proposes that freedom becomes associated with freedom of markets; one is free within the constraints of market rationality. Therefore, inequality characterizes this freedom, rather than equality being protected through the rule of law.[115] As stated above, neoliberalism is not about state non-intervention; it is about state intervention to optimize markets. As such, this "order [is] replete with contradiction and disavowal, structuring markets it claims to liberate from structure, intensely governing subjects it claims to free from government, strengthening and retasking states it claims to abjure."[116]

The language of freedom, borrowed from liberalism, is still in high use by neoliberal tenants ("free markets, free counties, free men"[117]), but this would be the "central ruse" of this governing rationality. Indeed,

> [s]ubjects, liberated for the pursuit of their own enhancement of human capital, emancipated from all concerns with and regulation by the social, the political, the common, or the collective, are inserted into the norms and imperatives of market conduct and integrated into the purposes of the firm, industry, region, nation, or postnational constellation to which their survival is tethered.[118]

Brown's words tie well with the aforementioned article on Nate Blecharczyk titled "Airbnb Co-Founder: Make Money Off Your Hobbies," when she states that "human capital is constrained to self-invest in ways that contribute to its appreciation or at least prevent its depreciation; [...] [this includes organizing its] leisure practices in value-enhancing ways,"[119] blurring the lines between personal hobbies and jobs, between the private and the work space.

In the context of free speech, Brown also addresses this through the eyes of a neoliberal governing rationality, which "supplants democratic political deliberation and voices with a formulation of speech as capital and free speech as an unhindered capital right."[120] Airbnb is seeking relief from strict regulations of the activities of its hosts on such a basis through its legal challenges related to freedom of speech provisions. It is seeking to be freed from constraints on its profits; many hosts support these actions in order to be free to monetize their space under the auspices of Airbnb, which is market- rather than state-driven.

Are Airbnb hosts truly finding freedom, from a schedule, from financial constraints, from regulation? After all, hosts are dependent on a guest wishing to secure a booking at a precise moment. Hosts are dependent on their pleasantness as hosts and the attractiveness of their space in competitive terms in order to monetize it to the point of freedom from financial worries, considering the additional financial burden of self-employment. Hosts are dependent on Airbnb as a platform, which makes some of the most impactful rules, such as the percentage it takes on each booking. Therefore, are hosts truly freed from potentially oppressive regulation, when Airbnb negotiates lenient regulations with governments?

Monetization is also key in the neoliberal project, but it is extended to the concept of economization. As such, monetization is to be understood in a greater context of economization of all the elements constituting social life, sometimes with the help of state regulation;[121] it can thus also be linked to the lure of monetizing everything, but also to applying the "model of the market" to all spheres, even those that are not "monetizable."[122] Brown gives the example of dating, quoting the manner in which online dating sites promote their services as helping one "maximiz[e] return on investment of affect, not only time and money."[123] Therefore, "both persons and states are expected to comport themselves in ways that maximize their capital value in the present and enhance their future value."[124] This gives true meaning to the term "governing rationality," as we are restricted, consciously or not, to thinking within this logic.

Orly Lobel, writing on the gig economy, states that "[l]eisure becomes work, work becomes leisure, socialization turns costly, and people price every interaction according to market value."[125] When Airbnb is promoted as providing hosts with the pleasure of having conversations with people from around the world on one's own patio, thus promoting meaningful engagements with guests as part of an optimized hosting labour act, does this not also promote the economization of friendship? Being especially friendly, in this case, can lead to better ratings on the host's profile. Moreover, Airbnb can also lead to monetizing one's attractiveness, in the context of hosts posting their pictures, or of guests posting theirs, waiting to be approved for a cheaper room on Airbnb than can be found in a hotel in the surrounding area. This leads to obvious problems, such as discrimination based on racialized physical features, which, of course, is prohibited in the hotel industry; but in the context of Airbnb, it is a free market, after all, and one can pick and choose. This was documented in a 2015 study, which proposed that the identity of guests not be revealed; however, "Airbnb, a standard-bearer of the so-called sharing economy, has argued forcefully that anonymity is incompatible with building trust between users."[126] This past September, Airbnb reacted with a new community commitment, as well as a nondiscrimination policy that users must accept.[127] Brown argues that neoliberal governance, namely, "devolv[es] authority, decision making, and the implementation of policies and norms of conduct."[128] Are Airbnb's regulations enough to curb discrimination, in a context of competition? Or, is there really just one guideline for all others—that of a "free" market?

2. Empowerment and Accountability for Oneself, Revisited

Empowerment, as discussed above, is often associated with entrepreneurship in the Airbnb context, or self-employment in general. Brown argues that beyond traditionally conceptualized entrepreneurship, under a neoliberal governing rationality, we seek "investors" in all spheres:

> [w]hether through social medial "followers," "likes," and "retweets," through rankings and ratings for every activity and domain, [...] the pursuit of education, training, leisure, reproduction, consumption, and more are increasingly configured as strategic decisions and practices related to enhancing the self's future value.[129]

Through Airbnb, are we empowering ourselves through the gamble that using this platform will give us more value than could be achieved through employment, in a context where competition is the name of the game, rather than equal opportunity?

Or, put differently, are the contours and limits of empowerment constricted within the governing rationality? Perhaps this helps us interpret how so many workers are moving towards "empowering" their labour through sharing economy platforms, seemingly oblivious to the labour rights they might be leaving behind.

Accountability for oneself thus appears central within a neoliberal governing rationality. Seeing that society in a competition framework is not characterized by equality, but rather is constituted of "a market formulation of winners and losers,"[130] one must take it upon himself or herself to not be a "loser." As such, "even as we are tasked with being responsible for ourselves in a competitive world of other human capitals, insofar as we are human capital *for* firms or states concerned with their own competitive positioning, we have no guarantee of security, protection, or even survival."[131] Hosts are human capital for Airbnb; the company does not offer any guarantees such as those stated above, even as it secures millions of dollars from manoeuvring its competitiveness in the accommodation industry, while hosts are accomplishing the substantial labour.

Brown argues that we are willing to sacrifice for the greater macroeconomic goal.[132] Following this argument, is it that we "understand" that the economy cannot offer costly labour rights to everyone, and thus self-employed workers must pay their due? Brown proposes that "bad citizenship" is namely characterized by workers that are "lazy consumers of benefits."[133] After all, we are "to become [...] responsible self-investor[s] and self-provider[s]."[134]

If we economize everything, then when are we accomplishing labour? How can we displace labour rights to such a context? How do we reconcile these rights with the logic of competition, in which inequality is naturalized?

Surely, many consumers feel advantaged by using Airbnb and do not question labour rights issues. But the fact is that many of these same consumers are susceptible to being at the receiving end of labour rights losses. This can occur whether they are workers in the hotel industry and face a downward pressure on labour rights through competition with Airbnb; if they decide to become Airbnb hosts themselves, perhaps even quitting their employee job in order to do so; or these losses can simply occur through our shifting conception of labour rights in the furtherance of the neoliberal governing rationality.

V. Conclusion

Resistance initiatives to the adverse effects of the so-called sharing economy are certainly emerging. A proposal gaining ground is that of a guaranteed basic income for all workers. This would contribute to levelling power relations for workers in the sharing economy.[135] As for financing this idea, well, "[h]ad they [Silicon Valley technology companies] paid more taxes, there would probably be less economic inequality to grapple with now in the first place."[136]

What might the future of labour rights look like if neoliberal rationality is to be consolidated and expanded? In the case of Airbnb, the discussion must be tied to one on subordination, prevalent in tourism studies. The carefree mindset often accompanying leisure tourism can potentially contribute to complicity in reproducing existing social subordinations, or in participating in subordination practices inherent to the guest-host relationship. Gender, racial, and class subordinations can thus be reinforced through the attitudes and behaviours of tourists. This is largely documented in the cases of practices of sexualisation of tourism promotion,[137] or of insisting on the exoticism of locals in the context of this promotion.[138] Similar reflections are possible concerning labour rights and Airbnb. Do tourists feel accountable for the labour rights situation of their Airbnb hosts, or of the hotel industry workers, for that matter, or do they feel that this is a national issue that they are not a part of? As in any tourism relation, playing the "game" of a market mindset, a strategy can be to concentrate on the power of the "guest," the consumer, and his or her awareness of national social issues.

Notes

1. Sabrina Tremblay-Huet is a doctoral candidate in law and lecturer at the University of Sherbrooke Faculty of Law. I wish to thank Orly Lobel and an anonymous reviewer for very helpful comments, as well as Finn Makela, Derek McKee, and Teresa Scassa for holding such a stimulating workshop.

2. See Philippe Orfali, "La loi anti-Airbnb est aisément contournée," *Le Devoir* (17 August 2016), online: <http://www.ledevoir.com/societe/actualites-en-societe/477891/la-loi-anti-airbnb-est-aisement-contournee>.

3. See Joshua Brustein & Christian Berthelsen, "N.Y. Governor Cuomo Signs Bill to Fine Illegal Airbnb Hosts," *Bloomberg* (21 October 2016), online: <https://www.bloomberg.com/news/articles/2016-10-21/n-y-governor-cuomo-signs-bill-to-fine-illegal-airbnb-hosts>.

4. Michel Foucault, *The Birth of Biopolitics: Lectures at the Collège de France, 1978–79* (Basingstoke, UK: Palgrave MacMillan, 2008).

5. Wendy Brown, *Undoing the Demos: Neoliberalism's Stealth Revolution* (New York: Zone Books, 2015).

6. *Act Respecting Labour Standards*, CQLR 1980, c N-1.1, s 1(10).

7. *Ibid*, s 2.

8. *Ibid*, ch IV, division I.

9. *Ibid*, ch IV, division II.

10. *Ibid*, ch IV, division III.

11. *Ibid*, ch IV, division IV.
12. *Ibid*, ch IV, division V.
13. *Ibid*, ch IV, division V.o.1.
14. *Ibid*, ch IV, division V.1.
15. *Ibid*, ch IV, division V.2.
16. *Ibid*, ch IV, division VI.
17. *Ibid*, ch IV, division VI.o.1.
18. *Ibid*, ch IV, division VI.1.
19. *Ibid*, s 93.
20. See Jean-Marc Piotte, "Les victoires des employéEs de l'hôtellerie québécoise," À bâbord! 28:1 (February–March 2009), online: <https://www.ababord.org/Les-victoires-des-employeEs-de-l>.
21. Yves-Thomas Dorval, "Salaire minimum à 15 $: le revers de la médaille," *La Presse* (22 November 2016), online: <http://www.lapresse.ca/debats/votre-opinion/201611/21/01-5043643-salaire-minimum-a-15-le-revers-de-la-medaille.php>.
22. CSN, "Lockout à l'Hôtel Pur de Québec—Le syndicat rétablit les faits," *Newswire* (13 November 2016), online: <http://www.newswire.ca/fr/news-releases/lockout-a-lhotel-pur-de-quebec---le-syndicat-retablit-les-faits-601015165.html>.
23. "Lock-out à l'Hôtel Pur de Québec: une grève déclenchée," *La Presse* (13 November 2016), online: <http://affaires.lapresse.ca/economie/quebec/201611/13/01-5040771-lock-out-a-lhotel-pur-de-quebec-une-greve-declenchee.php>.
24. Lia Lévesque, "11 hôtels à Montréal et Québec touchés par une grève vendredi," *La Presse* (8 September 2016), online: <http://affaires.lapresse.ca/economie/quebec/201609/08/01-5018273-11-hotels-a-montreal-et-quebec-touches-par-une-greve-vendredi.php>.
25. Chris Schenk, "Union Renewal and Precarious Employment: A Case Study of Hotel Workers" in Leah F Vosko, ed, *Precarious Employment: Understanding Labour Market Insecurity in Canada* (Montreal & Kingston: McGill-Queen's University Press, 2006) 335 at 336.
26. Hotel Association of Canada, News Release, "Government of Canada Recognizes Seasonal Nature of the Lodging Industry" (21 March 2016), online: <http://www.hotelassociation.ca/reports/news%20releases/Government%20of%20Canada%20Recognizes%20Seasonal%20Nature%20of%20the%20Lodging%20Industry.pdf>.
27. Hotel Association of Canada, News Release, "The Canadian Lodging Industry Defends the Temporary Foreign Worker Program" (24 April 2014), online: <http://www.hotelassociation.ca/reports/news%20releases/The%20Canadian%20Lodging%20Industry%20Defends%20the%20Temporary%20Foreign%20Worker%20Program.pdf>.
28. See Schenk, *supra* note 25 at 339.

29. See "Temporary Foreign Workers—Your Rights Are Protected," online: Government of Canada <https://www.canada.ca/en/employment-social-development/services/foreign-workers/protected-rights.html>.

30. Kendra Strauss & Siobhàn McGrath, "Temporary Migration, Precarious Employment and Unfree Labour Relations: Exploring the 'Continuum of Exploitation' in Canada's Temporary Foreign Worker Program," (2017) 78 Geoforum 199 at 200.

31. *Ibid* at 199.

32. *Ibid* at 203.

33. "Statement by the Minister of Employment, Workforce Development and Labour," *Newswire* (23 June 2016), online: <http://www.newswire.ca/fr/news-releases/statement-by-the-minister-of-employment-workforce-development-and-labour-584155711.html>.

34. See "Public Holidays," online: Éducaloi <https://www.educaloi.qc.ca/en/capsules/public-holidays>.

35. See "You Are a Self-Employed Worker," online: Revenu Quebec <http://www.rrq.gouv.qc.ca/en/travail/emploi_rrq/travailleur_autonome/Pages/travailleur_autonome.aspx>.

36. See "Understanding Québec's Occupational Health and Safety Plan" at 13, online: Commission de la santé et de la sécurité du travail du Québec <https://ilxcloud.s3.amazonaws.com/peer_resources/Understanding%20Qu%C3%A9bec%E2%80%99s%20Occupational%20Health%20and%20Safety%20Plan.pdf>.

37. See Leah F Vosko & Nancy Zukewich, "Precarious by Choice? Gender and Self-Employment" in Leah F Vosko, ed, *Precarious Employment: Understanding Labour Market Insecurity in Canada* (Montreal & Kingston: McGill-Queen's University Press) 67 at 72.

38. *Ibid* at 67.

39. Carolyn Said, "Window into Airbnb's Hidden Impact on S.F.," *San Francisco Chronicle* (June 2014), online: <http://www.sfchronicle.com/business/item/Window-into-Airbnb-s-hidden-impact-on-S-F-30110.php>.

40. Brad Tuttle, "Can We Stop Pretending the Sharing Economy Is All About Sharing?," *Time* (30 June 2014), online: <http://time.com/money/2933937/sharing-economy-airbnb-uber-monkeyparking>.

41. Katie Benner, "Airbnb Broadens Its Business with Tours and Travel Experiences," *The New York Times* (17 November 2016), online: <http://www.nytimes.com/2016/11/18/technology/airbnb-trips-travel-tours-tailored-experiences.html?_r=0>.

42. *Ibid*.

43. See Sam Levin, "Airbnb's Controversial Deal with Labor Union Falls Apart after Intense Backlash," *The Guardian* (21 April 2016), online: <https://www.theguardian.com/technology/2016/apr/21/airbnb-seiu-labor-union-deal-called-off-after-criticism>.

44. *Ibid.*
45. *Ibid.*
46. Sam Levin & Julia Carrie Wong, "Airbnb Negotiations with Powerful US Labor Union Facing Backlash," *The Guardian* (18 April 2016), online: <https://www.theguardian.com/technology/2016/apr/18/airbnb-seiu-backlash-labor-union-deal-new-york-california>.
47. See Justin Miller, "Uber, Airbnb and the Clash Between Workers and the On-Demand Economy," *Alternet* (2 May 2016), online: <https://www.alternet.org/labor/uber-airbnb-and-clash-between-workers-and-demand-economy>.
48. The definition of the labour force adopted here is the following: "[p]eople in jobs (wage work and self-employment) and the unemployed." See Leah F Vosko, ed, *Precarious Employment: Understanding Labour Market Insecurity in Canada* (Montreal & Kingston: McGill-Queen's University Press) at 457.
49. "Your Guide to Hosting Success on Airbnb," online: Airbnb <https://blog.atairbnb.com/guide-to-hosting-success>.
50. Ginia Bellafante, "Airbnb's Promise: Every Man and Woman a Hotelier," *The New York Times* (3 July 2014), online: <http://www.nytimes.com/2014/07/06/nyregion/airbnbs-promise-every-man-and-woman-a-hotelier.html?_r=0>.
51. Thank you to the anonymous reviewer for pointing out this very relevant hypothesis for the lack of attention to the labour force emerging through Airbnb.
52. Naomi Schoenbaum, "Gender and the Sharing Economy" (2016) 43:4 Fordham Urb LJ 1023 at 1030.
53. *Ibid* at 1031.
54. *Ibid* at 1028. The author analyses the sharing economy through the lens of gender using the aspects of identity and intimacy.
55. "Couchsurfing," online: <http://www.couchsurfing.com/about/about-us>.
56. James Dobbins, "Making a Living with Airbnb," *The New York Times* (7 April 2017), online: <https://www.nytimes.com/2017/04/07/realestate/making-a-living-with-airbnb.html?_r=1>.
57. Natasha Singer, "In the Sharing Economy, Workers Find Both Freedom and Uncertainty," *The New York Times* (16 August 2014), online: <http://www.nytimes.com/2014/08/17/technology/in-the-sharing-economy-workers-find-both-freedom-and-uncertainty.html?_r=0>.
58. Jacob Morgan, "Are Uber, Airbnb and Other Sharing Economy Businesses Good for America?," *Forbes* (17 December 2015), online: <http://www.forbes.com/sites/jacobmorgan/2015/12/17/are-uber-airbnb-and-other-sharing-economy-businesses-good-for-america/2/#517c34797de9>.

59. Ashley Parent, *Portable Bed & Breakfast: Empower Your Freedom Lifestyle with Airbnb*, Kindle ed (Amazon Digital Services, 2015).

60. Seb Linder, *Overnight Success: Achieve Financial Freedom through Airbnb*, Kindle ed (Amazon Digital Services, 2016).

61. Ben Carnes, "Did You Hear About the Tyranny of ... Legalizing Airbnb?," *Foundation for Economic Education* (17 May 2016), online: <https://fee.org/articles/did-you-hear-about-the-tyranny-of-not-banning-airbnb>.

62. Anthony Perucci, "City Begins to Consider More Freedom for Short-Term Rentals," *WGNO* (19 January 2016), online: <http://wgno.com/2016/01/19/city-begins-to-consider-more-freedom-for-short-term-rentals>.

63. "*Mais là, on décourage l'entrepreneuriat. On met des bâtons dans les roues des gens qui prennent des initiatives et profitent des nouvelles technologies* [...]," quoted in: Isabelle Ducas, "Airbnb: les propriétaires déchantent," *La Presse* (7 July 2016), online: <http://affaires.lapresse.ca/economie/immobilier/201607/07/01-4998700-airbnb-les-proprietaires-dechantent.php>.

64. See Hugo Martin, "Airbnb Sues Anaheim over Law That Makes the Rental Site Liable for Hosts Who Violate City Law," *Los Angeles Times* (28 July 2016), online: <http://www.latimes.com/business/la-fi-airbnb-anaheim-20160728-snap-story.html>.

65. See Katie Benner, "Airbnb Sues over New Law Regulating New York Rentals," *The New York Times* (21 October 2016), online: <http://www.nytimes.com/2016/10/22/technology/new-york-passes-law-airbnb.html>.

66. See Eric Newcomer, "Airbnb Sues Hometown San Francisco to Block Rental Rules," *Bloomberg* (28 June 2016), online: <https://www.bloomberg.com/news/articles/2016-06-27/airbnb-is-suing-hometeown-san-francisco-to-block-rental-rules>.

67. Martin, *supra* note 64.

68. "About Us," online: Airbnb <https://www.airbnb.ca/about/about-us?locale=en>.

69. Edgar Galeyev, *Practical Guide on How to Turn Your House into a Money-Making Machine: Achieve Financial Security Today*, Kindle ed (Amazon Digital Services, 2016).

70. Stephanie Buck, "Airbnb Co-Founder: Make Money Off Your Hobbies," *Mashable* (19 February 2013), online: <http://mashable.com/2013/02/19/airbnb-nate-blecharczyk/#PsY8DxSDGkqq>.

71. Alexandra Posadzki, "Putting Your Home on Airbnb? Here Are Some Things to Consider," *The Globe and Mail* (20 November 2016), online: <http://www.theglobeandmail.com/globe-investor/personal-finance/household-finances/more-people-flocking-to-airbnb-to-supplement-income/article32947832>.

72. Brad Stone, "The Sharing Economy: Monetize Your Life," *Bloomberg* (4 December 2014), online: <https://www.bloomberg.com/news/articles/2014-12-04/the-sharing-economy-monetize-your-life>.

73. Arthur C Brooks, "Start Helping the Helpers," *The New York Times* (17 October 2014), online: <http://www.nytimes.com/2014/10/18/opinion/arthur-c-brooks-start-helping-the-helpers.html?_r=0>.

74. Warren Bell, *The Airbnb Entrepreneur: How to Earn Big Profits, Even if You Don't Own a Property* (Melbourne: AirbnbHackers.com, 2014).

75. Scott Shatford, *The Airbnb Expert's Playbook: Secrets to Making Six-Figures as a Rentalpreneur*, Kindle ed (Amazon Digital Services, 2014).

76. "Airbnb Unveils Expansive Suite of Personalized Tools to Empower Hosts," online: Airbnb <https://www.airbnb.fr/press/news/airbnb-unveils-expansive-suite-of-personalized-tools-to-empower-hosts>.

77. "New Airbnb Partnership Empowers Rural Indian Women," online: Airbnb <https://www.airbnbcitizen.com/new-airbnb-partnership-empowers-rural-indian-women>.

78. "Celebrating and Empowering Women Around the World," online: Airbnb <http://blog.airbnb.com/celebrating-and-empowering-women-around-the-world>.

79. *Ibid.*

80. I will only mention the work of Leah F Vosko & Nancy Zukewich, noting that "dominant approaches to analyzing the dynamics of self-employment still rest on a narrow normative model—the male entrepreneur choosing risk, autonomy, and independence over stability and direct supervision." See *supra* note 37 at 67.

81. Jesse Hathaway, "How Peer-to-Peer Businesses Give Consumers a Lyft," *Chicago Tribune* (30 March 2015), online: <http://www.chicagotribune.com/news/opinion/commentary/ct-airbnb-uber-lyft-consumer-rideshare-heartland-perspec-0331-jm-20150330-story.html>.

82. Jeffrey Pfeffer, "How to Make a Fortune Without 'Doing' Anything: The Uber, Airbnb Story," *Fortune* (24 November 2014), online: <http://fortune.com/2014/11/24/uber-airbnb-sharing-economy-fallacy>.

83. Doug Henwood, "What the Sharing Economy Takes," *The Nation* (27 January 2015), online: <https://www.thenation.com/article/what-sharing-economy-takes>.

84. "Vancouver Airbnb Hosts Rely on Extra Income: Report," *Global News* (7 July 2016), online: <http://globalnews.ca/news/2809704/vancouver-airbnb-hosts-rely-on-extra-income-report>.

85. "Airbnb's Positive Economic Impact in Cities Around the World," online: Airbnb <https://www.airbnb.com/economic-impact>.

86. See Danielle Kubes, "How Airbnb Renters Are Helping Canadians Pay Off Their Mortgage in a Grey-Market Area," *Financial Post* (17 January 2015), online: <http://business.financialpost.com/personal-finance/

mortgages-real-estate/how-airbnb-renters-are-helping-canadians-pay-off-their-mortgage-in-a-grey-market-area>.

87. See Tara Siegel Bernard, "A Down Payment with a Catch: You Must Be an Airbnb Host," *The New York Times* (18 September 2017), online: <https://www.nytimes.com/2017/09/18/your-money/mortgages/loftium-airbnb-down-payment.html>.

88. See e.g. "Guesty," online: <https://www.guesty.com/features>.

89. "Wendy Brown," online: Berkeley Political Science <http://polisci.berkeley.edu/people/person/wendy-brown>.

90. Sheila Raju, "The Fare-ness of Uber, Airbnb, and the Sharing Economy," *Huffington Post* (18 October 2014), online: <http://www.huffingtonpost.com/sheila-raju/the-fareness-of-uber-airbnb_b_5686540.html>.

91. See Foucault, *supra* note 4 at 78.

92. *Ibid* at 117.

93. *Ibid* at 131.

94. *Ibid* at 118.

95. *Ibid* at 119.

96. *Ibid* at 131.

97. *Ibid* at 132.

98. *Ibid* at 139.

99. *Ibid* at 223.

100. *Ibid* at 147.

101. *Ibid* at 149-50.

102. Brown, *supra* note 5 at 30.

103. *Ibid* at 31.

104. *Ibid* at 83.

105. *Ibid* at 79.

106. *Ibid* at 64.

107. Foucault, *supra* note 4 at 121.

108. Brown, *supra* note 5 at 122.

109. *Ibid* at 126–27.

110. *Ibid* at 151.

111. *Ibid* at 209.

112. *Ibid* at 38.

113. *Ibid* at 65.

114. Harry W Arthurs, "Labour Law after Labour" in Guy Davidov & Brian Langille, eds, *The Idea of Labour Law* (New York: Oxford University Press, 2011) 13 at 21.

115. Brown, *supra* note 5 at 41.

116. *Ibid* at 49.

117. *Ibid* at 108.

118. *Ibid*.

119. *Ibid* at 177.

120. *Ibid* at 173.

121. *Ibid* at 62.

122. *Ibid* at 31.

123. *Ibid.*

124. *Ibid* at 22.

125. Orly Lobel, "The Gig Economy & The Future of Employment and Labor Law" (2017) 51 USF L Rev 51 at 54.

126. Mike McPhate, "Discrimination by Airbnb Hosts Is Widespread, Report Says," *The New York Times* (11 December 2015), online: <http://mobile. nytimes.com/2015/12/12/business/discrimination-by-airbnb-hosts-is-widespread-report-says.html?referer=>.

127. See Katie Benner, "Airbnb Adopts Rules to Fight Discrimination by Its Hosts," *The New York Times* (8 September 2016), online: <http://www. nytimes.com/2016/09/09/technology/airbnb-anti-discrimination-rules. html>.

128. Brown, *supra* note 5 at 129.

129. *Ibid* at 34.

130. Brown, *supra* note 5 at 41.

131. *Ibid* at 37.

132. *Ibid* at 211.

133. *Ibid* at 212.

134. *Ibid* at 84.

135. See Vili Lehdonvirta, "Can Universal Basic Income Counter the Ill-Effects of the Gig Economy?," *The Conversation* (12 April 2017), online: <https:// theconversation.com/can-universal-basic-income-counter-the-ill-effects-of-the-gig-economy-75581>.

136. *Ibid.*

137. A popular analysis is Cynthia Enloe's feminist take on governmental promotion of tourism. See Cynthia Enloe, *Bananas, Beaches and Bases: Making Feminist Sense of International Politics*, 2nd ed (Berkeley, CA: University of California Press, 2014).

138. Racialization of tourism in the Global South is namely deconstructed by postcolonial theorists. See e.g. Michael C Hall & Hazel Tucker, *Tourism and Postcolonialism: Contested Discourses, Identities and Representations* (New York: Routledge, 2004).

About the Contributors

Harry Arthurs is University Professor Emeritus and President Emeritus at York University. He has served as Dean of Osgoode Hall Law School (1972–77) and President of York University (1985–92). He is a former associate of the Canadian Institute for Advanced Research, a Fellow of the Royal Society of Canada, and a Corresponding Fellow of the British Academy.

Francesco Ducci is a doctoral candidate at the University of Toronto Faculty of Law. He specializes in competition law as well as economic analysis of law.

Marie-Cécile Escande-Varniol is a senior lecturer at the Institut d'Études du Travail de Lyon (IETL), Université Lumière Lyon 2 (France). She is director of the Master Droit social, mobilité internationale des travailleurs. She is a member of the CERCRID (*Centre de Recherche Critique sur le Droit.*

Vincent Gautrais is Full Professor and L. R. Wilson Chair in Information Technology and E-commerce Law at the Faculty of Law, Université de Montréal. He is also the director of the Centre de recherche en droit public. He previously held the Université de Montréal Excellence Chair in Security and Internet Law.

Michael Geist is Professor at the University of Ottawa Faculty of Law. He holds the Canada Research Chair in Internet and E-commerce Law. He is a former member of Canada's National Task Force on Spam.

Eran Kaplinsky is an Associate Professor of Law at the University of Alberta. His research and teaching interests include land use planning and regulation, municipal law, property law, expropriation and compensation, and economic analysis of law.

Finn Makela is Associate Professor at the Université de Sherbrooke Faculty of Law. He specializes in legal theory and epistemology, legal research methodology, labour and employment law, the law of higher education, common law, and transnational law. He previously practiced in the area of labour and employment law.

Derek McKee is Assistant Professor and Co-Director of Programs in Common Law and Transnational Law at the Université de Sherbrooke Faculty of Law. He specializes in administrative law, tort law, and transnational law.

Teresa Scassa is Professor at the University of Ottawa Faculty of Law, where she holds the Canada Research Chair in Information Law. She is a former member of the External Advisory Committee of the Office of the Privacy Commissioner of Canada, and of the Canadian Government Advisory Committee on Open Government.

Nofar Sheffi is a lecturer at the University of New South Wales Faculty of Law. She specializes in contract theory, law and technology, as well as critical and social legal theories.

Sabrina Tremblay-Huet. is a doctoral candidate and lecturer at the Université de Sherbrooke Faculty of Law. She specializes in tourism law, international human rights law, and critical legal theory.

Eric Tucker is Professor at York University's Osgoode Hall Law School, as well as a Distinguished Visiting Researcher, Cleveland-Marshall College of Law, Cleveland State University. He has written widely on labour and employment law issues including books on the history of occupational health and safety regulation and collective bargaining law in Canada.

Mariana Valverde is Professor at the Centre for Criminology and Sociolegal Studies at the University of Toronto, as well as its former Director from 2007 to 2013. She also holds a courtesy cross-appointment to the Department of Geography and Planning as well as the Faculty of Law. She has been a Fellow of the Royal Society of Canada since 2006.

Law, Technology and Media

Edited by Michael Geist

The *Law, Technology and Media* series explores emerging technology law issues with an emphasis on a Canadian perspective. It is the first University of Ottawa Press series to be fully published under an open access licence.

Previous titles in this collection

Karim Benyekhlef, Jane Bailey, Jacquelyn Burkell and Fabien Gélinas (eds.), *eAccess to Justice*, 2016

Jane Bailey and Valerie Steeves (eds.), *eGirls, eCitizens*, 2015

Michael Geist (ed.), *Law, Privacy and Surveillance In Canada in the Post-Snowden Era*, 2015

Michael Geist (ed.), *The Copyright Pentalogy: How the Supreme Court of Canada Shook the Foundations of Canadian Copyright Law*, 2013